DEC 3 1 2016

D0710288

DEC 1 1918

Praise for *The Mother of All Booklists*

"*The Mother of All Booklists* is amazing. A valuable resource and a good read in itself."—**Judy Allen, author of** *Awaiting Developments* **and winner of the Whitbread Children's Novel Award and the Friends of the Earth Award**

"A brilliant, heartfelt, beautifully written and well-chosen compilation of some of the best books for children, teens, and adults. A fabulous resource for teachers, librarians, and parents."—**Dianna H. Aston, author of** *A Rock Is Lively*, **a Boston Globe's Best Children's Book of the Year**

"A treasure trove for lovers of nonfiction!"—**Don Brown, award-winning author of** *He Has Shot the President!: April 14, 1865: The Day John Wilkes Booth Killed President Lincoln*

Martin's *The Mother of All Booklists* provides a terrific resource for teachers, students, librarians, and anyone who loves books. Its focus on nonfiction not only caters to professionals looking for Common Core materials but helps validate the interests of the huge number of readers who have always preferred factual books. Most of all, it's just a great read and will send people scurrying to the library.— **Sneed B. Collard, author of** *Animal Dads, The Prairie Builders*, **and** *Sneed B. Collard III's Most Fun Book Ever about Lizards*

"This is a resource I'll keep nearby, not just to guide my own reading but as a secret reference to use when people ask me to recommend good books for them to read. Martin's thorough and smart review of recent nonfiction will make me look smart when I'm asked to talk about books worth reading. This book is a must-have for school and public libraries. Patrons and librarians will wear out this resource in their search for great nonfiction books. Teachers at all levels will also find great value in it. Considering how much information this book contains, it's surprisingly easy to navigate, and the author has anticipated readers' needs by, for example, rearranging the master lists into smaller, subject-defined categories. I also appreciated the short biographies of twenty-five contemporary authors and the extensive bibliographies at the end of the volume. The annotations are engagingly written, and the range of books included is impressive. If this book can't help someone find a nonfiction book they want to read, I don't know what will."—**Chris Crowe, professor of English at Brigham Young University and author of** *Death Coming Up the Hill*

"Now that my children are teenagers, I seem to have forgotten how to select books for kids of any other age. Fortunately, I'm among readers who can 'listen to mother' to reliably make choices, and not just for children but for readers of all ages. The mother in this case is Bill Martin, author of *A Lifetime of Fiction: The 500 Most Recommended Reads for Ages 2 to 102* and its nonfiction sequel, *The Mother of All Booklists: The 500 Most Recommended Nonfiction Reads for Ages 3 to 103*. Bill took on the overwhelming task of delving into the opinions of a legion of book reviewers and researching multiyear booklists across the board so his selections represent the combined viewpoints of critics rather than the opinions of just one or a few. His exceptionally easy-to-use guide enables parents, teachers, and interested readers to quickly select books based on readers' ages, in five categories, from preschool through adult. Each category contains 100 titles and descriptions. Thank you, Bill, for creating such a valuable resource. Your book will no doubt be one of the most dog-eared in every school and public library."—**Jennifer Keats Curtis, award-winning author of *Kali's Story: An Orphaned Polar Bear Rescue***

"A wide-ranging and wonderfully varied celebration of nonfiction, proving that this genre provides a rich a nourishing diet to grow the minds of young readers. I wish we had this in the UK!"—**Nicola Davies, zoologist, children's author, and one of the original presenters of the BBC wildlife program *The Really Wild Show***

"This is the most comprehensive and well-organized nonfiction booklist I've ever seen. An absolute must-have resource for readers and educators."—**Matt de la Pena, author of the critically acclaimed young adult novel *The Living***

"What a useful resource William Martin's *The Mother of All Booklists* will be! This guide reflects the best of today's nonfiction for all ages."—**Kay Frydenborg, author of *Wild Horse Scientists***

"For those of us who know we're living in the Golden Age of Nonfiction, *The Mother of All Booklists* is a godsend. Bill Martin has done the heavy lifting for parents, teachers, and devoted readers, providing us with a one-stop source for acclaimed modern nonfiction organized by age, genre, and interest category. *Mother* testifies to the brilliance, beauty, and sometimes unbelievability of the truth found in great nonfiction."—**Gary Golio, author and illustrator of *Spirit Seeker*, one of the New York Public Library's 100 Titles for Reading & Sharing**

"*The Mother of All Booklists* is the mother of all nonfiction best book guides. It belongs in every home, school, community, and university library."—**Greg Grandin, professor of history at New York University and prize-winning** author of *The Empire of Necessity: Slavery, Freedom, and Deception in the New World*

"*The Mother of All Booklists* is a well-organized composite of major awards and booklists, a great time-saver for accessing the best nonfiction books for any age group. This guide will efficiently help educators, parents, and readers meet Common Core standards."—**Christy Hale, author and illustrator of *Dreaming Up: A Celebration of Building*, a Bank Street College of Education Best Children's Book**

"How do you find the best nonfiction books for yourself or a child in your life? This well-researched, well-written, comprehensive "mother list" is the perfect place to start. An invaluable resource!"—**Deborah Heiligman, author of *Charles and Emma: The Darwins' Leap of Faith*, winner of the first YALSA Excellence in Nonfiction Award**

"Think of *The Mother of All Booklists* as a treasure chest filled with ideas for great reads. William Martin profiles a huge variety of wonderful books sure to inform, entertain, and inspire readers of all ages."—**Barbara Kerley, award-winning author of *The Dinosaurs of Waterhouse Hawkins* and *A Home for Mr. Emerson***

The Mother of All Booklists

The 500 Most Recommended Nonfiction Reads for Ages 3 to 103

WILLIAM PATRICK MARTIN

ROWMAN & LITTLEFIELD
Lanham • Boulder • New York • London

Published by Rowman & Littlefield
A wholly owned subsidary of The Rowman & Littlefield Publishing Group, Inc.
4501 Forbes Boulevard, Suite 200, Lanham, Maryland 20706
www.rowman.com

Unit A, Whitacre Mews, 26-34 Stannary Street, London SE11 4AB

Copyright © 2015 by Rowman & Littlefield

All rights reserved. No part of this book may be reproduced in any form or by any electronic
or mechanical means, including information storage and retrieval systems, without written
permission from the publisher, except by a reviewer who may quote passages in a review.

British Library Cataloguing in Publication Information Available

Library of Congress Cataloging-in-Publication Data

Martin, William P. (William Patrick)
  The mother of all booklists : the 500 most recommended nonfiction reads for ages 3 to
103 / William Patrick Martin.
      pages cm
  Includes bibliographical references.
  ISBN 978-1-4422-3861-9 (cloth : alk. paper) — ISBN 978-1-4422-3862-6 (ebook)
  1. Best books—United States. I. Title.
  Z1035.M396 2015
  028.10973—dc23   2014021412

♾™ The paper used in this publication meets the minimum requirements of American
National Standard for Information Sciences—Permanence of Paper for Printed Library
Materials, ANSI/NISO Z39.48-1992.

Printed in the United States of America

For Mary Anne Zane,
reader and mother-in-law extraordinaire.

Contents

Acknowledgments

I thank the librarians, critics, educators, scholars, editors, and reporters that put so much of themselves into creating the booklists upon which *Mother* depends. We are all in their debt for recommending books of the highest caliber that inform, inspire, amuse, and edify, helping us know ourselves and the world a little better. I acknowledge Fallon Stoeffler for her able writing assistance, and I thank Robert Hayunga and Charles Harmon from Rowman & Littlefield for their continuing guidance and confidence in my work. As always, I am especially grateful to my wife, Marianne, for proofreading the manuscript and providing advice and support through all phases of the project.

Introduction

Imagine there was a gathering of the English-speaking world's most eminent booklist makers and critics from journalism, publishing, library science, education, and book-award organizations. The purpose for this distinguished assembly was to create uniquely authoritative age-group reading lists, establishing what culture critic Matthew Arnold would have called "the best that was thought and said" in the realm of nonfiction. In essence, the construction of these ultimate reading lists is the premise for *The Mother of All Booklists: The 500 Most Recommended Nonfiction Reads for Ages 3 to 103*, but instead of convening a panel of the most high-powered experts, *Mother* uses extensive past and present booklists created by these experts and their organizations.

Written for parents, grandparents, and teachers who confront the bewildering array of award and recommended reading lists, *Mother* is a composite of all the major booklists, as well as some that are lesser known. It brings together 155 of the most influential book awards and reading lists from leading magazines, newspapers, reference books, schools, libraries, parenting organizations, websites, and professional groups across the country. *Mother* is not the opinion of one book critic but the aggregate opinion of an army of critics. By pooling the talent of the foremost literary authorities, *Mother* becomes America's most reliable and trustworthy guide to nonfiction books.

Organized into five age-group lists, each with 100 books—preschoolers (ages 3–5), early readers (ages 5–9), middle readers (ages 9–13), young adults (ages 13–17), and adults (ages 18+)—*Mother* amalgamates the knowledge of the best English-language booklists in the United States as well as a few of the most noteworthy ones from Canada and Great Britain. Spanning early youth to late adulthood, this integrative guide supplies the best-of-the-best nonfiction-reading recommendations for countless educational needs and recreational interests.

The past and present booklists that make *Mother* a who's who of literary, professional, and journalistic excellence include the *New York Times'* Notable Books, the National Book Awards, the Pulitzer Prizes, the Los Angeles Times Book Prizes, the Boston Globe–Horn Book Awards, the Newbery and Caldecott Medals, and titles recommended by the *School Library Journal, Booklist, Kirkus Reviews, Publishers Weekly*, Chicago Public Library, Boston Public Schools, National Council of the Teachers of English, National Council for the Social Studies, and the National Science Teachers Association. The award lists include both winners and finalists, capturing information from the inception of the awards to the most current data available. The booklists vary greatly. Sometimes they are dedicated to a specific genre, topic, age group, or grade level, and sometimes they are defined by year, decade, or the "best of all time." All types of nonfiction books are included: biography, business, cooking, culture and society, current events, economics, environment, essays, foreign affairs, history, mathematics, medicine, narrative nonfiction, philosophy, politics, religion, science, sports, travel, true crime, and war. The booklists typically encompass multiple years of recommendations. Some of the nonfiction titles qualify as creative nonfiction. Using supposition and fictional techniques, they tell factually accurate stories in a compelling way.

Mother is a new type of best-book guide. Instead of relying on the knowledge and taste of a single expert or organization, *Mother* leverages the collective wisdom of a diverse body of authorities, creating a whole that is greater than the sum of its parts and establishing new common ground. To generate the reading lists, a database of over 20,000 booklist entries was created, with each book classified by age group. The ranked booklists that emerged from this meta-compilation were the ones upon which most experts agree.

This unique reference book further distinguishes itself from other best-book guides by addressing every age group—toddler through centenarian. Usually, books of this kind are limited to children, teens, or adults, or they focus on one genre; rarely do they encompass every developmental stage and survey the entire nonfiction field. Moreover, *The Mother of All Booklists* does not list its books willy-nilly, it rank orders them based on the number of "votes" they received from the experts. Like its predecessor, *A Lifetime of Fiction: The 500 Most Recommended Reads for Ages 2 to 102* (2014), *Mother* will be a one-stop resource and a comprehensive reading plan for some readers. With the confidence that comes from aggregating multiple knowledgeable opinions, *Mother* offers a single vision of the nonfiction most worth reading for every stage of life.

One driver behind *Mother*'s development is the adoption of the Common Core State Standards by public schools in most states. These standards dramatically increase the emphasis on nonfiction, requiring 12th-grade reading to be 70-percent nonfiction and elementary reading to be 50-percent nonfiction.

These benchmarks are intended to better prepare high school students for the complexity of modern life. *Mother* will enable teachers and parents to navigate this transformation by helping them to select the very best nonfiction titles. My other reason for creating this guide is that existing award lists and best-book guides often seem too idiosyncratic, telling us as much about the reviewers as the books they review. *Mother* counterbalances these natural predispositions, producing booklists that are more objective and comprehensive, reflecting the shared values of the literary establishment rather the opinion of one person or group.

Besides the annotated lists, *Mother* has a chapter on "Special Interests" that sorts the books into a collection of categories encompassing different age groups, well-established genres, and topics that reflect the unique character of this particular collection of recommended reads. The books are divided into adventure, African American experience, animal rescue, animals, art, bilingual books, biography, birds, business and economics, classics, concept books, crime, disasters, diversity, families and relationships, food, graphic novels, health and disease, history, insects and spiders, inspiration, life cycles, nature, ocean life, performing arts, religion, reptiles, science, sports, technology, war, wildlife and environmental conservation, and women's struggles and accomplishments. The categories were created to help readers locate their favorite subjects and to capture the collection's most distinctive and dominant themes.

No collection of best books would be complete without some acknowledgment of the authors who created them, so I included a chapter highlighting "25 Contemporary Writers You Should Know." *Mother* includes the work of great literary and historical figures such as Anne Frank, Rachel Carson, Virginia Woolf, Truman Capote, George Orwell, Malcolm X, Benjamin Franklin, and Charles Darwin, whose contributions are well established. Yet there are also many outstanding modern authors and illustrators whose lives and work demand more recognition. This stellar collection of contemporary storytellers represents a variety of backgrounds, interests, accomplishments, and age-group specializations. In each case, their biographical sketches include some insight or quote about how and why they conduct their work. Each writer and illustrator in this chapter has at least two books on *Mother*'s booklists, while two of them, Steve Jenkins and Russell Freedman, contributed an astonishing 15 and 10 books respectively! To be singled out just once by such a prestigious cross section of literary experts is a special achievement, but to have several books held in such high esteem is a remarkable feat.

To those who worry about the quality and standing of nonfiction writing, *The Mother of All Booklists* demonstrates that exceptional reality-based storytelling is flourishing. "While nonfiction has never been completely ignored, for a long time it was brushed off and pushed aside, as though factual books were socially inferior to the upper crust stuff we call literature," observed author Russell Freedman during his acceptance for the Newbery Medal for *Lincoln: A Photobiography*.[1] This guide leaves no doubt that nonfiction writing, no longer the ugly stepchild to fiction, now occupies a position of equality and respect on par with the finest literature, giving nonfiction lovers a rich array of choices for themselves, friends, and children that is without precedent. For readers looking to escape to exciting new worlds, fiction is no longer the automatic choice. As Mark Twain understood, "truth is stranger than fiction," and, as *Mother* demonstrates over and over again, reality literature in the right hands can become so interesting that it qualifies as escapist literature.

Note

1. *The Newbery & Caldecott Medal Books, 1986–2000: A Comprehensive Guide to the Winners* (Chicago: American Library Association, 2001), 73.

CHAPTER 1

Preschoolers (Ages 3–5)

There are many little ways to enlarge your child's world.
Love of books is the best of all.

—Jacqueline Kennedy

1. *Me . . . Jane.* Written and illustrated by Patrick McDonnell. (Little, Brown Books for Young Readers, 2011.) McDonnell's ink-and-watercolor account links the childhood dreams of Dr. Jane Goodall to her ultimate calling as the world's most famous primatologist. Young Jane is a studious and active girl who goes everywhere with her stuffed chimpanzee, Jubilee. She spends lots of time outside her English country home making sketches, taking notes, and dreaming of one day living in the African jungle like Tarzan and Jane. Jane is a keen observer of nature with an active imagination, visualizing herself swinging on a vine in the jungle. The book concludes with a message from Dr. Goodall and information for further study.

2. *Dave the Potter: Artist, Poet, Slave.* Written by Laban Carrick Hill. Illustrated by Bryan Collier. (Little, Brown Books for Young Readers, 2010.) Hill and Collier's picture-book biography tells the astonishing story of a South Carolina slave who managed to enrich and empower his bleak existence 200 years

ago by becoming a great artist and poet. Dave carves his words into his beautifully sculpted clay pots, his strength and dignity coming through in earth-toned watercolor illustrations showing the different stages of his creative process. This lost artist lived and died as a 19th-century slave, and not much is known about the details of his life. But his work lives on as an inspirational reminder of a man who triumphed over adversity and left behind objects of incredible beauty and utility. At the end of the book, there is a photo of some of Dave's creations.

3. *Stay: The True Story of Ten Dogs.* Written by Michaela Muntean. Illustrated by K. C. Bailey and Stephen Kazmierski. (Scholastic Press, 2012.) Michaela Muntean, along with the spousal team of K. C. Bailey and Stephen Kazmierski, tells the unique story of Luciano Anastasini and 10 ragtag mutts he adopts and transforms into an amazingly successful circus act. Luciano, who comes from a long line of circus performers, has his acrobatic career cut short by a debilitating fall from a high wire. In this photo essay, the resilient performer figures out a way to reinvent his act and give some abandoned dogs a second chance. Luciano becomes the most unorthodox animal trainer, closely observing each dog's quirks and letting the animals show him what they are best able to do. The result of his love and patience is a troupe of the most entertaining canine performers who appear in some of the best circuses in the country.

4. *In My Backyard.* Written by Valarie Giogas. Illustrated by Katherine Zecca. (Sylvan Dell Publishing, 2007.) In Giogas and Zecca's rhyming and counting book, preschoolers will learn to count to 10 and become familiar with baby and group names such as puppies belonging to a litter and pups belonging to a family of porcupines. Ten types of common woodland animals are colorfully and realistically portrayed with plenty of visual clues as to where the animals live and what they eat. Each page of this fun read-aloud book has close-ups and larger pictures designed for young readers to find and count the animals. There is information on how to observe backyard wildlife, how to care for an injured animal, how to keep a journal, and other interesting facts.

5. *Lightship.* Written and illustrated by Brian Floca. (Atheneum/Richard Jackson Books, 2007.) Floca tells the fascinating and little-known story of how lighthouses were once built aboard sturdy little ships anchored out to sea to guide sailors safely to port. Located in the Great Lakes and ocean harbors in places where conventional lighthouses could not be built, lightships were designed to ride out storms and cut through the fog by shining their lights and sounding their horns. Floca's ink-and-watercolor drawings skillfully show the crew at work and provide various diagrams and perspectives on the ships. These floating lighthouses occupy an important place in American history. They saved many lives, but in an era of deep underwater platforms, they are no longer needed.

6. *It's a Butterfly's Life.* Written and illustrated by Irene Kelly. (Holiday House, 2007.) Kelly wonderfully illustrates and explains the life cycle of butterflies and how they change into lovely creatures capable of traveling long distances to warmer climates. Kelly's simple prose and detailed watercolor images illustrate the metamorphosis from egg, to caterpillar, to chrysalis, and finally to a graceful winged creature. She identifies different species of butterflies and provides fascinating information about their body parts and activities. Children will be excited to hear remarkable facts such as the butterfly's ability to taste with its feet and its capacity to migrate 80 miles in one day. They will gain a new appreciation of these beautiful insects and get enough information to start their own butterfly garden.

7. *Where in the Wild? Camouflaged Creatures Concealed . . . and Revealed.* Written by David M. Schwartz and Yael Schy. Illustrated by Dwight Kuhn. (Tricycle Press, 2007.) Schwartz and Schy combine poetry, science, and full-page photography to produce an engrossing lift-the-flap book on how 10 animals conceal themselves from predators. Nature's color and camouflage is on display in this entertaining and educational book about large and small animals. Children will encounter a coyote, tree frog, fawn, weasel, moth, killdeer, crab spider, green snake, flounder, and red spotted newt and will sometimes be challenged to find the animals hiding in plain sight in their natural habitats. *Where in the Wild?* is an excellent introductory science book suitable for preschoolers and older children and would be a great addition to a home library.

8. *Fabulous Fishes.* Written and illustrated by Susan Stockdale. (Peachtree Publishers, 2008.) With rhyming text and striking drawings, Stockdale has created a unique introduction to the alphabet. This is a must-read preparation for a child's first visit to a public aquarium. With an underwater world of more than 20 types of fish, Stockdale's drawings come alive in vivid images of common and exotic varieties of fish in many different shapes and sizes. Preschoolers will learn about how swordfish capture their prey and about how remoras attach themselves to sharks and live off the remains of the large predator's meals. Stockdale does a wonderful job of depicting different aquatic environments, whether it is bright coral or a murky riverbed. The book has an excellent glossary with informative descriptions of each fish and its habitat.

9. *Big Blue Whale.* Written by Nicola Davies. Illustrated by Nick Maland. (Candlewick, 2001.) Davies and Maland pay tribute to the biggest and arguably the most majestic animal that ever lived through well-written descriptions and double-page spreads. Children will learn how the great creature feels, eats, travels, communicates, and cares for its young. The size of this leviathan is clear right from the start, as readers are shown a young man and woman near an elephant and a giraffe standing alongside a whale's tail. In a manner perfect for her young audience, Davies observes that the whale's eye is "as big as a teacup" and that its skin is "springy and smooth like a hard-boiled egg, and it's as slippery as wet soap."

10. *All the Water in the World.* Written by George Ella Lyon. Illustrated by Katherine Tillotson. (Atheneum/Richard Jackson Books, 2011.) Using verse and digital illustrations, Lyon and Tillotson introduce children to the water cycle, conveying how our lives depend upon this precious resource. Readers are shown water as it appears on our ocean-covered planet, water spouting from a hose, water running down mountains, water dropping from the sky, and water in short supply in bare and arid landscapes. The idea of evaporation is cleverly demonstrated by having the words swirl up the page from the ocean and into the sky. The message of the book is that all living things are connected to water, and we must protect it.

11. *Over and Under the Snow.* Written by Kate Messner. Illustrated by Christopher Silas Neal. (Chronicle Books, 2011.) Messner and Neal team up on a book guaranteed to pique children's interest and appreciation of nature. The story revolves around a young girl spending the day skiing with her father through the woods. She narrates this story of "the secret kingdom beneath the snow," which is populated by mice, shrews, squirrels, rabbits, bullfrogs, and deer, all tucked away beneath a wintery landscape, while animal predators watch and wait hoping for a meal. The girl catches glimpses of animal activity as she travels through the forest, while cutaway views nicely show what is happening below the ground. Neal's mixed-media illustrations and use of muted colors effectively capture the silent beauty of winter.

12. *Red-Eyed Tree Frog.* Written by Joy Cowley. Illustrated by Nic Bishop. (Scholastic Paperbacks, 1999.) Nic Bishop's spectacular close-up photographs document the nocturnal wandering of this cute Central American amphibian as he avoids predators and searches for food in the tropical rain forest. By posing questions and creating suspense, Cowley simply and engagingly amplifies the effect of the razor-sharp images. Preschoolers will be on the edge of their seats, finding out about tiny creatures that are sometimes the hunter and sometimes the hunted. In this pictorial adventure, the red-eyed protagonist narrowly escapes being eaten by a snake and encounters other forest creatures such as an iguana, ant, katydid, and caterpillar. The book ends with the little frog safely camouflaged and ready to sleep the day away.

13. *Leo the Snow Leopard: The True Story of an Amazing Rescue.* Written by Craig Hatkoff. Illustrated by Isabella Hatkoff. (Scholastic Press, 2010.) The Hatkoffs tell the remarkable story of Leo, an orphaned cub rescued by a shepherd in the snowy Himalayan Mountains, and how scientists ultimately find him a home in the Bronx Zoo. Focusing on the example of a hand-fed cub protected by a kindly shepherd and then taken in by the Wildlife Conservation Society, this is an inspirational story of international cooperation in protecting the world's endangered wildlife and a guide to how different people can work together to achieve common goals. The book concludes with interesting information on wildlife conservation and on the habitat of the snow leopard.

14. *Underground: Finding the Light to Freedom.* Written and illustrated by Shane W. Evans. (Roaring Brook Press, 2011.) Dramatic illustrations highlight Evans's excellent story of southern slaves who escape bondage using the Underground Railroad. The story is told by a group of slaves who must quietly crawl, run barefoot, sleep outdoors, and find refuge with strangers on their secret nighttime journey. With only a starry sky to guide their way, they meet supporters along the way and do everything they can to avoid being captured. The book comes to a satisfying conclusion when the fugitives finally reach their northern destination and are able to lift a newborn baby into the sunlight of freedom. Preschoolers will pay rapt attention to this exciting narrative.

15. *Never Smile at a Monkey: And 17 Other Important Things to Remember.* Written and illustrated by Steve Jenkins. (HMH Books for Young Readers, 2009.) Author and illustrator Steve Jenkins has produced a visually magnificent picture book with just enough danger to make it the perfect read-aloud for preschoolers and older children. Eighteen animals are highlighted, each exhibiting threats and hazards inherent in their unique natural defense mechanisms. The book manages to educate and startle as it points out that monkeys may view the showing of teeth as an act of aggression and that getting tangled up with some types of jellyfish could result in your death. Jenkins's book is attractively alliterative as he instructs readers to "never pet a platypus," "never harass a hippopotamus," and "never step on a stingray."

16. *Chameleon!* Written by Joy Cowley. Illustrated by Nic Bishop. (Scholastic, 2005.) "The chameleon rests in his tree. His skin has peaceful colors. He wakes up hungry for a juicy insect." Finding no insects nearby he climbs down from his safe spot in the tree and searches for food. This delightful book of photographs and lean text shows a day in the life of a male chameleon found in the Madagascar tropical rain forests. Cowley and Bishop show him encountering a frog, scorpion, and caterpillar, a source for his next meal. As he moves about, brilliant photographs document his changes in color. The protagonist encounters a female chameleon that accepts his foray into her territory, recognizing that he is no threat. *Chameleon!* is an excellent companion to Cowley and Bishop's *Red-Eyed Tree Frog.*

17. *Starfish*. Written by Edith Thacher Hurd. Illustrated by Robin Brickman. (HarperCollins, 2000.) Originally published in 1962, this preschool classic deserves a new generation of readers on the strength of Brickman's beautiful new watercolor collages. But Hurd's poetic writing is still the best introduction to the world of starfish and their many varieties. Children will be eager to learn how starfish look, grow, behave, eat, and lay eggs. They will see where starfish live, how they glide about looking for food, how they attack a clam, and what happens when one of these special sea animals loses an arm, also called a "ray." *Starfish* is an excellent choice for a child's first exposure to science and nonfiction.

18. *Winter's Tail: How One Little Dolphin Learned to Swim Again*. Written by Craig Hatkoff, Juliana Hatkoff, and Isabella Hatkoff. (Scholastic, 2009.) The Hatkoff family tells the inspirational story of a little orphaned bottlenose dolphin, Winter, who is rescued and fitted with the world's first and only prosthetic dolphin's tail. As a baby, she is caught in a crab trap, mangling her original tail. She is taken to Florida's Clearwater Marine Aquarium, where she is nursed back to health and given a second chance with a device that mimics her natural swimming movement. The book does an outstanding job of documenting the dramatic rescue, incredible recovery, and training. Children, especially those with physical disabilities, will be encouraged by this story of resilience and resourcefulness.

19. *About Hummingbirds: A Guide for Children*. Written by Cathryn Sill. Illustrated by John Sill. (Peachtree Publishers, 2011.) The Sills have created a charming and informative science book for young children that will ably introduce them to the diminutive powerhouses of the avian world. Preschoolers will be amazed to find that the unique hummingbird is the only bird that can fly backward, forward, and even upside down. Some hummingbirds are only two inches long, and others can use spider webs to paste their nests together. Clear, simple language and color palates cover a wide range of facts on how the birds eat, fly, fight, reproduce, and camouflage themselves. This is an ideal nature book that educates and entertains.

20. *Machines Go to Work in the City.* Written and illustrated by William Low. (Henry Holt, 2012.) Classically trained artist William Low's introduction to big machines is a surefire hit with preschoolers who seem endlessly fascinated with vehicles and how they work. His book is interactive, richly illustrated, and succeeds in finding excitement in commonplace activities. Set in a lively cityscape, this lift-the-flap book includes pictures of a bucket truck, airplane, train, and tower crane and plenty of information to keep readers engaged. Children learn, for example, that when the garbage truck picks up trash at its last stop, there is still more to the story, as the truck must make its way to a landfill to dump its trash. When cars are backed up because of a broken traffic light, a bucket truck arrives to save the day.

21. *Little Dog Lost: The True Story of a Brave Dog Named Baltic.* Written and illustrated by Mônica Carnesi. (Nancy Paulsen Books, 2012.) With simple language and eye-catching watercolor illustrations, Carnesi captures the drama and adventure of a real-life rescue of a little brown dog stranded on a chunk of ice and swept out on the Baltic Sea. Onlookers first spot the dog from along the banks of the Vistula River in Poland. Firefighters form a human chain, but are unable to complete the rescue. Against all odds, the terrified dog is still alive after two days at sea. Finally, a research vessel brings the frozen and terrified dog on board, where he continues to live as a member of the ship's crew.

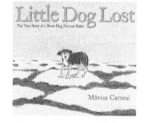

22. *Koko's Kitten*. Written by Francine Patterson. Illustrated by Ronald H. Cohn. (Scholastic, 1985.) Patterson and Cohn's story of the world famous, American Sign Language–speaking gorilla Koko is a touching account of the great ape's love for her pet kitten, All Ball. Dr. Patterson, a developmental psychologist, is the first person to ever communicate with a gorilla using sign language. With her language ability, the ape requests the tiny feline and establishes a close relationship through grooming, cuddling, and caring for her pet. The relationship comes to a tragic end when the kitten is killed in a car accident, and the gorilla's sorrow is perceptible. The book documents her grieving process. Happily, Koko is given a new kitten and is able to establish another intimate bond.

23. *Just One Bite*. Written by Lola Schaefer. Illustrated by Geoff Waring. (Chronicle Books, 2010.) Schaefer and Waring's oversized picture book dramatically illustrates the eating habits of animals large and small, and in particular, what they can consume in "just one bite." Packed with exciting facts and compelling images, the book highlights a variety of creatures. A whale eats a giant squid, an earthworm consumes a tiny speck of vegetable matter, a hummingbird sips drops of nectar, while a Komodo dragon snacks on a snake. Children will be fascinated by this gallery of creatures and will appreciate the additional information on each species contained in a foldout section at the end of the book.

24. *Elephants Can Paint, Too!* Written and illustrated by Katya Arnold. (Atheneum Books for Young Readers, 2005.) Arnold, an art teacher, tells the strange but true story of how she trained elephants to make paintings. "I teach in two schools," she writes. "One is in the city. The other is in the jungle. Some of my students have hands. Others have trunks." Arnold's human school is in New York City, and her elephant school is in an Asian jungle. On side-by-side pages, beautiful color photographs show the artwork of both types of students. Arnold's purpose is to help preserve this endangered species, which suffered neglect when the elephants began losing their jobs hauling lumber due to tree conservation efforts. The paintings are sold to raise money to support efforts to save the elephants.

25. *Bring On the Birds.* Written and illustrated by Susan Stockdale. (Peachtree Publishers, 2011.) Rhyming text and bold acrylic paintings make Stockdale's book an excellent introduction to the diverse world of birds. Budding preschool ornithologists will love this survey of 21 unique bird species from all over the planet. They will learn about birds that swim, birds that swoop and dive, birds with impressive plumage, and birds that thrive in extreme environments. While many varieties of bird life are presented, the central idea of this attractive text is that all birds have feathers and all were hatched from eggs. The book will work well as a teaching tool or for read-aloud enjoyment. More information and resources on the featured birds can be found at the back of the book.

26. *My Shapes/Mis Formas.* Written and illustrated by Rebecca Emberley. (Little, Brown, 2000.) Preschoolers and toddlers will enjoy Emberley's bilingual picture dictionary for its simple introduction to basic shapes. In double-page spreads, this board book has vibrantly colored paper-cut illustrations and large text. Each shape is paired with a familiar object that uses the shape. A circle is situated with a balloon and a triangle with a butterfly, and each is labeled in Spanish and English. Bold and sharp contrasts make *My Shapes/Mis Formas* visually appealing, encouraging young children to return often to learn new vocabulary. The book is part of a popular series that also introduces essential concepts such as color, number, and opposites.

27. *May I Pet Your Dog? The How-To Guide for Kids Meeting Dogs (and Dogs Meeting Kids).* Written by Stephanie Calmenson. Illustrated by Jan Ormerod. (Clarion Books, 2007.) Harry, a friendly dachshund, teaches a little boy the etiquette of how to safely interact with unfamiliar dogs. Calmenson and Ormerod's essential guidebook for youngsters takes Harry through the process step-by-step, beginning with the boy asking the owner's permission to pet the dog, allowing the pooch to sniff his hand, and approaching the dog from the side. How young children encounter dogs on the street is an essential topic in the book. This practical guide prepares children for their inevitable encounters with dogs by showing them a variety of canine breeds, sizes, and situations. Unavoidable meetings with unfriendly dogs are skillfully navigated in a way that is instructive and never threatening.

28. *A Second Is a Hiccup: A Child's Book of Time.* Written by Hazel Hutchins. Illustrated by Kady MacDonald Denton. (Arthur A. Levine Books, 2007.) Want to know the duration of a second? "A second is a hiccup—the time it takes to kiss your mom, or jump a rope, or turn around." Are you curious about the length of a week? It's seven sleeps. What about a year? It is the time it takes to grow into new shoes. Hutchins and Denton accomplish the challenging task of making the abstract notion of time intelligible in terms young children can really understand. With watercolor-and-ink drawings, three children are shown interacting with one another, their parents, and siblings. This is a charming and imaginative book. It will be invaluable to children learning the nature of time and the units we use for measuring it.

29. *The Tiny Seed.* Written and illustrated by Eric Carle. (Crowell, 1970.) Young readers will love Carle's nonfiction classic about a minute seed overcoming the odds and surviving the cold winter to blossom into a gorgeous spring flower. This collage picture book describes the life cycle of a plant, beginning with flower pods sending the seeds into the wind, with some making their way into the ground. When spring comes, one seed grows into a big flower, and when autumn arrives, the cycle repeats. Children learn that seeds are vulnerable and suffer heavy casualties. The sun scorches some seeds; birds, fish, or mice eat them; and some are blown into completely inhospitable environments. The illustrations are so good that the story can unfold without reading.

30. *What Do Wheels Do All Day?* Written by April Jones Prince. Illustrated by Giles Laroche. (HMH Books for Young Readers, 2006.) Large rhyming text and stunning paper collages make Prince and Laroche's tribute to wheels a guaranteed winner with young children. This interesting concept book has detailed illustrations of all kinds of wheeled objects. It's answer to the title question is an entertaining and informative display of people using wheels of all types and sizes for a variety of purposes. Windmills, pinwheels, bicycles, skateboards, Ferris Wheels, wheelchairs, trains, and tractors are only a few examples of wheels that are shown at work and play. This large book has plenty of close-ups and double-page spreads that will keep the attention of active preschoolers.

31. *Animal Dads.* Written by Sneed B. Collard III. Illustrated by Steve Jenkins. (HMH Books for Young Readers, 2000.) *Animal Dads* is a welcome addition to the countless children's books featuring mothers as the sole or primary caregiver of offspring. Collard and Jenkins's appealing pictures show how the males of various species perform a variety of parenting tasks including feeding, teaching, and protecting their young. From lions, to poison arrow frogs, to emperor penguins, strikingly vivid illustrations show animal parings in their natural habitats. Collard and Jenkins's book effectively serves different age groups with large and simple explanatory text for preschoolers and smaller print that conveys more complex and detailed ideas appropriate for older kids.

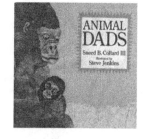

32. *Zoo Borns! Zoo Babies from around the World.* Written by Andrew Bleiman and Chris Eastland. (Simon & Schuster, 2010.) This book features color photographs of baby animals born in captivity, and it is difficult to imagine a more informative, adorable, and appropriate book for preschoolers. Bleiman and Eastland's catalog of interesting newborns includes a kangaroo, fox, hyena, tiger, mongoose, ocelot, anteater, spotted hyena, and many more. The book is clear that the critters are not pictured in their original environments. The preface explains that when animals live in the zoo, scientists can study them and then do a better job of helping to protect them in the wilderness. Cleverly written from the animal's perspective, the narrative is as engaging as the photographs.

33. *Ten Little Fingers and Ten Little Toes.* Written by Mem Fox. Illustrated by Helen Oxenbury. (HMH Books for Young Readers, 2010.) Rarely does one hear a preschool picture book described as profound or humanistic, but it might just apply to this exquisite little book that begins with the simple rhyme, "There was one little baby who was born far away. And another who was born on the very next day. And both of these babies, as everyone knows, had ten little fingers and ten little toes." Beautiful, laughing, different-looking babies from around the planet are wonderfully captured in bright watercolor illustrations. Fox and Oxenbury's focus on commonality across cultures is a tribute to tolerance. *Ten Little Fingers and Ten Little Toes* is the ideal read-aloud storybook.

34. *Biggest, Strongest, Fastest.* Written and illustrated by Steve Jenkins. (HMH Books for Young Readers, 1995.) Aided by full-color cut-paper collage illustrations, Jenkins addresses the perennial curiosity children have about animals that stand out or reign supreme in various ways. Kids will be fascinated to learn that the cheetah pictured on the book's cover is the world's fastest animal, the Etruscan shrew is so tiny that it can sleep in a teaspoon, one type of African elephant can eat 300 pounds of leaves and grass per day, and the world's biggest snake can swallow a deer whole. World records regarding 14 different animals and other surprising scientific facts will make Jenkins's book an informative favorite among young readers.

35. *The Bumblebee Queen.* Written by April Pulley Sayre. Illustrated by Patricia J. Wynne. (Charlesbridge Publishing, 2006.) With spare text and precisely rendered ink and watercolors, Sayre and Wynne provide captivating details about the busy life cycle of a queen bee. Young readers follow the bee beginning in spring when she awakens from her winter shelter, as she builds her hive in an abandoned mouse nest and collects nectar. Aspiring naturalists will learn about how the queen tends to her eggs and larvae and cares for the drones, workers, and new queens that hatch. The queen finally dies at the end of the summer, paving the way for the next generation of queen bees to start colonies of their own.

The Bumblebee Queen
April Pulley Sayre ❦ Illustrated by Patricia J. Wynne

36. *My Favorite Word Book: Words and Pictures for the Very Young.* Written and illustrated by Selina Young. (Doubleday Books for Young Readers, 1999.) There is no book that does a better job of introducing young children to basic vocabulary than *My Favorite Word Book.* This nicely illustrated, action-oriented picture book features over 500 commonly used words for common objects on bright double-page spreads with headings such as travel, parts of the body, pets, jobs, and toys. New Zealand illustrator Selina Young gets youngsters started on the road to reading by having cheerful characters named Zoe and Toby introduce kids to many things that are important in a child's world. Accompanied by some animal friends, the sister-and-brother team points out things such as frogs, bees, carrots, and toothpaste in recognizable locations including a home, garden, and supermarket. This colorful and energetic word book also has match-the-word games, hidden objects, and an index.

MY FAVORITE
WORD BOOK
Words and Pictures for the Very Young

SELINA YOUNG

37. *Here Come the Girl Scouts! The Amazing All-True Story of Juliette "Daisy" Gordon Low and Her Great Adventure.* Written by Shana Corey. Illustrated by Hadley Hooper. (Scholastic Press, 2012.) Rejecting the stuffy conventions of Victorian society, Juliette "Daisy" Gordon Low, the founder of the Girl Scouts, opened the door for girls to help others, while embracing exercise and outdoor activity and independence. Corey and Hooper's opening scene shows young Daisy wearing a petticoat, but hanging from a tree, underscoring the tension between social expectations that girls be prim and proper and their natural desire for excitement and adventure. At the first meeting of the Girl Scouts, Low's vision was made clear when she said, "They'd hike and camp and swim! They'd do good deeds. They'd learn to tie knots and survive in the wilderness and even save lives!"

38. *The Emperor's Egg.* Written by Martin Jenkins. Illustrated by Jane Chapman. (Candlewick, 2002.) Gender stereotypers beware! Jenkins and Chapman's picture book tells the true story of how the male emperor penguin stands out in the freezing cold for months guarding his mate's egg while she is out catching fish. Jenkins's light conversational style and Chapman's blue-and-purple acrylic paintings leave no doubt that this parental division of labor leaves the father temporarily underfed while the mother eats her fill of fish and squid. This cute family of anthropomorphized Antarctic birds will be very attractive to preschoolers. Readers will gain a new appreciation and definition of the idea of a present and devoted father.

39. *Hottest, Coldest, Highest, Deepest.* Written and illustrated by Steve Jenkins. (Houghton Mifflin, 1998.) The creator of *Biggest, Strongest, Fastest* succeeds in again providing young readers the fun and remarkable facts they crave. With eye-popping collage illustrations, Jenkins explores many of the greatest wonders of the natural world. This extraordinary primer of record-breaking geography takes young readers to earth's deepest ocean, highest mountain, and longest river. Jenkins also makes comparisons to put things in perspective. For example, he pictorially contrasts Russia's Lake Baikal, the world's deepest lake (5,134 feet) with New York's Empire State Building (1,250 feet). By presenting the planet as such an amazing and interesting place, Jenkins sparks the minds of curious learners and makes them want to learn more.

40. *How to Be a Baby . . . by Me, the Big Sister.* Written by Sally Lloyd-Jones. Illustrated by Sue Heap. (Schwartz & Wade, 2007.) Based on her six years of experience in this world, a sagacious big sister shares long lists of things a baby can't do and has lots of insights on the nature of infanthood. "When you're a baby, you just wear your pajamas ALL THE TIME and not real clothes" and "You don't read books. You eat them" and "When you're a baby, you don't carry a backpack. You go in one," intones the sassy and superior narrator. Lloyd-Jones and Heap's adorable story, with just the right mix of annoyance and love, is a clear standout among many books that focus on the reactions of older children to newborn babies.

41. *Tarra & Bella: The Elephant and Dog Who Became Best Friends.* Written and illustrated by Carol Buckley. (Putnam Juvenile, 2009.) With sensitive and tender descriptions and lots of color photographs, Buckley, founder and CEO of the Elephant Sanctuary in Middle Tennessee, has ably documented the unusual bond between a retired circus elephant and a stray dog. These unlikely buddies are inseparable. They play with one another, go on walks, share meals, and even nap together. When Bella is hurt, Tarra joins her at the animal hospital and remains by her side until she gets better. There even are pictures of Tarra petting Bella with her trunk. This heartwarming tale will be a favorite with young kids, and they will want to reread the book often.

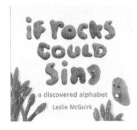

42. *If Rocks Could Sing: A Discovered Alphabet.* Written and illustrated by Leslie McGuirk. (Tricycle Press, 2011.) Over the course of 10 years, McGuirk assembled an amazing collection of 26 rocks to represent every letter of the alphabet. For the letter "B," for example, there is a bird-shaped rock on a nest with an egg. For "D," she has a dog rock with a collar, while "R" is a stone rabbit complete with a carrot. Through the imaginative arrangement of unusual ocean-sculpted rocks and the use of props, her unique alphabet book will teach valuable lessons and ensure that children never look at rocks the same way again. The book may inspire a generation of rock collectors, provide ideas for show and tell, or supply materials for arts and crafts.

43. *One Small Place in a Tree.* Written by Barbara Brenner. Illustrated by Tom Leonard. (HarperCollins, 2004.) Brenner and Leonard's book explores a hidden hole in a tree that has been the home of many animals. With detailed and realistic paintings, this description of the life cycle of a forest ecosystem shows what the tree would look like at different times over a number of years. The hole begins as a scratch from a bear. The orifice expands when woodpeckers eat its new inhabitants, timber beetles. When decay sets in, the hole grows into a small hollow and becomes home to birds and squirrels. Even when the tree falls to the ground, it provides refuge to spiders, mice, salamanders, and tree frogs. The message to would-be scientists is to look closely at nature and it will reveal fascinating secrets.

44. *Meet the Dogs of Bedlam Farm.* Written and illustrated by Jon Katz. (Henry Holt, 2011.) Katz, author of *A Dog Year* and other adult titles about dogs, makes a big splash in the world of children's books with his heartwarming picture book featuring four dogs that perform various jobs on his farm in upstate New York. Frieda, a Rottweiler–German Shepherd mix, is the farm's watchdog; Rose, a border collie, herds sheep; Izzy, also a border collie, is a therapy dog for sick people; and Labrador Retriever Lenore's only job is to be friendly and keep the rest of the pack happy. Color photographs show a successful and harmonious team with each member doing what he or she naturally does best.

45. *Pale Male: Citizen Hawk of New York City.* Written by Janet Schulman. Illustrated by Meilo So. (Knopf Books for Young Readers, 2008.) Crisp prose and luminous watercolors make Schulman and So's story of Central Park's famous red-tailed hawk a clear standout among other books about the bird and his mate who build their nest near the top of one of Fifth Avenue's luxury apartment buildings. Pale Male, named for his light color, develops a strong public following, but the building's residents become fed up with the bird droppings. When the building's owners remove the nest, there are protests and even an international outcry. The well-to-do residents lose the battle, and the birds are allowed to return to the high-rise to raise their chicks.

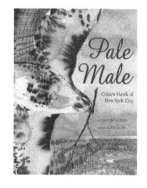

46. *Rosie, a Visiting Dog's Story.* Written by Stephanie Calmenson. Illustrated by Justin Sutcliffe. (HMH Books for Young Readers, 1998.) Calmenson and Sutcliffe's sensitive descriptions and expert color photography document the training that goes into a working dog that cheers people up in nursing homes, hospitals, and some schools. Not all dogs are suited for helping elderly, lonely, ill, or disabled people. They must, like Rosie, have a pleasant disposition, be a good listener, and be comfortable working around wheelchairs and special equipment. The book traces the Tibetan terrier puppy's stages of training and her preparation for visits, including pictures of her joyfully working in various settings. Young readers will appreciate this tribute to dogs that do so much to comfort others.

47. *Strong Man: The Story of Charles Atlas.* Written and illustrated by Meghan McCarthy. (Knopf Books for Young Readers, 2007.) McCarthy's comic-book panels tell the story of a cultural icon known for feats of strength and ability such as bending iron bars and tearing apart phone books. Charles Atlas, once the proverbial 98-pound weakling, became known as one of the world's most physically fit men. After his boyhood arrival from Italy, Charles found himself the target of bullies in his Brooklyn neighborhood. Inspired by powerful zoo animals and images of muscular Greek gods, he ended the mistreatment by becoming a bodybuilder. Charles created his own fitness program and inspired millions of people to lead healthier lives. The book has many charming illustrations including one of Charles straining to pull an actual train.

48. *My Visit to the Zoo.* Written and illustrated by Aliki. (HarperCollins, 1999.) This book is a must-read before a young child's first visit to a zoo. With lush illustrations, Aliki brings the Zoological Conservation Park to life by following two children on a tour, where they are introduced to many different animals, their habitats, and their countries of origin. Narrated by one of the children, the youngsters ride on a monorail, visit a rain forest, observe birds at the aviary, and pet young animals. The park is depicted as an animal sanctuary where the animals move about freely in natural settings. The final page has a world map showing the home of each of the 80 species mentioned.

49. *Step Gently Out.* Written by Helen Frost. Illustrated by Rick Lieder. (Candlewick, 2012.) There is something almost Zen in Frost and Lieder's simple poetry and captivating close-up photographs of the insect world. The book captures the flash of a firefly, the flight of a bumblebee, the leap of a cricket, the spin of a spider's web, and several other images in a manner that invites contemplation of their natural beauty. "Step gently out, be still, and watch a single blade of grass," Frost recommends. "A spider spins a silken thread to step across the air. A praying mantis looks at you—do you know she's there?" This meditative book would be perfect for bedtime.

50. *What Bluebirds Do.* Written and illustrated by Pamela F. Kirby. (Boyds Mills Press, 2013.) Kirby's  sharp color photos and straightforward captions feature the lives of a pair of Eastern bluebirds and five chicks. The book covers their courtship, nesting, laying of eggs, and rearing of the fledglings. Readers will feel like they have a front row seat on the baby birds' development as the birds grow toward self-sufficiency and are finally able to search for food on their own. The mated pair used a nesting box set up in the author's backyard, where she used a blind to get a number of great action and close-up pictures. The back matter of this first-rate book includes conservation information and ideas on how to support and attract bluebirds.

51. *Stars beneath Your Bed: The Surprising Story of Dust.* Written by April Pulley Sayre. Illustrated by  Ann Jonas. (Greenwillow Books, 2005.) At first blush, dust may seem like a paltry topic for a children's book, but Sayre and Jonas rise to the challenge, convincingly showing the importance of these ubiquitous specks and giving them the respect they deserve. In spare poetic words and impressionistic pictures they explain what dust is, how it moves, and how it sticks around forever. Young readers will be surprised to hear that dust is generated everywhere, from pollinating flowers to erupting volcanoes. The dust on your computer screen may have once been attached to a dinosaur, the dust under your bed may have come from a comet, and the dust in the air is what makes sunsets so colorfully magnificent.

52. *Two Bobbies: A True Story of Hurricane Katrina, Friendship, and Survival.* Written by Kirby Larson and Mary Nethery. Illustrated by Jean Cassels. (Walker Childrens, 2008.) Larson and Nethery tell the remarkable and moving story of an abandoned dog and cat in New Orleans who become best friends after Hurricane Katrina. Surviving on their own for months, Bobbi and Bob Cat wander through hazardous, storm-ravaged streets, desperately searching for food and water. Rescue workers soon find that the two cannot be separated, not only because of their emotional bond but also because Bob Cat is blind and Bobbi functions as his seeing-eye dog. After their story made national news, the two companions were happily adopted together. Watercolor illustrations provide glimpses of the city's devastation, making the book an appropriate introduction to Hurricane Katrina for a young audience.

53. *African Animal Alphabet.* Written by Beverly Joubert and Dereck Joubert. (National Geographic Children's Books, 2011.) Wildlife filmmakers and photographers Beverly and Dereck Joubert apply their expertise to children's literature with a captivating alphabet book. Powerful photographs bring African animals to life in entries for each letter of the alphabet, each accompanied by brief alliterative text. Preschoolers will enjoy pages such as "B is for Baboon: These boisterous baby baboons are bouncy little apes that like to babble and bicker" and "D is for dung beetle: Two dung beetles roll dirty dung into a decorative ball." The Jouberts, who are National Geographic "Explorers-in-Residence," include both popular and lesser-known creatures: cheetahs, elephants, lions, zebras, as well as the umbrette and Xenopus bullfrogs.

54. *Dinosaurs, Dinosaurs.* Written and illustrated by Byron Barton. (HarperCollins, 1989.) Barton makes skillful use of eye-popping colors, simple shapes, and appealing compositions to create the perfect preschool introduction to the exciting world of dinosaurs. Eager listeners will learn that dinosaurs lived a long time ago and that they came in many sizes and varieties. Some had spikes down their backs, some had boney heads, some had horns, and some had long tails. Without overwhelming his tender young audience, Barton shows that while some dinosaurs were scary, some were merely scared. The endpapers identify the beasts by their scientific name with helpful phonetic pronunciations. This simple book will keep listeners fully engaged.

55. *Alphabeasties and Other Amazing Types.* Written by Sharon Werner and Sarah Forss. (Blue Apple Books, 2009.) The special thing about Werner and Forss's lift-the-flap book is that their "alphabeasty" animals are constructed out of different typefaces. It is not just that alligators are built out of a's or that zebras are assembled with z's. Lift the flap, and K becomes a foot kicking a soccer ball, R suggests a rabbit ready to jump, G calls to mind a tall giraffe, and B conjures up gothic vampire bats. Using creative animal silhouettes, the book succeeds in teaching the alphabet and letter design. Nascent readers as well as veteran graphic designers will appreciate this animal alphabet book, and both groups will have reason to return to it again and again.

56. *The Wing on a Flea: A Book about Shapes.* Written and illustrated by Ed Emberley. (Little, Brown, 1961.) Emberley introduces the concept of shapes by encouraging children to see them in everyday things. With rhyming text and colorful images on a black background, a flea's wing becomes a triangle and the wheels on a truck can be visualized as circles. Most of Emberley's pictures are a combination of shapes, but the concept of a circle, triangle, and rectangle are clearly and separately discussed. This book is likely to inspire children to look at the world differently, finding geometric shapes embedded in common objects and situations. As the author puts it, "A circle could be a little green pea, or eyes in the dark, if you'll just look and see."

57. *Bugs! Bugs! Bugs!* Written and illustrated by Bob Barner. (Chronicle Books, 1999.) Daddy longlegs spiders, ladybugs, and butterflies are three of the very small creatures that stand out in Barner's playful picture book that begins emphatically with "Bugs! Bugs! Bugs! I want to see bugs!" The book's most interesting aspect is its bug-o-meter that lists interesting facts about each of the eight bugs featured, such as whether it can fly or sting, how many legs it has, and where it lives. Barner's vibrant multimedia illustrations of smiling bugs, insects, and arthropods will fascinate children, turning bug skeptics into bug lovers. This informative introductory book concludes with actual-size illustrations of the bugs that are sure to appeal to future entomologists.

58. *The Handiest Things in the World.* Written by Andrew Clements. Illustrated by Raquel Jaramillo. (Atheneum Books for Young Readers, 2010.) Clements and Jaramillo's tribute to the miraculous but unappreciated human hand looks at what the appendage can do and compares it to a variety of handy tools it has inspired. On double-page spreads, the first page shows photographs of a child performing some task with his hands, and the second page displays a comparable implement. This uncommon concept book examines 17 activities, such as catching an insect first with one's hands and then with a net, and digging in the ground with and without a garden tool. Rhyming text accompanies attractive close-up photos, providing a fresh look at our first and foremost mother of invention.

59. *I Face the Wind.* Written by Vicki Cobb. Illustrated by Julia Gorton. (HarperCollins, 2003.) This introductory science book makes young children begin to think scientifically by observing and experimenting with air and wind. Cobb's interactive text and Gorton's playful illustrations combine to explain many fun and informative hands-on activities. Children are asked to reflect on their experiences with wind and to name things wind can do. One simple exercise demonstrates that air has weight. Using a wire coat hanger as a rough scale, two empty balloons are shown to be in balance. When one balloon is inflated with air, the scale tilts in its direction. With some adult assistance, this easy-to-comprehend science primer is perfect for preschoolers and slightly older kids.

60. *How Many Baby Pandas?* Written and illustrated by Sandra Markle. (Walker Childrens, 2011.) Markle's fact-filled text and gorgeous close-up photos of baby pandas taken in the Woolong Giant Panda Breeding Center in China will interest children, who will surely see parallels with human development. The book focuses on 16 pandas from birth to age 2, showing how they grow, play, eat, nap, and other activities. As newborns, the cubs are surprisingly tiny, hairless, pink creatures with closed eyes. As they mature, they are pictured interacting with their mother and human caregivers. Markle's photo-essay has the additional benefit of serving as an addition book, posing basic questions, such as "How many baby pandas are eating?"

61. *Chameleons Are Cool.* Written by Martin Jenkins. Illustrated by Sue Shields. (Candlewick, 1998.) Jenkins and Shields's preschool science book illuminates the world of chameleons by looking at how they are different from other lizards and how they come in different varieties. Bright watercolor illustrations and age-appropriate text describe the chameleon's physical and behavioral attributes, especially their rotating eyes and ability to change color. One fun fact is that a chameleon's eye is mostly covered in skin and that it must use a peephole in the middle of the skin to see. This picture book is an exciting introduction to a very strange species and one that will leave the audience wanting to learn more.

62. *Harlem's Little Blackbird.* Written by Renée Watson. Illustrated by Christian Robinson. (Random House Books for Young Readers, 2012.) Born to parents who were once slaves, this remarkable story of Florence Mills is an inspiration to children and an important history lesson on how bigotry shapes a person's life. Watson and Robinson's picture book biography examines the triumphs and obstacles encountered by this trailblazing singer and dancer who achieved international success, managing to sing in London and on Broadway. Despite this, she constantly encountered discrimination. When Florence got her first chance to perform in Washington, D.C., her black friends were not permitted to be in the audience. Taking a stand for racial equality, Florence turned down an offer to become the first black woman to perform in the famous Ziegfeld Follies in favor of performing with other actors and singers in an all-black revue. Her trademark song is "I'm a Little Blackbird Looking for a Bluebird."

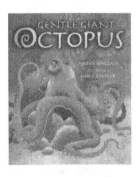

63. *Gentle Giant Octopus.* Written by Karen Wallace. Illustrated by Mike Bostock. (Candlewick, 2002.) Told in the form of a story about a mother octopus swimming through the ocean looking for a place to lay her eggs, this book succeeds as both science and entertainment. Wallace and Bostock show the vulnerable octopus, with her tentacles following behind her, being attacked first by a crab and then by an eel, who tears off a tentacle. She employs many tactics to defend herself, including camouflage, shooting backward through the water, and squeezing into small holes. When she finds a safe haven, she deposits thousands of eggs, which she protects until they hatch. Using dramatic watercolor images and few words, Wallace and Bostock show the sea creature disappearing into the ocean depths as her life cycle ends.

64. *Dig Dig Digging.* Written by Margaret Mayo. Illustrated by Alex Ayliffe. (Henry Holt, 2002.) "They can work all day" is Mayo's constant refrain as she describes the action-packed, noisy efforts of large vehicles going about their daily business. There is a lot of beeping, vrooming, whirring, and whizzing as busy machines work hard to get their jobs done. Ayliffe introduces 11 actively engaged machines, including fire engines, bulldozers, dump trucks, tractors, and helicopters, using bold cut-paper images. "Bulldozers," readers learn, "are good at push, push, pushing, over rough, bumpy ground," while "Helicopters are good at whir, whir, whirring, hovering and zooming, rotor blades whizzing." Children will be in awe of these enormous machines and will feel as if they can actually hear their engines roar.

65. *Seahorses.* Written by Jennifer Keats Curtis. Illustrated by Chad Wallace. (Henry Holt, 2012.) Curtis and Wallace's poetic text and luminescent digital artwork combine to tell the story of a male sea horse from birth to fatherhood. The book covers the little fish's growth, characteristics, and eating habits against the backdrop of a vivid coral-reef-and-sea-grass environment. Children will be surprised to discover that males are the ones that give birth to new sea horses and that they possess a chameleon's ability to camouflage themselves by changing color. This amazing life-cycle book deals sensitively with the mating ritual between the male and female, observing, "His fins become very dark brown as he waltzes around her to music only he can hear."

66. *Out of Sight.* Written by Francesco Pittau and Bernadette Gervais. (Chronicle Books, 2010.) This stunning, oversized, lift-the-flap book features more than 50 animals, each with its own flap, which reveals a surprising fact. Constructed entirely of cardboard, Pittau and Gervais's guess-the-animal picture book will captivate children with its beautiful, double-page spreads and startling information. Kids will learn

that hippopotami are actually more dangerous than sharks, marmots can whistle, buffalo can run 30 miles an hour, and some shrews are poisonous. Gervais provides plenty of visual clues, suggesting what is concealed under each flap, and some of the animals pop up when the flap is lifted. *Out of Sight* introduces the variety of the animal world in a truly fun and attention-grabbing way. Children will test the durability of the book as they return to it again and again.

67. *Ladybugs: Red, Fiery and Bright.* Written and illustrated by Mia Posada. (Carolrhoda Books, 2002.) Children may think they know all about these red-coated, flying beetles, but Posada's brightly colored, informational picture book will open new doors with its introduction to the life cycle of one of the most popular and approachable insects. With vivid close-ups and rhyming text well suited to reading aloud, the book covers what ladybugs eat, what kinds of predators can harm them, how they lay their eggs, and what they are called at different stages of development. At the end of the book, Posada has a helpful diagram showing the parts of the insect and includes pages of facts about different varieties of ladybugs.

68. *Oscar and the Bird: A Book about Electricity.* Written and illustrated by Geoff Waring. (Candlewick, 2011.) Waring's book introduces young children to the concept of electricity through a winning story of two animal friends, exciting illustrations, and supplemental activities. Oscar is a curious cat who finds a tractor in a field, hops aboard, and accidentally switches on its windshield wipers. Big-eyed Oscar does not know what is going on until a very knowledgeable and talkative bird joins him. His feathered friend explains that tractors and other machines are powered by electricity, and then he goes on to discuss batteries, generators, lightning, and even wind turbines. Readers who like *Oscar and the Bird* might consider trying other titles in the start-with-science series, such as *Oscar and the Bat: A Book about Sound* (2008) or *Oscar and the Snail: A Book about Things That We Use* (2009).

69. *I Fall Down.* Written by Vicki Cobb. Illustrated by Julia Gorton. (HarperCollins, 2004.) The award-winning author and illustrator of *I Face the Wind* takes on the topic of gravity in this outstanding science book. Cobb and Gorton are again advocating for adopting an investigational attitude in urging children to perform a series of experiments such as testing gravity by tossing objects into the air and observing the speed at which they fall. With appealing child-friendly illustrations and simple sentences, children are encouraged to explore and learn about the natural world. The recommended exercises will be great for parents and children to do together. *I Fall Down* is an excellent choice for the family library.

70. *Ones and Twos.* Written and illustrated by Marthe Jocelyn and Nell Jocelyn. (Tundra Books, 2011.) Acclaimed writer and illustrator Marthe Jocelyn and her daughter team up for the first time in producing a delightful counting book centering on two girls who meet up at the park and a mother bird who frequently crosses their path. Intended for toddlers and preschoolers, this simple book invites children to consider everyday objects alone or in pairs. In predictable verse and bright images, the girls are shown flying kites, eating snacks, and at the end of the day, having a sleepover. "One bird, two eggs, One girl, two legs" are the type of rhyming couplets that are encountered throughout the book. This Jocelyn collaboration works as a story of friendship and as a concept book.

71. *How Did That Get in My Lunchbox? The Story of Food.* Written by Chris Butterworth. Illustrated by Lucia Gaggiotti. (Candlewick, 2011.) Butterworth and Gaggiotti prove that asking children to think about the contents of their lunch box can be a valuable educational experience. The book encourages kids to ask who made the bread for their sandwich and who picked the fruit for their snack, having them look beyond the grocery store to where their food originated and how it got to market. Cheery

retro-style cartoon illustrations of food production and distribution activities include workers in fields, orchards, dairies, and factories. The book recommends better eating habits, including more fresh fruits and vegetables, and has a chart of the five basic food groups. After reading this book, children will see the food packed in their lunch box in a different light.

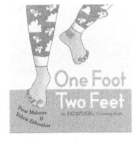

72. *One Foot Two Feet: An Exceptional Counting Book.* Written by Peter Maloney and Felicia Zekauskas. (Putnam Juvenile, 2011.) In this creative, dual-purpose counting-and-vocabulary book, a die-cut window displays one member of a group that will be seen on the subsequent page. With cartoon-style artwork and a light touch, Maloney and Zekauskas use the picture book to advance young readers' understanding of irregular plural nouns. Thus, by turning a page, one foot becomes two feet, one mouse become three mice, one die becomes six dice, and so forth. Providing comic relief, there is a little airplane shown flying from page to page, a device which entertains rather than distracts. There is also a handy row of images at the bottom of the pages to help readers keep track of where they are in the book.

73. *The Busy Body Book: A Kid's Guide to Fitness.* Written and illustrated by Lizzy Rockwell. (Dragonfly Books, 2008.) Two happy kids bouncing on pogo sticks on the book's cover set the tone for this pictorial fitness guide. Rockwell's well-intentioned book is a straightforward attempt to encourage kids to be more physically active and better able to personally resist the tide of childhood obesity. She stresses that the human body was made for vigorous movement, not just lounging on a couch. There are excellent diagrams that show the skeleton, muscles, heart, and blood vessels to give youngsters a firm grasp of what is taking place inside them. Rockwell suggests several games and activities—from dog walking to bike riding to wheelchair racing—that will give all types of children plenty of ideas for healthy exercise.

74. *One Boy.* Written and illustrated by Laura Vaccaro Seeger. (Roaring Brook Press, 2008.) Seeger teaches the numbers from 1 to 10 with simple cutout pages that entice preschoolers to turn page after page while guessing at what will come next. Her richly illustrated and cleverly designed book starts with a boy who appears alone in a cutout square. Readers see that he has a bag of paintbrushes and when they begin turning pages, they find two seals, three apes, and so on. At the end of the book, it is clear that it was the boy who painted the images. The special thing about this colorful concept book is its peek-a-boo quality. Every cutout reveals something about the larger picture that follows.

75. *My Painted House, My Friendly Chicken and Me.* Written by Maya Angelou. Illustrated by Margaret Courtney-Clarke. (Crown Books for Young Readers, 2003.) Poet laureate Maya Angelou and photojournalist Margaret Courtney-Clarke collaborate in telling a story about Thandi, a South African Ndebele girl, and the extraordinary artwork produced by the women of her tribe. Thandi, who in this first-person narrative addresses the reader as "stranger-friend," talks about her brother, her cherished chicken, and her village. Stunning color photographs document the traditional village culture through its wall paintings, beadwork, and blankets. This warm and positive introduction to a different way of life would be a good read-aloud selection. Young listeners will like Thandi's innocent voice and appreciate her touches of humor.

76. *Rah, Rah, Radishes! A Vegetable Chant.* Written and illustrated by April Pulley Sayre. (Beach Lane Books, 2011.) Sayre's cheerleading tribute to fresh vegetables is a passionate attempt to get young people to eat more of them. Vibrant and appealing photographs unite with rhyming and alliterative text to celebrate multiple veggie varieties and plug unabashedly for healthier eating. This ideal read-aloud book

includes common selections and introduces children to the probably unexplored territory of fennel, kale, kohlrabi, rutabagas, bok choy, and scallion. Kids who previously held to the conviction that they do not like vegetables might be convinced to give them another try. Sayre's comic endnote advises, "No vegetables were harmed or mistreated in the making of this book. Most, however, were later eaten."

77. *Museum ABC.* Written by Metropolitan Museum of Art. (Little, Brown Books for Young Readers, 2002.) *Museum ABC* is not your typical ABC book. Using the alphabet, this exceptional title provides a uniquely rewarding tour of the New York Metropolitan Museum of Art's world-renowned collection. With little text and many of the most spectacular pieces of art imaginable, this picture book will satisfy people of all ages. Beginning with "A is for Apple," readers will see a page of four paintings, including details from Roy Lichtenstein's *Red Apple* and Paul Cezanne's *Apples*, all taken from the Met's enormous collections. The book continues this pattern of abstracting common objects from uncommon pictures, representing a diverse range of artists, countries, and media.

78. *In the Trees, Honey Bees.* Written by Lori Mortensen. Illustrated by Cris Arbo. (Dawn Publications, 2009.) The best part of Mortensen and Arbo's exploration of the remarkable lives of honeybees are the close-up, inside-the-hive views of the queen and bee eggs in their wild colony. Brightly colored images focus on a beehive hidden in a tree trunk and include the surrounding landscape. Through the experience of short rhymes and detailed illustrations, young readers will find out how honeybees work and respond to threats. One picture shows bees warding off an attack from a hungry bear. Other illustrations show the relationship of bees to other animals and to beekeepers who depend on their honey. *In the Trees,*

Honey Bees is the best introduction for beginning readers to this enticing and important insect.

79. *Monarch and Milkweed.* Written by Helen Frost. Illustrated by Leonid Gore. (Atheneum Books for Young Readers, 2008.) This book deals with the interrelated life cycles of the lowly milkweed plant and the spectacular monarch butterfly that makes an annual intercontinental flight to lay eggs on the host plant. Frost and Gore's account of this special symbiotic relationship is told with precise poetic text and attractive pastel-and-acrylic illustrations. Their story starts with the growth of the milkweed shoot and the insect's northern migration from Mexico covering thousands of miles. Upon her arrival, the beautiful butterfly finds a mate, lays her eggs, and then departs. When the egg hatches, a tiny caterpillar emerges to eat the pale green leaves, grow into a chrysalis, and finally become a new monarch, while the milkweed seeds scatter in the wind. Endpapers provide a map of the butterfly's amazing journey.

80. *Slow Down for Manatees.* Written and illustrated by Jim Arnosky. (Putnam Juvenile, 2010.) When a motorboat seriously injures a pregnant Florida manatee, she is rescued and nursed back to health in a seaside aquarium facility. With sensitive acrylic artwork and straightforward text, Arnosky tells the story of the terrible accident, the recovery period, and the surprise birth of a healthy calf. The gentle manatee, a member of an endangered species, becomes a favorite with aquarium visitors. After the mother and child were released back into the canal where they were found, a sign was posted advising boaters to slow down for manatees. Young readers will learn the importance of protecting these majestic animals and acquire information about their behavior and habitat along the way.

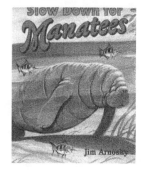

81. *Meet the Howlers!* Written by April Pulley Sayre. Illustrated by Woody Miller. (Charlesbridge Publishing, 2010.) Sayre and Miller's introduction to the howler monkeys of Central and South America is an entertaining and informative picture book. Against a leafy, verdant backdrop, the book shows the energetic rain forest creatures swinging through the branches loudly crying "Woo-hoo-hoo! AH-UH-OH," a refrain that appears throughout the book. There are lots of facts about their environment, traits, eating habits, facial expressions, and rude behavior, including a tendency "to urinate close to or on the invader to mark their territories." With watercolor crayons and pencil illustrations and engaging text, this playful book will be great for solitary readers or for reading aloud.

82. *Life-Size Zoo: From Tiny Rodents to Gigantic Elephants, An Actual Size Animal Encyclopedia.* Written by Teruyuki Komiya. Illustrated by Toyofumi Fukuda. (Seven Footer Press, 2009.) Arresting photographs taken at Japanese zoos give readers the unique opportunity to see zoo animals in their actual size. Wildlife photographer Toyofumi Fukuda accomplishes this by taking full-length photos of smaller animals, such as the prairie dog and meerkats, and headshots of larger animals, such as zebras and elephants. The close-ups of faces of the bigger animals are particularly striking and include unusual glimpses of the tongues of both a tiger and giraffe. This oversized book has pictures of 20 animals, with facts about their body dimensions and habitat in adjoining panels. Small whole-body images of the animals appear on the end pages with information about their locations throughout the world.

83. *An Island Grows.* Written by Lola M. Schaefer. Illustrated by Cathie Felstead. (Greenwillow Books, 2006.) Schaefer and Felstead's important story of the birth of an island traces its growth from an erupting undersea volcano to a fully developed island. Colorful collage illustrations show each stage of the island's development, from red-hot magma bubbling on the ocean floor, to an accumulating mound of rocks, to a thriving ecosystem with plants and animals. Finally, the island is shown hosting a vibrant community of people. At the end of the book, another undersea volcano erupts, and the primordial process of island birth begins again. *An Island Grows* concisely chronicles many significant transformations in ways that young readers can easily grasp. The book is introductory science at its best.

84. *An Orange in January.* Written by Dianna Hutts Aston. Illustrated by Julie Maren. (Dial, 2007.) How do ripe oranges find their way to grocery shelves? Aston and Maren answer this question with an interesting story of the life and journey of an orange, beginning with an orchard tree blossom and ending with the sweet, juicy fruit in the mouths of eager youngsters. In this celebration of one of nature's original pleasures, curious readers will find beautiful imagery and information about plant growth and the produce business. Starting with the hand of a worker plucking an orange and loading it on a truck, the long trip from tree to market culminates in the hands of a lucky boy who shares it with friends.

85. *In the Wild.* Written by David Elliott. Illustrated by Holly Meade. (Candlewick, 2013.) Elliott's smart, lyrical text and Meade's stunning woodcuts combine to create memorable portraits of 13 wild animals and their habitats. In full-spread illustrations, the featured creatures include an elephant, buffalo, lion, sloth, panda, tiger, rhino, and polar bear, each seeming to jump off the pages. A panda is pictured in a bamboo forest and a jaguar is seen prowling in the jungle, while an Arctic polar bear disappears into the snow, cleverly alluding to the bear's status as an endangered species. The poetry is equally engaging: "When peaceful, silent; when angry, loud. Who would have guessed the Elephant is so much like a cloud?"

86. *Sign Language ABC.* Written and illustrated by Lora Heller. (Sterling Children's Books, 2012.) Heller, who teaches American Sign Language to babies and toddlers in New York City, has produced a book that extends her commitment to finger spelling to a much wider audience. She immediately hooks her audience with the suggestion, "Imagine being able to tell your friend a secret from way across the playground." Presenting hand signing as a fun and useful skill, Heller shows small hands in a range of skin tones forming letters within inset circles. Next to the circles are cute cartoon illustrations that simply state that A is for Astronaut, C is for Crab, J is for Juggle, R is for Robot, and so forth.

87. *First the Egg.* Written and illustrated by Laura Vaccaro Seeger. (Roaring Brook Press, 2007.) Seeger's unusual concept book is about the wonder of transformations, particularly those in nature. Minimal text and simple die-cuts on each page show a repeating first-then pattern: first an egg and then a chicken, first a caterpillar and then a butterfly, first a seed and then a flower, and so on. The book concludes with some examples that are more abstract, such as paint becoming a picture and a word becoming a story. Children will enjoy poking their fingers through the die-cut holes and flipping the durable pages to further consider these momentous changes. *First the Egg* provides not only tactile stimulation but also a first introduction to the classic conundrum, "Which came first, the chicken or the egg?"

88. *On the Farm.* Written by David Elliott. Illustrated by Holly Meade. (Candlewick, 2008.) The fast-fading family farm is captured nostalgically in Elliott's rich poetry and Meade's bold woodcuts. Set in double pages, the idyllic farmhouse and barnyard feature a large cast of animal characters from busy bees to strutting roosters to head-butting rams. A stealthy snake winding his way in the garden is the only thing that disturbs this rustic scene. Elliott and Meade, the same team who produced *In the Wild*, have produced another winning combination of lyrical text and eye-grabbing woodcuts. Children and adults will love its old-fashioned beauty. Starting with the crowing rooster on the front cover and continuing inside to the grazing cows, the book exemplifies the ideal of the American farm.

89. *The Boy Who Loved Math: The Improbable Life of Paul Erdös.* Written by Deborah Heiligman. Illustrated by LeUyen Pham. (Roaring Brook Press, 2013.) This is a picture-book biography of a world famous Hungarian genius who spent all of his time living out of suitcases and traveling to solve math problems. Heiligman and Pham compellingly and compassionately show Paul Erdös to be an unconventional man with great contradictions. From a very early age, he had the ability to calculate in his head the number of seconds a person was alive. Yet even as an adult, he still needed his mother to do his laundry and even butter his bread. Paul didn't fit in at school, and was homeschooled by his mother, who was a mathematics teacher. To illustrate Paul's single-minded fascination with numbers, Pham shows complex math puzzles floating around him and scattered in his environment.

90. *Why? The Best Ever Question and Answer Book about Nature, Science and the World around You.* Written by Catherine Ripley. Illustrated by Scot Ritchie. (Owlkids Books, 2010.) Why do cows moo? Why is soap so slippery? How does soda get fizzy? Why are some eggs white while others are brown? Why do cats' eyes shine in the dark? Why are peaches fuzzy? How do bees make honey? With cheery cartoon illustrations and an amazing array of spot-on topics, Ripley and Ritchie's question-and-answer book supplies basic information about everyday questions and childhood interests. Six sections sort the questions into familiar categories such as supermarket, kitchen, nighttime, outdoor, and farm animal. This query-based book works because it responds to children's curiosity in a very engaging and effective way.

91. *My Light.* Written and illustrated by Molly Bang. (Scholastic, 2004.) In this original treatment of the sun and other related sources of energy, Bang cleverly has the sun narrate the story. Kids will be drawn to the sun's voice as it proclaims, "I am your sun, a golden star. You see my radiance as light." The sun explains how rain carries "my energy" down until it is captured in a dam. "The water spins the turbines round and round. It spins my energy to generators, which make electricity." Compelling images work in tandem with the text to show how energy comes from water, wind, earth, and sun. This ambitious book also describes the weather cycle, windmills, fossil fuels, and solar cells.

92. *Pop! The Invention of Bubble Gum.* Written and illustrated by Meghan McCarthy. (Simon & Schuster/Paula Wiseman Books, 2010.) With easy-to-understand language and funny illustrations, McCarthy uses her signature cartoon characters and imagery to tell the story of Walter Diemer, the creator of bubble gum. McCarthy acknowledges that gum has been around since the time of the ancient Greeks, but it took a candy factory accountant tinkering with different formulas to perfect one of history's most beloved treats. Walter is an exemplar of enterprise and trial-and-error persistence as he helps his business become more successful. This picture biography and history of gum is edifying, but what really stands out are the many pictures of happy people blowing their first pink bubbles.

93. *Are You a Snail?* Written by Judy Allen. Illustrated by Tudor Humphries. (Kingfisher, 2000.) The life of a slimy blob is no walk in the park. With short, simple sentences and colorful watercolor and pencil drawings, Allen and Humphries show that there are many challenges that go into changing from an egg to a grown up snail. In the course of a lifetime, snails must constantly find food and water, do their best to avoid predators, and somehow survive the winter. Preschoolers and early readers will love this close-up examination of the common backyard snail and will never look at the creature the same way again. Allen and Humphries have teamed up on other "Are You" books that include portraits of grasshoppers, butterflies, bees, ladybugs, and dragonflies.

94. *Snowflakes Fall.* Written by Patricia MacLachlan. Illustrated by Steven Kellogg. (Random House Books for Young Readers, 2013.) MacLachlan and Kellogg celebrate the precious beauty and uniqueness of every human life in this touching tribute to the victims of the Sandy Hook Elementary shootings in Newtown, Connecticut, that occurred in 2012. The book is an affirmation of life written in continuous verse and illustrated to show how the world renews itself through changes in season. MacLachlan writes, "Snowflakes / Fall / Drift / And swirl together / Like the voices of children," in a powerful metaphor and reminder of the fragile and fleeting nature of childhood. Kellogg, a 35-year resident of the village of Sandy Hook, raised his family there.

95. *Hachiko.* Written by Pamela S. Turner. Illustrated by Yan Nascimbene. (HMH Books for Young Readers, 2004.) Turner and Nascimbene tell the true story of a devoted Tokyo dog who became famous because of his daily trips to a train station. Hachiko accompanied his owner to the train every day, and, after his master passed away, he continued for 10 years to go to the station each day to keep vigil for the deceased man. The dog's story is told through the eyes of a young boy named "Kentaro," who along with others provided the faithful dog with food and water. The story, exuding dignity rather than sentimentality, is illustrated with pictures of women in kimonos and other images that make its Japanese setting clear. Hachiko died of old age at the train station and a bronze statue was erected there in his honor.

96. *Market!* Written and illustrated by Ted Lewin. (HarperCollins, 1996.) Lewin's detailed watercolor paintings of six markets from around the world are a vivid showcase of cultural and ethnic diversity. This exciting tour features a rich array of goods: Ecuador's sweaters, ponchos, bowls, and spices; Nepal's woodcarvings; Ireland's horses; Uganda's meats and bananas; New York City's fish; and Morocco's pottery and dates. With several double-page spreads per country, Lewin shows the commonality and differences of far-flung buying and selling activities on busy streets, country roads, and in desert conditions. Lewin's lively compositions resemble photographs. Concise text complements the pictures by further describing the settings and the items for sale.

97. *Redwoods.* Written and illustrated by Jason Chin. (Flash Point, 2009.) When a boy finds an abandoned book about the redwood forests and starts reading it, his normal subway trip is transformed into an adventurous, educational visit to old-growth redwoods. As he begins to read and consider the age of the ancient trees, imagined dinosaurs can be seen in the subway windows, and the boy is pictured sitting next to a Roman Legionnaire wearing a toga. Exiting the subway, he explores the forest, learning about the redwood's growth patterns and properties and is in awe of their immensity. When he returns from his reverie, a girl picks up the book to start her own adventure. Chin's imaginative story is a brilliant mixture of fiction and nonfiction, succeeding as straightforward information and as pure fantasy.

98. *My First Day.* Written by Steve Jenkins and Robin Page. Illustrated by Steve Jenkins. (HMH Books for Young Readers, 2013.) Covering both well-known and exotic animals, Jenkins and Page, a creative team, describe what 23 different newborns can do with and without their parents' help on the first day of life. In a book that differentiates based on degrees of independence, human babies and Siberian tigers are relatively helpless as they enter the world. But other species hit the ground running or hit the water swimming, such as the wood duck that is pictured jumping out of the nest and immediately paddling after its mother. A self-sufficient wildebeest similarly announces, "On my first day, I trotted along with my mother. My herd was on the move, and I had to keep up!" Beautiful cut-paper illustrations and short paragraphs narrated by the animals combine to document the crucial few hours for the emperor penguin, polar bear, sea otter, and many other animals.

99. *Swirl by Swirl: Spirals in Nature.* Written by Joyce Sidman. Illustrated by Beth Krommes. (HMH Books for Young Readers, 2011.) Sidman and Krommes have created a unique tribute to a naturally occurring shape that has a design that is both beautiful and valuable. With poetry and illustrations of elegant simplicity, the book supplies an incredible array of spiral examples in snail shells, rushing rivers, elephant tusks, flower buds, space galaxies, funnel tornados, ocean waves, curled up chipmunks, and even the human ear. Celebrating the spiral's utility (as in the tight grasp of a spider monkey's tail) and its perfection as a mathematical construct (as in the Fibonacci sequence), *Swirl by Swirl* will be a memorable experience, producing a heightened awareness and appreciation of this special pattern in the natural world.

100. *Goodnight, Goodnight Construction Site.* Written by Sherri Duskey Rinker. Illustrated by Tom Lichtenheld. (Chronicle Books, 2011.) "The sun has set, the work is done; It's time for trucks to end their fun. So one by one they'll go to bed, To yawn and rest their sleepy heads, Then wake up to another day, Of rough-and-tough construction play!" Rinker and Lichtenheld's unusual bedtime book introduces toddlers and preschoolers to five big hardworking trucks that at the end of the day prepare to go to sleep. With the sun setting on their construction site, these cute anthropomorphized machines lie down to rest one

by one. The crane truck folds his boom, the cement mixer takes a bath, the dump truck begins to snore, while the bulldozer and excavator also settle in with their nightly rituals. Against a starlit sky, soothing illustrations of the trucks and engaging rhythmic text make *Goodnight, Goodnight Construction Site* an ideal read-aloud selection.

CHAPTER 2

Early Readers (Ages 5–9)

For inquisitive kids there is nothing better than well-written nonfiction.

—Marilyn Courtot

1. *Actual Size.* Written and illustrated by Steve Jenkins. (HMH Books for Young Readers, 2011.) Taking on the concept of scale, award-winning master of collage illustration Steve Jenkins creates one of his greatest books yet for young readers and listeners. In this large picture book, he shows 18 life-size animals in whole or part, sometimes making their actual size clear through comparisons with everyday objects. Though he supplies ample textual information, the startling images most effectively tell the story. Among these are a giant squid eye that is larger than a human head, a massive gorilla hand, a tiny dwarf goby, a two-inch pygmy shrew, and a saltwater crocodile with a face so large it requires a multipage foldout. Kids who view size as a personal matter will appreciate the book's size-and-weight information and love the extreme images of big and small.

2. *The Beetle Book.* Written and illustrated by Steve Jenkins. (HMH Books for Young Readers, 2012.) This large-format picture book opens with the astounding fact that 25 percent of every type of plant and animal on the planet is a beetle. Jenkins explores the fascinating variety and special nature of beetles, including their structure, function, and topics such as how they feed, communicate, reproduce, and defend themselves. Early readers and listeners will be astonished by the fact that there are over 350,000 different types of beetles, and they will be riveted by the colorful collage illustrations, including dark silhouettes showing the beetles' actual size. This introduction to the world's most ubiquitous insect is packed with little-known facts and arresting images.

3. *Black Jack: The Ballad of Jack Johnson.* Written by Charles R. Smith Jr. Illustrated by Shane W. Evans. (Roaring Brook Press, 2010.) In verse and collage artwork, Smith and Evans tell the important story of the first African American fighter to become the heavyweight champion of the world. Children will be interested in how young Jack stood up to bullies at the urging of his mother and how he then worked hard to become one of the most renowned athletes of the 20th century. Jack Johnson, the son of former slaves, was a source of pride and inspiration to black people, and his accomplishments reverberated inside and outside the world of sports. Jim Jeffries, the reigning champ, was so concerned about losing a fight to a black man that he retired. When Jeffries finally decided to fight Johnson, Jeffries was defeated.

4. *Monsieur Marceau: Actor without Words.* Written by Leda Schubert. Illustrated by Gerard DuBois. (Flash Point, 2012.) Schubert and DuBois tell the little-known story of the teenage World War II hero in Nazi-occupied France who grew up to become the world's most famous mime. As a child, Marcel idolized Charlie Chaplin and practiced miming for his friends. When he was a young man, he bravely helped Jewish children escape to Switzerland and hid U.S. parachutists, preventing their capture. After the war, Marcel Marceau studied mime and created his famous persona known for its whiteface, red lips, and rumpled stovepipe hat. This excellent biography depicts Marcel in costume expressively and wordlessly acting out situations such as tug of war, fighting a bull, and chasing butterflies.

5. *When Marian Sang: The True Recital of Marian Anderson.* Written by Pam Muñoz Ryan. Illustrated by Brian Selznick. (Scholastic Press, 2002.) Ryan and Selznick team up to tell the story of one of America's greatest singers, African American contralto Marian Anderson. This large picture book with rich sepia-toned illustrations begins with young Marian singing in her south Philadelphia church choir and moves on to her lifelong struggle against racism. Marian is excluded from many American venues but achieves great success and popularity in Europe. The climactic ending of the book shows the great vocalist finally getting to perform in an American setting commensurate with her ability, before an audience of 75,000 at a 1939 Lincoln Memorial concert.

6. *Astronaut Handbook.* Written and illustrated by Meghan McCarthy. (Knopf Books for Young Readers, 2008.) McCarthy's picture book follows the exciting progress of four bug-eyed cartoon astronauts getting ready to travel into space. Young readers and listeners will follow these aspiring recruits as they receive rigorous training, attend astronaut classes, take fitness tests, get measured for their space suits, and finally blast off. Would-be adventurers will learn that not all astronauts are trained for the same jobs: some are scientists, some fly the spacecraft, and others repair equipment. As part of their preparation, astronauts are passengers in a plane called the "Vomit Comet," which enables them to experience weightlessness. This informative book includes helpful pictures of critical equipment such as the space suits and space shuttle toilet.

7. *On Earth.* Written and illustrated by G. Brian Karas. (Perfection Learning, 2008.) Describing the earth as a giant merry-go-round, Karas encourages his young readers to think big as he invites them to climb aboard our planet for a ride through space. With text and cartoon pictures of admirable simplicity, he ambitiously delves into concepts such as rotation and revolution, the passing of seasons, and even the tilt of the earth's axis. Children will realize, possibly for the first time, that they live on a planet that is in constant motion, spinning and circling in a vast universe of planets and stars. *On Earth* is a charming, illustrated, and informative first science book that early readers will want to study on their own and hear read aloud.

8. *Country Road ABC: An Illustrated Journey through America's Farmland.* Written and illustrated by Arthur Geisert. (HMH Books for Young Readers, 2010.) Although it is organized alphabetically, Geisert's beautiful and informative picture book is not really a preschooler's ABC book but a showcase of contemporary American farm life better suited to early readers and listeners. Young children are pictured traveling along an Iowa landscape and witnessing agricultural activities through a careful selection of 26 words and detailed color scenes, while on the lower portion of the page, a country road cleverly forms a continuous panorama. The book has a glossary to help with vocabulary and explain concepts such as ammonia fertilizer, soil erosion, and z-braces (used to stabilize barns). Geisert's book is not a nostalgic walk down memory lane but a realistic rendering of the present-day lives of farmers.

9. *Soar, Elinor!* Written by Tami Lewis Brown. Illustrated by François Roca. (Farrar, Straus & Giroux, 2010.) Admirers of Amelia Earhart will be delighted to find this gem of a book about a lesser-known woman aviator, Elinor Smith. Beginning flying lessons at the age of 10, she became the youngest person to earn a pilot's license in America at the age of 16. As a teenager, she became famous for flying beneath four of New York City's bridges, and at 89 years of age, she was honored by being invited to operate NASA's space shuttle simulator. Roca's realistic paintings excellently accompany Brown's catalog of her many accomplishments. *Soar, Elinor!* was based on Brown's interviews with Elinor before the legendary pilot passed away in 2010.

10. *Just a Second.* Written and illustrated by Steve Jenkins. (HMH Books for Young Readers, 2011.) Teaching young children about the passage of time is no small challenge, and Jenkins succeeds admirably in this dazzling, fact-filled book. This extraordinary picture book not only makes units of time intelligible, it also sparks curiosity in science, math, and the earth's history. Accompanied by his signature collages, Jenkins stretches the mind by having readers and listeners consider that a bumblebee's wings can beat 200 times per second, a ladybug can eat 500 aphids in a week, or a person standing at the equator is actually moving at a rate of 18 miles per minute as the planet rotates. Adults may be just as enthralled as early readers with this book.

11. *A Weed Is a Flower: The Life of George Washington Carver.* Written and illustrated by Aliki. (Prentice Hall, 1965.) This is the inspirational story of a man who rose above his modest beginnings to become a scientist and devote his life to helping others, particularly poor southern farmers. Although he was born a slave, through diligence and hard work he was able to make numerous discoveries involving common peanuts. Dr. Carver studied agricultural science at the Tuskegee Institute and taught farmers about the importance of rotating crops. Aliki's account of the life of George Washington Carver is informative and boldly illustrated. This biography will help early readers and listeners appreciate the importance of diligence and scientific discovery.

12. *Around One Cactus: Owls, Bats and Leaping Rats.* Written by Anthony D. Fredericks. Illustrated by Jennifer DiRubbio. (Dawn Publications, 2003.) During daylight hours, a child sees a saguaro cactus standing alone and assumes that there is nothing else to observe in the dry desert. Fredericks and DiRubbio show a nocturnal transformation, a scene that comes alive with a variety of creepy, crawly, fascinating creatures. The reality of a complex ecosystem is made clear through rhyming verse and vibrant illustrations. The animal life in and around the cactus includes a scorpion, rattlesnake, owl, and Gila monster, which the author observes are there to "play or prey." The picture book's field-notes section provides plenty of information on the animals, including the fact that all of them can be found in the Sonoran Desert.

13. *Ballet for Martha: Making Appalachian Spring.* Written by Jan Greenberg and Sandra Jordan. Illustrated by Brian Floca. (Flash Point, 2010.) Greenberg, Jordan, and Floca have produced an important book about the collaboration of three master artists who worked together to create one of the world's most-renowned ballets, *Appalachian Spring.* This behind-the-scenes story of choreographer Martha Graham, composer Aaron Copland, and set designer Isamu Noguchi explains the development of the iconic performance about American pioneers. Through sparse text and elegant watercolors, readers witness the diverse talents laboring intensely to prepare for the ballet's inaugural performance at the Library of Congress in 1944. This historical picture book captures the excitement of the creative process and the artists that brought *Appalachian Spring* to life.

14. *Life in the Ocean: The Story of Oceanographer Sylvia Earle.* Written and illustrated by Claire A. Nivola. (Farrar, Straus & Giroux, 2012.) This outstanding picture book biography of Sylvia Earle shows her development from her simple curiosity about nature, to her growth into a world-renowned scientist and explorer, and, finally, to her becoming a passionate protector of the oceans. Earle began her love affair with the sea as a young girl swimming in the Gulf of Mexico. Nivola's vivid and detailed pictures show young Sylvia studying a dragonfly surrounded by pond creatures and later swimming in the vast blue ocean. Years later Sylvia, now a marine scientist, lived for two weeks in a deep-sea station and helped design devices that allowed divers to go to astounding underwater depths. An author's note asks for action to protect the endangered oceans from the hazards of oil spills, overfishing, and pollution.

15. *Living Sunlight: How Plants Bring the Earth to Life*. Written by Molly Bang and Penny Chisholm. (Blue Sky Press, 2009.) In this sequel to *My Light*, Molly Bang coauthors with MIT professor Penny Chisholm to describe photosynthesis, with the sun again serving as narrator and star of the show. Responsible for giving life to everything on earth is no small task. Fortunately, the sun is up to the challenge, bestowing its energy on plants, and then, on animals and people. Bang and Chisholm ably explain the remarkable cycle of converting energy into the building blocks of plant life and how animal life depends on plants for food and oxygen, but photosynthesis is an inherently challenging concept. Early readers and listeners will want and need to return to this wonderful picture book again and again to understand this miraculous process.

16. *An Egg Is Quiet*. Written by Dianna Hutts Aston. Illustrated by Sylvia Long. (Chronicle Books, 2006.) Aston and Long's attractive and informative guide to the world of eggs is surprising in its variety. It features 60 types of eggs in different shapes, colors, textures, and sizes, each elegantly illustrated and succinctly described with distinctive cursive font and poetic text. This album includes eggs from ladybugs, hummingbirds, ostriches, snakes, fishes, frogs, sea turtles, emperor penguins, and even fossilized dinosaur eggs.

Young readers will learn that some eggs are camouflaged to blend in with their environment and that some eggs from species such as the seabird are pointy "so if they're laid on rock ledges, they roll around in safe little circles, not off the cliff."

17. *The Extraordinary Mark Twain (According to Susy).* Written by Barbara Kerley. Illustrated by Edwin Fotheringham. (Scholastic Press, 2010.) In 1885 and 1886, Susy Clemens, Mark Twain's 13-year-old daughter, eager to show that her famous father was much more than a mere humorist, decided to set the record straight by writing a biography of him. She spent these two years documenting the celebrated writer's life. Her work was finally published in its entirety in 1985, and Kerley includes excerpts in Clemens's own handwriting in this large-format picture book. Liberally quoting from Susy's account, Kerley enhances this tender and admiring portrait. While Susy sought to expand her father's reputation beyond comedy, the irony of Fotheringham's best illustrations is that they are comedic.

18. *Can We Save the Tiger?* Written by Martin Jenkins. Illustrated by Vicky White. (Candlewick, 2011.) In this thoughtful introduction to endangered species, Jenkins and White ask not only "Can we save the tiger" but also can we save the kakapo, bison, sawfish, partula snail, ground iguana, white-rumped vulture, and many other near-extinct animals. There are thousands of species that are in danger of disappearing unless steps are taken to protect them. With its clear, concise, and simple discussion of complicated issues and detailed color illustrations, this call to action is well suited to a young audience. Children will feel a sense of responsibility for helping to take care of these rare creatures and will be heartened by the book's success stories.

19. *How to Clean a Hippopotamus: A Look at Unusual Animal Partnerships.* Written by Steve Jenkins and Robin Page. Illustrated by Steve Jenkins. (HMH Books for Young Readers, 2010.) This talented husband-and-wife partnership is on firm scientific ground in their exploration of fascinating symbiotic animal relationships. When an egret hitches a ride on the back of a large antelope, the bird benefits by eating the grasshoppers that fly up from the grazing animal. The antelope likewise benefits by getting early warnings from the egret about approaching predators. In attractive page layouts that resemble a graphic novel, the book supplies many examples of mutually beneficial interactions, including those between humans and dogs, crabs and jellyfish, and little turtles who partner with gigantic hippopotamuses. This attention-grabbing book is packed with diet, size, and habitat information for more than 50 animals.

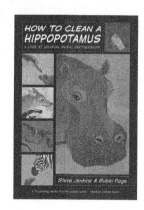

20. *Insect Detective.* Written by Steve Voake. Illustrated by Charlotte Voake. (Candlewick, 2012.) The Voake cousins have produced an exciting fact-filled introduction to the planet's most abundant creature. According to the book, "there are more insects living in the world than all the other animals put together—that's about 20,000,000 insects for every single person." What's more, these six-legged creatures are all doing strange and wonderful things for those who care to investigate. The Voakes' large-format book, written with brief prose and gracefully illustrated, is an invitation to go outdoors. Children are encouraged to look closely and find insects hunting for food, building nests, and living together underground. They will learn that ants communicate by touching their antennae and wasps use their strong jaws to collect wood. Readers will be well rewarded for their detective work.

21. *Pelé, King of Soccer/El rey del fútbol.* Written by Monica Brown. Illustrated by Rudy Gutiérrez. (Rayo, 2008.) Brown and Gutiérrez's tale of the legendary soccer superstar Pelé begins with his impoverished Brazilian childhood and his dream of one day winning the World Cup. Pelé, the first man in the history of soccer to score 1,000 goals, is shown playing the game with his boyhood friends and father, joining a professional team at age 15, and realizing the full extent of his adult abilities in executing his famous "bicycle kick." The images show a determined man bursting with energy and enthusiasm at the top of his profession. This energetic and inspirational picture story is told in both English and Spanish.

22. *Sea Horse: The Shyest Fish in the Sea.* Written by Chris Butterworth. Illustrated by John Lawrence. (Candlewick, 2006.) The world of the cautious and mysterious sea horse comes alive in this engaging book about one of the ocean's endangered species. With a curled tail like a monkey, a head resembling a horse, and "tiny prickles down his back, like a dragon," this unusual creature is extremely wary of danger. Always alert for predators, a male sea horse carefully navigates through gorgeously illustrated waving sea grass, changing color to match his environment. Butterworth and Lawrence do a particularly good job depicting its mating behavior. Children may be surprised to learn that sea horses mate for life. Through intricate engravings and lyrical text, they will learn about the sea horse's mating dance, the deposit of the female's eggs in the male's pouch, and the birthing process where baby sea horses "swirl around him in the water like smoke."

23. *Coral Reefs.* Written and illustrated by Jason Chin. (Flash Point, 2011.) Chin begins with the same exciting premise that he used in *Redwoods*, where a child who finds a mysterious book is transported to a new world. With *Redwoods*, a boy on a train ends up in the forest; in *Coral Reefs*, a girl reading a book in a library is suddenly underwater swimming among animals and plants. With arresting images and clear text, the book becomes a straightforward introduction to the ecosystem of the Caribbean reefs. Effectively marrying the magic of fiction to the fact-filled power of nonfiction, Chin is on to something. Readers of all ages will be hoping that he writes at least one more imaginative information-picture book along this line.

24. *Energy Island: How One Community Harnessed the Wind and Changed Their World.* Written and illustrated by Allan Drummond. (Farrar, Straus & Giroux, 2011.) Drummond's picture book introduces the windy Danish island of Samso, an inspiring true story of energy independence. The cheery cover sets the tone with a group of adults and children, pinwheels in hand, standing in front of a windmill erected off the coast of their island. On the first page, children learn how ordinary people became extraordinary when they decided to drastically cut their carbon emissions with the help of the abundant wind. Light-and-airy watercolor sketches and brief text tell the story largely from a child's perspective. The idea for conserving energy and being self-sufficient came from the people on the island who built their own wind turbines. When a big storm cut the island's power cable, the turbines were still going strong. Soon the whole island was on board with projects ranging from solar panels to bicycles.

25. *Looking at Lincoln.* Written and illustrated by Maira Kalman. (Nancy Paulsen Books, 2012.) A little girl passes a man in the park who looks a lot like the man on the penny and five-dollar bill. She goes to the library and finds out some interesting things about Abraham Lincoln, our legendary 16th president. With brightly colored pictures and textual enthusiasm, Kalman creates a child-friendly portrait with quirky little facts about Lincoln, such as his dog's name being Fido and his habit of keeping notes in his famous stovepipe hat. These fun facts are seamlessly integrated with momentous information, such as his signing of the Emancipation Proclamation, his delivery of the Gettysburg Address, and his remembrance at the Lincoln Memorial, the monument boldly illustrated on the book's cover.

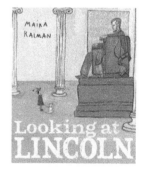

26. *One Tiny Turtle.* Written by Nicola Davies. Illustrated by Jane Chapman. (Candlewick, 2005.) Loggerhead turtles are one of nature's great mysteries. Davies and Chapman tell the astonishing story of how a loggerhead covers thousands of miles of the ocean in a span of 30 years, only to return to the exact beach spot where she was born, to mate and lay her eggs. Growing from a tiny hatchling into a huge lumbering animal with an inexplicable homing beacon, this lone creature faces frequent danger, never more so than when it is first born and must race for its life to the water while predators lie in wait. Chapman does a great job of illustrating this dramatic odyssey, nicely complementing Davies' lyrical and informative text.

27. *So You Want to Be President?* Written by Judith St. George. Illustrated by David Small. (Philomel, 2004.) Judith St. George and David Small's humorous portrait of American presidents will captivate its childhood audience and cause its adult readers to perhaps fret because of its irreverence. The point of the book is that presidents, like everyone, have their vices and virtues, and that our mixed group of leaders are both more and less than the icons on Mount Rushmore (shown on the book's cover). In the style of a political cartoonist, Small shows a naked and obese William Howard Taft being lowered into a bathtub, and Richard Nixon striking an oddly forced victory pose in the White House bowling alley while Henry Kissinger and others wait their turn to throw the ball. This collection of quirks and quotes from 42 presidents will ignite an interest in history and biography and motivate kids to want to learn more.

28. *Brothers at Bat: The True Story of an Amazing All-Brother Baseball Team.* Written by Audrey Vernick. Illustrated by Steven Salerno. (Clarion Books, 2012.) During the 1930s in Long Branch, New Jersey, a family formed its own semipro baseball team, and it became the longest-running all-brother team in baseball history. The Acerra family had 16 kids, 12 of them boys, who all loved to play baseball. Salerno's period artwork dazzles, emulating an old-time comic book, and Vernick's sentences convince, distilling interviews from two surviving brothers. The story shows how they supported one another on and off the field, how the team needed to be temporarily suspended during World War II, and how the gang was inducted into the Baseball Hall of Fame. The narrative has occasional sad moments, such as when one brother lost an eye after being struck by a baseball, and funny scenes, such as one brother running at night with toilet paper in hand to the family's outhouse.

29. *Fifty Cents and a Dream: Young Booker T. Washington.* Written by Jabari Asim. Illustrated by Bryan Collier. (Little, Brown Books for Young Readers, 2012.) Asim and Collier's story of Booker T. Washington's burning desire for education is an important message for children and an excellent tribute to one of America's great historical figures. Young Booker was born into slavery. At the end of the Civil War, upon gaining his freedom, he made an amazing 500-mile trek on foot from his home in West Virginia to attend school, with only 50 cents in his pocket. This difficult journey foreshadowed the demanding leadership role Booker would later play in the African American community. Impressive artwork and compelling descriptions of this thoughtful and determined young man make *Fifty Cents a Dream* an attractive addition to any home library.

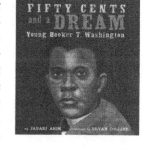

30. *How Much Is a Million?* Written by David M. Schwartz. Illustrated by Steven Kellogg. (HarperCollins, 1985.) If a goldfish bowl could hold 1,000,000 goldfish, then it would be big enough to hold a whale. If 1,000,000 children formed a human tower, they would be higher than an airplane could fly. And if 1,000,000,000 kids climbed on one another's shoulders, they would reach the moon. To get a handle on an even-more-astronomical concept, mathematician David Schwartz and illustrator Steven Kellogg suggest counting to a trillion, an exercise that

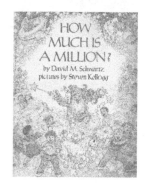

would take 2,000 years. The outcome is comically pictured in gravestones, establishing that everyone involved would not live long enough to make a dent in this task. Schwartz and Kellogg team up to produce many clever and well-illustrated examples that enable children to tangibly grasp truly immense numbers.

31. *Martin's Big Words: The Life of Dr. Martin Luther King, Jr.* Written by Doreen Rappaport. Illustrated by Bryan Collier. (Hyperion, 2007.) This picture-book introduction and tribute to one of the world's greatest civil rights leaders begins with his young days as a minister's son and continues up to his tragic assassination in 1968. Impressed by his father's preaching, young Martin promises, "When I grow up, I'm going to get big words, too." With many quotes and spectacular illustrations, Rappaport and Collier show him following through on that pledge, most notably in the historic march on Washington. This portrait of the American spiritual and political leader most identified with nonviolent change shows him as a man of faith and determination battling against prejudice and segregation. This impressive book ends with the statement, "His big words are alive for us today."

32. *Nic Bishop Spiders.* Written and illustrated by Nic Bishop. (Scholastic, 2012.) "There are more than 38,000 types of spiders. They live everywhere, even in your basement," reports renowned photographer-biologist Nic Bishop. Dramatic close-up photographs and startling facts make his large-scale spider book a certain winner with young audiences. Bishop points out that spiders predate dinosaurs and have turned out to be much more resilient and diverse predators. Some spiders are as tiny as a grain of sand, while one South American tarantula is so big it can eat a bird. There are 15 brilliant photos of these scary little meat eaters, including one of a fishing spider with his foot resting on the water's edge and another shot of a jumping spider suspended in midair. Fans of Bishop's book will find similar ones written by him devoted to snakes, frogs, lizards, and more.

33. *Owen & Mzee: The True Story of a Remarkable Friendship.* Written by Isabella Hatkoff, Craig Hatkoff, and Paula Kahumbu. Illustrated by Peter Greste. (Scholastic Press, 2006.) The idea for this photo essay originated when Craig Hatkoff and his 6-year-old daughter Isabella saw a newspaper article about a baby hippo orphaned by a cataclysmic tsunami. The article included a photograph taken by Peter Greste of Owen: a baby hippo snuggling with an old giant tortoise. The animal was rescued by Kenyan villagers and taken to an animal sanctuary, where he formed the surprising attachment with the tortoise. Tender photos show the unlikely mammal-and-reptile duo swimming, eating, and playing together. Aided by Paula Kahumbu, manager of the sanctuary, this noteworthy story includes lots of information about the animals and their caregivers.

34. *You Never Heard of Sandy Koufax?!* Written by Jonah Winter. Illustrated by André Carrilho. (Schwartz & Wade, 2009.) Winter and Carrilho tell the story of the best left-handed pitcher in baseball history, who faced discrimination because he was Jewish. Shy-and-modest Sandy got off to a slow start playing for the Brooklyn Dodgers, but a few years after the team moved to Los Angeles, his career skyrocketed, and he led the Dodgers to many wins. Eye-catching, elongated, cartoonish illustrations capture his grace and power as he delivers fastballs over the plate. Refusing to play in the first game of the 1965 World Series because it fell on Yom Kippur brought Sandy criticism, but it also earned him the pride of the Jewish community. The legendary athlete abruptly retired from baseball at the peak of his powers, probably because of his painfully overworked pitching arm.

35. *Snowflake Bentley*. Written by Jacqueline Briggs Martin. Illustrated by Mary Azarian. (HMH Books for Young Readers, 1998.) *Snowflake Bentley* is a gorgeous biography about a Vermont farm boy who spent 50 years pioneering snowflake photography and becoming famous for his scientific expertise on ice crystals. When Bentley was 16, his parents spent their life savings on a special microscope camera so the teenager could record the images of snowflakes. Azarian's beautifully detailed woodcuts tinted with watercolors earned him America's most prestigious award for children's illustration. Three of Bentley's photographs of snowflakes are also included. Children will be inspired by Martin's simple descriptions of Wilson Bentley's passion and determination and the support he received from his family.

36. *The Boy Who Invented TV: The Story of Philo Farnsworth*. Written by Kathleen Krull. Illustrated by Greg Couch. (Knopf Books for Young Readers, 2009.) For readers who take technology for granted, Krull asks them to imagine what it would be like to be young Philo Farnsworth at the beginning of the 20th century. Philo was born into a world with no indoor bathrooms, refrigerators, radio, television, cell phones, and Internet, yet he possessed the genius to figure out how to transmit the world's first television image. Soft, mixed-media illustrations and well-explained scientific concepts are the defining features of this inspiring picture-book biography. This story of the boy who came up with the idea for television while plowing a field on his family's farm concludes with an afterword that discusses the lawsuit he needed to wage against RCA to get credit for one of the greatest inventions of all time.

37. *Down, Down, Down: A Journey to the Bottom of the Sea*. Written and illustrated by Steve Jenkins. (HMH Books for Young Readers, 2009.) "Half the earth lies beneath water more than a mile deep, but most of this watery world is a mystery to us," writes Jenkins, who then drops the startling fact that "more people have walked on the moon than have visited the deepest spot in the ocean." In *Down, Down, Down,* Jenkins again shows the knack for explicating exciting facts, presenting odd animals, and using cut-paper illustrations to make the wonder of nature accessible to youngsters. The book has more than 50 strange creatures from above the water down to the depths of the Mariana Trench. In Jenkins's skilled hands, there is no need to embellish children's nonfiction: his judicious selection of material speaks for itself.

38. *Moonshot: The Flight of Apollo 11.* Written and illustrated by Brian Floca. (Atheneum/Richard Jackson Books, 2009.) Floca's informational picture book marvelously captures the adventure and drama of this epic human journey to the moon. From the pictures of the Saturn V rocket pulling away from the launch pad, to images of floating clutter inside the spaceship, to shots of men actually setting foot on the moon's surface, the book effectively conveys the idea that Apollo 11 was "a giant leap for mankind." This story of great men and machines working in harmony in the summer of 1969 is well told, well illustrated, and well researched. Endpapers supply plenty of additional detail on the chronology of the mission and the history of the lunar program.

39. *A Drop of Water: A Book of Science and Wonder.* Written and illustrated by Walter Wick. (Scholastic Press, 1997.) Photographer Walter Wick's eye-catching introduction to H_2O shows the substance in all its protean varieties. Brilliant, stop-action, color photographs capture water in its different states—gas, liquid, and solid—and in different arrangements, such as a crown created by a splash in a pool, soap bubbles, dew in a spider's web, snowflakes, frost, and a prism. Wick also addresses condensation, evaporation, capillary action, and surface tension, the latter concept strikingly shown in a photo of a steel pin seeming to float magically on the surface of water. Accompanying the photos are straightforward and informative paragraph-length captions. The book concludes with a list of simple experiments that a young audience will be eager to try.

40. *It Jes' Happened: When Bill Traylor Started to Draw.* Written by Don Tate. Illustrated by Gregory Christie. (Lee & Low Books, 2012.) Bill Traylor, a self-taught American folk artist who was born a slave, started drawing pictures at age 85. Tate and Christie tell the true story of a man who survived the Civil War, raised a family and outlived them, and ended up sleeping on the street in Montgomery, Alabama. In 1939, he began creating art on sidewalks and discarded cardboard until an established artist took an interest in his work. Traylor began to exhibit his work and is now recognized as one of the greatest self-taught artists of the 20th century. One of Traylor's drawings is reproduced at the end of the book.

41. *Sonia Sotomayor: A Judge Grows in the Bronx/La juez que creció en el Bronx.* Written by Jonah Winter. Illustrated by Edel Rodriguez. (Atheneum Books for Young Readers, 2009.) Winter and Rodriguez's bilingual picture book is the story of a little girl from the South Bronx who grew up to become the first Latina appointed to the nation's highest court. Sonia's mother, a single parent living in a housing project, "worked night and day" as a switchboard operator to pay for school tuition, while Sonia worked just as hard to earn academic honors and attend Princeton University. Sotomayor is shown as a model of diligence, overcoming juvenile diabetes and the early death of her father to become a classic American success story. Impressive artwork of Sotomayor's home and neighborhood, along with the inspiring story told in English and Spanish on each page, makes this a very attractive volume.

42. *Nic Bishop Snakes.* Written and illustrated by Nic Bishop. (Scholastic, 2012.) Award-winning photographer-biologist Nic Bishop introduces the world of snakes and does not mince words about how scary they can be. With his signature close-up photography and meticulous research, he makes it clear that these varied reptile predators can crush their victims, inject them with toxic venom, and even swallow them whole. He writes that there are over 3,000 types of snakes, one weighing over 400 pounds, and another stretching 30 feet long. There are even flying snakes that flatten themselves and sail through the rain forest. Making absolutely sure that he always has his audience's attention, Bishop conveys one fascinating fact after another.

43. *Planting the Trees of Kenya: The Story of Wangari Maathai.* Written and illustrated by Claire A. Nivola. (Farrar, Straus & Giroux, 2008.) Wangari Maathai, winner of the 2004 Nobel Peace Prize, grew up in Kenya, a country covered with fig trees. She studied biology at a Benedictine college in Kansas and returned home to Kenya to find her land stripped of trees for commercial farming and the society in disarray. Dismayed by the ruination, Maathai became an activist and founded the Green Belt Movement, where she encouraged people to restore their country through sound environmental practices such as planting trees. Nivola's rich panoramic illustrations of Kenya's highlands and her pictures of Maathai's college campus dotted with Catholic nuns are beautifully executed. This story of the conservation activities of the first African woman to receive the world's most prestigious prize will inspire children to follow her lead.

44. *The Camping Trip That Changed America.* Written by Barb Rosenstock. Illustrated by Mordicai Gerstein. (Dial, 2012.) After John Muir, a world-famous environmentalist, goes on a wilderness camping trip with President Theodore Roosevelt, the young president decides to help protect America's vanishing forests by establishing national parks. Their three-day visit to the giant sequoias in the Yosemite forest in 1903 had far-reaching consequences for our country. It led to the creation of a system of national parks, wildlife sanctuaries, and national forests. Rosenstock's folksy text and Gerstein's colorful pictures, particularly of the two men standing by colossal

sequoias and then talking by the light of a campfire will capture the imaginations of young readers and listeners. It may even make children feel grateful that someone had the wisdom to conserve this shared national resource.

45. *Eleanor, Quiet No More.* Written by Doreen Rappaport. Illustrated by Gary Kelley. (Disney-Hyperion, 2009.) Kelley's evocatively muted illustrations and Rappaport's effective use of Eleanor Roosevelt's quotations are the high points of their spot-on portrait of America's greatest First Lady. While other girls from her privileged upper class were having fun at parties, the bookish and independent Eleanor was spending her time teaching the poor in New York City. Tracing Eleanor's development from a lonely childhood to a passionate political advocate, the book captures many of Eleanor's important causes, including her advocacy on behalf of women, the poor, and black Americans. When her husband dies in office, Eleanor stays committed to the principles of equality and justice, continuing to inspire America's social conscience.

46. *The Dinosaurs of Waterhouse Hawkins: An Illuminating History of Mr. Waterhouse Hawkins, Artist and Lecturer.* Written by Barbara Kerley. Illustrated by Brian Selznick. (Scholastic Press, 2001.) Back in the mid-19th century when almost no one knew about dinosaurs, Waterhouse Hawkins was the first person to ever create full-size models of them. Growing up in London, Hawkins had a passion for drawing and sculpting the ancient creatures, and he came up with the idea of building model dinosaur replicas to scale from fossil remains that had been unearthed. To gain the approval of England's top scientists, Hawkins staged a special New Year's party for them inside the life-size model of an iguanodon. Some of his models are still on display in England. Kerley's informative narrative is enough to keep young readers engaged, but Selznick's intricate drawings in stunning double-page spreads are absolutely striking.

47. *Meadowlands: A Wetland Survival Story.* Written and illustrated by Thomas F. Yezerski. (Farrar, Straus & Giroux, 2011.) *Meadowlands* is a story of how thousands of acres of New Jersey wetlands, once flourishing with life, were trashed and polluted by several generations of people but are now making a comeback thanks to the work of dedicated environmental activists and others. Yezerski's pictorial history includes shameful images of burning mountains of garbage and junk piles. His watercolors render the once prevalent birdlife that was destroyed when industrial pesticides weakened the shells of their eggs. In the last 40 years, some wildlife has been able to return, but the ecosystem remains fragile. This book documents at least a partial triumph of environmental recovery over degradation.

48. *Thunder Birds: Nature's Flying Predators.* Written and illustrated by Jim Arnosky. (Sterling, 2011.) Arnosky's white-chalk acrylic paintings realistically depict more than 20 avian predators, including eagles, owls, herons, vultures, loons, pelicans, ospreys, falcons, cormorants, and gannets. With informative text and exquisite images, the recognized naturalist and illustrator explains why vultures have featherless heads and how an owl's feathers allow it to fly so silently. The book has six giant gatefolds that provide life-size illustrations and many close-up pictures of birds' regal heads, glassy eyes, and sharp beaks. Arnosky describes his predators as awe-inspiring and magnificent. The same can be said for Arnosky's book, the splendid product of many years of research and thousands of miles traveled.

49. *Ocean Sunlight: How Tiny Plants Feed the Seas.* Written by Molly Bang and Penny Chisholm. (The Blue Sky Press, 2012.) The award-winning combination of Bang and Chisholm continues to delight and educate in this introduction to the oceanic world. As they did with *My Light* and *Living Sunlight*, this volume manages to be both ambitious and simple in its explanation and illustration of critical scientific concepts. Consistent with the other books, the sun

narrates its role in the ocean's ecosystems. "I am your sun," states the immodest protagonist. "All ocean life depends on me; so does all life on land." The book explains photosynthesis and phytoplankton, the "great invisible pasture of the sea," and its role in the food chain. Bang's dramatic and dynamic painting, done in marine greens and blues, adds an element of wonder to this fact-filled volume.

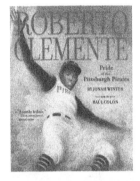

50. *Roberto Clemente: Pride of the Pittsburgh Pirates.* Written by Jonah Winter. Illustrated by Raúl Colón. (Perfection Learning, 2008.) Winter and Colón's picture-book biography of this great athlete makes it clear why he was such a beloved role model. Roberto Clemente, who rose from poverty to become an all-star player for the Pittsburgh Pirates, was the first Latino inducted into the Baseball Hall of Fame. Besides leading his team to two World Series, Clemente was a good family man and humanitarian dedicated to helping others. Clemente died tragically in a plane crash off the shores of his native Puerto Rico while on his way to provide aid to earthquake victims in Nicaragua. Soft illustrations and powerful narration create a portrait of a true sports hero.

51. *UnBEElievables: Honeybee Poems and Paintings.* Written and illustrated by Douglas Florian. (Beach Lane Books, 2012.) Florian marries wordplay and science in a colorful poetry collection about the lives of honeybees. In his latest winning poetry book about animals, anthropomorphized bugs are described in verse while straightforward acts appear alongside. Drone bees resemble kids, and a regal queen bee appears in a jeweled crown and pink robe holding a mobile phone. Early readers and listeners will love the book's playfulness, which includes, "All day we bees / Just buzz and buzz. / That's what we duzz / And duzz and duzz" and "I'm a nectar collector. / Make wax to the max. / A beehive protector. / I never relax." There are 14 poems in all, each of them wonderfully illustrated in drawings that resemble children's chalkboard art.

52. *What Do You Do with a Tail Like This?* Written by Steve Jenkins and Robin Page. (HMH Books for Young Readers, 2003.) The accomplished team of Jenkins and Page creates a guessing-game book that explores what animals can do with their ears, eyes, mouths, noses, feet, and tails. Jenkins employs his award-winning collages to illuminate different parts of animal anatomy. In answer to the question "What do you do with a nose like this?" Jenkins and Page point out that if you are an elephant, you can use your nose to give yourself a bath, and if you are a mole, you can use your nose to navigate underground. The book's title question about tails receives answers such as "If you're a lizard, you break off your tail to get away" and "If you're a scorpion, your tail can give a nasty sting." Readers can find more illustrations and information on the featured animals at the end of the book.

53. *I Have a Dream.* Written by Martin Luther King Jr. Illustrated by Kadir Nelson. (Schwartz & Wade, 2012.) "I have a dream that one day this nation will rise up and live out the true meaning of its creed: 'We hold these truths to be self-evident: that all men are created equal.'" This rendering of Dr. King's iconic "I Have a Dream" speech is illustrated with 16 wonderful oil paintings by award-winning artist Kadir Nelson. King's historic speech was delivered in 1963 on the steps of the Lincoln Memorial and is considered one of the most important statements on freedom and equality in American history. Nelson pictures the civil rights leader standing before a bank of microphones speaking to the vast audience and has images of earnest people marching, listening, and holding hands. The entire speech is included at the back of the book along with an audio CD.

54. *What Presidents Are Made Of.* Written and illustrated by Hanoch Piven. (Atheneum Books for Young Readers, 2012.) Piven's whimsical gallery of 17 U.S. presidents is creatively constructed out of small toys and objects, each one of which represents some aspect of a president's image or personality. Each colorful caricature is accompanied by an anecdote that sheds light on the chief executive's character or describes some episode of his life or presidency. The face of Andrew Jackson, the leader known for his public duels, is assembled with bullets for eyes, a boxing glove for a nose, and a pistol for a mouth. The personage of Abraham Lincoln has a cannon for an eye and broken chains for a beard. Known for his humility but not his good looks, Lincoln humorously replies to the charge that he is two-faced, "If I had another face, do you think I would wear this one?" The book concludes with small standard portraits from Washington to Obama, along with their terms in office.

55. *Harvesting Hope: The Story of Cesar Chavez.* Written by Kathleen Krull. Illustrated by Yuyi Morales. (HMH Books for Young Readers, 2003.) Krull and Morales's biographical tribute to one of America's great civil rights champions begins in his shy boyhood and culminates in his organization of a mass protest against terrible working conditions for itinerant farmworkers in California. The Chavez family, forced by drought to leave their Arizona farm, was always on the move, with Cesar attending 35 different schools. For Chavez, that translated into adversity for him both as a laborer and as a student. In one incident, a teacher hung a sign on him that said, "I am a clown. I speak Spanish." Morales's attractive earth-toned illustrations and bright acrylics engagingly portray the countryside and the lives of the people. An author note states that before Chavez founded the National Farmer Workers Association, migrant farmworkers had the longest hours, lowest pay, shortest lives, and least protection of any workers in America.

56. *Wilma Unlimited: How Wilma Rudolph Became the World's Fastest Woman.* Written by Kathleen Krull. Illustrated by David Diaz. (HMH Books for Young Readers, 2000.) Krull and Diaz's picture-book biography begins with the statement, "No one expected such a tiny girl to have a first birthday." Yet this underweight African American baby grew from a little girl who overcame polio and scarlet fever to the first American woman to win three gold medals in a single Olympics. Refusing to accept that she would never walk again, Wilma Rudolph exercised relentlessly for many years, shed her steel brace, steadily increased her speed, and in 1960 represented the United States as a world champion. With Diaz's vivid watercolors framed in sepia-toned photographic backgrounds and Krull's unsentimental, conversational text, this account of Wilma Rudolph's ceaseless determination is testament to the indomitable human spirit. Readers and listeners will need to remind themselves that this remarkable story is fact, not fiction.

57. *14 Cows for America.* Written by Carmen Agra Deedy and Wilson Kimeli Naiyomah. Illustrated by Thomas Gonzalez. (Peachtree Publishers, 2009.) When Wilson Kimeli Naiyomah returns home to Kenya and tells his people about the horrific September 11, 2001, attacks in the United States, where he has been attending medical school, his Maasai people decide to give the American people a healing gift of 14 sacred cows. This selfless act of compassion and heartfelt generosity from a tiny, remote village is a story of friendship that transcends political boundaries. Gonzalez's brilliant colored pencil-and-pastel illustrations and Deedy's concisely elegant sentences give meaning to her statement that "there is no nation so powerful it cannot be wounded, nor a people so small they cannot offer mighty comfort."

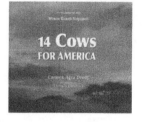

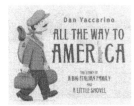

58. *All the Way to America: The Story of a Big Italian Family and a Little Shovel.* Written and illustrated by Dan Yaccarino. (Knopf Books for Young Readers, 2011.) Dan Yaccarino traces his family roots from Sorrento, Italy, to New York City, linking generations with a little shovel that is passed down from fathers to sons. This charming tale begins with the author's great-grandfather, a farmer who leaves Italy in search of a better life in America. After his arrival on Ellis Island, he opens a market and teaches his family to work hard and to love life. The family heirloom shovel, more of a grocer's scoop, is the story's constant thread. Bright digital pictures show it being used on a farm and in a bakery, restaurant, and barbershop. This happy story is a timely reminder that America is a nation of hardworking immigrants.

59. *The Boy Who Drew Birds: A Story of John James Audubon.* Written by Jacqueline Davies. Illustrated by Melissa Sweet. (HMH Books for Young Readers, 2004.) Davies and Sweet's portrait of America's greatest painter of birds begins in 1804 in the Pennsylvania countryside. Determined to solve the mystery of the seasonal comings and goings of birds, the 18-year-old Audubon pioneered a technique for tracking birds that verified for the first time that the same birds that left in the winter returned to the same location in the spring. Sweet's mixed media relies on pencil sketches, ink drawings, watercolors, and photos to illuminate the work of this master ornithologist and painter, while Davies's narration captures Audubon's passionate love of the outdoors and scientific curiosity. *The Boy Who Drew Birds* is an excellent introduction to the early life of the naturalist for whom the National Audubon Society is named.

60. *Growing Frogs.* Written by Vivian French. Illustrated by Alison Bartlett. (Candlewick, 2003.) A little girl thinks that frogs have the capacity to grow very big, and her mother assures her that even grown-up frogs will grow no larger than the parent's hand. To test this claim, mother and daughter visit a pond, collect frog spawn, and take the gelatinous mass of eggs home to an aquarium to observe the hatching. With engaging descriptions and precise colorful images in multiple frames, French and Bartlett show the step-by-step metamorphosis of the jellylike eggs hatching into tadpoles and tadpoles developing into baby frogs. French advises her young readers that frogs are an endangered species and should be returned to their natural habitat.

61. *Harriet and the Promised Land.* Written and illustrated by Jacob Lawrence. (Aladdin, 1997.) Spare text and spectacular illustrations are the defining qualities of Jacob Lawrence's tribute to Harriet Tubman and her persistent struggle to free her people from slavery via the Underground Railroad. Having escaped the yoke of slavery, Tubman is shown returning to the South many times to lead her people to freedom. "Some were afraid, / But none turned back, / For close at their heels / Howled the bloodhound pack," writes Lawrence on the constant dread of being killed or recaptured. Lawrence's paintings are bold, frenetic, infused with urgency, and packed with scenes of her clandestine travels. This portrait of an American heroine will inspire young readers.

HARRIET AND
THE PROMISED LAND
by JACOB LAWRENCE

62. *Mermaid Queen: The Spectacular True Story of Annette Kellerman, Who Swam Her Way to Fame, Fortune and Swimsuit History.* Written by Shana Corey. Illustrated by Edwin Fotheringham. (Scholastic Press, 2009.) Annette Kellerman, who founded water ballet, revolutionized women's swimsuits, and was the first woman to attempt to swim the English Channel, was an early feminist who helped make it possible for women to enjoy the water and be more fully engaged in sports. As a child in Australia, Annette became an endurance swimmer to strengthen her weak legs, becoming a skillful athlete and performer. Powerful images and simple text show her winning races, touring Europe and America, and yet being forced to cover up her bare legs. Eventually, she got arrested for her unwillingness to wear heavy, uncomfortable swimwear, but her bold action helped liberate women from unfair social restraints.

63. *Bug Zoo.* Written by Nick Baker. (DK Publishing, 2010.) Bug-loving kids will really value this well-organized guide to catching backyard insects and making small habitats for them. Insect identification books are interesting and plentiful, but naturalist Nick Baker's practical advice will be deeply appreciated for addressing an important problem for early readers. Kids will be eager to learn how to construct a spider house, bee box, wormery, and ant farm. With easy to follow instructions and excellent photos, Baker focuses on 13 different insects, including ladybugs, crickets, wood lice, and mosquito larvae. He includes facts about the prospective pets and suggests what to feed them. There is even a section on zoo tools such as a plastic spoon, a magnifying lens, and a paintbrush for gently nudging the bugs along.

64. *Dogs and Cats.* Written and illustrated by Steve Jenkins. (HMH Books for Young Readers, 2012.) Jenkins has created another fact-filled book that cleverly allows children to read about one pet, flip the book over, and find out about the other pet. The two halves intersect with a large picture of the perennial foes lying together on a rug. His trademark collages work amazingly well to illustrate copious amounts of information about the two animals' origins, behavior, anatomy, socialization, life cycle, domestication, and breeds, as well as unusual trivia. *Dogs and Cats* will leave kids with a completely new understanding of America's favorite house pets. They will join Jenkins's considerable nonfiction fan base when they enjoy visiting this uniquely styled, two-for-one book again and again.

65. *The Chiru of High Tibet.* Written by Jacqueline Briggs Martin. Illustrated by Linda Wingerter. (Houghton Mifflin Books for Children, 2010.) Native to the remote northern plains of Tibet, the chiru is the source of the world's warmest and softest wool. This distinction has made the antelope-like creatures targets of poachers, pushing the species to near extinction because to make just one shawl, poachers may kill up to five of the small animals. Martin and

Wingerter tell the remarkable adventure story of conservationist George Schaller and his team's arduous trek to Tibet to find the valley where chiru females give birth. Finding this birthing ground and getting the Chinese government to protect it was Schaller's solution to the survival of the species. Martin's dramatic narrative and Wingerter's lush watercolor landscapes trace the difficult task of following the animals over cold, treacherous terrain.

66. *My Senator and Me: A Dog's-Eye View of Washington, D.C.* Written by Edward M. Kennedy. Illustrated by David Small. (Scholastic, 2006.) Charmingly told by Splash, Senator Kennedy's Portuguese water dog, this story introduces the political process by focusing on a typical day in the nation's capital. Splash provides a quick tour of the Beltway's major monuments and buildings, rides the underground tram between the Senate and Capital, and plays on the lawn. Small's ink-and-watercolor images endearingly render the senator and his pooch attending a press conference, visiting a committee meeting, being photographed, and even finding time for a dog treat. Splash barks when a committee reaches an impasse on a bill, but there are no government shutdowns, only tidy resolutions, in this sweet depiction of Washington politics.

67. *Ladybugs.* Written by Gail Gibbons. (Holiday House, 2012.) Easy-to-grasp descriptions, straightforward information, and colorful artwork combine to thoroughly introduce these beautiful insects. Gibbons does a particularly good job describing the stages of a ladybug's growth and also covers different ladybug species, body parts, eating habits, predators, defenses, habitat, and mating. She explains that ladybugs are beneficial because they consume aphids that harm crops and other plants. Gibbons notes that there are about 5,000 varieties of ladybugs, including some that can swim and others that can fly at speeds up to 15 miles an hour. Early readers needing an age-appropriate resource for preparing a report would be well served by this quality book.

68. *Vulture View.* Written by April Pulley Sayre. Illustrated by Steve Jenkins. (Henry Holt, 2007.) Kids will squeal in delight at Sayre and Jenkins's treatment of the disgusting eating habits of these important scavengers that seek food that many in the animal kingdom would gladly pass up. Turkey vultures adore food that is already deceased and often in a state of rancid decay. These birds are attracted to all things rotten, feasting themselves on food that Sayre describes frankly as a reeking mess. Jenkins's illustrations capture the vultures from many different perspectives and do not shy from their unpleasant appearance. The book's solid educational message is that turkey vultures are a vital part of nature's clean-up crew and occupy an important place in the wildlife ecosystem.

69. *A Butterfly Is Patient.* Written by Dianna Hutts Aston. Illustrated by Sylvia Long. (Chronicle Books, 2011.) Long's spectacular watercolors and Aston's fact-filled text work in tandem to create a stylish picture book that explains why a butterfly has to be patient as it develops from minute egg to a caterpillar, creating a chrysalis that transforms into its final form. This valuable introduction to butterflies describes metamorphosis, pollination, camouflage, migration, and how butterflies differ from moths. Aston artfully explains that the wing scales of some butterflies are "stacked like shingles on a roof," while other butterflies are so tiny that their wingspan is "about the length of a grain of rice." This book is as well researched as it is well written, and is the perfect companion to Aston and Long's equally attractive *An Egg Is Quiet* (2006) and *A Seed Is Sleepy* (2007).

70. *Noah Webster and His Words.* Written by Jeri Chase Ferris. Illustrated by Vincent X. Kirsch. (HMH Books for Young Readers, 2012.) Ferris and Kirsch's amusing picture book tells the story of the American educator responsible for publishing Webster's American Dictionary, one of the all-time favorite books published in English, and authoring the first American schoolbooks. It made no sense to Noah for each person and government entity to have different versions of the same language. His dictionary idea grew out of the conviction that his fledgling nation could be unified through standardized spellings and definitions. Kirsch's cartoon drawings illustrate key moments with funny illustrations, such as when Webster tremblingly completes the final entry: ZY-GO-MAT-IC (adj.: related to the cheek bone). After 20 years of work, 70-year-old Noah Webster published his magnum opus dictionary in 1828.

71. *What to Do about Alice? How Alice Roosevelt Broke the Rules, Charmed the World, and Drove Her Father Teddy Crazy!* Written by Barbara Kerley. Illustrated by Edwin Fotheringham. (Scholastic Press, 2008.) This picture-book biography of irrepressible Alice Roosevelt Longworth confirms President Roosevelt's famous quote about his daughter, "I can be president of the United States, or I can control Alice. I cannot possibly do both." Kerley and Fotheringham's enthralling portrait shows Alice as an outspoken, unconventional, and uncommonly intelligent girl who had the run of the White House. Fotheringham's illustrations show Alice as pure energy in motion, as she greets important White House visitors with her pet snake and rides trays down the White House stairs with her younger siblings. Children will love this spirited girl and appreciate the inside look at one of the country's first families.

72. *A Nation's Hope: The Story of Boxing Legend Joe Louis.* Written by Matt De La Peña. Illustrated by Kadir Nelson. (Dial, 2011.) De La Peña and Nelson's story of boxer Joe Louis focuses on his 1938 world heavyweight rematch with German Max Schmeling. The historic boxing match between the African American sharecropper's son and the symbol of Hitler's "master race" was viewed in political terms as a proxy battle between American and Nazi ideologies. Spare verse and stunningly realistic pictures show the

great drama and importance of the contest. Louis did not want to be a disappointment to his country or to the black community, and he knocked out his opponent in the first round before a crowd of 70,000 fans in Yankee Stadium. Though he had lost to Schmeling in 1936, the victory in the second fight made Louis a national hero.

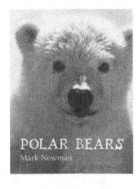

73. *Polar Bears.* Written and illustrated by Mark Newman. (Henry Holt, 2010.) Newman's icy-blue photos and informative text tell the fascinating story of the world's largest species of bear, including facts about its habitat, physical characteristics, life cycle, and threats it faces because of global warming. Young listeners and readers will be surprised to learn that the polar bear's skin color is black, that it is an excellent swimmer, that it weighs only one pound at birth, and that its chances of survival after the first three years of life are slim in the harsh Arctic environment. The book also includes many appealing photographs of adult and baby bears and an explanation from the author on how he took them.

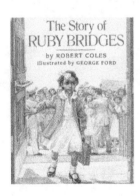

74. *The Story of Ruby Bridges.* Written by Robert Coles. Illustrated by George Ford. (Scholastic, 2010.) Six-year-old Ruby Bridges made history when she had the courage to face angry mobs of white parents to become the first African American sent to first grade in an all-white school. This true story of how a little girl had to endure months of the most overt and ugly racism is dramatically articulated and powerfully illustrated by Coles and Ford. While the protesting parents refused to send their children to school with Ruby, she prayed for them. The final page of the book reprints Ruby's daily prayer of asking God to forgive these parents. Youngsters who read and listen to this important book will be inspired by Ruby's strong faith and heroism.

75. *Orani: My Father's Village.* Written and illustrated by Claire A. Nivola. (Farrar, Straus & Giroux, 2011.) Illuminated by her beautiful gouache paintings evoking a simple way of life, Nivola reminisces about her idyllic childhood summers in the small village in Sardinia where her father and many of her relatives still resided. This 1950s story of a nurturing village suspended in time is memorable for its depiction of the richest of everyday life, including family feasts, traditional three-day weddings, and horses dashing through narrow streets. Nicola roamed freely through the town with her cousins in tow and reflected on how close-knit Orani differed from her life in America. Children will enjoy the intimacy and simplicity of this Mediterranean island and get a glimpse of a fulfilling life that did not require gadgets and high-speed communication.

76. *Sixteen Years in Sixteen Seconds: The Sammy Lee Story.* Written by Paula Yoo. Illustrated by Dom Lee. (Lee & Low Books, 2010.) In 1948, Sammy Lee became the first Asian American to win an Olympic gold medal. Paula Yoo and Dom Lee's telling of this stirring true story begins with Sammy, a Korean American boy in California, watching white children enjoy a public pool he's only allowed to use on Wednesdays when it is available to people of color. Besides discrimination, Sammy must also contend with his father, who wants him to forgo training to be a diver in favor of becoming a medical doctor. Sammy works out a compromise with his father that eventually leads him to achieve Olympic and career success. After 16 years of determined effort, the story comes to a satisfying conclusion with Sammy's award-winning 16-second dive.

77. *Those Rebels, John and Tom.* Written by Barbara Kerley. Illustrated by Edwin Fotheringham. (Scholastic Press, 2012.) In the style of narrated political cartoon, Kerley and Fotheringham's portrait of two of America's founders goes into detail about John Adams and Thomas Jefferson's many differences and their roles in developing the Declaration of Independence. Adams was argumentative, short, and stout; Jefferson was contemplative, tall, and lean, but what they had in common was their commitment to unifying the American colonies and separating from England. An author's note acknowledges the coincidence that both men died on July 4, 1826, within hours of each other. This important relationship in American history is a timely reminder of how political leaders overcame differences and worked together to serve the public interest.

78. *One Giant Leap.* Written by Robert Burleigh. Illustrated by Mike Wimmer. (Philomel, 2009.) This commemoration of the first moon landing conveys the unique excitement of one of the greatest episodes in human history. With short sentences written in dramatic free verse, Burleigh tells the story of astronauts Armstrong and Aldrin as they land the Eagle on the surface of the moon, while Collins keeps the Columbia spacecraft in the moon's orbit. Wimmer's breathtaking illustrations show a variety of perspectives, including the first steps on the moon and the planting of the American flag. In a media environment saturated with fanciful tales about space travel, children will appreciate hearing about an actual "One small step for man; one giant leap for mankind."

79. *You Are Stardust.* Written by Elin Kelsey. Illustrated by Soyeon Kim. (Owlkids Books, 2012.) Kelsey and Kim's picture book introduces children to the idea that they are part of the natural world, composed of atomic particles from stars that exploded eons before their birth. Based on science, Kelsey's book shows our connectedness to nature with examples such as "Like fish deep in the ocean, you called salt water home. You swam inside the salty sea of your mother's womb" and "The water swirling in your glass once filled the puddles where dinosaurs drank." Meanwhile, Kim's diorama art give the images a unique three-dimensional look. Tracing their origins to the ancient stardust at the beginning of the universe, this important book gives young children a lot to contemplate.

80. *Amazing Sharks!* Written by Sarah L. Thomson. (HarperCollins, 2006.) This is a splendid beginner book for children who are interested in sharks, and it would be particularly helpful to kids looking for an accessible resource for a school report or project. Packed with facts and large color photographs from the Wildlife Conservation Society, this book discusses the diversity of the species and their dramatic differences in size. The book is filled with information about their teeth, how they use their senses to find prey, how they reproduce, and how their habitats are endangered by human activity. Thomson has included a helpful pronunciation guide and appropriate explanations of new vocabulary. Children will come away with a better understanding of the role these skilled predators play in the ocean and an understanding of why they should be protected.

81. *You Forgot Your Skirt, Amelia Bloomer!* Written by Shana Corey. Illustrated by Chesley McLaren. (Scholastic Press, 2000.) Amelia Bloomer started her own newspaper to champion equal rights for women and their right to vote, but she is best remembered for her battle against the restrictive clothing women were expected to wear. Corey and McLaren's humorous treatment of Bloomer's place in American social history will resonate with kids, and they will understand why she rebelled against being a "proper lady." As an alternative to insanely impractical hoop skirts, heavy petticoats, and tight corsets, she popularized a more sensible and comfortable approach to fashion that involved wearing a knee-length skirt over baggy pants. From that point on, it seemed only fitting that "bloomers" be named after their chief advocate. Bloomer continued to work for women's equality along with well-known suffragists such as Elizabeth Cady Stanton.

82. *The Boy on Fairfield Street: How Ted Geisel Grew Up to Become Dr. Seuss.* Written by Kathleen Krull. Illustrated by Steve Johnson and Lou Fancher. (Dragonfly Books, 2010.) "Once upon a time, there lived a boy who feasted on books and was wild about animals" is the auspicious beginning of the team's wonderful biography. Before he became the legendary Dr. Seuss, Ted Geisel was a quirky and imaginative kid who enjoyed drawing the animals in his father's zoo. Illustrated by old-timey, nostalgic paintings, along with delightful characters from Seuss's books, this is a story of a determined doodler who succeeded in spite of a warning from his high school art teacher that he had no future in art. The book happily concludes with 22-year-old Ted living in Greenwich Village, ready to launch a career as one of the most acclaimed children's author/illustrators of all time.

83. *Frida.* Written by Jonah Winter. Illustrated by Ana Juan. (Arthur A. Levine Books, 2002.) This is the unique story of Frida Kahlo who overcame polio and a near-fatal bus accident to emerge as a world-renowned painter. With sparse narrative and brilliant surrealistic illustrations taken from Mexican folklore, Winter and Juan's biography explains Frida's art and life as transcendence over catastrophic injury and chronic pain. "Instead of crying, she paints pictures of herself crying," Winter writes. Young readers will be fascinated by images of traditional figures such as a skeleton, devil, jaguar, and monkey. They will come away with an understanding of how the difficult life of a resilient young woman was transformed into breathtaking art.

84. *Bugs Are Insects.* Written by Anne Rockwell. Illustrated by Steve Jenkins. (HarperCollins, 2001.) Easy-to-read text and bright illustrations make Rockwell and Jenkins's introduction to common backyard insects a winner with preschoolers and early readers. "Count its legs. Count how many parts make up its body," Rockwell suggests, clearly defining insects as "anything with six legs and three body parts" and explaining bugs as insects with "a mouth like a beak and a head that forms a triangle." This well-explained account uses the correct terminology—words such as skeleton, antennae, and abdomen—to explain basic insect characteristics, and the collage illustrations are artfully and realistically rendered. As with their other books for a young audience, Rockwell and Jenkins have produced another high quality nonfiction title.

85. *Dolphin Baby!* Written by Nicola Davies. Illustrated by Brita Granström. (Candlewick, 2012.) When a baby bottlenose dolphin first comes into the world, he arrives tail first, quickly swimming to the surface for air. So begins zoologist Nicola Davies's lively story of the first few months in the life of a calf. Clear text and energetic illustrations show him being helped by his mother, learning how to suckle for milk, figuring out how to whistle, catching his first fish, playing with other young calves, and exploring his bright blue ocean world. With a sentence or two of narrative description per page, the little dolphin gradually becomes more independent, although he has not yet had to contend with predators.

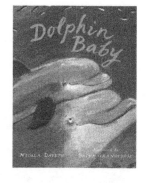

86. *Caterpillar, Caterpillar.* Written by Vivian French. Illustrated by Charlotte Voake. (Candlewick, 2009.) Prompted by her grandfather's surprising decision to grow stinging nettles in his garden, a little girl finds out about the miraculous transformation of caterpillars into butterflies. Her grandfather points out that the nettles are a hospitable home to butterfly eggs and invites her to observe their hatching and development. French's decision to have the girl narrate the story in the first person is a wise one because it strongly conveys the child's wonder and delight in experiencing the arrival of a peacock butterfly from its chrysalis. French's text and Voake's ink-and-watercolor artwork capture not only the metamorphosis of these insects but also the warm relationship between the girl and her grandfather.

87. *Fireboat: The Heroic Adventures of the* John J. Harvey. Written and illustrated by Maira Kalman. (Putnam Juvenile, 2002.) First launched in 1931, the *John J. Harvey* was the premier fireboat of its time, but by 1995, it was retired from service and considered no longer needed. That opinion changed on September 11, 2001, when New York City asked if the fireboat could help battle its worst fire ever and firefighters attached their hoses to the boat and fought the fires from the terrorist attack for several days. Maira Kalman's story and illustrations do a masterful job of tying together some of the Big Apple's best and worst days. She notes, for example, that the *John J. Harvey*'s 1931 launch coincided with the building of the Empire State Building and Babe Ruth hitting his 611th home run.

88. *Creep and Flutter: The Secret World of Insects and Spiders.* Written and illustrated by Jim Arnosky. (Sterling Children's Books, 2012.) With informative field notes and amazing gatefold illustrations, naturalist Jim Arnosky illuminates the diverse world of insects and spiders. There are remarkable images of silverfish, beetles, butterflies, mosquitoes, moths, mayflies, dragonflies, spiders and more, each of them well described. Arnosky personalizes this excellent nonfiction title by touching on some of his experiences, such as observing a lady beetle crash near his woodstove or watching a mayfly hatch in a pond. Many of the drawings are intricate, revealing details of the secret habitats of spiders and insects. Children will enjoy their visit to this unnoticed world and will be inspired to do their own investigations.

89. *Dreaming Up: A Celebration of Building.* Written and illustrated by Christy Hale. (Lee & Low Books, 2012.) In this ingenious introduction to famous architecture, Christy Hale connects the building abilities of children to some of the great buildings of the world. With 14 two-page spreads and poetry, she shows young kids building with various objects and then describes what they are creating. In one spread, children are shown stacking paper cups into a tower, and on the opposite side is the photo of the Petronas Twin Towers, one of the world's tallest buildings. Another pairing compares a child playing with wooden blocks to Frank Lloyd Wright's Fallingwater. Preschoolers will identify with the young children pictured at play, while older kids will appreciate the back matter, which includes notes on the architects and more information about each building.

90. *Animal Talk: How Animals Communicate through Sight, Sound and Smell.* Written by Etta Kaner. Illustrated by Greg Douglas. (Kids Can Press, 2002.) Kaner and Douglas's excellent overview of the many ways animals "talk" includes velvet monkeys, sea lions, birds, lemurs, moths, dolphins, insects, zebras, and more. Filled with interesting information about each animal's relevant physical characteristics, the book covers communication behaviors such as warning for danger, attracting a mate, or delimiting territory. In one case, a firefly is pictured sending light messages, and in another case, a peacock is shown displaying its feathers to a peahen. Realistic illustrations make *Animal Talk* especially appealing, while chapters such as "Saying It with Sound" and "Saying It with Smell" make the organization easy for children to follow.

91. *Exploding Ants: Amazing Facts about How Animals Adapt.* Written by Joanne Settel. (Atheneum Books for Young Readers, 1999.) Kids will absolutely love biology professor Joanne Settel's lurid descriptions of the incredible things that some animals must do to survive. With chapter headings such as "Murderous Nest Mates," "Gulping Eyeballs," and "Dog Mucus and Other Tasty Treats," it is clear from the start that this is not just another science book. Children will be horrified to know that braconid wasps lay eggs under a caterpillar's skin to enable the young wasp to feast on the insect as it grows. Readers will also learn

intriguing facts: "Some ticks take in so much blood," Settel writes, "they swell to nearly four times their normal size. That's like an adult human expanding to the height of a two-story building!" This attractive book has excellent color photos, clearly explained scientific terms, and a glossary.

92. *Just Ducks!* Written by Nicola Davies. Illustrated by Salvatore Rubbino. (Candlewick, 2012.) An observant young girl who lives near a river filled with mallard ducks learns quite a bit just by watching them. Narrating the story, she hears the ducks quack in the morning, notices them eating as she goes to school, and even recognizes their mating behaviors: "I like it when a drake shows off his handsome feathers to the ducks, trying to get one to be his girlfriend." The book comes to a pleasing close that sounds like a bedtime story: "The bridge is quiet, and there's just the sound of rushing water and the stillness of the night." Davies's gentle descriptions and Rubbino's soft watercolor paintings combine to produce a very handsome picture book that has many of the same charms as classic fiction.

93. *Face to Face with Lions.* Written by Beverly and Dereck Joubert. (National Geographic Children's Books, 2008.) Drawing on their years of experience documenting African wildlife, National Geographic field researchers Beverly and Dereck Joubert supply crystal clear close-up photographs and abundant information on the lion's diet, physical traits, habitat, family structure, and behavior. The husband-and-wife team begins with a description of a close encounter with a charging male, goes on to supply plenty of lion facts and personal anecdotes, and includes interesting lists on topics such as "How not to get eaten by a lion" and "How to live with lions." The Jouberts explain the risks human beings create for these regal animals and advocate for conservation efforts.

94. *From Seed to Plant.* Written and illustrated by Gail Gibbons. (Holiday House, 1993.) Gail Gibbons's clear introduction to plant growth and reproduction provides stimulating facts on the life cycles of flowers, trees, fruits, and vegetables. Covering pollination through full growth, her vivid illustrations and easy-to-read text will help young readers and listeners understand the complex relationship between seeds and the plants they engender. There are additional fun facts about seeds and plants at the end of the book and simple instructions on how children can grow their own bean plant. *From Seed to Plant* would be an excellent addition to a home library or a great classroom science text.

95. *Guess What Is Growing inside This Egg.* Written and illustrated by Mia Posada. (Millbrook Press, 2006.) Structured as a guessing game, Mia Posada's repeated refrain, "Can you guess what is growing inside this egg?" provides young readers with clues, such as the image of an animal parent, as to what is growing. Turn the page and there is a wealth of factual information on a variety of egg layers, including spiders, octopuses, penguins, alligators, ducks, and sea turtles. Teachers and young aspiring zoologists will appreciate the information about the animals' habitats, nurturing, and eating habits, and especially what the babies look like inside their eggs. Posada's collage pictures are magnificent and will invite close examination and discussion.

96. *I Feel Better with a Frog in My Throat: History's Strangest Cures.* Written and illustrated by Carlyn Beccia. (Houghton Mifflin Books for Children, 2010.) With an entertaining question-and-answer format, Carlyn Beccia explores many of the crazy things people over the ages have tried in order to cure themselves of sickness. Readers are given three possible answers to a malady question and are challenged to guess which cure has been most effective. Beccia then discloses which cures are effective, why they

work, and where they might have gotten their start. This look at some of history's most bizarre remedies includes people putting mustard on their heads, applying mummy powder to wounds, drinking a glass full of millipedes, and getting a dose of frog soup. Beccia's funny illustrations and text, based on solid science, is a fascinating mystery tour that will test the stomachs and excite the imaginations of both young and older readers.

97. *Balto and the Great Race.* Written by Elizabeth Cody Kimmel. Illustrated by Nora Koerber. (Paw Prints, 2008.) When dozens of children in Nome, Alaska, get diphtheria, a heroic sled dog name Balto travels 650 miles through a terrible snowstorm with the antitoxin serum to save the day. In this true 1925 story, the Siberian husky and his team of dogs overcome daunting obstacles to reach an isolated location that could not be reached by any other means. Children will be gripped by Koerber's bold black-and-white illustrations and Kimmel's exciting story, made even more lucid through her inventive rendering of the dog's thoughts and feelings. This fast-paced title would be a perfect choice for readers looking to attempt their first chapter book.

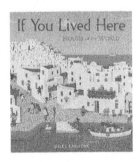

98. *If You Lived Here: Houses of the World.* Written and illustrated by Giles Laroche. (HMH Books for Young Readers, 2011.) Giles Laroche's gorgeous picture book presents 16 unique homes across many locations and time periods to explain how different people live. From a house carved out of a mountain to one constructed in a tree, each dwelling begins with a paragraph that starts with the phrase "If you lived here." Detailed, bas-relief collage illustrations show a tremendous variety of homes including yurts, boathouses, stilt houses, trailers, and log cabins. The text includes fascinating facts about house types, materials, locations, and histories. Readers will be able to imagine different modes of existence, such as people fishing from their bedroom windows and people rotating their homes to watch the sunrise and sunset.

99. *There Goes Ted Williams: The Greatest Hitter Who Ever Lived.* Written and illustrated by Matt Tavares. (Candlewick, 2012.) Growing up in San Diego, Ted Williams had only one purpose—to some day become baseball's best hitter, a goal that he accomplished while playing his entire career for the Boston Red Sox. Matt Tavares's story of the slugger's amazing career focuses on Williams's hard work and determination and his tours of duty as a fighter pilot in World War II and the Korean War. The Hall of Famer's most noteworthy season was 1941 when he batted a staggering .406. Williams's long professional career lasted until 1960, when he hit a home run in his last time at bat. Children will be inspired by this well-written tribute and will be mesmerized by the striking watercolor pictures of the gaunt baseball legend.

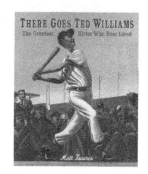

100. *What Is the World Made Of? All about Solids, Liquids, and Gases.* Written by Kathleen Weidner Zoehfeld. Illustrated by Paul Meisel. (HarperCollins, 1998.) The great virtue of *What Is the World Made Of?* is its amazing accessibility. Zoehfeld and Meisel introduce science concepts usually reserved for older kids in a way that is age appropriate, information rich, and just plain fun. The differences between solids, liquids, and gases are explained with easily recognizable, everyday items. Readers will find out about gases by smelling the scent dispersed from a bottle of perfume, or learn how liquid behaves as demonstrated by a glass of spilled milk. Examples are provided for each state of matter, and there is a page of easy home exercises requiring some assistance from adults. Meisel's mixed-media drawings and conversation balloons give this informational picture book an amusing touch.

CHAPTER 3

Middle Readers (Ages 9–13)

It's not just how much students read that matters, but also what they read.

—Bryan Goodwin and Kirsten Miller

1. *Amelia Lost: The Life and Disappearance of Amelia Earhart.* Written by Candace Fleming. (Schwartz & Wade, 2011.) Fleming's brilliant account of Amelia Earhart's life and her doomed final flight reads more like a suspense novel than history or biography. Alternating chapters between her childhood and the exhaustive search for her missing plane, the author introduces an element of drama not often encountered in nonfiction. Aided by plenty of black-and-white photographs, sidebars, maps, and handwritten notes, the trailblazing aviatrix emerges as a complex and intriguing character with many achievements and just as many occasions for self-promotion. From the beginning of her early life to her famous disappearance in 1937, *Amelia Lost* is a gripping read and a perfect choice for mid-level students.

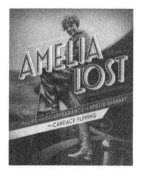

2. *Temple Grandin: How the Girl Who Loved Cows Embraced Autism and Changed the World.* Written by Sy Montgomery and Temple Grandin. (HMH Books for Young Readers, 2012.) Temple Grandin is a woman who triumphed over great odds, including a father who thought she should have been institutionalized for mental retardation, to become an animal welfare expert, advocate, and professor at Colorado State University. Her work has helped reduce the cruelty in the livestock industry, yet as a withdrawn autistic child, she had to overcome enormous barriers and prejudice. Temple's mother recognized her potential and fought to get her daughter an education that allowed this unusual girl to make productive use of her unique and talented way of seeing the world. This portrait will make autism more understandable to children and encourage them to consider that some ways of thinking may be more a gift than a disability.

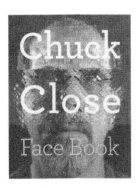

3. *Chuck Close Face Book.* Written by Chuck Close. (Abrams Books for Young Readers, 2012.) In this autobiographical, question-and-answer narrative, the groundbreaking artist answers questions posed by a dozen fifth graders from Brooklyn who visited his studio. The children ask Close straightforward questions such as "How do you start a painting?" and "Why do you make so many self-portraits?" He supplies answers that are fascinating and unassuming. This portrait introduces the discipline of art and the life of an artist through the lens of his serious health issues. Close, who is bound to a wheelchair and paints with a brush strapped to his arm, became quadriplegic when at age 48 a blood vessel burst in his back, leaving him almost completely paralyzed. Since childhood, Close has also had to contend with severe dyslexia and face blindness (prosopagnosia), which got him started on the subject of what made faces uniquely recognizable. The book contains 14 striking self-portraits and a chronology of the artist's life.

4. *Moonbird: A Year on the Wind with the Great Survivor B95.* Written by Phillip Hoose. (Farrar, Straus & Giroux, 2012.) B95 is nicknamed "Moonbird" because during his long lifetime, this tiny shorebird has flown the distance to the moon and halfway back again. Tagged with his official B95 leg band, each year he travels a staggering 18,000 miles round trip from the bottom tip of South America to the Canadian Arctic. Though he can fly for several days without food or sleeping, he must occasionally rest and eat. Because human activity has disrupted the migratory patterns of Moonbird and his flock, their population has drastically declined and they face extinction. Phillip Hoose's solidly researched and remarkably well-written account includes profiles of the scientists who study these marathon fliers and supplies suggestions on how the beleaguered birds can be saved.

5. *Almost Astronauts: 13 Women Who Dared to Dream.* Written by Tanya Lee Stone. (Candlewick, 2009.) This is the story of 13 women who demonstrated the grit and ability to be astronauts and passed all the endurance tests but were prevented from going into space because of their gender. In the early 1960s, the "Mercury 13" had already proven themselves as pilots, and one of them, Jerrie Cobb, had even logged more hours in the air than did John Glenn. But prevailing attitudes and the actions of powerful people kept these women on the sidelines. Stone notes that it took until 1978 for a woman to be allowed into space and 16 more years for a woman to be permitted to command a mission. Middle readers will benefit from knowing about this important chapter in the struggle for women's equality.

6. *Heart and Soul: The Story of America and African Americans.* Written and illustrated by Kadir Nelson. (Balzer & Bray, 2011.) Intimately narrated in the feisty voice of an aged woman looking back on her life, Nelson's epic history of African Americans is a story of struggle, inspiration, and bravery. Illustrated with dozens of magnificent full-page paintings, this

tour de force covers the most notable people and events from the American Revolution to the election of President Obama. This is the story of leaders, such as Frederick Douglass, Rosa Parks, Langston Hughes, Joe Lewis, Louis Armstrong, and Martin Luther King Jr., and of slavery, Jim Crow laws, the Civil War, the Ku Klux Klan, the Tuskegee Airmen, persistent discrimination, and the civil rights movement. "You have to know where you came from so you can move forward," writes Nelson in his epilogue. This comprehensive history of the black experience in America counts as one of those steps forward.

7. *Michelangelo*. Written and illustrated by Diane Stanley. (HarperCollins, 2003.) Stanley's picture-book biography of one of the world's greatest artists pays tribute to Michelangelo's achievements while also recognizing his problems and disappointments. Her account of the Italian Renaissance master begins with him being taken in by a stonecutter's family, where he developed his lifelong love of the medium. Even though Michelangelo's father beat him when he wanted to become apprenticed to an artist, the budding artist still remained committed. This exceptionally well-researched portrait recognizes Michelangelo's mastery as a sculptor and painter, including his famous statue of David and his paintings of the Sistine Chapel. Photos of Michelangelo's art were enhanced by computer, blending nicely into Stanley's illustrations.

8. *Beyond Courage: The Untold Story of Jewish Resistance during the Holocaust*. Written by Doreen Rappaport. (Candlewick, 2012.) Doreen Rappaport debunks the myth "Jews went like lambs to the slaughter" in Nazi-occupied Europe during World War II, describing 20 inspiring Jewish resistance efforts. Accompanied by stirring black-and-white photographs and original research, Rappaport profiles brothers who led refugees into the forest to raise a guerilla army, resisters who ambushed a train to release

scores of imprisoned Jews, and a 12-year-old boy who hid explosives in his violin case and blew up German officers in a hotel moments after entertaining them. Example after example shows dauntless men, women, and children finding ways to organize and sabotage Hitler's genocidal plan. These important stories are a tribute to the strength of the human spirit.

9. *Drawing from Memory.* Written and illustrated by Allen Say. (Scholastic Press, 2011.) With exquisite illustrations and poignant text, Caldecott Medalist Allen Say recounts learning to draw under the direction of Japan's leading cartoonist, Noro Shinpei, in postwar Tokyo. Say's graphic novel and coming-of-age story describes his father's opposition to his artistic career aspirations and the close bond he formed with his sensei, who took Say on as a student at age 13. Up-and-coming artists will be surprised to learn that Say began living on his own at age 12, when he was able to work single-mindedly on his art. Readers can find out more about Allen Say in his autobiographical novel for older readers, *The Ink-Keeper's Apprentice* (1979).

10. *Bomb: The Race to Build—and Steal—the World's Most Dangerous Weapon.* Written by Steve Sheinkin. (Flash Point, 2012.) In *Bomb*, Steve Sheinkin shows that true-life nonfiction can be exemplary history and, at the same time, exude the same thrill and suspense as a high-octane spy novel. His story of the international race to build the first atomic bomb begins in Germany in 1937, when a chemist discovers that a Uranium atom can be split in two. This discovery spawns the most intense international race in human history. The goal was achieved in Los Alamos, New Mexico, by America's most capable scientists. Sheinkin's powerful book includes accounts of Soviet espionage, descriptions of commando attacks on Germany's heavy water plant in Norway, and the dropping of the first bomb over Hiroshima. *Bomb* succeeds in capturing the "strange mix of pride and horror" that scientists felt in winning World War II while also bequeathing to the world its most lethal weapon.

11. *We Are the Ship: The Story of Negro League Baseball.* Written and illustrated by Kadir Nelson. (Hyperion Books for Children, 2008.) Upon the occasion of his founding of the Negro National League, Rube Foster remarked, "We are the ship; all else the sea." Kadir Nelson invites readers to hop aboard this proverbial ship as he takes his audience on a fascinating tour of a neglected slice of American social and political history. The book is anonymously narrated in the first person in a style that projects authenticity and casual intimacy. Cleverly organized into nine innings, the book begins in 1920 with the formation of a separate baseball league for black players and concludes in 1947 when Jackie Robinson breaks the color barrier, joining the previously all-white major league. Nelson's writing is fresh and informative, and his paintings are breathtaking. *We Are the Ship* is a truly outstanding book, the award-winning artist's first as both author and illustrator.

12. *A Black Hole Is NOT a Hole.* Written by Carolyn Cinami DeCristofano. Illustrated by Michael Carroll. (Charlesbridge Publishing, 2012.) DeCristofano and Carroll boldly go where few children's writers would dare visit in a title that explores the exotic world of black holes, quasars, gravity, singularities, and the notion of an event horizon. The team does an impressive job of introducing some of the most sophisticated scientific concepts imaginable in this mind-expanding book. With a lively conversational tone and lovely illustrations, diagrams, charts, and photos, the volume communicates the vastness of space and the role that scientists such as Newton, Einstein, and Reber played in advancing our understanding of the universe. Readers of all ages will appreciate how DeCristofano and Carroll have made the esoteric realm of astronomers and physicists comprehensible and attractive as a topic of further study.

13. *Abraham Lincoln and Frederick Douglass: The Story behind an American Friendship.* Written by Russell Freedman. (Clarion Books, 2012.) This well-researched book portrays Abraham Lincoln and former slave Frederick Douglass, the most famous African American of his era, as friends and allies who shared many traits, core ideas, and personal histories. Both men were born poor and were self-educated, and they were united in the belief that no person should ever be allowed to own another. When these towering figures first met in 1863—Douglass visited the president in the White House—the nation was already embroiled in the Civil War. Although they only met on three occasions, the relationship was anchored in mutual admiration and respect. Fans of *Abraham Lincoln and Frederick Douglass* will want to also read Freedman's *Lincoln: A Photobiography* (1987), for which the noted biographer won the Newbery Medal.

14. *An American Plague: The True and Terrifying Story of the Yellow Fever Epidemic of 1793.* Written by Jim Murphy. (Clarion Books, 2003.) Science, politics, and descriptions of widespread panic converge in this tour-de-force rendering of the devastation inflicted on Philadelphia in 1793 by a lethal yellow fever epidemic. Jim Murphy adroitly covers not only the disease and its symptoms but also the crisis posed by having the young nation's capital and largest city completely paralyzed. With 10 percent of the city's population dead from the deadly disease, President Washington was unable to convene Congress in the fear-and-plague-ridden city. The author recognizes the gallant role that Philadelphia's free blacks played in nursing the stricken city residents. *An American Plague* is generously illustrated with reproductions of paintings, maps, and newspaper articles.

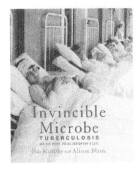

15. *Invincible Microbe: Tuberculosis and the Never-Ending Search for a Cure.* Written by Jim Murphy and Alison Blank. (Clarion Books, 2012.) Murphy and Blank's engrossing history of "the greatest killer of humans in the history of the world" begins with over-500,000-year-old fossilized evidence of TB and continues to the present day where it still poses a deadly threat to millions of people. Antibiotics have been a great help in fighting the disease, but the emergence of drug-resistant tuberculosis is still cause for alarm. This comprehensive look at the seemingly invincible microbe includes an account of its diagnosis and development, the various treatments over time, and a description of how society has acted toward its victims. There are numerous photographs, illustrations, and source notes, as well as a bibliography and an index in this meticulously researched volume.

16. *The Day-Glo Brothers.* Written by Chris Barton. Illustrated by Tony Persiani. (Charlesbridge Publishing, 2009.) In this uniquely stylized book, Barton tells how Bob and Joe Switzer experimented for years before finding the formula for creating an intense fluorescent paint. Persiani illustrates the early years of the boys' lives in black and white, gradually introduces colors, and concludes with vibrant images in yellow, green, and orange. The boys are quite different, both temperamentally and vocationally, with studious Bob wanting to become a doctor and carefree Joe hoping for a career in show business. When an industrial accident leaves Bob recuperating in a poorly lit basement, they turn their sights on creating paints that glow with special intensity. These products are now widely used in a variety of useful and artistic ways. Early and middle readers will enjoy this outstanding nonfiction picture book.

17. *Hand in Hand: Ten Black Men Who Changed America.* Written by Andrea Davis Pinkney. Illustrated by Brian Pinkney. (Hyperion, 2012.) Andrea Davis and Brian Pinkney, a husband-and-wife team, have assembled authoritative narratives and beautiful color portraits of 10 of the most accomplished and influential African American men in U.S. history, including Frederick Douglass, W. E. B. Du Bois, Thurgood Marshall, Jackie Robinson, Martin Luther King Jr., and Barack Obama. Each sketch is prefaced by a poem that sets the stage for a vignette of their lives and times. The compelling stories highlight childhood events, important influences, and the impact the men have had on American society. These profiles of the most important black men are perfectly suited for middle readers who are always hungry for role models. Children will also be interested in the book's civil rights time line and sources for further reading.

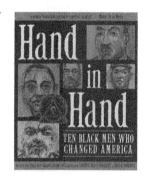

18. *The Great and Only Barnum: The Tremendous, Stupendous Life of Showman P. T. Barnum.* Written by Candace Fleming. Illustrated by Ray Fenwick. (Schwartz & Wade, 2009.) This illustrated biography of the world's greatest showman is like the circus that it describes. Full of eye-catching sidebars, vintage posters, and period photographs, this fully drawn, warts-and-all portrait of the legendary Phineas Taylor Barnum is a nonfiction masterpiece. The book not only acknowledges the accomplishments of the man responsible for "The Greatest Show on Earth," but distinguishes itself in revealing P. T. Barnum's dark side, including hucksterism, the mistreatment of animals, and the exploitation of human deformities and handicaps. "Amusement may not be the great aim of life, but it gives zest to our days," Barnum once remarked to a reporter who questioned the worth of Barnum's life's work. Amusement and zest are, likewise, not the only aims of nonfiction, but this frank biography delivers more of these commodities than is commonly found in material recommended for children. Young readers will be hooked on this larger-than-life biography.

19. *Kakapo Rescue: Saving the World's Strangest Parrot.* Written by Sy Montgomery. Illustrated by Nic Bishop. (HMH Books for Young Readers, 2010.) Take a 10-day trip to a remote island off the coast of New Zealand with Montgomery and Bishop and experience the work of a team determined to save the last of these beautiful nocturnal ground-dwelling parrots. With spectacular photographs and enthusiastic descriptions, *Kakapo Rescue* documents an exciting mission to preserve these unusual creatures that once numbered in the millions in New Zealand but now number less than 90 in their last refuge on Codfish Island. Montgomery and Bishop were given special permission from the New Zealand government to accompany a recovery team, where they endured strong wind and rain to track and monitor these vulnerable parrots.

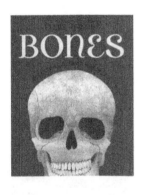

20. *Bones: Skeletons and How They Work.* Written and illustrated by Steve Jenkins. (Scholastic, 2010.) "Bones are alive. They grow as an animal grows, get stronger when they are strained, and repair themselves if they get broken," writes Steve Jenkins. They come in a range of shapes and sizes, each with its own place and function. With his customary fine-paper-craft collages and fact-filled text, Jenkins broadly surveys the animal kingdom, showing remarkable similarities across species. One page compares the arm structure of a mole, human, and spider monkey, while another page shows the skeletal forelimbs of a turtle, whale, and fruit bat. The author makes good use of humor to liven the text, with subheadings such as "That's a Handful," "Big Foot," "Arm Yourself," and "Head Case." Readers will be given information about bone joints, symmetry, and motion, and be treated to fascinating asides about exoskeletons.

21. *Extreme Animals: The Toughest Creatures on Earth.* Written by Nicola Davies. Illustrated by Neal Layton. (Candlewick, 2009.) Humorous illustrations and fascinating facts harmonize in Davies and Layton's catalog of amazing animals that can easily surpass delicate humans in their ability to withstand extreme temperatures or go without food or water. Some of the most tenacious survivors include emperor penguins, polar bears, reptiles, and camels—not to mention sea creatures enduring the deepest oceans and bacteria that thrive inside active volcanoes. This natural-history book brilliantly showcases the variety and ruggedness of different creatures by comparing them to humans. Young readers, accustomed to thinking about humanity as earth's foremost species, will learn a little humility as they place our survival attributes in a more realistic perspective.

22. *The Wall: Growing Up behind the Iron Curtain.* Written by Peter Sis. (Farrar, Straus & Giroux, 2007.) Peter Sis's illustrated autobiography tells about his life as a developing artist growing up in communist Czechoslovakia. As a child, he followed the party line, and while at school, his artist leanings were strictly controlled and channeled. As information from the West slipped into his country, Sis and other young people wanted to listen to the Beatles and read Allen Ginsberg. But when the Soviet Union invaded in 1968, the hope of political and cultural reform came crashing down. One picture shows Sis fleeing from the secret police. At the end of the book, Sis escapes to freedom as the Berlin Wall falls, traveling to America to become a successful animator. This story of stultifying conformity undone by creative expression will resonate with young readers.

23. *The Great Fire.* Written by Jim Murphy. (Scholastic, 2010.) Chicago's great fire of 1871 was one of the greatest disasters in American history, nearly obliterating the city and leaving 100,000 people homeless. Setting aside the folklore about Mrs. O'Leary and her cow, Murphy's riveting and well-researched account of the horrific three-day fire suggests that the fire could have been contained if not for poor communication, unfortunate high winds, and the shameful fact that the blaze would have been

met more aggressively if it had started in a wealthy section rather than in a working-class neighborhood. Street maps show the progression of the fire, and newspaper accounts supply personal anecdotes, while illustrations dramatically show the conflagration and destruction.

24. *Into the Unknown: How Great Explorers Found Their Way by Land, Sea, and Air.* Written by Stuart Ross. Illustrated by Stephen Biesty. (Candlewick, 2011.) This introduction to the boldest explorers of all time features dramatic stories, colorful maps, and intricate cross-sectional illustrations of the vehicles used in the various expeditions. Ross and Biesty's engaging guide highlights the deeds of 14 adventurers and the challenges they faced. Arranged chronologically, these narratives of discovery cover the lives and times of historic figures, including Marco Polo, Zheng He, Christopher Columbus, Magellan, Edmund Hillary, Mary Kingsley, Jacques Piccard, and Neil Armstrong. The text speaks to the explorers' motivations and contains abundant detail about navigation, locations, technology, and other essential concepts. *Into the Unknown* is a slice of world history that is guaranteed to spark the interests and imaginations of readers.

25. *Team Moon: How 400,000 People Landed Apollo 11 on the Moon.* Written by Catherine Thimmesh. (Houghton Mifflin Company, 2006.) Where other Apollo 11 books focus exclusively on the actions of a handful of famous astronauts, Catherine Thimmesh's valuable account expands the credit for the moon landing to embrace many unsung contributors. Readers who know something about this historic mission probably never considered the important role played by space suit seamstresses and designers, engineers, telescope operators, photographers, flight directors, record keepers, and thousands of others who contributed to this epic journey. The Kennedy Space Center alone had 17,000 behind-the-scenes workers. Arresting photographs and quotes from many of those who were involved with the project add to the credibility and authenticity of Thimmesh's book.

26. *Knucklehead: Tall Tales and Mostly True Stories about Growing Up Scieszka.* Written and illustrated by Jon Scieszka. (Viking Juvenile, 2008.) The cover of this very funny autobiography sets the tone with a young, helmeted Jon Scieszka imagining himself riding aboard a tank in the midst of a fierce battle. Styled like a vintage comic book, this collection of anecdotes about growing up as one of six brothers provides a hilarious peek into the creative mind of the author of *The Stinky Cheese Man* (1992) and *The True Story of the 3 Little Pigs!* (2009). Parents naturally want their children to read edifying nonfiction, but they would be wise to remember the importance of reading that is purely recreational. *Knucklehead* will not convey knowledge of important concepts or events, but it will serve the high purpose of hooking youngsters on the pleasure of reading.

27. *Electric Ben: The Amazing Life and Times of Benjamin Franklin.* Written and illustrated by Robert Byrd. (Dial, 2012.) Robert Byrd makes the astonishingly productive life of Benjamin Franklin fully accessible to young readers in his detailed portrait of a Renaissance man who stands out among our country's founders. With intricate double-page illustrations that nicely depict colonial America and text that conveys a wealth of information, Franklin emerges as an energetic, world-class statesman, printer, author, philosopher, scientist, and inventor. Byrd separates Franklin's life into 17 imaginative sections arranged chronologically, highlighting various accomplishments, such as his experiments with electricity and his ideas to form fire departments and lending libraries. *Electric Ben* is historical biography for children at its very best.

28. *America Is under Attack: September 11, 2001: The Day the Towers Fell.* Written and illustrated by Don Brown. (Flash Point, 2011.) Writing for an audience that had not been born in 2001, Brown uses restraint and empathy to document the terrible events of the morning of September 11th. Without sensationalizing, Brown's watercolors and straight-forward minute-by-minute chronology capture the plane hijackings, the crashes at the World Trade Center, the Pentagon, and Shanksville, Pennsylvania, the fiery collapse of the twin towers, and the heroic rescue efforts. Adults for whom this day is still a vivid memory will recognize Brown's picture book as authentic history. Weaving together the horrendous events with the experiences of some of those who were directly affected, this solidly presented account will allow parents and teachers to talk about this tragedy with children.

29. *Boys of Steel: The Creators of Superman.* Written by Marc Tyler Nobleman. Illustrated by Ross Mac-Donald. (Knopf Books for Young Readers, 2008.) Colorfully illustrated in a style reminiscent of retro comic books and harmonized with a compelling narrative that will captivate middle readers, MacDonald and Nobleman's picture book is about writer Jerry Siegel and illustrator Joe Shuster, the creators of the character that personified the idea of superhero. After being rejected by several publishers, DC Comics published the Superman comic in 1938. The young partners sold their work to the publisher for a mere $130, and the book's afterword discusses their very difficult compensation battle with the comic-book company. Siegel and Shuster are presented both as important creative artists and as nerdy outcasts, more like mild-mannered Clark Kent than like the Man of Steel.

30. *Cathedral: The Story of Its Construction.* Written and illustrated by David Macaulay. (HMH Books for Young Readers, 1973.) David Macaulay's tribute to the Gothic cathedral, one of humankind's most majestic architectural wonders, shows its step-by-step construction in breathtakingly intricate pen-and-ink drawings. This nonfiction classic captures every stage of the structure's growth from its planning to the erection of the walls, vaulting, and towers. The cathedral is set in 1252 in a fictitious French town whose people decide to build this imposing glory to God after their church is struck by lightning. Macaulay, who was once an architectural student at the Rhode Island School of Design, is clearly a master of his craft. People of all ages will never grow tired poring over the details of this award-winning book.

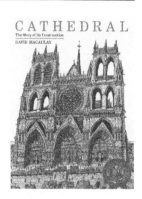

31. *Phineas Gage: A Gruesome but True Story about Brain Science.* Written by John Fleischman. (HMH Books for Young Readers, 2002.) In 1848, Phineas Gage had a hideous accident. An explosion sent an iron rod through his head, but instead of dying, he miraculously recovered and underwent a dramatic personality change. Phineas could work and communicate, but he went from being steady and well liked to becoming crude and impulsive, losing mental functions such as social intelligence and the ability to assess risk. Science writer Fleischman's story of this railroad construction foreman injured on the job is an important story because the case was a landmark in brain science. The 11-year study of this unfortunate man vastly contributed to our scientific knowledge of the central nervous system.

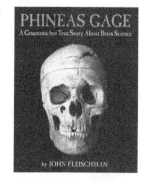

32. *Candy Bomber: The Story of the Berlin Airlift's "Chocolate Pilot."* Written by Michael O. Tunnell. (Charlesbridge Publishing, 2010.) This is a story of a small act of kindness with large ripple effects. Following World War II, when the United States began airlifting supplies to Russian-blockaded West Berlin, cargo pilot Lieutenant Gail Halvorsen began secretly bringing candy and gum to the city's suffer-

ing children. After meeting some of the children, he began dropping the sweets by tiny parachutes. The "Candy Bomber" became a symbol of hope. Soon the pilot's generous deeds became an officially sanctioned operation, and tons of candy were delivered to the children who gathered in the plane's flight path. *Candy Bomber* is liberally illustrated with many of Halvorsen's own black-and-white photographs.

33. *Zombie Makers: True Stories of Nature's Undead.* Written by Rebecca L. Johnson. (21st Century, 2012.) Aided by vivid color photographs, Rebecca L. Johnson's book presents a collection of fungi, worms, viruses, and wasps that occupy bodies and take over the brains of their victims. These zombie makers are not for the faint of heart. The author introduces worms that cause crickets to take their own lives and wasps that turn cockroaches into repositories for their larvae. Each chapter introduces an organism, explains its life cycle, describes how it attacks its host, and ends with a section called "The Science behind the Story." In a literary environment inhabited by so many books about zombies, it is good to see one that grabs the interests of readers with solid scientific research.

34. *Citizen Scientists: Be a Part of Scientific Discovery from Your Own Backyard.* Written by Loree Griffin Burns. Illustrated by Ellen Harasimowicz. (Henry Holt, 2012.) Children who are interested in nature and science will be delighted to find out from Burns and Harasimowicz how they can assist with real-life, seasonal science projects. Under the banner of "citizen science," which Burns defines as "the study of the world by the people who live in it," this engaging, photographically rich book describes four exciting scientific projects and how people of any age can get involved with data collection. Aided by color photos that show children doing observations, the book details seasonal projects such as the winter bird count, the summer ladybug project, the spring frog monitoring, and the fall monarch butterfly tagging. One of the most interesting things about *Citizen Scientist* is its vision of science as a shared democratic enterprise, not just the exclusive province of a few experts.

35. *The Elephant Scientist.* Written by Caitlin O'Connell and Donna M. Jackson. Illustrated by Timothy Rodwell. (HMH Books for Young Readers, 2011.) This close look at the work of scientist Caitlin O'Connell focuses on the amazing discovery she made while observing African elephants in Etosha National Park in Nambia. She learned that elephants, like the insects she previously studied, actually detect sound with their limbs. When she noticed the animals stopping abruptly in a uniform manner, she got the idea that they were all sensing vibrations through their feet. The book allows readers to experience the research as it developed from this hypothesis, including lab work on the cells of elephant feet and trunks, and sound vibration experiments in the field with elephant herds. Attractive photographs of the elephants and their surroundings illuminate this intriguing investigation.

36. *My Season with Penguins: An Antarctic Journal.* Written and illustrated by Sophie Webb. (HMH Books for Young Readers, 2000.) Ornithologist and artist Sophie Webb provides a candid firsthand account of what it was like to spend two months on a remote island off the coast of Antarctica studying Adélie penguins. Illustrated with watercolors that amplify her detailed journal, Webb discusses the habitat and mating rituals of the penguins, discusses some unusual methods of collecting data, and mentions some of the realities of living in this subzero world. The difficulties range from adjusting to 24 hours of sunlight, to needing to add alcohol to the paint to prevent it from turning to slush, to complaining about going to the bathroom outdoors when it's cold and windy. Webb helpfully states the scientific questions that guided the expedition and includes a glossary to assist with some of the technical vocabulary.

37. *Freedom Walkers: The Story of the Montgomery Bus Boycott.* Written by Russell Freedman. (Holiday House, 2006.) This essential story of the American civil rights movement begins with the unjust Montgomery, Alabama, law that required African Americans to sit in the back of buses and to even relinquish their seats to whites when the bus was at full capacity. When Rosa Parks politely refused to give up her seat to a white man, this simple, strategic act precipitated a national movement for racial equality. Parks was arrested and a boycott of the city buses ensued. Freedman's well-researched historical account discusses how the successful 310-day strike brought the bus company to its knees and how the U.S. Supreme Court eventually declared Alabama's bus segregation laws unconstitutional. Compelling black-and-white photos powerfully add to the impact of this necessary book.

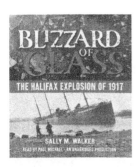

38. *Blizzard of Glass: The Halifax Explosion of 1917.* Written by Sally M. Walker. (Henry Holt, 2011.) Nearly 2,000 people perished on December 6, 1917, when two ships collided in Halifax Harbor creating the largest man-made blast prior to the dropping of the atomic bomb at Hiroshima. The tragedy was made even more unbearable when the following day a blizzard dumped more than a foot of snow on the area, immobilizing relief efforts. The ship explosion flattened more than 16 square miles, breaking windows 50 miles away. Two large maps and numerous black-and-white photos help tell the story of how the Canadian towns of Halifax and Dartmouth were devastated in this accident involving ships destined for service in World War I. Walker's compelling narrative tells the story of the explosion, aftermath, and rebuilding through the eyes of five local families.

39. *The Case of the Vanishing Golden Frogs: A Scientific Mystery.* Written by Sandra Markle. (Millbrook Press, 2011.) In the late 1990s, Panamanian golden frogs began to disappear, triggering a scientific investigation and rescue effort for these national symbols of Panama. With eye-catching color photographs and lucid text, Sandra Markle's book does an excellent job of exploring the mysterious plight of these little yellow creatures. Unlike other endangered species, they were not being hunted to extinction. Were they being killed by pollution? Was the problem climate change? Were their habitats being destroyed? As is sometimes the case in science, there was no definite solution to this puzzle. Even though they did not fully understand the source of the disease, scientists did find evidence that a fungus was undermining the frogs' ability to keep their skin moist.

40. *A Dream of Freedom: The Civil Rights Movement from 1954 to 1968.* Written by Diane McWhorter. (Scholastic, 2004.) Motivated by her own privileged childhood in racially segregated Birmingham, Alabama, Pulitzer Prize–winning author Diane McWhorter describes modern civil rights history in a way that is personal and political. "I couldn't tell you then what civil rights meant," McWhorter writes frankly of her sixth-grade perspective, "but grown-ups sounded so disgusted when they mentioned them that I figured they had to be bad words." No longer blind to the history of black oppression, the author vividly covers the major milestones of the civil rights movement from the 1954 *Brown v. Board of Education* Supreme Court decision to the 1968 assassination of Martin Luther King Jr. Sidebars, newspaper reprints, and photographs of the period ably supplement this stirring narrative.

41. *For the Birds: The Life of Roger Tory Peterson.* Written by Peggy Thomas. Illustrated by Laura Jacques. (Boyds Mills Press, 2011.) The passion of famous bird lover and creator of the popular Peterson Field Guides comes alive in this first-ever children's biography of Roger Tory Peterson. This accessible picture-book portrait shows Peterson as a skilled writer, gifted artist, educator, and environmental activist who worked tirelessly to protect the habitats of birds around the world. In 1934, he published *A Field Guide to the Birds* and later produced guides

to insects, fish, mammals, reptiles, amphibians, and plants that have sold in the millions. Illuminating illustrations of his long career and spectacular pictures of many bird species add to this fascinating read. This rendering of Peterson's sense of wonder and commitment will make readers want to get their hands on Peterson's guides and do their own outdoor investigations.

42. *Lincoln: A Photobiography.* Written by Russell Freedman. (Clarion Books, 1987.) The Newbery Medal has rarely been awarded to works of nonfiction, but Russell Freedman's portrait of the great Civil War president earned this prestigious honor in 1988. The book comprehensively spans Lincoln's childhood, his work as a country lawyer, his marriage to Mary Todd, his election to the presidency, his wartime leadership, and subsequent assassination. Freedman carefully collected over 80 photographs, and they work hand in glove with his extensive research. Young readers will come away with a new understanding of the controversies and challenges Lincoln faced in leading a deeply divided country. *Lincoln: A Photobiography* is clearly the standout title for children among the many portraits of this iconic leader.

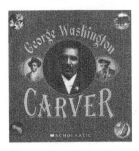

43. *George Washington Carver.* Written by Tonya Bolden. (Scholastic, 2009.) Among the several biographies of George Washington Carver, this lavishly illustrated picture book stands out by virtue of its well-sourced narrative, carefully selected photographs, and the man's own paintings and botanical drawings. Tonya Bolden traces Carver's life from his humble beginnings as a slave to the height of his career as a pioneering scientist, conservationist, and educator. This fresh portrait discusses not just his well-known peanut studies but also his considerable research on, and product development from, many plants. In Bolden's hands, this trailblazing genius is recognized as a man who wanted to waste nothing and had a prescient vision that society's needs can be satisfied by renewable natural resources.

44. *How They Croaked: The Awful Ends of the Awfully Famous.* Written by Georgia Bragg. Illustrated by Kevin O'Malley. (Walker Childrens, 2012.) The horrific ends of 19 of history's most famous people are laid bare by Bragg's irreverent style and O'Malley's black-and-white cartoon illustrations. Readers will learn, for example, that George Washington was treated with blister beetles, draining most of the blood from his ailing body, and that the corpse of Henry VIII was believed to have exploded in its coffin while he lay in state. One of the book's many indelicate sectional subtitles is "Marie Curie: You Glow Girl!" referring to the famous scientist's death from radioactivity. In a book that generally panders to the sometimes-lurid appetites of young readers, this fascinating volume more than redeems itself through its information-rich text. Its most saving grace is that it will attract even the most disinclined readers.

45. *Seven Miles to Freedom: The Robert Smalls Story.* Written by Janet Halfmann. Illustrated by Duane Smith. (Lee & Low Books, 2012.) In this picturebook portrait, Halfmann and Smith sketch a portrait of Robert Smalls and his daring escape from slavery during the Civil War. Through dutiful service to his master, Smalls learned so much about ships and sailing that he was promoted to the position of wheelman. He used this knowledge to great benefit. In 1862, he stole a ship loaded with Confederate cannons and led his crew and family north to a Union fort. In this uncommon act of skill and courage, Smalls became the first African American captain of a U.S. vessel and the first black to have a ship named after him. Smalls went on to serve in the South Carolina legislature and in the U.S. Congress.

46. *Nurse, Soldier, Spy: The Story of Sarah Edmonds, a Civil War Hero.* Written by Marissa Moss. Illustrated by John Hendrix. (Harry N. Abrams, 2011.) The old saw about truth being stranger than fiction receives a strong endorsement in this intriguing story about a 19-year-old woman from Canada who disguised herself as a man in order to serve in the Union Army during the U.S. Civil War. Sarah Emma Edmonds came to the United States to escape an arranged marriage and became a male nurse in the army under the name of Frank Thompson. Sarah's performance was so exemplary that she was then asked to be a spy behind enemy lines, where she also served with distinction. Hendrix's bold caricatures and Moss's lively use of dialogue make *Nurse, Soldier, Spy* a very exciting story for young readers.

47. *Poop Happened! A History of the World from the Bottom Up.* Written by Sarah Albee. Illustrated by Robert Leighton. (Walker Childrens, 2010.) Yes, this is a history of excrement and the public health challenges that accrue from its management and disposal. This cartoon book announces that it is the "number one book on number two" and proves its point with topics such as "The Age of Shovelry," "The Origin of Feces," "Reeking Renaissance," "Hellenic Hygiene," and "How Do Astronauts Use the Toilet in Space?" Albee and Leighton's social history traces the development of human sanitation practices from ancient ages to the present with particular attention to Western civilization. Flush with scatological puns, the book sheds serious light on the need of increasingly populated civilizations for efficient waste disposal.

48. *Shipwrecked! The True Adventures of a Japanese Boy.* Written by Rhoda Blumberg. (HarperCollins, 2003.) Aided by well-chosen maps and drawings, Rhoda Blumberg tells the true story of a poor Japanese boy who becomes instrumental in opening up his isolationist society to the West in the 1800s. When 14-year-old fisherman Manjiro is shipwrecked hundreds of miles away from Japan, he is rescued by an American whaling ship and taken to America, where he is educated and learns navigation, mining, and many things about American society. During this era, Japan was xenophobic, likely to execute anyone who would leave the country for another and then return, yet Manjiro decided to return to his home country. He was thrown in prison, eventually released, became a samurai, teacher, and interpreter, playing a historic role in promoting trade and acceptance of Western society.

49. *Bodies from the Ash: Life and Death in Ancient Pompeii.* Written by James M. Deem. (HMH Books for Young Readers, 2005.) In 79 AD, the city of Pompeii, one of the largest in the Roman Empire, was buried when Mount Vesuvius erupted, entombing its inhabitants. Hundreds of years later, archeologists began excavating the city, unearthing a treasure trove of historical and cultural artifacts. Deem's comprehensive story of this lost city includes its time as a thriving metropolis and its rediscovery in the 1700s, and it has impressive descriptions of how plaster casts of the disaster victims have shed light on their lives and times. There are many excellent color photos of the bones and relics that have been unearthed over the years. Middle readers would be well served to learn about one of the world's greatest catastrophes from Deem's respectful and thoroughly researched book.

50. *Queen of the Falls.* Written and illustrated by Chris van Allsburg. (HMH Books for Young Readers, 2011.) Chris van Allsburg's venture into nonfiction has the same exquisite visual quality that earned him Caldecott Medals for *Jumanji* (1981) and *The Polar Express* (1985). The unusual topic of his sepia-tinted illustrations is the story of a 62-year-old woman who seeks fame and fortune by being the first person to survive going over Niagara Falls in a wooden barrel. Annie Edson Taylor, a widow and retired charm-school instructor, accomplished this dangerous stunt

in 1901, and then toured the country talking about her deed. Early and middle readers will find much to engage them in this suspenseful story of an unlikely daredevil.

51. *And Then What Happened, Paul Revere?* Written by Jean Fritz. Illustrated by Margot Tomes. (Puffin, 1996.) Fritz and Tomes take a somewhat humorous look at the man immortalized for his famous midnight ride to warn his fellow patriots that the British were coming. This illustrated biography includes a harrowing account of Paul Revere's historic Revolutionary War journey and some little-known information, such as his manufacturing of a silver collar for someone's pet squirrel, his whittling of false teeth in his spare time to supplement his silversmith income, and his raising a family of 16 children. Particularly helpful is the map illustrating Revere's ride through Boston, Concord, and Lexington. This humanistic portrait will make a great read-aloud text for young and older elementary-age children.

52. *Ubiquitous: Celebrating Nature's Survivors.* Written by Joyce Sidman. Illustrated by Beckie Prange. (HMH Books for Young Readers, 2010.) Skillfully mixing poetry and science, this fascinating gallery of biological success recognizes various species for their astonishing ability to adapt and flourish in often severe environments. Sidman and Prange show why, while many other life forms have become extinct, some have turned out to be so resilient. Their varied collection of survivors includes bacteria, beetles, geckos, mollusks, lichens, sharks, diatoms, ants, squirrels, coyotes, crows, and humans. Prange's vivid watercolor-and-linoleum cuts meld with Sidman's fine verse to impart not just information about this diverse assemblage but also a sense of wonder about how some life forms have lasted so long in the natural world. In a publishing landscape where ordinary children's literature often seems ubiquitous, this beautiful collection ranks as extraordinary.

53. *Sadako and the Thousand Paper Cranes.* Written by Eleanor Coerr. Illustrated by Ronald Himler. (Penguin Group, 2009.) Originally published in 1977, *Sadako and the Thousand Paper Cranes* is a special book that has been translated into many languages and often used for peace education programs. Sadako Sasaki was two years old when the United States dropped an atomic bomb near her home in Hiroshima on August 6, 1945. Her life as a school athlete was cut short when she developed leukemia, which her mother called the "atom bomb disease." Given only a year to live, Sadako was inspired by a Japanese legend that held that if an ill person could fold 1,000 cranes, the gods would make her well again. The 11-year-old girl managed to fold 644 cranes before passing away on October 25, 1955. Friends and family took up the task of folding the remaining cranes and buried them with the little girl.

54. *Spirit Seeker: John Coltrane's Musical Journey.* Written by Gary Golio. Illustrated by Rudy Gutierrez. (Clarion Books, 2012.) The highs and lows in the life of legendary jazz musician John Coltrane are admirably portrayed in this fantastically illustrated and movingly told biography. The product of a deeply religious family, Coltrane played the saxophone in his North Carolina high school and then studied jazz in Philadelphia. Touring with his band led not only to his addiction to drugs but also to the development of his music. A constant student of philosophy and world religions, he remained committed to the vision of using music to express his spiritual longings. With the help of his second wife, he overcame his drug problem to emerge as an iconic figure in the history of American music, performing with other artistic giants such as Miles Davis and Thelonious Monk.

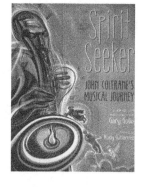

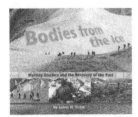

55. *Bodies from the Ice: Melting Glaciers and the Recovery of the Past.* Written by James M. Deem. (HMH Books for Young Readers, 2008.) This book describes the movement of glaciers, convincingly showing that the artifacts and bodies preserved in them provide an important glimpse into the past. In 1991, for example, mountain climbers in the Austrian Alps found the oldest human ever preserved in ice, with radiocarbon techniques dating its age at 5,300 years. Aided by excellent photographs and illustrations, Deem's book devotes several chapters to the mortal dangers climbers face investigating glaciers. Disturbingly, more discoveries are likely to be made because of glacial melting due to global warming. This book nicely complements two of the author's other critically acclaimed titles: *Bodies from the Bog* (1998) and *Bodies from the Ash* (2005).

56. *Come Back, Salmon: How a Group of Dedicated Kids Adopted Pigeon Creek and Brought It Back to Life.* Written by Molly Cone. Illustrated by Sidnee Wheelwright. (Sierra Club Books for Children, 2001.) A polluted, junk-filled stream near Jackson Elementary School in Everett, Washington, was so bad that salmon could no longer return to it to spawn. *Come Back, Salmon* describes the inspiring and determined efforts of the school children and community to adopt Pigeon Creek and restore it to good health. Lively text based on recorded conversations and color photos of the children in action convey the excitement and enthusiasm the project inspired, as the community cleaned up the stream, hatched Coho salmon eggs from a state hatchery, stocked the stream, learned about the life cycle of the fish, and kept Pigeon Creek as an unpolluted spawning ground. Though many naysayers said that the salmon would never return to Pigeon Creek, the fish did come back, much to the children's delight.

57. *Escape! The Story of the Great Houdini.* Written by Sid Fleischman. (Greenwillow Books, 2006.) Newbery Medalist Sid Fleischman, who once worked as a magician, is the perfect author of a biography of the world's most-celebrated magician, escape artist, and self-promoter. "No jail cell, no hand cuffs, and no manacles could hold him," writes Fleischman of the man who reportedly walked through walls, escaped from a straitjacket while suspended upside-down from a building, and performed countless other amazing tricks. Particularly interesting is the illusionist's early career performing in vaudeville, small medicine shows, and traveling circuses. This lively and affectionate profile of Houdini's life and accomplishments, along with an impressive list of annotated sources, includes rare photographs the author obtained from Houdini's wife. Fleischman's unique relationship with his subject, coupled with his insider's knowledge of show business, makes *Escape!* a truly magical read.

58. *The Endless Steppe.* Written by Esther Hautzig. (Penguin, 1971.) When Esther and her family are accused of being capitalist enemies, they are taken from their wealthy Vilna, Poland, home by Soviet troops and sent to a forced labor camp in Siberia. Crowded into cattle cars, they are exiled to a cruel life of backbreaking work with barely enough food and clothing to survive. This shocking firsthand account of the horrors of her existence also includes accounts of the kindness of local villagers without whom she would not have survived. Ironically, when the war ends and her family is told they may return home, Esther finds that she has grown to love Siberia's endless, unspoiled steppe.

59. *The Fairy Ring, or, Elsie and Frances Fool the World.* Written by Mary Losure. (Candlewick, 2012.) Nine-year-old Frances is a real believer in fairies. When she and her cousin Elsie, age 15, create photographs of cutout paper fairies to get their families to stop teasing her, word spreads of this supposedly authentic photographic evidence and quickly spirals out of control. The photos even find their way into the

welcome hands of Sir Arthur Conan Doyle—famous for his Sherlock Holmes stories—who publishes them in an article as proof of the existence of fairies. This remarkable true story so ably told by Mary Losure offers a sympathetic portrait about people clearly in over their heads and feeling unable to undo a hoax that lingered for 60 years. Fortunately, Losure includes reproductions of famous fairy photos, allowing readers to experience firsthand what stirred up this intense yearning for magic in early 20th-century England.

60. *George vs. George: The American Revolution as Seen from Both Sides.* Written and illustrated by Rosalyn Schanzer. (National Geographic Children's Books, 2007.) This disarmingly mature look at the American Revolution distinguishes itself by making the important point that there are two sides to every story. Framing the war as a comparison between King George III of England and George Washington, commander of the Continental Army, may at first glance seem simplistic, but it makes the conflict very accessible to young readers and opens the door to a discussion of important and debatable questions involving taxation and other causes of the war. Parents who want to introduce their children to this historic conflict would be well served by *George vs. George.* While it has appealing cartoonlike illustrations and dialogue balloons, this is not "dumbed down" history but an unusually balanced and sophisticated account of a vital period in the history of England and America.

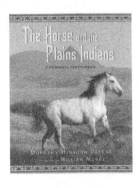

61. *The Horse and the Plains Indians: A Powerful Partnership.* Written by Dorothy Hinshaw Patent. Illustrated by William Muñoz. (Clarion Books, 2012.) The image of Native Americans on horseback is so thoroughly ingrained in our cultural consciousness that young readers might be forgiven if they thought this close relationship between man and animal always existed, perhaps assuming the horse was a species indigenous to North America. Patent and

Muñoz's enlightening history makes it clear that this transformative union did not begin until the 16th century, when the Spaniards first introduced horses. Prior to horses becoming an integral part of their culture, the Plains Indians used dogs to transport their belongings and hunted buffalo on foot. Engaging descriptions, along with beautiful illustrations and photographs, make this a very attractive title. Fans of this book should also consider reading Patent and Muñoz's *The Buffalo and the Indians: A Shared Destiny* (2006), which focuses on the special relationship between the buffalo and the Plains Indians.

62. *Black Elk's Vision: A Lakota Story.* Written by S. D. Nelson. (Harry N. Abrams, 2010.) S. D. Nelson, a member of the Standing Rock Sioux tribe of the Dakotas, has skillfully created a first-person account of the life of Lakota medicine man Black Elk that is a unique and refreshing take on American history. Starting with Black Elk's childhood visions, the narrative documents his involvement in the battles of Little Big Horn and Wounded Knee, as well as his travels with Buffalo Bill's Wild West Show. This recounting of the Native American experience provides a sense of what it must have been like to have their main food source, the buffalo, slaughtered by interlopers and to have their people herded into reservations. Captioned black-and-white archival photographs and colorful artwork add to the feeling of authenticity and intimacy in this large-format book.

63. *Kubla Khan: The Emperor of Everything.* Written by Kathleen Krull. Illustrated by Robert Byrd. (Viking Juvenile, 2010.) With Byrd's beautifully detailed illustrations, Krull's lively biography of Kubla Khan acknowledges his many accomplishments, such as ruling over the largest empire of his time, building the lavish Imperial City, which later became Beijing, and establishing a great postal system. Kubla was trained as a warrior like his grandfather Ghengis Khan, but wisely supported the arts, sciences, and technology in

ways that placed China at the forefront of the world. Ruling in the 13th century, Kubla Khan inherited an empire held together by fierce Mongol tribes and had advisors from many religions and nationalities. Much of what we know about the leader comes from the writings of Marco Polo, the famous Venetian merchant traveler.

64. *How Angel Peterson Got His Name.* Written by Gary Paulsen. (Perfection Learning, 2004.) Gary Paulsen takes an amusing and nostalgic look at his northern Minnesota boyhood of the 1950s, focusing on the stunts he and his friends performed that would be considered risky even by today's standards. The exploits include jumping three barrels on a bicycle, hang gliding with an Army surplus kite, riding over a waterfall in a pickle barrel, wrestling with a live side-show bear, and skiing behind a hot-rodding car. The point of this narrative is not to encourage foolhardiness but to provide a glimpse of how preadolescent boys often consider themselves to be invincible and will do almost anything to impress their peers.

65. *Jimi: Sounds Like a Rainbow: A Story of the Young Jimi Hendrix.* Written by Gary Golio. Illustrated by Javaka Steptoe. (Clarion Books, 2010.) This is the tale of a creative genius determined to behave and interpret music in his distinct way. Gary Golio and Javaka Steptoe's rendering of Jimi Hendrix, the 1960s rock star, begins with his Seattle childhood, living with his father in a boarding house. Devoted to drawing and music as a young man, the stirrings of Hendrix's unique vision began to emerge with his wondering if someone could paint pictures with sound. Steptoe's intense color illustrations are a good fit for Golio's rich and informative text. The story concludes when Hendrix is at the zenith of his artistic success, while his heartbreaking death is handled in an author's note along with suggested resources regarding drug abuse.

66. *My Librarian Is a Camel: How Books Are Brought to Children around the World.* Written by Margriet Ruurs. (Boyds Mills Press, 2005.) Throughout most of the United States, it is easy to take the availability of public library books for granted. But as Margriet Ruurs demonstrates in this informative photo essay, many remote areas of the world are not so lucky. In this intriguing tour of 13 countries, she shows how books are delivered in strange ways, including by donkey cart, bicycle, boat, elephant, wheelbarrow, and train. There are maps and descriptions of each of the featured countries and many excellent color photographs of kids with books, often taken by librarians on the front lines of providing a service that is so critical to a functioning literate society.

67. *Sit-In: How Four Friends Stood Up by Sitting Down.* Written by Andrea Davis Pinkney. Illustrated by Brian Pinkney. (Little, Brown Books for Young Readers, 2010.) Elementary school-age children will appreciate this picture book based on the historic sit-in by four African American college students who sought to integrate a Woolworth's lunch counter in Greensboro, North Carolina, in 1960. The Pinkneys do a wonderful job of showing how the peaceful protesters challenged unjust authority in the form of racial discrimination. This protest inspired other sit-ins, leading up to the signing of the Civil Rights Act of 1964 and eventually leading to the 1966 ruling by the Supreme Court forbidding this type of segregation. The poetic narrative is replete with food metaphors, while the graceful watercolor-and-ink artwork captures the energy of this historic act of civil disobedience.

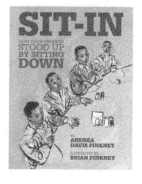

68. *Truce: The Day the Soldiers Stopped Fighting.* Written by Jim Murphy. (Scholastic, 2009.) World War I, known for its senseless brutality and carnage, had a brief shining moment of peace and sanity on Christmas Day in 1914 when troops on both sides of the Western Front openly defied orders by stopping the fighting and spontaneously celebrated the holiday with their enemies. Through excellent research based

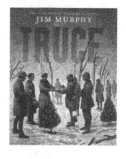

on primary sources and careful use of black-and-white photos, Murphy has created a truly valuable history not just of this famed Christmas miracle but also of the entire calamitous war. Murphy's excellent book includes an account of the events that led to World War I, and it has a time line, valuable source notes, and other resources.

69. *Action Jackson.* Written by Jan Greenberg and Sandra Jordan. Illustrated by Robert Andrew Parker. (Square Fish, 2007.) Affectionately named "Action Jackson" for his dynamic, paint-splattered canvases, Jackson Pollock is considered one of the great artists of the latter 20th century. *Action Jackson* is an excellent introduction to Pollock's life and work not just for middle readers but for readers of all ages. This book focuses on a critical two-month period of Jackson's life when he did one of his most important paintings, known as *Number 1, 1950,* or *Lavender Mist.* Young readers will get the sense that they are observing the artist in his barn studio as he engages in his intensely creative process. With energetic prose—"He swoops and leaps like a dancer, paint trailing from a brush that doesn't touch the canvas"—and vibrant impressionistic watercolors, this collaboration of Greenberg, Jordan, and Parker provides real insight into what it means to be an artist.

70. *William Shakespeare and the Globe.* Written and illustrated by Aliki. (HarperCollins, 2000.) With her lively, well-researched text and detailed cartoon pictures, Aliki creates an excellent introduction to the world's most famous playwright and the famous Globe Theatre, where many of Shakespeare's works were performed. Cleverly dividing her work into five "acts," the book covers Elizabethan theater history, including Sam Wanamaker's modern rebuilding of the Globe. In deference to the Bard's rare talent, numerous quotations from his plays are found throughout the book. Aliki's text also has very useful charts listing each of Shakespeare's plays, a chronology of his life, and even a sampling of words and expressions he contributed to the Western lexicon.

71. *Adventure beneath the Sea: Living in an Underwater Science Station.* Written by Kenneth Mallory. Illustrated by Brian Skerry. (Boyds Mills Press, 2010.) What would it be like to be an aquanaut and live for a week 60 feet underwater in the ocean in a vehicle that resembles a mobile home? Mallory and Skerry richly answer this question in their informative and visual account of living on the science station Aquarius, located on a coral reef off the Florida keys. The purpose of the Aquarius project is to allow researchers to electronically tag fish and to track their whereabouts without being limited to short visits. After extensive safety training, the author and photographer live with scientists in cramped living quarters and go scuba diving daily to observe the fish (and use the undersea outhouse). *Adventure beneath the Sea* provides a unique description of scientists at work and a striking photographic view of the beauty of underwater life.

72. *Airborne: A Photobiography of Wilbur and Orville Wright.* Written by Mary Collins. (National Geographic Children's Books, 2003.) *Airborne* has engaging text, but 60 duotone archival photos are the main attraction of Mary Collins's impressive book about the legendary Wright Brothers, who designed and flew the first powered aircraft, ushering in a new era of transportation. These mechanical geniuses, who ran a bicycle shop, essentially became the world's original aeronautical engineers when, in 1903, they made their historic flight at Kitty Hawk, North Carolina. Collins's narrative sheds light on the personalities of the inventors and methodically addresses key technical issues involved in controlling the movement of the plane, which had to be mastered to achieve controlled flight. The author's meticulous research is on display in her portrayal of Wilbur and Orville as detail men who left nothing to chance. The brothers selected North Carolina's Outer Banks as their test

site only after checking with the National Weather Service about optimal wind speeds and temperatures.

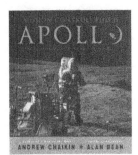

73. *Mission Control, This Is Apollo: The Story of the First Voyages to the Moon.* Written by Andrew Chaikin and Victoria Kohl. Illustrated by Alan Bean. (Viking Juvenile, 2009.) This handsome, highly readable volume describes the 1969 Apollo 11 moon landing and key missions in space history from Mercury through Apollo 17, but its most noteworthy distinction is its illustrator and writer. The book is illustrated by astronaut Alan Bean, the fourth man to walk on the moon during Apollo 12, and was coauthored by the exceptionally well-qualified Andrew Chaikin, who had already written a critically acclaimed book on space travel, *A Man on the Moon* (2002), for which he interviewed 28 former Apollo astronauts. *Mission Control* has a wealth of personal anecdotes, information on accidents and tragedies, illustrations showing where the lunar landings took place, and attractive diagrams of space vehicles. Readers will be delighted by the book and be motivated to learn more about the Apollo missions.

74. *Alex the Parrot: No Ordinary Bird.* Written by Stephanie Spinner. Illustrated by Meilo So. (Knopf Books for Young Readers, 2012.) Animal psychologist Irene Pepperberg overturned conventional scientific belief when she refuted the assumption that intelligence was an automatic reflection of brain size. In 1977, when Pepperberg was a graduate student, she bought an African grey parrot in a pet store and named him Alex, short for Avian Learning Experiment. To the amazement of the world, she taught the bird to add and subtract; recognize shapes, sizes, and colors; and vocalize and understand hundreds of words, something that other animals had never done. Spinner and So portray the close bond between Irene and Alex and the groundbreaking research in a light-

hearted conversational manner with striking multimedia illustrations. Children will fall in love with
Alex, seeing him transform from a frightened creature
to a bird that becomes a bossy show-off.

75. *If Stones Could Speak: Unlocking the Secrets of
Stonehenge.* Written by Mark Aronson. (National
Geographic Children's Books, 2010.) This exciting
archeology-in-progress book addresses one of the
world's most mysterious stone monuments—a site
that has spawned many theories over the centuries on
its origins, ranging from an early calendar, religious
temple, and a sacrificial site. Mark Aronson joins the
Riverside Project research team on the Stonehenge
dig and provides an informative firsthand account of
the research that has transformed our understanding
of this ancient stone circle. The team looked for clues
in the surrounding area and unearthed the biggest
Neolithic village ever found in England. The new
theory is that Stonehenge was used "to usher, to welcome, the honored dead into their permanent home,"
while their living relatives lived nearby in wooden
structures.

76. *Animals Up Close.* Written and illustrated by Igor
Siwanowicz. (DK Publishing, 2009.) Igor Siwanowicz, a biologist at Munich's Max Planck Institute
of Neurobiology, used advanced macrophotography
to produce a visually astounding book of close-ups
of animal textures, patterns, shapes, and colors that
has to be seen to be believed. There are spectacular
shots of creatures, including gerbils, centipedes, lo-
custs, geckos, flying fox bats, tarantulas, stag beetles,
axolotls, jellyfish, and their habitats. Each animal is
featured in a dramatic double-page spread that can't
help but evoke a sense of wonder. Ideal for children
looking to do reports, the book also has facts about
animal life spans, sizes, scientific names, and whether
they are on the list of threatened species.

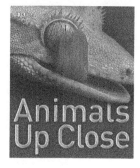

77. *How to Talk to an Autistic Kid.* Written by Daniel Stefanski. (Free Spirit Publishing, 2011.) Daniel Stefanski, a 14-year-old boy with autism, has written a practical and personal guide to help children understand some of the difficulties children with autism face in everyday social interactions and offers tips on how to better get along. "Not all people with autism are exactly alike," writes Daniel, "just like not all 'regular' kids or teenagers are exactly alike," but there are still many recurring issues, such as bullying, teasing, and excluding that are often products of misunderstanding. He explains that kids with autism often have trouble reacting to certain stimuli and understanding figures of speech and body language, but that they want to be treated with kindness and respect. "Even though my brain is different, I'm still a kid," he writes in his matter-of-fact way. This book would be the perfect choice for parents, teachers, and therapists for introducing and discussing the topic of autism with children.

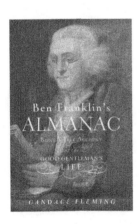

78. *Ben Franklin's Almanac: Being a True Account of the Good Gentleman's Life.* Written by Candace Fleming. (Atheneum Books for Young Readers, 2003.) This unique scrapbook-style portrait of the most accomplished American founder is modeled on the format of Ben Franklin's own *Poor Richard's Almanack* (2007). Packed with concisely packaged facts, quotations, anecdotes, maps, artifacts, newspaper ads, etchings, cartoons, lists, and inventions, Fleming's book deftly introduces young readers to the astonishing scope of Franklin's accomplishments. The book is designed so that readers can easily open the book anywhere and find a foothold, and there is also a helpful time line to help keep the fascinating man's life in proper sequence. This is an inspired rendering of the achievements of an individual too large to be easily captured in a conventional book.

79. *Little People and a Lost World: An Anthropological Mystery.* Written by Linda Goldenberg. (Twenty-First Century Books, 2006.) *Little People* is a story of an exciting archeological find on an Indonesian island and the scientific controversy that ensued over its meaning. When Australian and Indonesian archeologists found a small 12,000-year-old skeleton in a cave, they at first thought it was a child, but upon further study concluded that it was the remains of a three-foot-tall adult woman. The resulting scientific debate hinged on whether the skeleton was merely a small human, perhaps with a medical problem, or an entirely new species of human ancestor. Supported by color photographs, Linda Goldenberg succinctly explains the arguments and counterarguments surrounding the 2003 discovery, as well as who is entitled to claim ownership of the find. The most valuable lesson young readers may learn from this book is that science is often defined by conflict between rival paradigms rather than on the mere accumulation of settled facts.

80. *Big Wig: A Little History of Hair.* Written by Kathleen Krull. Illustrated by Peter Malone. (Arthur A. Levine Books, 2011.) Krull and Malone's playful picture-book history makes it clear that humans have been obsessing about their hair from the times of ancient Egypt and the Incan Empire. With clever illustrations and solid information, the book demonstrates that hair has been a matter not only of style and fashion but also of social class and status. The book gets off to a comical and informative start in discussing human prehistory. "In the beginning, everyone is furry," Krull writes. "People make friends by grooming each other. That is, picking the bugs out of the other guy's fur coat." Hair becomes the vehicle to take readers to many different times and places, with the familiar visages of Cleopatra, George Washington, Queen Elizabeth, and others in starring roles along the way.

81. *Around the World.* Written and illustrated by Matt Phelan. (Candlewick, 2011.) Matt Phelan's eye-catching graphic novel tells the story of three real-life journeys inspired by Jules Verne's timeless fictional adventure, *Around the World in Eighty Days* (1873). The three solo adventurers and the date of their global circumnavigations are miner-turned-bicyclist Thomas Stevens in 1884, reporter Nellie Bly in 1889, and sea captain Joshua Slocum in 1895. Accompanied by maps and epilogues, each story reverberates with attractively detailed illustrations and thrilling narrative. Phelan's illustrated nonfiction will hook children with its palatable sense of adventure and the knowledge that these amazing journeys really occurred. Don't be surprised if kids want to read Verne's classic to see how it measures up to real treks around the world.

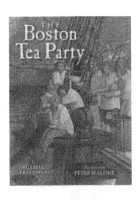

82. *The Boston Tea Party.* Written by Russell Freedman. Illustrated by Peter Malone. (Holiday House, 2012.) In protests opposing taxation without representation and affirming the right to control their own destinies, colonialists dumped tea into the Boston Harbor setting the stage for the American Revolution. Malone's gauzy watercolor paintings and Freedman's lucid storytelling capture the spirit of determination and rebellion of the colonists who meet at the Old South Church and then, disguised as Mohawk Indians, board three merchant ships, ejecting 226 chests of fine tea into the water. Freedman quotes from firsthand accounts of the 1773 episode and styles his writing to appeal to a middle-level readership. This pivotal event is meticulously well sourced and includes a bibliography, time line, historical map, and index.

83. *One Times Square: A Century of Change at the Crossroads of the World.* Written and illustrated by Joe McKendry. (David R. Godine, 2012.) The history of this bustling intersection made world famous by the New Year's Eve ball drop is skillfully told in words and pictures by Joe McKendry in a way that will make readers appreciate why it came to be called "The Crossroads of the World." Once the headquarters of the *New York Times*, One Times Square, at the intersection of Broadway and Seventh Avenue, is portrayed as a unique public space where people have assembled at important moments in history such as the end of World War II in 1945 or the Stock Market Crash of 1929. With lush watercolors and informative prose, McKendry traces the evolution of this iconic location from its early days as a dirt path to its current incarnation as a glitzy mecca visited by millions of tourists each year.

84. *The Emperor's Silent Army: Terracotta Warriors of Ancient China.* Written by Jane O'Connor. (Viking Juvenile, 2002.) When three famers accidently unearth a pottery head near Xi'an, China, it leads to the discovery of a hidden tomb containing an army of life-size statues, one of the most momentous archeological finds of modern times. The farmers, in the process of digging a well in 1974, had no idea that they had uncovered a site that turned out to cover several acres and entombed as many as 7,500 statues. Jane O'Connor's account of this archeological treasure explains that Qin Shihuang, China's first emperor, commissioned the creation of this model army of distinctly individualized soldiers. The excavated site also included hundreds of bronze swords, daggers, battle-axes, and other artifacts. Excellent color photographs show amazingly detailed terracotta warriors fully suited, standing at attention, and ready for battle.

85. *Built to Last: Building America's Amazing Bridges, Dams, Tunnels, and Skyscrapers.* Written by George Sullivan. (Scholastic, 2005.) Seventeen of America's greatest engineering projects are on display in George Sullivan's tribute to the nation's ingenuity. He has nothing but praise for the people who designed, built, and completed each architectural masterpiece, including the Transcontinental Railroad, Hoover Dam, Golden Gate Bridge, Brooklyn Bridge, Chesapeake Bay Bridge-Tunnel, Cascade Tunnel, and the Sears Tower. Accompanied by photographs and artist

renderings that show the scale of these projects, this informative narrative proceeds chronologically to explain the social and historical forces that drove the construction and the technological innovations that were achieved. "Engineers and architects are problem solvers," writes Sullivan, in a story that inspires, even as America now often fails to maintain the grand infrastructure that was such a great source of pride.

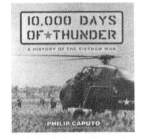

86. *10,000 Days of Thunder: A History of the Vietnam War.* Written by Philip Caputo. (Atheneum Books for Young Readers, 2005.) With *10,000 Days of Thunder,* Pulitzer Prize–winning journalist Philip Caputo has written the best and most complete overview yet of the Vietnam War for a middle and young-adult audience. This in-depth introduction to the "most unpopular war in American history and the only war America ever lost" covers 48 topics, including French colonialism, the Gulf of Tonkin, the Viet Cong, the My Lai Massacre, Watergate, the Pentagon Papers, antiwar protests, and the fall of Saigon. The actions of key historical figures such as Lyndon Johnson, Richard Nixon, General William C. Westmoreland, Ho Chi Minh, and Martin Luther King Jr. are also part of this thoughtful and dynamic history. The book has dramatic photographs, informative sidebars, and a time line.

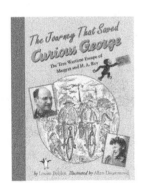

87. *The Journey That Saved Curious George: The True Wartime Escape of Margret and H. A. Rey.* Written by Louise Borden. Illustrated by Allan Drummond. (HMH Books, 2005.) Curious George fans will not be the only readers caught up by this engaging story of the lives of authors Margret and H. A. Rey and their dramatic bicycle escape through France during World War II. With the invading German Army at their heels, the Reys fled their Paris home with manuscripts, including a draft of what was to become the children's classic *Curious George* (1941) about a cheerful and hardy little monkey. Louise Borden and Allan Drummond's large-format book captures the story with lively prose and action illustrations, made even more effective through the use of Hans Rey's diary entries, and historical and family photographs. Children will love this richly detailed book and will perhaps view some of the Reys' fiction in a new light.

88. *Discovering Black America: From the Age of Exploration to the Twenty-First Century.* Written by Linda Tarrant-Reid. (Harry N. Abrams, 2012.) *Discovering Black America* is an epic history of African Americans, comprehensively covering 400 years of struggle and accomplishment beginning with a black sailor accompanying Christopher Columbus and continuing to the election of Barack Obama. Supplemented by carefully chosen reproductions of historical documents, photographs, and sidebars, journalist Linda Tarrant-Reid writes engagingly on an extensive array of topics and people. Her account includes slavery, the Civil War, Jim Crow, Reconstruction, the Mississippi Freedom Riders, the civil rights movement, and historical figures such as poet Phillis Wheatley, Booker T. Washington, and W. E. B. Du Bois; the book also provides a rare glimpse of the communications between Martin Luther King Jr. and Malcolm X. This book would be a fine addition to any family library.

89. *What the World Eats.* Written by Faith D'Aluisio. Illustrated by Peter Menzel. (Tricycle Press, 2008.) "For the first time in history, more people are overfed than underfed. And while some people still have barely enough to eat, others overeat to the point of illness," writes Faith D'Aluisio, who, along with photographer Peter Menzel, traveled around the world visiting 25 families in 21 countries to interview, describe, and photograph what people eat in the course of a week. This visually amazing collection shows families surrounded by their foods and includes the cost of the foods in U.S. currency. *What the World Eats* covers wide-ranging food traditions around the globe as well as the stark differences in access to

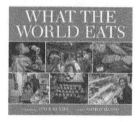

proper nutrition. Young readers may be surprised to discover that food abundance is not an automatic ticket to better health, as some wealthy counties contend with diabetes and obesity.

90. *Eleanor Roosevelt: A Life of Discovery.* Written by Russell Freedman. (HMH Books for Young Readers, 1997.) Russell Freedman is in his best form as a writer in this masterful, Newbery Honor study of Eleanor Roosevelt. Tracing her evolution from a shy and awkward young girl to an outspoken political activist, Eleanor emerges from an unhappy childhood to become an internationally known progressive advocate who redefined the position of First Lady, and helped found the United Nations. One hundred forty superb black-and-white photographs round out this portrait of an inspiring role model. Russell deftly handles sensitive issues in Eleanor's life, such as FDR's marital infidelity, his polio, and his death while in office. This portrait makes it clear why Eleanor Roosevelt, with her prodigious writing, wide-ranging interests, and irrepressible spirit, is one of the most admired women in American history.

91. *Who Was First? Discovering the Americas.* Written by Russell Freedman. (Clarion Books, 2007.) It is one of the interesting paradoxes of American national life that Christopher Columbus is still unequivocally celebrated as the discoverer of America when ample evidence exists to suggest otherwise. Russell Freedman's fresh examination of this elemental historical topic suggests that plenty of explorers, nomads, and traders from around the world visited America long before 1492. Useful maps and illustrations detail the early travels of the Chinese, Vikings, Mayas, and Incas. For young readers, the important takeaway from *Who Was First?* will not be a definitive new answer to the question of discovery but of history as a dynamic process of revision in light of new evidence.

92. *Far from Shore: Chronicles of an Open Ocean Voyage.* Written by Sophie Webb. (HMH Books for Young Readers, 2011.) Sophie Webb brings all her talents as an author, illustrator, and scientist to bear in her detailed journal of life aboard a research vessel over very deep waters in the eastern tropical Pacific Ocean. During a four-month voyage, she and her colleagues collect samples of a variety of life including seabirds, dolphins, and whales. Though the author is a member of the research team tasked with counting seabirds, she uses time and expertise to observe and document many activities and to illustrate them gracefully in watercolor and pencil. *Far from Shore* is both a real-life adventure and a candid portrayal of science, including its bursts of excitement and inevitable periods of drudgework.

93. *Girls Think of Everything: Stories of Ingenious Inventions by Women.* Written by Catherine Thimmesh. Illustrated by Melissa Sweet. (HMH Books for Young Readers, 2002.) Although their accomplishments have often been ignored or minimalized, girls and women have been responsible for some of our most useful inventions. Thimmesh profiles many little-known inventors and discusses where they got their ideas and what helped make them a reality, while Sweet supports the text with outstanding collage artwork. Readers will learn that His-ling-shi, a Chinese empress, discovered silk; Mary Anderson invented windshield wipers; Ann Moore created the Snugli baby carrier; and Beulah Henry received a patent for an ice cream freezer and invented a "liquid paper" substance for correcting typewriter errors. This book helps set the record straight on the small and large ways that girls and women have used their ingenuity to make life better.

94. *An Extraordinary Life: The Story of a Monarch Butterfly.* Written by Laurence Pringle. Illustrated by Bob Marstall. (Scholastic, 1996.) Pringle personalizes what could have been just another life-cycle book through the observation of one monarch he names "Danaus" after its species name. In a story that captivates rather than just informs, Danaus starts out as an egg on a milkweed plant, goes through her metamorphosis from caterpillar, to chrysalis, to butterfly, and makes the long flight from Massachusetts to Mexico. This oversized book has many colorful paintings of anthropomorphized Danaus at home in her habitat eating, mating, and flying clear of predators. This highly readable narrative has attractive maps, informative sidebars, clear captions, and a list of recommended readings.

95. *Harriet Tubman: Conductor on the Underground Railroad.* Written by Ann Petry. (Amistad, 2007.) This is a portrait of a heroic woman who led hundreds of people out of slavery into freedom. Relying on both imagined conversations and solid research, Ann Petry brings Harriet Tubman to life in a narrative that is accessible, well written, and informative. Born a slave on the eastern shore of Maryland, Tubman escaped to the North to secure her own freedom. Tubman was known as "Moses" because of her selfless efforts to help others escape bondage. This electrifying biography of the most famous Underground Railroad conductor shows Tubman as a symbol of strength to African Americans and a scourge to money-hungry plantation owners.

96. *Dogs on Duty: Soldiers' Best Friends on the Battlefield and Beyond.* Written by Dorothy Hinshaw Patent. (Walker Childrens, 2012.) Readers of all ages will find something to like about this story of specially trained military dogs, particularly in the photos showing the affectionate bonds that exist between them and human partners. Dorothy Hinshaw Patent writes that dogs have been part of military units throughout history, with 9,000 dogs serving in World War II and 4,000 devoted canines participating in the Vietnam War. These special dogs have had critical roles in Iraq and Afghanistan, prominently coming to the public's attention for the role they played in the raid on Osama Bin Laden's compound. Patent does a great job of describing how the dogs are trained and equipped, what they are expected to do on the battlefield and other missions, and how they are cared for when they retire from service.

97. *How It Feels When Parents Divorce.* Written by Jill Krementz. (Knopf, 1984.) With poignant stories and sensitive photographs, Jill Krementz provides valuable insights for parents and children on how to survive family breakups. Told in the children's own words, these stories of divorce are based on interviews with 19 boys and girls who share their raw feelings of anger, pain, fear, and confusion about the crisis in their lives. By considering the gamut of their thoughts and feelings, Krementz hopes children will recognize that the strong emotions they are experiencing are normal and that there are productive ways to navigate through this trying period. With so many children in the United States affected by divorce, this book is a useful guide and welcome reminder of how resilient kids can be.

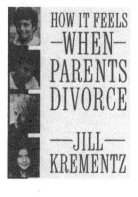

98. *Case Closed? Nine Mysteries Unlocked by Modern Science.* Written by Susan Hughes. Illustrated by Michael Wandelmaier. (Kids Can Press, 2010.) Hughes and Wandelmaier skillfully marry modern technology and history in their look at nine perplexing cases, devoting one full chapter to each mystery. The book, for example, describes the case of Hatshepsut, the first female pharaoh, who disappeared around 1457 BC; the case of the vanished ancient Arabian Peninsula city of Ubar; and the famous case of Amelia Earhart, who was never found. With great photos, maps, diagrams, and illustrations, *Case Closed* is a tribute to how modern science has shed light on some of

history's most fascinating and bewildering puzzles, although not every listed case is closed. The book's glossary and index will be helpful to student report writers.

99. *Guinea Pig Scientists: Bold Self-Experimenters in Science and Medicine.* Written by Leslie Dendy and Mel Boring. Illustrated by C. B. Mordan. (Henry Holt, 2005.) Unwilling to ask others to be party to their often dangerous experiments, some devoted scientists and physicians throughout history have used themselves as guinea pigs. Dendy, Boring, and Mordan collaborate to profile 10 cases of men and women who subjected themselves to risky experimentation for the good of humanity, sometimes paying the ultimate price for their scientific zeal. The experiments cover a daunting list of topics, for example, digestion, yellow fever, heart catheterization, and heat tolerance, and are well supported by ink portraits and black-and-white photos. The authors treat these scientists as bold and devoted heroes but caution aspiring scientists to never use themselves as guinea pigs.

100. *John Muir: America's First Environmentalist.* Written by Kathryn Lasky. Illustrated by Stan Fellows. (Candlewick, 2006.) Fellows's pleasant acrylic paintings and Lasky's inspiring text work together to tell the story of John Muir, beginning in his native Scotland and going on to his travels to many locales, including Wisconsin, Canada, Alaska, Florida, and California. This picture-book biography portrays Muir as a resilient outdoorsman and true lover of nature in all its manifestations, including tundra, swamps, farmland, and ancient sequoia forests. Young readers will appreciate the stature of the man credited with founding the Sierra Club and helping to create the national park system, and they will feel the affection that he had for the unspoiled wilderness. They will view the desire to protect the environment as a worthy calling and an important part of American tradition.

CHAPTER 4

Young Adults (Ages 13–17)

> Read the best books first, or you may not have a chance to read them all.
>
> —Henry David Thoreau

1. *The Diary of a Young Girl.* Written by Anne Frank. (Bantam, 1993.) A beloved world classic published in 60 languages, *The Diary of a Young Girl* is the detailed record kept by Anne Frank while she was in hiding for two years with her family during the Nazi occupation of the Netherlands. Secretly cloistered in the attic of an old office building, this remarkable Jewish teenager made thoughtful and intimate journal entries chronicling her love, fear, and claustrophobic living conditions. After being apprehended by the Gestapo, she died of typhus in the Bergen-Belsen concentration camp. Anne Frank's diary has become a symbol of nobility and courage in the face of evil. It is essential reading for anyone hoping to understand World War II and the Holocaust. The book was first published in the United States in 1952.

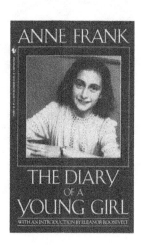

2. *The Mighty Mars Rovers: The Incredible Adventures of* Spirit *and* Opportunity. Written by Elizabeth Rusch. (HMH Books for Young Readers, 2012.) One of the most riveting things about this book is how it tells the story of the enormously successful

mission to Mars while framing it through the eyes of the mission's lead scientist, Cornell professor Steven Squyres. Award-winning author Elizabeth Rusch structures this tale of the robot vehicles named *Spirit* and *Opportunity* as a great adventure story charged with emotion. The purpose of the trip to this hostile environment was to gather information and images and to determine if Mars ever had water, suggesting the possibility of life. *Spirit* and *Opportunity* were expected to last only a few months, but continued to gather data for years. This detailed and meticulously researched look at a complex scientific mission should not be missed. In addition to shots of the mighty rovers, the book features stellar photographs of the red planet and of the scientific team at work.

3. *The Quest for the Tree Kangaroo: An Expedition to the Cloud Forest of New Guinea.* Written by Sy Montgomery. Illustrated by Nic Bishop. (HMH Books for Young Readers, 2006.) This is both an adventure story and an informational tour de force about an expedition to a truly remote ancient forest in Papua New Guinea to radio-collar the tree-dwelling kangaroo. Sy Montgomery and Nic Bishop, an experienced team, not only show scientists at work but enable readers to feel their exhilaration in climbing mountains and finding rarely studied creatures. As always, Bishop's close-up and panoramic color photos are spectacular, while Montgomery communicates the thrill of research and discovery, skillfully providing middle and young-adult readers with a fact-rich understanding of what the trip is all about.

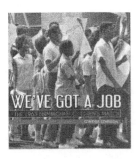

4. *We've Got a Job: The 1963 Birmingham Children's March.* Written by Cynthia Levinson. (Peachtree Publishers, 2012.) When civil rights leaders needed to increase the size of their nonviolent protest, they called on thousands of Birmingham's young African Americans to take to the streets. In this captivating photo essay, Cynthia Levinson movingly describes how almost 4,000 children and teenagers marched and were jailed for protesting the city's discrimination practices. The participation of young people turned out to be critical because in 1963 many adults still lacked confidence in the effectiveness of mass civil disobedience and many were worried about being fired from their jobs. With well-selected black-and-white photographs, the author chronicles the important but often overlooked contribution of young people by focusing on the brave participation of four individuals.

5. *The Notorious Benedict Arnold: A True Story of Adventure, Heroism, and Treachery.* Written by Steve Sheinkin. (Flash Point, 2010.) In a biography that reads more like action adventure than actual history, Steve Sheinkin has crafted an exciting narrative that is guaranteed to win over even the most hardcore teenage nonreader. The book's greatest appeal is how it convincingly shows that the infamous Benedict Arnold was as capable of being a hero as he was capable of being a traitor to the American Revolution. After distinguishing himself as a fearless fighter in the invasion of Canada, Arnold is passed over for promotion, then plots with British officer John Andri to turn West Point over to the British. When the plot is revealed, Andri is hanged, and Arnold flees to England, where he lives the rest of his life, despised and dishonored.

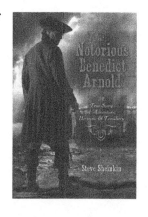

6. *Charles and Emma: The Darwins' Leap of Faith.* Written by Deborah Heiligman. (Square Fish, 2011.) In this book about the history of science, Deborah Heiligman does an admirable job demonstrating the revolutionary significance of the theory of evolution. As a biography, her text works as a deeply personal portrait of one of humankind's intellectual giants. Where the book truly shines, however, is as a romance and marriage of opposites between Emma, an open-minded and devoutly religious Christian, and her scientifically minded husband Charles, with whom Emma was lovingly at odds. Although Emma supported and edited Charles's work, she feared that her mate's scientific doctrines could send him to hell. *Charles and Emma* is a book that succeeds on so many levels that it can be read rewardingly over and over again.

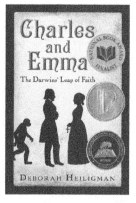

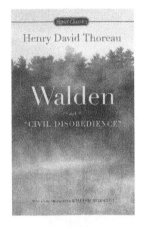

7. *Walden and "Civil Disobedience."* Written by Henry David Thoreau. (Signet Classics, 2012.) Believing that "the mass of men lead lives of quiet desperation," Henry David Thoreau wrote *Walden* as a kind of manifesto for solitude, self-reliance, naturalism, and simple living. Almost universally ranked as one of the greatest works of American literature, the book is a memoir and spiritual statement with worldwide influence. In its most quoted passage, Thoreau writes, "I went to the woods because I wished to live deliberately, to front only the essential facts of life, and see if I could not learn what it had to teach, and not, when I came to die, discover that I had not lived." Thoreau's essay on civil disobedience is an argument for disobeying the actions of an unjust government.

8. *Claudette Colvin: Twice toward Justice.* Written by Phillip Hoose. (Farrar, Straus & Giroux, 2009.) Months before civil rights pioneer Rosa Parks famously refused to give up her seat to a white person on a Montgomery, Alabama, bus, a 15-year-old girl named Claudette Colvin was actually the first African American to perform this brave act. This little-known story is about a teenager who, after being arrested and jailed, was shunned by her classmates and ignored by the community. Undeterred, Claudette became an active participant in the city's bus boycott and a witness during the trial that overturned the bus segregation law, yet her deeds were not celebrated. The author suggests that because she was pregnant and unmarried, protest leaders thought that Rosa Parks would create a more wholesome image for the civil rights movement.

9. *The Tarantula Scientist.* Written by Sy Montgomery. Illustrated by Nic Bishop. (HMH Books for Young Readers, 2007.) Montgomery and Bishop provide another informative and eye-popping look at scientists at work as they describe the research of arachnologist Samuel Marshall in the dense rain forest of French Guiana. Readers get close-up looks of the scientist encouraging hairy tarantulas to come out of their burrows and the largest comparative spider laboratory in America. The book is filled with color photographs that are so clear they may make readers squeamish, and it is packed with so much information about the eight-legged creatures—including the biggest spider on earth, the Goliath bird-eating tarantula—that readers might take Montgomery's advice on how to observe their own local spiders.

10. *Written in Bone: Buried Lives of Jamestown and Colonial Maryland.* Written by Sally M. Walker. (Carolrhoda Books, 2009.) Walker's book highlights nine colonial-era graves to show what can be revealed when forensic archeologists deploy the skills of the best crime-scene investigators. Through precise investigation of what is "written in bone," scientists examine human remains and their surroundings to unlock the mysteries of the past. Illustrated with color photos of skulls, skeletons, and excavations, the book shows researchers analyzing soil samples to estimate the time of burial; looking at skeletons for evidence of accidents, dietary deficiency, or violence; and checking teeth and bones to discern the age, gender, and ethnicity of the deceased. Walker's illuminating book follows investigators into the past lives of several people, including an enslaved African girl, a ship's captain, and a teenager who may have been beaten to death and buried in a cellar.

11. *The Autobiography of Malcolm X.* Written by Malcolm X and Alex Haley. (Ballantine Books, 1992.) Malcolm X's philosophy of black pride, anger, and struggle is the cornerstone of this classic autobiography. Considered one of the most important books in late-20th-century American society, the memoir is coauthored by journalist Alex Haley and is based on extensive interviews conducted between 1963 and 1965, the year of Malcolm X's assassination. This book covers many topics including a critique of white racism and a call for African American self-help. The autobiography traces Malcolm X's transformation

from a criminal to his embrace of political activism and the Muslim faith. Readers will be moved by this strong voice of social reform and will recognize that the book's themes are still relevant today.

12. *Flesh and Blood So Cheap: The Triangle Fire and Its Legacy.* Written by Albert Marrin. (Knopf Books for Young Readers, 2011.) The time was March 25, 1911, and the location was New York City's Triangle Shirtwaist Factory. In a story of the unsafe working conditions in the textile industry, *Flesh and Blood So Cheap* recounts the tragic, horrific, and avoidable deaths of 146 people, most of them women, in one of the most disastrous workplace fires in American history. The immigrant garment workers were trapped inside the factory because its doors were locked, ensuring that workers stayed put. In the aftermath of this calamity, reforms were finally enacted. Aided by archival black-and-white photographs, Albert Marrin does a masterful job of describing this era, before labor unions and government regulation, when greedy companies could act with impunity.

13. *Hitler Youth: Growing Up in Hitler's Shadow.* Written by Susan Campbell Bartoletti. (Scholastic, 2005.) "I begin with the young. We older ones are used up . . . but my magnificent youngsters! Look at these men and boys! What material! With them, I can create a new world," proclaimed Adolf Hitler in 1933, launching the most aggressive program of political indoctrination of children in modern times. Award-winning author Susan Campbell Bartoletti has written a masterpiece based on oral histories, diaries, letters, and interviews with people who once belonged to the Hitler Youth, or *Hitlerjugend*, that is as informative as it is chilling. Her description of how history's most reviled dictator was able to command the loyalty of millions of young people is a remarkable read and very relevant in a world still vulnerable to right-wing extremism.

14. *Janis Joplin: Rise Up Singing.* Written by Ann Angel. (Harry N. Abrams, 2010.) Ann Angel has written a well-researched tribute biography about one of the most intriguing and influential performers in rock-and-roll history, covering a musical career that spanned only three years. Joplin, who died of an overdose of drugs and alcohol at age 27, comes across as an enormously talented, wildly rebellious, heartbreakingly insecure, and, ultimately, self-destructive young woman. Featuring more than 60 photographs, this book captures the bohemian spirit of 1960s pop culture and is a warning about its excesses. *Janis Joplin: Rise Up Singing* is a must-read for aspiring musicians and for anyone who wants to understand the struggles, flaws, and accomplishments of this gifted artist.

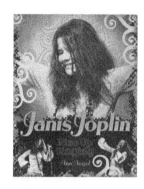

15. *Lafayette and the American Revolution.* Written by Russell Freedman. (Holiday House, 2010.) The is an elegantly illustrated story of the legendary French aristocrat who came to the colonies to fight in the American Revolution and ended up becoming a close confidant of George Washington. Russell Freedman, who is no stranger to writing history and biography for the younger set, makes this biography of Marquis de Lafayette come alive. He describes Lafayette's secret departure from France against the orders of his king and his path to becoming the youngest general in the Continental Army at the age of 19. This 10-chapter book includes Lafayette's meetings with the Iroquois Confederacy, his leadership at Yorktown, and his key role in getting the French government to send troops to aid the American insurgents.

16. *Something Out of Nothing: Marie Curie and Radium.* Written by Carla Killough McClafferty. (Farrar, Straus & Giroux, 2006.) Educated in her native Russian-occupied Poland, Curie moved to Paris to continue her studies at the Sorbonne and stayed there to discover two new elements, pioneer the science of radioactivity, and earn two Nobel Prizes for her groundbreaking scientific work. McClafferty's

extensively documented study traces Curie's life from her modest beginnings as a poor Polish girl, to her happy marriage to fellow scientist Pierre Curie, to her stunning success as a scientist, and finally to her illness and death from overexposure to radium. This first-ever woman Nobel laureate was single minded in her dedication to pure research and constantly in need of money to support her work. She never took out any patents for her discoveries, even as others profited from their use and abuse.

17. *The Way Things Work.* Written by David Macaulay and Neil Ardley. Illustrated by David Macaulay. (DK Publishing, 2004.) *The Way Things Work* is nothing short of encyclopedic. The detailed illustrations, diagrams, and entertaining explanations of everyday machines and inventions are organized into four sections: "Movement," "Harnessing the Elements," "Working with Waves," and "Electricity and Automation." Some of the everyday gadgets explained are lawn sprinklers, space shuttles, electric guitars, compact discs, smoke detectors, zippers, hang gliders, televisions, and refrigerators. This wide-ranging tour of modern technology and its scientific underpinnings is so nicely designed and easy to understand that it will convince even the most mechanically inept that they can understand how things work. There are several editions of *The Way Things Work* and *The New Way Things Work.* They are all extraordinary introductions to seemingly ordinary technology.

18. *Tracking Trash: Flotsam, Jetsam, and the Science of Ocean Motion.* Written by Loree Griffin Burns. (HMH Books for Young Readers, 2007.) Loree Griffin Burns is talking trash, but not the kind that leads to an exchange of blows. Instead, it is a description of the unusual work of an oceanographer who keeps track of debris as its travels great distances on Pacific Ocean currents. Burns's focus is Curtis Ebbesmeyer, who, along with a community of scientists and beachcombers, collects information with the goal of understanding and protecting the ocean. Aided by maps and fine color photos, the book describes how computer-modeling programs of ocean currents can predict the landfall of drifting trash ranging from sneakers to bathtub toys. The book concludes with an alarming look at how plastic waste is harming marine wildlife and destroying the environment.

19. *I Know Why the Caged Bird Sings.* Written by Maya Angelou. (Ballantine, 2009.) Originally published in 1969, this memoir about the Arkansas childhood of African American writer and poet Maya Angelou, the first in a seven-volume series, is a modern classic. This 1930s-and-1940s coming-of-age story shows Maya's transforming from being a victim of racism to her growing into a strong and capable young woman able to handle whatever life sends her way. Young Maya was routinely subjected to racial oppression and humiliation in her tiny Arkansas town, was raped by her mother's boyfriend, and subsequently witnessed and was traumatized by his murder. Maya's love of literature became her refuge and helped save her from despair. With its sexual content, strong language, and compelling narrative, this title is best suited for mature teens and adults.

20. *Hole in My Life.* Written by Jack Gantos. (Farrar, Straus & Giroux, 2002.) The author of Newbery Award–winning *Dead End in Norvelt* (2011) made an equally eminent contribution to American literature in the publication of his riveting memoir about time spent in federal prison at age 20 for drug smuggling. Gantos said he hoped to make $10,000 after graduating from high school by helping to transport a ton of hashish from Florida to New York City. Describing his time of incarceration as the bleakest time of his life, Gantos gives no hint of romanticizing this experience, conveying mostly regret for a stupid adventure gone bad. Gantos used his scared-straight time in prison to turn his life around and dedicate it to a career as a writer.

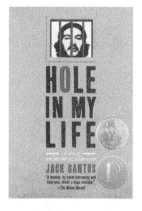

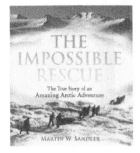

21. *The Impossible Rescue: The True Story of an Amazing Arctic Adventure.* Written by Martin W. Sandler. (Candlewick, 2012.) When eight whaling ships were stranded in Arctic ice and hundreds of sailors faced starvation, three men traveled over 1,500 miles of the most hazardous Alaskan terrain, often in blizzard conditions, to bring them herds of reindeer for food. This 1897 rescue mission was ordered by President McKinley and depended on the assistance of indigenous Alaskans. Sandler's engaging account of this true adventure is built from journal entries and is enhanced by helpful maps and amazing photographs of the courageous rescuers, the whaling ships, and the frigid landscape. The book has detailed source notes and a time line of key events.

22. *The Race to Save the Lord God Bird.* Written by Phillip Hoose. (Farrar, Straus & Giroux, 2010.) This book is about efforts to save the ivory-billed woodpecker, the first modern endangered species, from the tragedy of extinction. The woodpecker was once abundant in the southeastern United States and Cuba, but as settlers and loggers eliminated its habitat and hunters killed it for sport, the bird has not been spotted since 1987. Hoose's multifaceted story covers 200 years of history and introduces important figures such as artist John James Audubon, bird collector William Brewster, and conservationists James Tanner and John Baker. His book has informative sidebars and archival photos, including shots of women with feathered hats, shedding light on another reason the bird became extinct.

23. *Secrets of a Civil War Submarine: Solving the Mysteries of the* H. L. Hunley. Written by Sally M. Walker. (Carolrhoda Books, 2005.) When the Union successfully blocked ships from bringing war supplies to the southern Confederacy, Horace L. Hunley made up his mind to create a submarine that would be able to blow up enemy ships. After many failed attempts, a Confederate submarine finally succeeded in sinking the USS *Housatonic* in 1864. The *H. L. Hunley* never returned to port and was not found until 1995. With the aid of informative diagrams, maps, and photos, Walker's story of the design, construction, deployment, and discovery of this Civil War vessel describes an interesting and little-known slice of naval history. Readers will also enjoy Walker's explanation of the complex archeological techniques used to raise the sub and recover its contents.

24. *Tasting the Sky: A Palestinian Childhood.* Written by Ibtisam Barakat. (Farrar, Straus & Giroux, 2007.) Ibtisam Barakat's autobiography describes the experiences of a child caught up in the entrenched Israeli-Palestinian conflict. Her story begins when she was 6 years old during the 1967 Six Days War, when she and her family were on the run from Israeli solders. Ibtisam discusses her difficult life as a refugee and her elation over the discovery of the written word. The book is not a partisan political polemic but a touching expository on the devastating effects that war has on children. Ibtisam movingly compares her shattered life to that of street dogs: "I knew that they were dying and that they had come to our door only because, like us, they were seeking refuge. But instead of understanding, we shot at them, the way the warplanes shot at us."

25. *The Federalist Papers.* Written by Alexander Hamilton, James Madison, and John Jay. (Simon & Schuster, 2004.) Arguing for faith in strong central government and the ratification of the U.S. Constitution, the Federalist Papers began appearing in three New York newspapers beginning in 1787. This collection of 85 essays written under the pen name "Publius" is perhaps the most important set of political statements in the history of the country. "If men were angels, no government would be necessary," wrote Madison. "In framing a government which is to be administered by men over men, the great difficulty lies in this: you must first enable the government

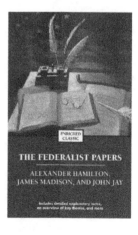

to control the governed; and in the next place oblige it to control itself." When federal judges and others interpret the Constitution, they often use the Federalist Papers to help determine the intentions of its framers.

26. Titanic: *Voices from the Disaster*. Written by Deborah Hopkinson. (Scholastic, 2012.) On April 15, 1912, the "most luxurious ship the world had ever seen" struck an iceberg in the North Atlantic, and of the 2,208 people on board, only 712 of them survived. This well-known story gets an updated interpretation in Deborah Hopkinson's intertwining of the voices of passengers and crew members who survived the sinking of the RMS *Titanic*. In fascinating detail and with an abundance of archival photographs and facts about the magnificent ship, she describes how the disaster unfolded. The material on the sinking of the ship, the rush for lifeboats, and the dreadful wait to be rescued is more informative and every bit as dramatic as the movie versions of this ill-fated voyage.

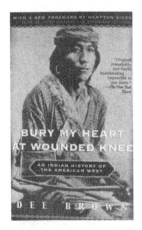

27. *Bury My Heart at Wounded Knee: An Indian History of the American West*. Written by Dee Brown. (Holt, Rinehart & Winston, 1970.) Dee Brown's history of the settlement of the American West is written from the point of view of its original inhabitants, who were victims of broken treaties, forced relocations, massacres, and policies that were designed to destroy their way of life. This chronicle of abuse and betrayal begins with the Native Americans first conducting themselves in a generally peaceful way toward the arriving Europeans, then experiencing gradual encroachment, and finally resisting only after their land is being seized. This well-sourced and heartbreakingly honest book fundamentally changed how many Americans view the country's westward expansion by showing how Indian tribes were systematically annihilated.

28. *Dear Miss Breed: True Stories of the Japanese American Incarceration during World War II and a Librarian Who Made a Difference.* Written by Joanne Oppenheim. (Scholastic, 2006.) This book recounts one of American history's most troubling episodes in the unfair treatment of Japanese Americans on the West Coast following the Pearl Harbor attack. The focus of the narrative is Clara Breed, a San Diego librarian, and her correspondence with children and teens who were "relocated" because of their Japanese ancestry. The imprisoned kids wrote to Miss Breed from their concentration camps, and she wrote back and enclosed care packages with books and candy. Oppenheim skillfully employs quotes from the letters to weave her story into a broader account of the period. Readers will gain an appreciation of the fear and uncertainty experienced by these children and will be inspired by the actions of Clara Breed, who worked for their release.

29. *Marching for Freedom: Walk Together Children and Don't You Grow Weary.* Written by Elizabeth Partridge. (Viking Juvenile, 2009.) Partridge's photo essay takes a close look at the tumultuous three months of nonviolent protests in Alabama that reached their apex in the historic march from Selma to Montgomery in 1965. Her story is told from the perspective of children and teens who marched courageously alongside Martin Luther King Jr. demanding that African Americans be granted the right to vote. Through lively text, vivid quotations, and stunning black-and-white photos, the author shows how protesters were attacked with whips, clubs, and tear gas in this pivotal and terrifying moment in the civil rights movement. In a time when voting rights are again under attack, this book should inspire young readers (and eventual voters) to be more active and vigilant in defense of their basic democratic inheritance.

30. *A Life in the Wild: George Schaller's Struggle to Save the Last Great Beasts.* Written by Pamela S. Turner. (Farrar, Straus & Giroux, 2008.) This is the biography of George Schaller, one the world's great field biologists, wildlife conservationists, environmentalists, and explorers. Over a career that spans decades and took him all over the world, Schaller transformed his field by demonstrating that dangerous animals, such as the snow leopard, mountain gorilla, and Serengeti lion, could be studied in their own habitats. Illustrated with the scientist's own photographs, the book includes maps and progress reports on the species he has studied and advice on how to get involved with conservation efforts. Readers will be impressed with how much land Schaller has convinced governments to set aside for nature preserves and how he has lived a truly impactful life out in the wildness.

31. *Narrative of the Life of Frederick Douglass: An American Slave.* Written by Frederick Douglass. (Simon & Schuster, 2004.) First published in 1845, Douglass's memoir was the most famous and influential piece of abolitionist literature to appear in the 19th century. In 11 chapters, the legendary orator recounts his life as a slave and his desire to become a free man. Douglass was despised by slave-owning plantation owners because he was the living embodiment of everything they said that black people could not be: people with the same human capabilities and rights as any white American citizen. In the book, he reports that he was whipped on a weekly basis and worked to the point of exhaustion. Douglass writes that the turning point in his life was his being sent from his Maryland plantation to the city of Baltimore, where he was given the opportunity to read. Every teenager will benefit from reading this eye-opening classic.

32. *Shipwreck at the Bottom of the World: The Extraordinary True Story of Shackleton and the* Endurance. Written by Jennifer Armstrong. (Paw Prints, 2008.) Excellent writing and a riveting story converge in *Shipwreck at the Bottom of the World*, creating a dramatic story of survival about Ernest Shackleton and his men, who were attempting to become the first explorers to cross the frozen continent of Antarctica. When their ship *Endurance* got trapped in the ice, the rugged team spent months camping on ice floes. They then made a difficult journey in lifeboats to remote Elephant Island, where a handful of men navigated hundreds of miles of open sea to find a rescue ship. Almost two years after the *Endurance* became icebound, Shackleton was finally able to go back and rescue his men. This harrowing adventure story includes 40 photographs of the ill-fated expedition.

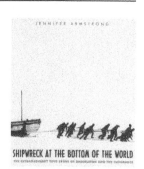

33. *The War to End All Wars: World War I.* Written by Russell Freedman. (HMH Books for Young Readers, 2013.) World War I was the first world conflict in which powerful modern weapons, including machine guns, poison gas, flamethrowers, tanks, and airplanes, were used. With the extent of its carnage, it was called "The War to End All Wars," because it was thought that mankind would never again subject the world to such cruel and devastating weapons of mass destruction. From the 1914 assassination of Archduke Franz Ferdinand to the punitive 1918 Treaty of Versailles, Russell Freedman's photo essay and lucid, well-researched text masterfully tell the story of this complex war, suggesting how it sowed the seeds of future conflict.

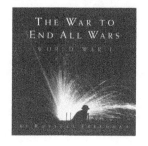

34. *Sir Walter Raleigh and the Quest for El Dorado.* Written by Marc Aronson. (Clarion Books, 2000.) This excellent biography skillfully portrays the successes and failures of the momentous life of a man with prodigious talent. Perhaps best known for his efforts to gain favor with Queen Elizabeth I, Sir Walter Raleigh is noted in legend for laying down his cape to cover a mud puddle for the monarch. Sir Walter

"Ralegh"—as scholars say is the proper spelling of his name—was a kind of Renaissance man who rose from humble beginnings to enjoy great wealth and influence. Soldier, courtier, explorer, poet, writer, and friend to many of the most important people of his day, Raleigh helped crush the Irish rebellion, wrote a book of world history, conducted raids on Spanish ships, and was finally undone by his ill-fated expeditions to South America in search of the mythic treasure of El Dorado.

35. *Spies of Mississippi: The True Story of the Spy Network That Tried to Destroy the Civil Rights Movement.* Written by Rick Bowers. (National Geographic Children's Books, 2010.) Rick Bowers's astonishing description of this previously unknown history centers around how the state of Mississippi created a commission in 1956 that was used as a spy network intent on crushing the civil rights movement within the state. Relying on primary source materials, interviews, and oral histories, the author demonstrates how white politicians recruited and paid blacks and whites to infiltrate a variety of groups and organizations. Neighbors, teachers, and even ministers willingly spied on people close to them, helping to delay integration and voting rights efforts and propping up a morally bankrupt system of white supremacy. This shadowy Mississippi agency spread segregationist propaganda and employed covert methods to harass, harm, and spy on its citizens, evoking comparisons to Soviet- and Nazi-style oppression.

36. *Terezín: Voices from the Holocaust.* Written by Ruth Thomson. (Candlewick Press, 2011.) Following the Nazi invasion of Czechoslovakia, the town of Terezín was used by Germany as a ghetto and transit camp for thousands of Jews on their way to death camps. Through artwork and secret diary entries and autobiographies of its resident inmates, Ruth Thomson shows how the town functioned as a propaganda show camp, as people were used as props to hide the truth about the sordid reality of the Holocaust. The point of this Nazi ruse was to convince the world that its treatment of Jews was humane, but the reality was that of the almost 100,000 prisoners who passed through Terezín, only 132 survived.

37. *1776*. Written by David McCullough. (Simon & Schuster, 2005.) Written as a companion work to his acclaimed biography *John Adams* (2001), McCullough's *1776* is the product of extensive archival research in both America and England. This powerful book from a master historian focuses on military rather than political events at the start of the American Revolution. Readers will be absorbed in the decisions of General Washington, who had never before led an army, and captivated by material on King George III, William Howe, the British commander, and his troops. As McCullough's gripping narrative makes clear, King George, in control of the world's most potent army, greatly underestimated the will of the American colonists. An illustrated edition of *1776* was released in 2007.

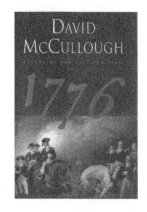

38. *They Called Themselves the KKK: The Birth of an American Terrorist Group.* Written by Susan Campbell Bartoletti. (HMH Books for Young Readers, 2010.) With material from many sources, Bartoletti's well-researched chronicle of America's most notorious homegrown terrorist organization is a thoughtful history of the tumultuous post–Civil War period. Besides an account of the Reconstruction Era, it is also a story of lynching, fear, and hate crimes committed throughout the South by hooded thugs claiming to be members of an invisible empire. This account of domestic terrorism is a reminder that American democracy is not immune from secret societies and organized violence. The quality of the writing and illustrations will enthrall everyday readers, while serious students will appreciate the author's scholarship as conveyed in her informative narrative, civil rights time line, bibliography, and notes.

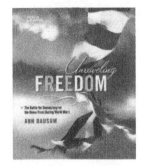

39. *Unraveling Freedom: The Battle for Democracy on the Home Front during World War I.* Written by Ann Bausum. (National Geographic Children's Books, 2010.) During World War I and in the aftermath of the horrific sinking of the *Lusitania* by a German torpedo, the United States was caught up in a hysteria that led to the suppression of basic freedoms. Under the banner of "making the world safe for democracy," German Americans were persecuted and the Espionage Act of 1917 and the Sedition Act of 1918 curtailed free speech. Socialists such as Eugene Debs were jailed for their antiwar views, and many other peace activists were silenced. In Ann Bausum's excellent book, young readers will learn that the unraveling of freedom during World War I was not an anomaly. She includes a thought-provoking "Guide to Wartime Presidents," identifying eight periods of war in America and a discussion of the democratic freedoms sacrificed in the name of democracy.

40. *Birmingham Sunday.* Written by Larry Dane Brimner. (Calkins Creek, 2010.) On Sunday, September 15, 1963, a terrorist bomb exploded at the 16th Street Baptist Church in Birmingham, Alabama, claiming the lives of four innocent black girls. Brimner explains that the church was not a random target but a frequent headquarters for civil rights leaders such as Martin Luther King Jr., who used it for meetings and the training of activists. Instead of creating fear and submission, this brutal act stirred the conscience of the nation and led to the passage of the landmark Civil Rights Act of 1964. Aided by black-and-white photographs, the author puts this brutal bombing in social and political context by reference to other civil rights issues such as the Jim Crow laws and the *Brown v. Board of Education* Supreme Court ruling.

41. *Vincent van Gogh: Portrait of an Artist.* Written by Jan Greenberg and Sandra Jordan. (Delacorte Books for Young Readers, 2001.) According to Greenberg and Jordan, van Gogh spent his early years at elite schools in Holland where he took a variety of courses including freehand drawing. "The drawing classes were considered part of a well-rounded gentleman's education, not preparation for a career," the authors observe, but in the case of this irascible and gifted boy, they planted the seed for what would become a burning commitment to his craft. After first trying his hand at being a preacher and art dealer, at age 27, van Gogh took up painting and didn't look back. The legendary artist, known for his vibrant style and for pioneering new techniques, is portrayed not as a loner but as someone who had many friends. He was especially close to his brother Theo, with whom he lived in Paris. This valuable book features van Gogh–family photographs and exemplary color reproductions of many of the artist's paintings.

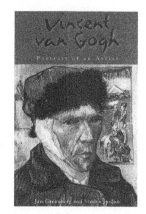

42. *Wild Horse Scientists.* Written by Kay Frydenborg. (HMH Books for Young Readers, 2012.) This book recounts the work of veterinarians Ron Keiper and Jay Kirkpatrick, who study and protect the lives of the wild horses who live on Maryland's Assateague Island. To keep the island's fragile ecosystem in balance, the scientists manage the horse population with a contraceptive vaccine injected into wild mares with darts fired from a distance. The goal is to limit the mares to a single foal per lifetime. Aided by sidebars and beautiful color photographs, Kay Frydenborg explains the history of the wild horses and effectively describes both laboratory and fieldwork, including the innumerable hours the veterinarians must spend watching and charting the lives of their equine subjects.

43. *Common Sense, Rights of Man, and Other Essential Writings of Thomas Paine.* Written by Thomas Paine. (Penguin Group, 2003.) At a time when the issue of independence from Great Britain was still unresolved, Paine's *Common Sense* had a decisive impact on American colonists. Structured like a sermon with biblical references, this classic was directed at the common man rather than Enlightenment intellectuals. Frequently read aloud at public gatherings to colonists who could not read for themselves, the slim book had a galvanizing effect. Paine argued for equality of rights, rejected reconciliation with England, and attacked the idea of a hereditary monarchy. Written in clear and straightforward language, the 1776 polemic was such a powerful and unequivocal call for independence that no reader or listener was left sitting on the fence. Published in 1791 and 1792, *Rights of Man* argues that popular political revolution is permissible when a government does not protect the natural rights of its people.

44. *The Wright Brothers: How They Invented the Airplane.* Written by Russell Freedman. (Holiday House, 1994.) Nonfiction master Russell Freedman employs lively, informative prose and excellent photographs to document the early aviation efforts of Wilbur and Orville Wright, culminating in their historic flight at Kitty Hawk, North Carolina. Freedman's fully realized portraits show the unmarried brothers to be tireless workers who methodically created the first powered, sustained, and controlled human flight. The brothers painstakingly tinkered and experimented until they perfected their flying machine and then with equal zeal successfully promoted and profited from their invention. Readers will come away from *The Wright Brothers* with a better appreciation of the process of invention and the degree of single-minded dedication that is required to solve complex problems.

45. *21: The Story of Roberto Clemente.* Written and illustrated by Wilfred Santiago. (Fantagraphics, 2011.) Roberto Clemente, one of the most inspirational figures in baseball history, gets his due in this graphic novel by Wilfred Santiago. Growing up in Puerto Rico, Clemente excelled at all aspects of the game, was recruited by professional scouts, and ended up playing in the American big leagues. Playing for the Pittsburgh Pirates, he led his team to World Series victories, amassed a career batting average of .317, and was voted the National League's Most Valuable Player for 1966. But it was his conduct off the field that established his humanitarian reputation, most notably in his direction of a relief mission to Nicaragua to assist earthquake victims. While on this 1972 trip to bring medical supplies, he died when his plane went down in the Caribbean Sea. With its artistic treatment of the game's greatest Latino ballplayer, Santiago's informative biography demonstrates the power of the comic-book form.

46. *Bad Boy.* Written by Walter Dean Myers. (Amistad, 2002.) Set on the streets of Harlem, Walter Dean Myers's stirring memoir is a portrait of a difficult childhood and coming-of-age. His tumultuous upbringing included getting into trouble, playing basketball, being raised by loving foster parents, suffering from a speech impairment, and dropping out of high school to join the army. Even as a dropout, Myers wrote and read in secret, absorbing the best works of literature. After years of working odd jobs, he finally devoted himself to writing full-time. Myers has written over 50 books, both fiction and nonfiction, and is best known for his powerful books about young African Americans.

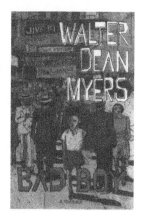

47. *Night.* Written by Elie Wiesel. (Hill & Wang, 2006.) Nobel laureate Elie Wiesel has dedicated his life to bearing witness to the horror of the Holocaust, and his masterpiece, *Night*, ranks with Anne Frank's *The Diary of a Young Girl* as one of the definitive classics about the Nazi attempt to exterminate the Jewish people. His autobiography describes the daily terrors that he, as a teenager, faced with his father in the Nazi death camps. The book's larger statement is about his encounter with evil and his loss of faith in God and mankind. Wiesel's candid and terrifying record about what really happened in the concentration camps carries with it the hope that what happened to the Jewish people should never be forgotten or repeated.

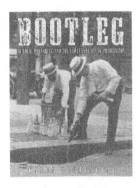

48. *Bootleg: Murder, Moonshine, and the Lawless Years of Prohibition.* Written by Karen Blumenthal. (Flash Point, 2011.) Karen Blumenthal's balanced and comprehensive history traces the urge to ban alcohol from the time of the Puritans, through the Civil War, up to the passage of the ill-fated 18th Amendment establishing Prohibition, and then to its repeal. When Prohibition was the law of the land, instead of the intended moral strengthening and the end of alcohol abuse, America saw widespread corruption and lawlessness and the emergence of gangsters such as Al Capone. Yet the amendment also had the desired effect of lowering the consumption of alcohol and related diseases. In the present time when states and municipalities are moving to decriminalize marijuana, readers will no doubt be interested in using *Bootleg* as a resource to make connections with the comparable well-intentioned effort to prohibit the use of pot.

49. *Every Bone Tells a Story: Hominin Discoveries, Deductions, and Debates.* Written by Jill Rubalcaba and Peter Robertshaw. (Charlesbridge Publishing, 2010.) "Most people think the dead are silent, but to an archaeologist they're boisterous storytellers," write Rubalcaba and Robertshaw in their introduction to the work of archeologists and paleontologists that focuses on four hominids who existed before recorded history. The fossils that they analyze are Turkana Boy, Lapedo Child, Kennewick Man, and Ötzi the Iceman, which are the remains of ordinary people. The authors explain how and where their remains were discovered and shed light on how they lived and died. Of particular interest are the lively debates that surround these discoveries, illuminating these complex fields of study. The dead may be willing storytellers, but scientists do not always agree on what they have to say.

50. *Children of the Great Depression.* Written by Russell Freedman. (Clarion Books, 2005.) With his usual narrative talent and with pictures from legendary photographers such as Dorothea Lange and Walker Evans, Russell Freedman builds an account of the lives of children during the Great Depression. Using diaries, memoirs, letters, and other sources, the author looks at the enormous challenges faced by youth from a variety of demographics, including migrant farmworkers, children who were forced to ride the rails, and kids who lived in American cities. This information-rich history succeeds in placing a human face on the economic malaise of the 1930s. Admirers of this photo essay will want to read Freedman's noteworthy *Children of the Wild West* (1992).

51. *Feynman.* Written by Jim Ottaviani. Illustrated by Leland Myrick. (First Second, 2011.) By all accounts Richard Feynman was one of the most brilliant minds of the 20th century. The Nobel Prize–winning physicist, known as an irreverent showman, worked on the Manhattan Project that developed the atomic bomb and is credited for being the scientist who figured out that the O-rings were the cause of the spacecraft *Challenger* explosion. The incredible curiosity and wide-ranging, larger-than-life talents of this rare polymath are on full display in this graphic novel. Ottaviani and Myrick team up to show Feynman as an important popularizer of science who,

when he wasn't doing quantum electrodynamics, learned how to play the bongos and crack safes. Feynman fans would also profit from reading his own *"Surely You're Joking, Mr. Feynman!" Adventures of a Curious Character* (1997).

52. Witches! *The Absolutely True Tale of Disaster in Salem.* Written and illustrated by Rosalyn Schanzer. (National Geographic Children's Books, 2011.) Rosalyn Schanzer's powerful story of the mass hysteria that gripped this Massachusetts colonial village is well told and outstandingly illustrated in black and white with touches of red. When illness mysteriously struck two Puritan girls, the community decided that they were bewitched and launched the famous Salem Witch Trials. Once the frenzy of accusations began, no one—not even household pets—was safe from being considered in league with the devil. This bizarre witch hunt destroyed lives and led to the deaths of dozens of people. The stylized pictures include images of witches flying through the air and girls having crazy courtroom fits.

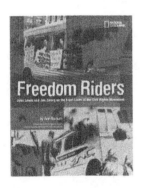

53. *Freedom Riders: John Lewis and Jim Zwerg on the Front Lines of the Civil Rights Movement.* Written by Ann Bausum. (National Geographic Children's Books, 2005.) Ann Bausum's unique historical sketch focuses on the perspectives and biographies of two young men of different backgrounds and races who participated in the Freedom Rides into the Deep South in 1961. Poor black John Lewis and middle-class white Jim Zwerg first met in Tennessee at a training session on how to contest segregated lunch counters and movie theaters. In the course of their involvement with the civil rights movement, like so many others, they were harassed and beaten by white mobs for having the courage to stand up to segregation. Vivid storytelling and dramatic black-and-white photographs will make this a memorable read for those who are not familiar with this important part of American history.

54. *Harlem Stomp! A Cultural History of the Harlem Renaissance.* Written by Laban Carrick Hill. (Little, Brown Books for Young Readers, 2009.) This image-and-information-packed history is the first aimed at introducing the Harlem Renaissance to a teenage readership. Covering mostly the early decades of the 20th century, Hill's book documents the musical, artistic, and literary energy of African American culture and the blossoming of a new sense of racial identity. Young readers will be introduced to the opposing philosophies of the cautious Booker T. Washington and more activist W. E. B. Du Bois and learn about the contributions of cultural icons such as Louis Armstrong, Zora Neale Hurston, James Baldwin, and Langston Hughes. Vivid colors and lively text make *Harlem Stomp* an attractive and informative read.

55. *Democracy in America.* Written by Alexis de Tocqueville. (Library of America, 2004.) Sent by the French government to study the American prison system in 1831, Alexis de Tocqueville instead spent nine months traveling about the new country making a larger study of its society. The work, originally published in two volumes in 1835 and 1840, was immediately popular in France and the United States and is now regarded as a political science classic. Tocqueville rightly predicted that America would be torn apart over the issue of slavery, warned that wealthy elites could come to dominate our country's politics, and was one of the first social critics to pay attention to the status of women. Predicting today's political gridlock, the Frenchman wrote, "I cannot help fearing that men may reach a point where they look on every new theory as a danger, every innovation as a toilsome trouble, every social advance as a first step toward revolution, and that they may absolutely refuse to move at all."

56. *The Hive Detectives: Chronicle of a Honey Bee Catastrophe.* Written by Loree Griffin Burns. Illustrated by Ellen Harasimowicz. (HMH Books for Young Readers, 2013.) What happened to all the bees? When beekeepers first encountered the destruction of their hives in 2006, a team of scientists went to work to find out the cause. Burns and Harasimowicz profile the scientists and the nature of the catastrophe that caused millions of bees across the country to simply vanish. While no sure cause has been found, the scientists did come up with a name for the problem, colony collapse disorder (CCD). As the book title suggests, more light is shed on the detectives and their methods than on a solution to the puzzle. According to the prevailing view, the honeybee disaster was attributable to a combination of factors, including pesticides, mites, and viruses. Readers will appreciate the book's valuable information on the essential role that bees play as pollinators.

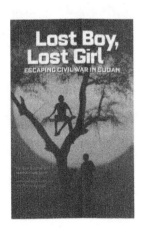

57. *Lost Boy, Lost Girl: Escaping Civil War in Sudan.* Written by John Bul Dau, Martha Arual Akech, Michael S. Sweeney, and K. M. Kostyal. (National Geographic Children's Books, 2010.) The book describes the heartbreaking stories of John and his wife Martha, both Christians from South Sudan, who were forced to flee hundreds of miles and endure the most treacherous conditions before arriving in UN refugee camps and finding sanctuary in the United States. The backdrop for this survival story is the still-brewing civil war between Muslim Arabs in the northern part of the country and Christian Africans in the South, which has caused thousands to be displaced from their families and towns and to face starvation and murder. After decades of war, in 2011 South Sudan separated from Sudan, making it the world's youngest nation, but the violence continues.

58. *I Am Scout: The Biography of Harper Lee.* Written by Charles J. Shields. (Henry Holt, 2008.) This portrait of the notoriously reclusive and unconventional author of *To Kill a Mockingbird* highlights Lee's creation of this acclaimed novel and her lifelong friendship with Truman Capote. Shields investigates the similarities between Lee and Scout, the narrator of her novel, looks at the role Lee played in helping Capote do research for his own classic, *In Cold Blood,* and explores the mystery of why she never published another book. *I Am Scout* is a reworking of Shields's popular *Mockingbird: A Portrait of Harper Lee* (2006), adapted for young-adult readers. Shields based his books on extensive documentary and interview research, but did not have access to Harper Lee.

59. *John Lennon: All I Want Is the Truth.* Written by Elizabeth Partridge. (Viking Juvenile, 2005.) Elizabeth Partridge's vivid photo biography of the legendary musician traces his life from his birth during a German air raid on Liverpool in 1940 to his murder in front of his Manhattan apartment in 1980. She astutely describes how Lennon and the Beatles became the most financially successful and critically regarded rock-and-roll band in history and sheds light on the breakup of the group and on the nature of his relationship with Yoko Ono. Lennon is presented as a rebellious, self-centered musical genius, always struggling to make sense of his fame and art. There is a wealth of photos covering every stage of Lennon's life.

60. *The Bat Scientists.* Written by Mary Kay Carson. Illustrated by Tom Uhlman. (HMH Books for Young Readers, 2010.) Bats loom large in the popular imagination but are not often the subject of scientific study. In *Bat Scientists*, Mary Kay Carson and Tom Uhlman follow the uncommon work of preeminent scientist Merlin Tuttle, who founded Bat Conservation International, a group that protects the small mammals and their habitats throughout the world. Tuttle has been studying bats his whole life and is

now working to save them from extinction due to a deadly fungus known as white-nose syndrome. The book features many striking color photographs, taken by Uhlman and Tuttle, of the hairy creatures; lots of information about bat biology and behavior; and a map of the habitats of bats around the globe.

61. *The Life and Death of Adolf Hitler.* Written by James Cross Giblin. (Clarion Books, 2002.) Giblin goes beyond the popular façade of this Austrian-born leader, tracing his transition from an ordinary child to a second-rate artist, decorated World War I soldier, gifted orator, prison-house author of *Mein Kampf,* to his appointment as chancellor of Germany, and ultimately to his becoming the most villainous figure of the 20th century. The arch of Hitler's complex career is interwoven with penetrating descriptions of the social, economic, and political milieu that were so favorable to his stunning acquisition of power. Giblin's final chapter, titled "Hitler Loves," chillingly describes the rise of neo-Nazism in America and Europe. Beginning with the icy gaze of Hitler on the book cover, many compelling black-and-white photos add power to this important portrait.

62. *The Manatee Scientists: Saving Vulnerable Species.* Written by Peter Lourie. (HMH Books for Young Readers, 2011.) Lourie's book highlights the work of three veteran scientists who work in different parts of the world protecting one of nature's gentlest aquatic creatures. Readers can follow the investigations of John Reynolds in Florida, Fernando Rosas in Brazil, and Lucy Keith in West Africa as they try to save manatees from extinction. There are many photos of the docile species in the clear waters of Florida where they attract tourists, and in the cloudy, remote rivers of Brazil and West Africa where they are hunted for food. Besides being used for nourishment, the manatee is also subject to environmental hazards, disease, and human intrusions into their habitats.

63. *Soul Surfer: A True Story of Faith, Family, and Fighting to Get Back on the Board.* Written by Bethany Hamilton, Sheryl Berk, and Rick Bundschuh. (MTV Books, 2006.) The 13-year-old homeschooled girl who lost her left arm in a shark attack in Hawaii describes how her belief in God helped her cope with the event and return to competitive surfing. The book begins with an account of the 2003 shark attack on the island of Kauai and goes on to describe Bethany's upbringing in a Christian family and the challenges of her recovery process. The teenager writes candidly about adjusting to her new life, coping with people's stares, and drawing strength from her faith. "I don't pretend to have all the answers to why bad things happen to good people," she writes. "What I do know is that I want to use what happened to me as an opportunity to tell people that God is worthy of our trust, and to show them that you can go on and do wonderful things in spite of terrible events that happen."

64. *This Land Was Made for You and Me: The Life and Songs of Woody Guthrie.* Written by Elizabeth Partridge. (Viking Juvenile, 2002.) Partridge has written an outstanding portrait of the free-spirited, itinerant artist who wrote thousands of songs but is best known for the legendary American ballad "This Land Was Made for You and Me." Woody Guthrie, a giant among 20th-century folk musicians, gave voice to union organizers, migrant farmworkers, antiwar protesters, and underdogs in all walks of life. Enhanced by black-and-white photographs and lyrics from Guthrie's songs, this biography provides insight into his many relationships and the complex issues and events that shaped him. The passionate musician strongly influenced other great singer-songwriters, such as Bob Dylan, Joan Baez, and Bruce Springsteen. In 1967, at age 55, Guthrie died in a mental institution ravaged by Huntington's disease.

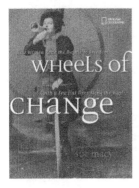

65. *Wheels of Change: How Women Rode the Bicycle to Freedom (with a Few Flat Tires along the Way).* Written by Sue Macy. (National Geographic Children's Books, 2011.) Sue Macy's refreshing and energetic book zeroes in on how the bicycle helped women in their early struggle to secure more mobility, freedoms, and rights in the late 1800s. With the advent of this simple mode of travel, women were able to take advantage of new opportunities, change how they dressed, get more vigorous exercise, and begin to change traditional ideas of femininity. Aided by a variety of eye-catching newspaper clippings and photographs, the book offers an exciting take on women's history that will be very appealing to middle and young-adult readers. *Wheels of Change* is also an excellent vehicle for addressing the larger question of how technology transforms society.

66. *The Year of Goodbyes: A True Story of Friendship, Family and Farewells.* Written by Debbie Levy. (Disney-Hyperion, 2010.) In 1938, Jutta Salzberg and her Jewish family escaped Nazi Germany and traveled to the United States to avoid being sent to a concentration camp and an almost certain death. During this poignant "year of goodbyes," 12-year-old Jutta collected inscriptions from friends and relatives in her autograph book. Many decades later, Jutta's adult daughter, Debbie Levy, fashioned her book of verse from this album, skillfully interweaving her poetry with material from the momentous year. Levy does her homework in this remarkable book, determining the fate of most of her mother's childhood friends, many of whom did not survive the Holocaust. The presentation of history from a young girl's perspective will be a memorable read for a middle-level and teenage audience.

67. *The Amazing Harry Kellar: Great American Magician.* Written by Gail Jarrow. (Calkins Creek, 2012.) Once America's most famous magician and a mentor to Harry Houdini, Harry Kellar had an incredible career that started as a magician's assistant and eventually led to performing stage shows for President Theodore Roosevelt and other heads of state, and to tours of five continents. Unlike other illusionists who hailed from Europe, Kellar came from Erie, Pennsylvania, and became the first dean of the Society of American Magicians. Young readers will be interested to know that Kellar was most likely the real-life inspiration for *The Wonderful Wizard of Oz* (1900). Gail Jarrow's late 19th- and early 20th-century biography is impressive: it includes reproductions of promotional posters, sidebars, a time line, notes, a bibliography, and a list of recommended readings.

68. *Charles Dickens and the Street Children of London.* Written by Andrea Warren. (HMH Books for Young Readers, 2011.) Warren's well-researched biography of Charles Dickens describes how his impoverished childhood led to the use of his writing to achieve social change. Warren's focus is based on Dickens's empathy for the children living in the poverty and squalor he observed in Victorian London, conditions the world now calls "Dickensian." History has already judged Charles Dickens to be one of history's greatest writers. Thanks to Andrea Warren's book, it is now clear that he was also one of history's great social reformers. Readers may be inspired to read Dickens's novels, with *Oliver Twist* (1837–1839) being the novel where he displays the most explicit social consciousness.

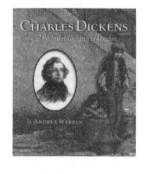

69. *The Autobiography of Benjamin Franklin.* Written by Benjamin Franklin. (Dover Publications, 1995.) Franklin's self-help memoir written over a 20-year period is considered the first great American book, and it is credited with helping to create the modern rags-to-riches autobiographical literary form. His book provides valuable insight into his life in Boston and Philadelphia, an account of his many accomplishments, and a picture of colonial life, but the most noteworthy aspect of this American classic is Franklin's passion for self-improvement. The

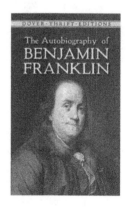

self-portrait contains his famous 13 virtues for living: temperance, silence, order, resolution, frugality, industry, sincerity, justice, moderation, cleanliness, tranquility, chastity, and humility. Unfortunately, Franklin's autobiography does not tell his entire life story, as he died in 1790 before he could complete it.

70. *The Dark Game: True Spy Stories from Invisible Ink to CIA Moles.* Written by Paul B. Janeczko. (Candlewick, 2010.) In the current era of massive surveillance, readers will be interested in at least a partial explanation of how the U.S government got to this point. From the American Revolution through the Cold War and beyond, Paul Janeczko serves up two centuries of spies and their methods, covering everything from invisible ink to cryptology to surveillance satellites. Stories of shadowy intelligence operations are inexorably linked to technological advances in this fascinating collection of stories. A brief passage at the end of the book touches on some current events. But to address the data-gathering sea change that occurred following the September 11, 2001, attacks, Janeczko says would require another book.

71. *Escape from Saigon: How a Vietnam War Orphan Became an American Boy.* Written by Andrea Warren. (Square Fish, 2008.) With the North Vietnamese Army marching on Saigon in 1975, the U.S.-led Operation Babylift frantically evacuated over 2,000 children who had little chance of a future in war-ravaged Vietnam. Andrea Warren's touching story focuses on Long, a mixed-race Amerasian boy, who was 9 years old at the time of the airlift. The story describes Long's abandonment by his American father, his Vietnamese mother's suicide, and his grandmother's difficult decision to put him up for adoption. In America, under the care of a Mennonite family, Long becomes Matt Steiner, and embarks on a new life that leads to his becoming a high-school valedictorian, a star athlete, and a medical doctor. As an adult, Matt travels back to Vietnam to reconcile his past and present life. Generously illustrated with photographs, the well-written story will give readers access to Matt's many emotional struggles.

72. *Friday Night Lights: A Town, a Team, and a Dream.* Written by H. G. Bissinger. (Da Capo Press, 1990.) *Friday Night Lights,* a book about a 1988 high school football team in West Texas, is widely considered one of the best books ever written about sports. The aim of the book, fully realized, was to understand the role that football plays in American culture, particularly in certain struggling rural communities. To write this masterpiece, Bissinger moved to Odessa where he spent the entire season immersing himself in the lives of the residents of the depressed oil town and following the stresses and aspirations of its Permian Panthers, the most successful high school football team in Texas history. In this compelling sociological portrait of a town, football seems to permeate every aspect of life. On Friday nights during football season, the game inspires a passionate intensity bordering on religious zeal.

73. *Faces from the Past: Forgotten People of North America.* Written by James M. Deem. (HMH Books for Young Readers, 2012.) Deem's introduction to the use of clay models, from sometimes centuries-old skeletons, for facial reconstruction is a stimulating look at how scientists probe more deeply into the origins and nature of ancient North Americans, a people often forgotten in history books. The process of humanizing unknown people from their burial remains helps bring their stories to light and often recognizes them through museum displays. The narrative begins with the human remains found in Nevada that are more than 10,000 years old and moves ahead to more recent finds, such as Mexican soldiers killed at the battle of the Alamo and Civil War–era slaves. Photos of skulls, casts, and masks nicely supplement the informative text.

74. *George Washington and the Founding of a Nation.* Written by Albert Marrin. (Dutton Juvenile, 2001.) Albert Marrin's excellent biography of America's most preeminent founder fills a void between an abundance of biographies designed for elementary students and those that are more scholarly adult works. The author frankly assesses Washington's role in history from multiple perspectives, including as commander of the Continental Army, slaveholder and plantation owner, and America's first president. The life, character, and contradictions of the revered leader are explored in the context of the colonies' fight for independence. Marrin makes good use of many of Washington's quotes, including one prophetic remark made toward the end of his life: "I can clearly foresee that nothing but the rooting out of slavery can perpetuate the existence of our union."

75. *The Letter Q: Queer Writers' Notes to Their Younger Selves.* Edited by Sarah Moon and contributing editor James Lecesne. (Arthur A. Levine Books, 2012.) Sixty-three award-winning writers and artists use their considerable skills, life experiences, and honesty to imaginatively tell their younger selves what they wish they had known about being lesbian, gay, bisexual, or transgendered in their youth. The collection of thoughtful and heartfelt letters cover a gamut of stories, including feelings of isolation and suicide brought on by bullying. Some of the letters are also quite funny, but all of them carry the message that life will get better. Young-adult readers will benefit from the contributors' wise and confidence-building counsel and become better able to embrace their sexual identity with love, understanding, and pride.

76. *Getting Away with Murder: The True Story of the Emmett Till Case.* Written by Chris Crowe. (Dial, 2003.) Chris Crowe describes one of American history's most egregious examples of injustice in his account of a 14-year-old black teenager who was murdered by two white men in Money, Mississippi, for allegedly whistling at a white woman. In 1955, Emmett Till was beaten to death, and his body was discovered floating in the Tallahatchie River. An all-white jury quickly acquitted the accused men, who confidently smoked cigars and read newspapers during their trial. A few months later they bragged in a *Look* magazine interview that they did commit the murder. The book has many photographs, including a shocking and widely viewed picture of the boy's bloated corpse in a casket. "The Emmett Till case was not the sole cause of the civil rights movement, but it was the final indignity that caused the flood of outrage to overflow the dam of racial injustice," writes Crowe.

77. *The Lincolns: A Scrapbook Look at Abraham and Mary.* Written by Candace Fleming. (Schwartz & Wade, 2008.) "They were like two pine trees that had grown so close their roots were forever intertwined," Candace Fleming writes in this fascinatingly unique dual biography. The author's treatment of the lives of Abraham and Mary Lincoln makes creative use of paintings, church documents, handwritten notes, anecdotes, letters, engravings, maps, cartoons, and rare period photographs to provide a visual and informational feast. The book is packed with significant historical and personal events, and it includes their childhoods, their tumultuous relationship, the Civil War, the loss of three of their children, the president's assassination, and Mary's little-known commitment to an insane asylum. Readers attracted to Fleming's innovative format will be motivated to read her *Our Eleanor: A Scrapbook Look at Eleanor Roosevelt's Remarkable Life* (2005).

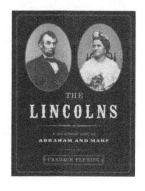

78. *Ghosts in the Fog: The Untold Story of Alaska's WWII Invasion.* Written by Samantha Seiple. (Scholastic, 2011.) Little has been written about the invasion of Alaska by Japanese forces in 1942, and Seiple's book is the first nonfiction narrative for teenagers to tell the story of this brutal World War

II battleground. Enhanced by more than 80 photographs, this almost-forgotten story is told from the perspective of the civilians who were captured on the Aleutian Islands and taken prisoner. Over 15,000 American troops were sent to Alaska to repel the Japanese, although the U.S. government denied that the invasion happened. Because of the persistently foggy weather, thousands of men were forced to engage in bloody hand-to-hand combat and more lives were lost in this island chain than in the Pearl Harbor attack. *Ghosts in the Fog* will be a surprising read for a general audience and an essential title for students of World War II history.

79. *Hidden Worlds: Looking through a Scientist's Microscope.* Written by Stephen Kramer. Illustrated by Dennis Kunkel. (HMH Books for Young Readers, 2003.) Readers are invited to follow the fascinating work of David Kunkle as he employs powerful microscopes to enter worlds not available to the naked eye. Unlike other scientists who focus on specialized content, Kunkle gets to explore wide-ranging fields because of his technical microscopy expertise, his focus ranging from examining muscle cells to investigating the effect of volcanic ash on algae. The book explains how Kunkel produces photographs and how scientists use them. Spectacular color photographs taken through an electron microscope—producing startling images of uncommon beauty—steal the show in this important book. Teenagers will be eager to look through a microscope and experience the excitement firsthand.

80. *Good Brother, Bad Brother: The Story of Edwin Booth and John Wilkes Booth.* Written by James Cross Giblin. (Clarion Books, 2005.) There are plenty of stories about families whose members fought on opposite sides of the Civil War, but there is none more powerful and vividly contrasted than the tale of the Booth brothers. Thoughtful, introspective Edwin Booth, considered the best classical actor of his time, supported Abraham Lincoln and the Union. Younger brother John Booth, also an actor and known for his passionate intensity and his love of the Confederacy, hated Lincoln so much that he assassinated him. The author covers the events leading up to and including the assassination, the plots he and his coconspirators had to kidnap the president, and the activities to bring the group to justice. Giblin's engaging book concludes with Edwin attempting to continue his theatrical career in the shadow of his reviled sibling who was shot by a Union soldier.

81. *The Longitude Prize.* Written by Joan Dash. Illustrated by Dusan Petricic. (Farrar, Straus & Giroux, 2000.) This is an in-depth story of John Harrison, a little-known 18th-century tinkerer without a formal university education who accomplished what the world's most brilliant minds could not: he created a device to enable sailors to reliably determine their east-west location—that is, their longitude. Hoping to avoid shipwrecks, the British government incentivized the process by promising an enormous prize, roughly equivalent to 12,000,000 of today's dollars, to the successful inventor. Even the renowned Sir Isaac Newton competed for the money and recognition. Dash's informative text and Petricic's clever illustrations move the story to its unsatisfying conclusion. Harrison, a lowly village carpenter, spent 50 years trying to collect his prize money and died before receiving acknowledgment for his great accomplishment.

82. *The Good Fight: How World War II Was Won.* Written by Stephen E. Ambrose. (Atheneum Books for Young Readers, 2001.) It would be difficult to suggest a more accessible World War II overview and resource for young adults than Stephen Ambrose's *The Good Fight,* which is structured as a series of one-page essays. This highly readable photo survey concisely covers not only the key battles but also many critical topics. The narrative addresses the origins of the war for both Germany and Japan, Hitler's climb to power, the launch of the Manhattan Project, the

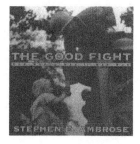

decision to drop the first atomic bombs at Nagasaki and Hiroshima, the creation of concentration camps, the institution of the Marshall Plan, the conduct of war crimes trials, and what life was like in the 1930s and 1940s for ordinary soldiers and their families.

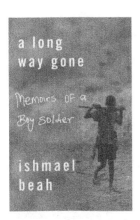

83. *A Long Way Gone: Memoirs of a Boy Soldier.* Written by Ishmael Beah. (Sarah Crichton Books, 2008.) The worst brutality of war is made clear in this haunting and heartfelt memoir about a boy who was forced to fight and kill in Sierra Leone, Africa. Ishmael Beah was an ordinary 12-year-old child when he was separated from his family when rebels attacked his hometown. He was then equipped with an AK-47 rifle and transformed into a ruthless killing machine. Beah tells his life-shattering story without an ounce of self-pity. He is living proof that some children possess a boundless reservoir that allows them to retain their humanity in the face of the starkest violence and cruelty. *A Long Way Home* is an essential insider's chronicle about a tragedy happening around the world: thousands of children are being conscripted into armies and militias. It is also a basis for hope.

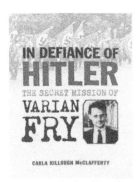

84. *In Defiance of Hitler: The Secret Mission of Varian Fry.* Written by Carla Killough McClafferty. (Farrar, Straus & Giroux, 2008.) American journalist Varian Fry traveled to Marseilles, France, on a two-week mission in the summer of 1940 to find and rescue approximately 200 artists, authors, and musicians who were marked for death in Nazi-occupied France. Varian stayed in France for over a year and ended up saving more than 2,000 people. McClafferty does a wonderful job of describing how Fry, at great personal risk, worked in a hostile environment under the noses of the authorities to save people he did not know. Most of the rescued people were Jews who would have faced death in concentration camps. Fry's heroic efforts stand in contrast to the attitudes of many Americans at that time who were not paying attention to the behind-the-scenes atrocities in Europe.

85. *King of the Mild Frontier: An Ill-Advised Autobiography.* Written by Chris Crutcher. (Greenwillow Books, 2003.) Chris Crutcher's life growing up in a small town in Idaho in the 1960s is the subject of this certainly not ill-advised autobiography. The book is full of painful and funny vignettes that include his regret for not being good enough at sports in a town where athletics was everything. It also includes his adolescent crushes, struggles with religion, and family dysfunction, leading to his becoming a child and family therapist. *King of the Mild Frontier* will be a satisfying read, particularly for teenage boys. For fans of Crutcher's popular young-adult fiction, the book will be an extra treat because it reveals the real-life origins of some of his characters.

86. *Navajo Code Talkers.* Written by Nathan Aaseng. (Walker Childrens, 1994.) Recreational readers and especially students of World War II or Native American culture will be captivated by this little-known story of how the Navajos created a complex, indecipherable code based on their native language to thwart Japanese interceptors. Nathan Aaseng describes how the American Marines depended on hundreds of Navajo men to help win the Pacific war, while the Navajos endured prejudice and other difficulties arising out of cultural differences. By all accounts, the Navajo code talkers did a masterful job for the war effort, working around the clock leading up to the Battle of Iwo Jima. They deserve a large measure of credit for its successful outcome.

87. *Miles to Go for Freedom: Segregation and Civil Rights in the Jim Crow Years.* Written by Linda Barrett Osborne. (Harry N. Abrams, 2012.) Osborne's outstanding book is the companion to her well-received *Traveling the Freedom Road* (2009), which covered the antebellum South, the Civil War, and Reconstruction for the period 1800 to 1877. *Miles to Go for Freedom* chronicles the Jim Crow era, from 1896, the date of the infamous "separate but equal"

Plessy v. Ferguson Supreme Court decision, to 1954, the date of the *Brown v. Board of Education* decision, overturning *Plessy*. With informative text and arresting photographs, Osborne's book documents the lengths to which mainly southern states went to deny voting rights to blacks and create "widespread discrimination, cruel prejudice and daily humiliation." Some readers will undoubtedly recognize some similarities to present-day efforts to limit and disenfranchise minority voters.

88. *The Mysteries of Beethoven's Hair.* Written by Russell Martin and Lydia Nibley. (Charlesbridge Publishing, 2009.) At Beethoven's deathbed, a 15-year-old musician snipped a lock of hair from the corpse of the world's greatest composer and placed it in a locket. This remembrance of the celebrated genius remained encased in this way from 1827 until 1994, when collectors acquired it at a Sotheby's auction. The collectors used the hair to seek a scientific explanation for Beethoven's talent and lifelong emotional and physical problems, including his deafness. Martin and Nibley's carefully crafted tale addresses this scientific detective story as well as the lock's intriguing odyssey from Vienna to Denmark and finally to Arizona. This excellent book, suitable for middle-level and young-adult readers, follows on the success of Martin's *Beethoven's Hair* (2000) written for adults.

89. *The Secret of the Yellow Death: A True Story of Medical Sleuthing.* Written by Suzanne Jurmain. (HMH Books for Young Readers, 2009.) Against the backdrop of the Spanish-American War, Walter Reed and his team of doctors went to Cuba to study yellow fever and determine its cause. Suzanne Jurmain peppers her writing with such vivid and gory details that readers will feel they can actually experience the fever of the stricken soldiers, see their lemon-colored eyes, and smell their foul odor. The author adopts an inviting conversational tone as she describes how the doctors systematically examined the origins and spread of the illness, finally concluding it was transmitted through mosquito bites. Young-adult readers of all kinds, and particularly those inclined to pursue a heath-care career, will appreciate this insalubrious slice of medical history.

90. *The Poet Slave of Cuba: A Biography of Juan Francisco Manzano.* Written by Margarita Engle. Illustrated by Sean Qualls. (Square Fish, 2011.) Written in free verse and well illustrated, this unique biography is about the cruelty Juan Francisco Manzano had to endure as a slave in a rich Cuban household as he secretly learned to read and write. In the first poem of this title, Juan resentfully refers to himself as a "pet" and "new kind of poodle" because he is at the beck and call of his owner's wife, expected to use his verbal talents to entertain her friends. Other verses refer to the African Cuban's barbaric treatment at the hands of a madwoman, concluding with his escape from bondage. This lyrical portrait, based on Juan's autobiographical writings, effectively alternates between his perspective and those of other characters.

91. *Pyongyang: A Journey in North Korea.* Written by Guy Delisle. (Drawn and Quarterly, 2007.) In this entertaining graphic novel, cartoonist Guy Delisle provides a rare glimpse of life in the most secretive and belligerent country in the world. In 2001, he was granted limited access to North Korea's capital city for work he was doing on a children's cartoon show. His encounter with totalitarian society lasted two months and produced striking illustrations and a personal account that includes descriptions of his work, bouts of boredom and isolation, humanizing details of the few North Koreans he got to know, cravings for Western food and coffee, and an overabundance of statues, portraits, and propaganda praising the "wise" leadership of this impoverished nation.

92. *Mysterious Messages: A History of Codes and Ciphers.* Written by Gary Blackwood. (Dutton Juvenile, 2009.) This chronicle of secret messaging comprehensively covers the field from ancient Sparta to the modern-day CIA. The book is exceedingly accessible, with helpful photos, images, and sidebars on almost every page, and it has an enjoyable mixture of facts about people, events, and technology. Blackwood's convincing point is that in matters of war and national security, cryptography has always played a decisive role. This narrative history of codes and ciphers will be a natural fit for middle- and high-school-age students, who are often considered undecipherable by their parents and teachers. Readers will be delighted to find that *Mysterious Messages* is filled with puzzles that they can solve for themselves.

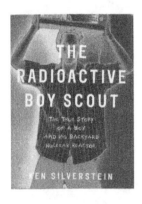

93. *The Radioactive Boy Scout: The True Story of a Boy and His Backyard Nuclear Reactor.* Written by Ken Silverstein. (Random House, 2004.) Some science projects go a little too far, particularly when they emit toxic levels of radiation, putting thousands of lives at risk. This is just what happened in a Detroit suburb when an unsupervised teenager got the bug for nuclear physics while working on his atomic energy badge for the Boy Scouts. Ken Silverstein does an admirable job of capturing the alarm and surrealism that surrounded David Kahn's construction of a nuclear reactor in his backyard garden shed. Remarkably, the boy found the outline for the reactor in a physics textbook, and he was able to construct a working model by acquiring his materials by mail order and from everyday items such as smoke detectors and old glow-in-the-dark clocks.

94. *The Complete Maus: A Survivor's Tale.* Written by Art Spiegelman. (Pantheon, 1996.) This mixed-genre comic book about the Holocaust has received extraordinary acclaim, becoming the first graphic novel to win the Pulitzer Prize. Created by avant-garde artist and writer Art Spiegelman, the book portrays humans as different species of animals: Germans are depicted

as cats, Jews as mice, and Poles as pigs. Told with
stark and shocking realism, the book shows the mice
being hunted and herded toward their deaths. It is
also a story of the author's difficult relationship with
his aging father, who survived the Holocaust. This
definitive edition of Spiegelman's *Maus* writings collects material that has been published in other books
and magazines. Readers may initially struggle with
the incongruity of finding this format applied to such
a terrible tragedy.

95. *Sir Charlie Chaplin: The Funniest Man in the
World.* Written by Sid Fleischman. (Greenwillow
Books, 2010.) Sid Fleischman's well-researched tribute is a classic rags-to-riches story of Chaplin's rise
from the London slums to become one of Hol-
lywood's biggest, funniest, and richest movie stars.
The Little Tramp was known for his mustache-cane-
and-bowler-hat persona and slapstick comedy, which
made him a silent-film legend. Chaplin became a
producer, director, and movie mogul, and later in
his career, he was knighted by Queen Elizabeth II.
Chaplin moved to Switzerland in 1952, returning to
the United States two decades later to receive a special
Academy Award. Abundant photographs and a time
line help make the book a memorable read. The Library of Congress selected Chaplin's first full-length
movie, *The Kid*, for preservation.

96. *Profiles in Courage.* Written by John F. Kennedy.
(Harper, 1964.) Kennedy's Pulitzer Prize–winning
book, written in the mid-1950s when he was recov-
ering from back surgery, describes the uncommon
political bravery that eight U.S. senators displayed
at different critical times in the country's history.
By crossing party lines, they did what was right and
necessary in the public interest. The profiled senators
are John Quincy Adams, Daniel Webster, Thomas
Hart Benton, Edmund G. Ross, Lucius Lamar,
George Norris, Sam Houston, and Robert A. Taft.
"A man does what he must—in spite of personal
consequences, in spite of obstacles and dangers, and

pressures—and that is the basis of all human morality," wrote Kennedy. This soon-to-be president's call for nonpartisan statesmanship is particularly relevant to today's ultrapartisan political climate.

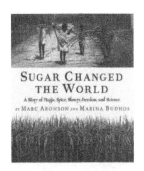

97. *Sugar Changed the World: A Story of Magic, Spice, Slavery, Freedom, and Science.* Written by Marc Aronson and Marina Budhos. (Clarion Books, 2010.) It is a rare book indeed that allows you to look at history in a fundamentally different way, and that is just what Aronson and Budhos's volume accomplishes. The authors detail the ancient discovery of sugar, its use in religious ceremonies, and especially its role as an all-purpose sweetener for candy, desserts, and beverages. Most critically, though, they discuss the central role sugar has had in the global economy, claiming that it has done more to transform the world than has any leader, empire, or war. Africans by the millions were brutally enslaved to work on Caribbean sugar plantations to enable businessmen to make vast fortunes. After reading this meticulously researched work about the impact of the sugar trade, young people will gain a new appreciation of how multinational corporations can shape world events.

98. *To Dance: A Ballerina's Graphic Novel.* Written by Siena Cherson Siegel. Illustrated by Mark Siegel. (Atheneum/Richard Jackson Books, 2006.) Siena and Mark Siegel, a husband-and-wife team, collaborate to tell the autobiographical story of how ballet became the most important thing in Siena's life. With fluid and graceful illustrations, the author's world of dance jumps from the page as she is shown leaping and spinning her way from her home in Puerto Rico, onward to dance instruction in New York City, and upward to performances with the city ballet. Siena's life spent rehearsing and performing, dealing with her parents' divorce, and handling a career-ending injury gives this picture story realism and poignancy. The graphic novel turns out to be the perfect vehicle for illustrating the dedication and growth of a young dancer. People of all ages who ever dreamed of becoming a dancer will be transfixed by the memoir.

99. *The Boy Who Harnessed the Wind.* Written by William Kamkwamba and Bryan Mealer. (Harper Luxe, 2009.) When African teenager William Kamkwamba first got the idea to build a windmill from discarded junk for his impoverished village, the townspeople called him crazy, but when he succeeded in creating electricity and a water pump, he was declared a hero. Motivated to improve living conditions in his famine-and-disease-stricken southern-Africa homeland, he collected and assembled scrap metal, bicycle and tractor parts, and PVC pipe to create a functional windmill that seemed like a miracle to local residents. Teenage and adult readers will be inspired by this story of tenacity and resourcefulness. An illustrated and simplified version of the book is available for early readers.

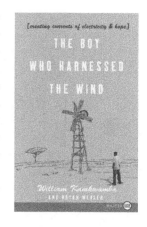

100. *Andy Warhol: Prince of Pop.* Written by Jan Greenberg and Sandra Jordan. (Random House, 2004.) The same pair who wrote the acclaimed biography *Vincent van Gogh: Portrait of an Artist* again team up to render the flamboyant life and work of a complex artist. Warhol, who immortalized Campbell's soup cans and famously predicted "in the future everybody will be world famous for 15 minutes," is described rising from poverty, attending art school in Pittsburgh, and bursting forth as an iconic hipster and media superstar. Although the book does not have many samples of his work, this well-researched narrative does establish the celebrity artist as someone who changed the art world by blending high and low culture.

CHAPTER 5

Adults (Ages 18+)

Always read something that will make you look good if you die in the middle of it.

—P. J. O'Rourke

1. *Silent Spring.* Written by Rachel Carson. (Houghton Mifflin, 1962.) *Silent Spring* was instrumental in launching the American environmental movement. The book documented the harmful effects of pesticides, such as DDT, on the environment and accused the chemical industry of spreading false information to protect its profits. Carson argued that the uncontrolled use of chemical poisons was harming or killing humans and many species of animals, particularly birds. The image she invokes is of a silent spring where no birdsongs can be heard. Carson's book discusses ways of controlling insects other than using toxic pesticides. Her book is important and is considered a warning about the limits of the technological control of nature.

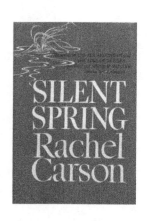

2. *Behind the Beautiful Forevers: Life, Death, and Hope in a Mumbai Undercity.* Written by Katherine Boo. (Random House, 2012.) In narrative nonfiction that reads like the best fiction, Boo opens a window on the hidden world of the global poor who, in this case, exist in the tumultuous "undercity" of one of the world's great metropolises. Her impossible-to-forget

Dickensian characters live in Annawadi, a sprawling slum located near the Mumbai airport. They strive for a better life but are held back by global recession, corruption, weather, and ethnic and interpersonal conflict, all the while fearing that the owners of the airport might bulldoze their shantytown into oblivion at any time. Boo's book is impressively researched and is based on several years of immersive investigation in India.

3. *The Emperor of All Maladies: A Biography of Cancer.* Written by Siddhartha Mukherjee. (Scribner, 2010.) Science-writer and cancer-specialist Siddhartha Mukherjee's landmark historical overview covers centuries of efforts to conquer this dreaded disease, starting with ancient surgeries and extending into the future. Drawing from a multitude of resources, *The Emperor of Maladies* is not just a medical history but also a masterful work of literary nonfiction. The erudite Columbia University professor focuses most of his attention on treatment regimens used since the 1950s, covering radiation treatments, chemotherapy, and biotechnical targeting of genes. This impressive chronicle is unusually accessible, treating cancer as a relentless and elusive enemy matched against an equally unyielding and resourceful medical establishment.

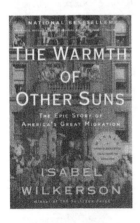

4. *The Warmth of Other Suns: The Epic Story of America's Great Migration.* Written by Isabel Wilkerson. (Random House, 2010.) Wilkerson's meticulously researched account of the great exodus of millions of African Americans fleeing the Jim Crow South to an uncertain future in the North and Midwest is one of the great and largely untold stories of the modern era. The book synthesizes a wealth of sociological data and digests interviews with over a thousand people, but the narrative's most exemplary feature is how it moves the story along through the profiles of three people who made the historic journey: Ida Gladney, who left Mississippi for Chicago; George, who traveled from Florida to Harlem; and Robert Foster, who made his trek from Louisiana to California. Each story is unique, but these in-country migrants each possessed a desire to find a better life, only to encounter more segregation and inequality. Covering the period 1915–1970, *The Warmth of Other Suns* is the definitive study of the modern-day relocation of black America.

5. *The Double Helix: A Personal Account of the Discovery of the Structure of DNA.* Written by James D. Watson. (Atheneum, 1968.) Watson's intimate autobiographical story of the discovery of the double helix structure of DNA is essential reading for anyone who wants to understand the foundations of modern biology. The account collects Watson's impressions of the early-1950s events that led to the breakthrough and awarding of the Nobel Prize to Francis Crick and himself. This scientific classic has been praised for its frank portrayal of the petty rivalries among scientists and criticized for how it characterizes and assigns credit to researchers who contributed to the discovery of the structure of DNA. A new version of the classic, *The Annotated and Illustrated Double Helix* (2012), is now available.

6. *In Cold Blood.* Written by Truman Capote. (Signet, 1965.) Capote details the savage murders of farmer Herbert Clutter, his wife, and two of their four children in Holcomb, Kansas. Two ex-convicts killed the bound and gagged family with shotguns. With suspense and empathy, Capote reconstructs the murder and the investigation that led to the killers' capture, trial, and execution. His research depended on extensive interviews with local residents and the killers, and his friend Harper Lee, who wrote *To Kill a Mockingbird*, assisted him. Six years in the making, Capote's book made him a celebrity. It is considered a true-crime masterpiece and the original nonfiction novel. It virtually created the new genre of creative nonfiction.

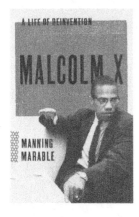

7. *Malcolm X: A Life of Reinvention.* Written by Manning Marable. (Viking, 2011.) Years in development, *Malcolm X* is the most complete and authoritative account ever written of the legendary black activist, minister, and leader. The book has new details on many aspects of his life, including more information about his time in Africa and his 1965 assassination. Marable, a professor of African American studies at Columbia University, unearths how the FBI infiltrated the Nation of Islam and possibly colluded in the leader's assassination. The book chronicles Malcolm X's early years as a street hustler, his time in prison, his religious conversion, and how he inspired hundreds of thousands of blacks to form stronger communities. Marable goes well beyond Malcolm X's autobiography to provide a more rich and informative portrait of this complex and controversial man.

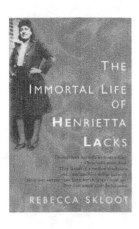

8. *The Immortal Life of Henrietta Lacks.* Written by Rebecca Skloot. (Crown, 2010.) Science-writer Rebecca Skloot's book is a towering achievement that succeeds as literary reportage, medical biography, and detective story, and as an inquiry into bioethics, poverty, racism, and greed. The astonishing story of Henrietta Lacks is about a poor black farmer whose cells were taken from her and subsequently used to develop a host of scientific breakthroughs such as the polio vaccine, gene mapping, and cloning. The cells were acquired without her knowledge or compensation in the early 1950s, while she and her family lived in poverty. Henrietta ended up in an unmarked grave; over 60 years later, her cells remain "immortally" alive, still making millions of dollars and fueling medical advances.

9. *A Heartbreaking Work of Staggering Genius.* Written by Dave Eggers. (Vintage, 2001.) When Dave Eggers's father died of lung cancer and his mother died of stomach cancer a month later, it became his responsibility to parent his eight-year-old younger brother Toph. In this brilliant and moving memoir, Dave's main challenge is to figure out how to be both brother and parent to Toph and try to lead the normal life of a man in his early 20s. Feeling that he has been robbed of his youth, Dave works on a magazine, obsesses about having sex, and worries about whether he is doing the right things with his younger brother. This book is a creative nonfiction classic, somehow managing to be both heartbreaking and funny.

10. *The Passage of Power: The Years of Lyndon Johnson.* Written by Robert A. Caro. (Knopf, 2012.) Historian Robert Caro's *The Passage of Power* is the fourth book in the acclaimed multivolume biography *The Years of Lyndon Johnson.* Instead of growing weary of Caro's encyclopedic writing about Johnson's life and times, the critics have become even more effusive in their praise, some considering the book to be the best political biography ever written. Chronicling the years 1958 to 1964—including Johnson's assumption of the presidency following Kennedy's assassination—Caro's book is by any measure an outstanding contribution to the understanding of one of American history's greatest progressive reformers and political schemers. History buffs will be eager to read the other parts of this monumental portrait and will anticipate the publication of his fifth and final book in this series.

11. *Homage to Catalonia.* Written by George Orwell. (Penguin Books, 1978.) When George Orwell went to Spain in 1936 to report on the civil war, he became caught up in the leftist revolutionary spirit and joined the fight against the fascists of General Francisco Franco. Originally published in England in 1938, *Homage to Catalonia* describes Orwell's wartime experiences and his political analysis of the intrigues and different agendas that led to the defeat of the socialists, anarchists, and communists by Franco's Nazi-backed forces. "Human beings were behaving as human beings and not as cogs in the capitalist machine," wrote Orwell of the anti-fascist impulse. Orwell used the experience of the Spanish Civil War to help write his classic dystopian novels *Animal Farm* (1945) and *Nineteen Eighty-Four* (1949).

12. *The Looming Tower: Al-Qaeda and the Road to 9/11.* Written by Lawrence Wright. (Knopf, 2006.) Lawrence Wright's book is a thorough and gripping account of the antecedents of the September 11 attacks and the most authoritative history of terrorism. The *New Yorker* staff writer explains the development of Islamic fundamentalism and describes the American counterterrorism efforts to track Al-Qaeda, concluding that the September 11 attacks could have been prevented if the FBI, CIA, and NSA had worked together. Based on hundreds of interviews conducted around the world and five years of solid research, this meticulously crafted and comprehensive narrative overshadows other books of its kind. *The Looming Tower* also packs an emotional wallop due to its in-depth explorations of the character and motives of key individuals, both Arab and American.

13. *Cleopatra: A Life.* Written by Stacy Schiff. (Little, Brown and Company, 2010.) Stacy Schiff's nuanced portrait of this mythologized queen sympathetically presents her as a shrewd and able ruler who shaped the ancient world rather than a woman solely defined by her sexual liaisons with Julius Caesar and Mark Antony. The biography unravels the Cleopatra myth with a narrative that gives the monarch her due for skillfully wielding power, sometimes ruthlessly, to become the most influential woman of her time. This realistic treatment of Cleopatra was long overdue. It does not eliminate the spicy details of the queen's legendary life, but instead balances them with a more comprehensive assessment of her reign as the last pharaoh of Egypt.

14. *The Information: A History, a Theory, a Flood.* Written by James Gleick. (Pantheon, 2011.) In a chronicle that includes African drums, written alphabets, Morse code, and binary signaling, James Gleick ambitiously traces the history of information technologies from their rudimentary origins to our present age, where gluts of information fundamentally shape and define us. Aided by portraits of key historical figures, the author investigates the increasingly vast and complex ways that we handle information, including the flood of news, blogs, tweets, and images that we continuously process via the Internet. With its discussion of quantum physics, information theory, molecular biology, and advanced mathematics, this daunting intellectual history will challenge the recreational reader.

15. *Nickel and Dimed: On (Not) Getting By in America.* Written by Barbara Ehrenreich. (Picador, 2011.) Undercover social-critic Barbara Ehrenreich's shocking exposé describes what life is like for millions of Americans forced to subsist on poverty-level wages. Working at minimum-wage jobs in three different cities, she found that her salary couldn't begin to cover the basic necessities of food and housing, much less health coverage. This journalist with a Ph.D. in cell biology found her jobs to be physically and mentally exhausting. The "working poor," Ehrenreich observes, "are in fact the major philanthropists of our society. They neglect their own children so that the children of others will be cared for; they live in substandard housing so that other homes will be shiny and perfect; they endure privation so that inflation will be low and stock prices high." Readers will be moved by this book and wonder what happened to the American Dream.

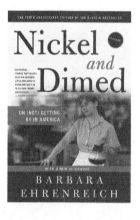

16. *Just Kids.* Written by Patti Smith. (Ecco, 2010.) New York City's intoxicating art and music scene of the late 1960s and early 1970s comes alive in this illustrated memoir and love story of singer-poet-songwriter Patti Smith and artist Robert Mapplethorpe, known for his provocative and erotic photography. Out of this creative milieu, these two "kids" forged a friendship that survived being broke and homeless and becoming celebrities who kept company with other legendary figures such as Bob Dylan, Allen Ginsberg, Andy Warhol, William Burroughs, and Sam Shepherd. Before Mapplethorpe died of complications arising from AIDS in 1989, Smith promised her friend that she would tell their story. *Just Kids* is

a remarkable elegy not just to Mapplethorpe, but also to a singularly irreplaceable bohemian way of life.

17. *The Lost City of Z: A Tale of Deadly Obsession in the Amazon.* Written by David Grann. (Vintage, 2010.) Following in the footsteps of lost British explorer Percy Fawcett, journalist David Grann journeyed to the Amazon jungle to investigate one of the great adventure mysteries of the 20th century. In 1925, Fawcett traveled into the depths of the jungle seeking the treasures of a lost ancient kingdom, and he never returned. Many others before and after the famed explorer went into the hostile jungle searching for gold, and Grann could not resist becoming one of them. In this excellent work of narrative nonfiction, the author capably interweaves Fawcett's story with his own, bringing both escapades to a satisfying conclusion.

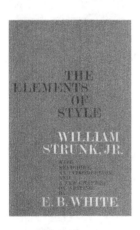

18. *The Elements of Style.* Written by William Strunk Jr. and E. B. White. (Macmillan, 1959.) *The Elements of Style* is often considered the definitive writing guide. In 1957, E. B. White acquired a version of this legendary little book that his former professor William Strunk Jr. had self-published in 1918. White admired its clear, concise advice and revised it to comprise elementary rules of usage, basic principles of composition, a few matters of form, and lists of expressions and words commonly misused and misspelled. Before publishing the revised book, White wrote in the *New Yorker* that Strunk's intent was to "cut the vast tangle of English rhetoric down to size and write its rules and principles on the head of a pin."

19. *The Age of Wonder: How the Romantic Generation Discovered the Beauty and Terror of Science.* Written by Richard Holmes. (Pantheon, 2009.) British biographer Richard Holmes presents a series of stories that provide a history of the men and women whose 18th-century discoveries and inventions ushered in the Romantic Age of Science. The author argues that Romanticism was both a reaction against the Enlightenment's scientific discoveries and an outgrowth of them. From Holmes's perspective, the ideals that drove scientists and poets were often not that different. Leading scientists such as astronomers William and Caroline Herschel and inventor Humphrey Davy are seen as influencing writers such as Coleridge, Wordsworth, Shelley, and Keats. The book contains a handy alphabetical list of key individuals in 18th-century science.

20. *Guns, Germs, and Steel: The Fates of Human Societies.* Written by Jared Diamond. (W. W. Norton, 2005.) Why weren't Africans, Australians, or Americans the ones to colonize Europe, rather than the other way around? Why did some people become literate and industrial while others did not? Evolutionary biologist Jared Diamond deftly addresses the huge and potentially explosive topic of why certain early people acquired more wealth and power. He does this not by resorting to discredited racial theories but by linking food production to the development of social organization, technological innovation, and immunity to infectious diseases. "History followed different courses for different peoples because of differences among peoples' environments, not because of biological differences among peoples themselves," concludes Diamond. When it was first published in 1997, *Guns, Germs, and Steel* won the Pulitzer Prize. The 2005 edition contains new illustrations and a chapter on Japan.

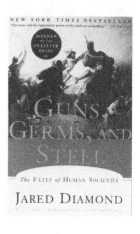

21. *The Civil War: A Narrative* (3 vols.). Written by Shelby Foote. (Random House, 1958–1974.) Shelby Foote's three-volume military history of the American Civil War is regarded as one of the foremost historical narratives of the 20th century. This comprehensive history touches on political, economic, and social developments, but the author's main contributions are in his lucid descriptions of the torment and strife of the war and in the way he has marshaled his facts, making the decisions of the key players and

the actions on the battlefield intelligible to a wide audience. The volumes in this monumental work are *Fort Sumter to Perryville* (1958), *Fredericksburg to Meridian* (1963), and *Red River to Appomattox* (1974). Some critics have jokingly observed that it took Foote five times as long to write about the Civil War as its participants took to fight it.

22. *Gödel, Escher, Bach: An Eternal Golden Braid.* Written by Douglas R. Hofstadter. (Basic Books, 1999.) This wide-ranging intellectual read does not lend itself to neat summarization, but it could be characterized as a breakthrough in the visualization of complex mathematical concepts. What Hofstadter has done is to find points of contact among the minds of mathematician Kurt Gödel, artist M. C. Escher, and composer Johann Sebastian Bach to discern the systems that underlie all mental activity. The author, a professor of computer science and cognitive science, provides keen insights into the nature of artificial and human intelligence, and he is upbeat on the former achieving the status of the latter. In a later edition of this groundbreaking title first published in 1979, he describes it as "a very personal attempt to say how it is that animate beings can come out of inanimate matter."

23. *A Brief History of Time: From the Big Bang to Black Holes.* Written by Stephen Hawking. (Bantam Books, 1995.) Hawking's book is a milestone in scientific writing and a mind-stretching summation of what theoretical physicists think about the origins and nature of the universe. Sprinkled with humor and written for a popular audience, the wheelchair-bound scientist's cosmological treatise lucidly explains the most exotic topics: antimatter, quarks, gravity, time, and space. His book is part of the physics community's perennial search for a grand unifying theory that would tie together the general theory of relativity and quantum mechanics—that is, one to explain the universe and everything in it. Hawking holds the Isaac

Newton's chair as Lucasian Professor of Mathematics at the University of Cambridge and is often seen as Newton and Einstein's successor.

24. *In the Garden of Beasts: Love, Terror, and an American Family in Hitler's Berlin.* Written by Erik Larson. (Crown, 2011.) After several other candidates turn him down, FDR plucks University of Chicago history professor William E. Dodd out of relative obscurity to serve as ambassador to Germany, where Hitler and the Nazis had recently gained power. Dodd and his flamboyant 24-year-old daughter Martha are the central figures in this true historical account. The professor at first believes that Nazism will moderate, while Martha has an affair with a Gestapo official and initially becomes an apologist for the revolutionary spirit and enthusiasm of the "New Germany," even as the Jews begin to be persecuted. There is nothing stale about Larson's narrative history of this critical period. *In the Garden of Beasts* reads like a political thriller.

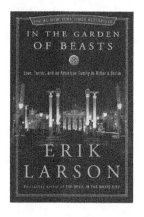

25. *The Making of the Atomic Bomb.* Written by Richard Rhodes. (Simon & Schuster, 2012.) Rhodes's definitive account traces the development of the world's ultimate apocalyptic weapon from its origins as a problem in theoretical physics to its devastating culmination at Hiroshima and Nagasaki. The book is also a chronicle of the personalities and greatest minds of the 20th century—especially Robert Oppenheimer, Niels Bohr, Leo Szilard, Enrico Fermi, Edward Teller, and Ernest Lawrence—and their contributions to developing the atomic bomb. Rhodes does a masterful job in explaining the Manhattan Project, with a host of details on everything from laboratory experiments to training of bombing pilots. First published in 1986, this meticulously researched and sweeping drama also includes information on the German and Japanese struggles to build a workable bomb.

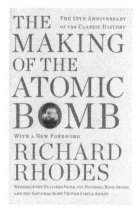

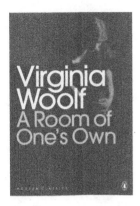

26. *A Room of One's Own.* Written by Virginia Woolf. (Penguin Books, 2002.) First published in 1929, Virginia Woolf's book-length essay is a landmark in modern feminist criticism. Her groundbreaking classic takes on the literary and social patriarchy that impedes women. It argues that women must have an income and a room of their own—literal and figural space—in order to have the freedom to create. Woolf was barred from formal education by her father's belief that schooling was an exclusively male domain, yet her book was based on a series of lectures she delivered at Newnham College and Girton College at Cambridge University in 1928. "The history of men's opposition to women's emancipation is more interesting perhaps than the story of that emancipation itself," wrote the renowned novelist, also famous for writing *Mrs Dalloway* (1925) and *To the Lighthouse* (1927).

27. *Columbine.* Written by Dave Cullen. (Twelve Books, 2009.) Dave Cullen's thoroughly researched and vividly detailed book provides the most complete account of the school massacre committed by two boys at Columbine High School in 1999 that resulted in the death of 13 people and the injury of 24 others who tried to escape. Eric Harris and Dylan Klebold are portrayed as hateful psychopaths with lots of friends and, surprisingly, not as victims of bullies as was widely reported. This is not a story of lonely nerds looking for revenge on a jock culture, but of malevolent terrorism. Ten years in the making, Cullen profiles the teenagers' evolution leading up to the shooting and the challenges the survivors faced in its aftermath. Several critics have compared Cullen's crime analysis to Capote's classic *In Cold Blood.* *Columbine* should be read not only to correct the entrenched myths surrounding the tragedy but also to glimpse the human capacity for evil.

28. *Speak, Memory: An Autobiography Revisited.* Written by Vladimir Nabokov. (Penguin Classics, 2000.) *Speak, Memory* is the memoir of one of the world's most internationally recognized novelists, poets, and short-story writers. This classic memoir of the acclaimed multilingual writer focuses on his happy, pampered childhood in czarist Russia and his flight, with his aristocratic family, from the Bolsheviks in 1918 to an impoverished émigré existence in Berlin and Paris. His nonlinear story touches sparingly on his years at Cambridge and concludes with his departure for the United States. The autobiography was first published in the United States in 1951 under the title *Conclusive Evidence.* Nabokov is best known for his novel *Lolita* (1958), dealing with a middle-aged man's obsession with a young girl.

29. *Electric Universe: How Electricity Switched on the Modern World.* Written by David Bodanis. (Broadway Books, 2006.) Science writer David Bodanis's history of the science of electricity is a journey of discovery, as it vividly describes the work of the many scientists and pioneers who unlocked and applied electricity's invisible secrets. This narrative includes information on a fascinating cast of characters, including Thomas Edison, Alexander Graham Bell, Michael Faraday, Alessandro Volta, Samuel Morse, Alan Turing, James Clerk Maxwell, and Cyrus West Field. This popular history makes electricity clear both as a force of nature and as an integral part of modern society. Bodanis's book was originally distributed under the title *Electric Universe: The Shocking True Story of Electricity* (2005).

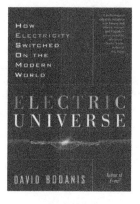

30. *The Structure of Scientific Revolutions.* Written by Thomas S. Kuhn. (University of Chicago Press, 1971.) *The Structure of Scientific Revolutions* is one of the most frequently cited books of the 20th century, influencing many fields and disciplines beyond its subject, the history and philosophy of science. Kuhn's book is important because it challenges the conventional notion of science as the accumulation of facts.

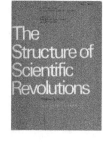

Kuhn's breakthrough is to show that progress is more revolutionary than evolutionary, with new paradigms overturning normal science. What seems to remain is a relativistic world with competing communities operating with incommensurable assumptions. Kuhn's idea of a paradigm has become ubiquitous; it is used to describe differing worldviews in the humanities, social sciences, and business.

31. *Into Thin Air: A Personal Account of the Mt. Everest Disaster.* Written by Jon Krakauer. (Pan Books, 2011.) Jon Krakauer's eyewitness account describes in riveting detail the terrible cost in lives lost climbing the earth's highest mountain in 1996. "Among my five teammates who reached the top, four . . . perished in a rogue storm that blew in without warning while we were still high on the peak. By the time I'd descended to Base Camp nine climbers from four expeditions were dead, and three more lives would be lost before the month was out," writes Krakauer, a journalist sent to Nepal to write about a guided ascent of Mt. Everest. Readers will be at the edge of their seats as they gain insight into what motivates people to throw caution to the wind and endure such extreme hardship and risk.

32. *The Forever War.* Written by Dexter Filkins. (Knopf, 2008.) Experienced *New York Times* foreign correspondent Dexter Filkins's modern classic in war reporting describes the rise of the Taliban and the wars in Afghanistan and Iraq with the authority and knowledge of someone who seems to have seen everything. His affecting vignettes are packed with memorable characters and shocking scenes that candidly report the brutal absurdity of war in some of the world's most hostile places. As suggested by the title of the book, this account is a bleak assessment of the seemingly endless conflict with Islamic fundamentalism and of the pattern of violence that extends into the future. Readers will be edified and moved by the author's unforgettable descriptions of bravery and tragedy.

33. *John Adams.* Written by David McCullough. (Simon & Schuster, 2001.) Master writer and historian David McCullough follows John Adams's life from childhood to his participation in the American Revolution and his positions of vice president and president, portraying him as blunt, brilliant, irascible, and often at odds with Thomas Jefferson. This magnificent portrait also features stimulating descriptions and accounts of other key figures, such as Washington, Franklin, Hamilton, his wife Abigail, and his son John Quincy, who would also go on to become president. In this biography that reads like a novel, Adams gets his due, becoming for readers what friend and rival Jefferson called "the colossus of independence." Admirers of McCullough's writing and historiographical skill would be well advised to read the author's other presidential biography, *Truman* (1992).

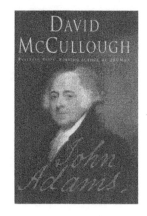

34. *Pilgrim at Tinker Creek.* Written by Annie Dillard. (HarperCollins, 2007.) "I am a fugitive and a vagabond, a sojourner seeking signs," writes Annie Dillard. *Pilgrim at Tinker Creek* is a record of Dillard's thoughts and observations on nature, solitude, religion, and other topics over the period of a year as she meanders around the creek close to her home near Virginia's Blue Ridge Mountains. The author's metaphysical pilgrimage is full of fresh insights and beautiful descriptions befitting the work of a great poet. One of Dillard's important topics has to do with the harshness and cruelty of the natural world, and on this theme, the book has a famous passage describing a frog being sucked dry by a giant water beetle. Critics see Dillard's writing as part of the tradition of American Transcendentalism and have compared her introspective and naturalistic masterpiece to the writings of Henry David Thoreau.

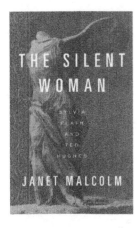

35. *The Silent Woman: Sylvia Plath and Ted Hughes.*
Written by Janet Malcolm. (Vintage, 1995.) Janet
Malcolm's postmodern portrait of Sylvia Plath and her
marriage to Ted Hughes explores the life and suicide of
the acclaimed poet and writer and the efforts of various
biographers to spin the story of her complex existence.
Key characters in Malcolm's narrative are biographer
Anne Stevenson and Ted Hughes's sister Olwyn
Hughes. The book also has important material on A.
Alvarez, author of *The Savage God* (1972), a study of
suicide that included the suicide of his friend Sylvia
Plath. This innovative book is also a look at the morally ambiguous role of the journalist and biographer,
who Malcolm lampoons as "a professional burglar,
breaking into a house, rifling through certain drawers
. . . and triumphantly bearing his loot away."

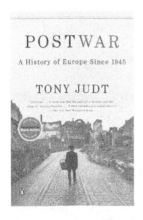

36. *Postwar: A History of Europe since 1945.* Written by
Tony Judt. (Penguin Press, 2005.) This sweeping, integrated narrative of how Eastern and Western Europe
rose from the ashes of World War II is unsurpassed in
its analysis of the Marshall Plan, the intricate and con-
flicted relationship with the United States, the transition away from Soviet Communism, and the formation of the European Union. With broad strokes and
carefully selected details, Tony Judt's hefty book covers
social developments, economic changes, and cultural
swings. *Postwar* succeeds as an authoritative reference
and as a well-told story. Even those who do not often
read European history will be left wanting more from
Judt, the director of New York University's Remarque
Institute, a multidisciplinary think tank.

37. *Angela's Ashes: A Memoir.* Written by Frank Mc-
Court. (Scribner, 1996.) "Worse than the ordinary
miserable childhood is the miserable Irish childhood,
and worse yet is the miserable Irish Catholic childhood," begins Frank McCourt, in a powerful book
that will make readers laugh and cry. McCourt writes
eloquently about his desperately impoverished life in
the slums of Depression-era Brooklyn, New York,

and Limerick, Ireland, made worst by an alcoholic father, a clinically depressed mother (Angela), and the loss of three siblings. The writing is infused with beauty rather than self-pity, and the author finds humor even in the most pitiful circumstances, such as when Frank's brother Malachy puts his father's false teeth in his mouth, where they become stuck, necessitating rushing him to the hospital to have them removed.

38. *The Selfish Gene.* Written by Richard Dawkins. (Oxford University Press, 2006.) Rather than focusing on evolution from the perspective of the organism or group, Dawkins's brilliant book provides a new twist on Darwin's theory by looking at it from a gene's perspective. His scientific classic uses the word "selfish" not to anthropomorphize or convey selfishness but to make the metaphorical point that the genes that get passed on to subsequent generations are the ones whose evolutionary consequences serve their interests. From Dawkins's vantage point, apparent acts of altruism are grounded in biology, and when creatures sacrifice themselves to protect their group, they are actually protecting the interests of their gene pool. Originally published in 1976, Dawkins's book created quite a stir in the scientific community, and its nontechnical language extended its influence to a wide audience.

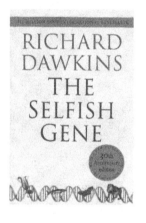

39. *Chaos: Making a New Science.* Written by James Gleick. (Penguin Books, 2008.) First published in 1987, this is the first book for a popular audience on the fundamentals of chaos theory. It chronicles its colorful history with entertaining stories about its eccentric pioneers, while laying bare the paradox that the universe is wildly random yet stable, and that mathematics can be used to understand complex natural systems that otherwise would have too many variables to investigate. Aided by sketches, photographs, and penetrating prose, former *New York Times* science writer James Gleick elucidates such

arcane topics as nonlinear dynamics, the Mandelbrot set, Julia sets, Lorenz attractors, and the Butterfly Effect. *Chaos* is a groundbreaking book that opens the door to a revolutionary new view of nature and to the geniuses responsible for discovering it.

40. *Unbroken: A World War II Story of Survival, Resilience, and Redemption.* Written by Laura Hillenbrand. (Random House, 2010.) Louie Zamperini was an American athlete who competed in the 1936 Berlin Olympics. When his B-24 crashed into the Pacific Ocean during World War II, this sole survivor spent 47 days on a life raft, enduring shark attacks and extreme hunger and thirst, before being captured by the enemy. In the hands of the Japanese, the presumed dead lieutenant suffered two years of beatings, starvation, and degradation and returned from the war a broken man. A random encounter with evangelist Billy Graham inspired him to turn his life around and commit himself to evangelical ministry. Laura Hillenbrand's inspiring tale of survival and redemption is based on impressive documentary research and 75 interviews with nonagenarian Zamperini.

41. *Cheever: A Life.* Written by Blake Bailey. (Knopf, 2009.) This in-depth literary biography of John Cheever, one of the foremost American fiction writers of the 20th century, is the first to be written with copious amounts of documentation coming from unprecedented access to the Cheever estate. Blake Bailey's empathetic narrative describes Cheever not only as a tormented alcoholic and self-hating bisexual but also as an oddly lovable man, even as he maintained difficult relationships with his family and literary peers such as Saul Bellow and John Updike. This authoritative biography will not be the last word on the iconic novelist and short-story writer, but it will be studied alongside Cheever's body of work for years to come.

42. *The Feminine Mystique.* Written by Betty Friedan. (Dell/Laurel, 1984.) In this feminist classic, one of the landmark books of the 20th century, Friedan objects to the mainstream image of women because it limits them to the role of housewife, largely wastes their potential, and leaves them unfulfilled. Identifying "the problem that has no name," she discusses the lives of several housewives who were justifiably unhappy, despite having material comforts and leading lives that seemed conventionally idyllic. First published in 1963, *The Feminine Mystique* is widely credited with having begun second-wave feminism and the women's liberation movement. Friedan went on to help found the National Organization for Women and served as its first president.

43. *The Omnivore's Dilemma: A Natural History of Four Meals.* Written by Michael Pollan. (Penguin Press, 2007.) In his introduction titled "Our National Eating Disorder," Pollan asks, "How did we ever get to a point where we need investigative journalists to tell us where our food comes from and nutritionists to determine the dinner menu?" Lifting the veil from our modern agriculture complex, the author attempts to solve the "omnivore's dilemma" by looking at four different food chains from source to mealtime: industrial, industrial-scale organic, local and sustainable, and hunter-gatherer. Pollan raises serious questions about many aspects of food production and animal conditions, and readers will find the material so disturbing that they may never want to eat meat again. A young-readers' edition of *The Omnivore's Dilemma* (2009) is also available, encouraging kids to become food detectives and to consider the health and environmental implications of their dietary choices.

44. *The Big Short: Inside the Doomsday Machine.* Written by Michael Lewis. (W. W. Norton, 2010.) If readers were to have just one book explaining the nation's most-recent economic crisis, *The Big Short* would be the logical choice. Michael Lewis describes how a few investment managers detected early on the emerging bubble in the mortgage bond market and made fortunes betting against it. The author inquires into who saw the real estate market for the trap it would become and explains how they made billions of dollars from that iconoclastic insight. Although this book is intended for general readers, the ones who are most likely to appreciate this character-driven analysis are financial insiders, who already have a working knowledge of collateralized debt obligations, credit default swaps, and other financial instruments.

45. *The Assassins' Gate: America in Iraq.* Written by George Packer. (Farrar, Straus & Giroux, 2005.) This is the story of America's poorly planned Iraq war and occupation, the country's most unpopular and controversial overseas venture since the Vietnam War. Using his experience on the front lines reporting for the *New Yorker*, George Packer chronicles the people and ideas that created the Bush administration's war policy and the struggles of American and Iraqi soldiers on the ground. Packer's book differs from others because it traces the evolution of the author's original support of the war to his recognition that it was terribly mismanaged. His book highlights the role that neoconservative ideology played in all aspects of the war effort.

46. *The Dark Side: The Inside Story of How the War on Terror Turned into a War on American Ideals.* Written by Jane Mayer. (Doubleday, 2008.) In this dramatic exposé, the Bush administration's "War on Terror" is shown to have disastrously eroded American ideals as well as the nation's moral standing around the world. Mayer details the ugly underbelly of the war as it was manifested in water boarding, stress positions, harsh interrogations, open-ended detentions without due process, extraordinary renditions, secret CIA prisons, warrantless wiretappings, sleep deprivation, sexual humiliation, and other gross violations of the U.S. Constitution and the Geneva Conventions. This provocative and hard-hitting book argues that America's embrace of torture was not just immoral but also seriously undermined efforts to stop Al-Qaeda. Mayer's work on *The Dark Side* helped earn her a prestigious Guggenheim Fellowship.

47. *Zeitoun.* Written by Dave Eggers. (McSweeney's, 2009.) Eggers's restrained yet enthralling account of what happened to Abdulrahman Zeitoun in New Orleans during Hurricane Katrina is sure to prompt feelings of outrage and demand an answer to the question "How could this have happened here?" When the family of housepainter Zeitoun left the city as the storm approached, he stayed behind to watch over their property and ended up using his canoe to travel about helping his neighbors and feeding animals abandoned by their owners. In a confluence of disaster management, racial profiling, and the war on terror gone wildly amok, Zeitoun was arrested by military men with M-16 rifles and swept into a Kafkaesque bureaucratic maze.

48. *The Great War and Modern Memory.* Written by Paul Fussell. (Sterling, 2012.) Originally published in 1975, *The Great War and Modern Memory* focuses on the English literary response to the harsh reality of trench war in World War I. Paul Fussell relies on material from many primary sources—including books, personal correspondence, and newspaper accounts—to elucidate the meaning of the war for individuals and our perception of the modern world. This unusual marriage of literary criticism and the horrors of combat is a truly original undertaking in explaining how "the war to end all wars" changed the sensibilities of a generation. This illustrated edition features a wide range of rare period photographs, illustrations, advertisements, and maps.

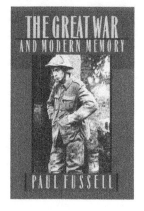

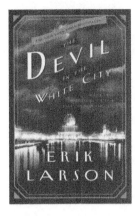

49. *The Devil in the White City: Murder, Magic, and Madness at the Fair That Changed America.* Written by Erik Larson. (Crown, 2003.) Written with his characteristic novelistic flair, Erik Larson tells the true story of two men, one the architect of the 1893 Chicago World's Fair and the other a serial killer responsible for the deaths of scores of young women around the city. The account balances descriptions of the work of industrious Daniel H. Burnham, who faced daunting obstacles to make the vast project a reality, and diabolical H. H. Holmes, who, while pretending to be a doctor, lured his victims to their deaths in his elaborately constructed hotel, crematorium, and gas chamber. Larson's well-told story and quality prose is everything readers hope to find in serious nonfiction.

50. *The Education of Henry Adams.* Written by Henry Adams. (University of Virginia Press, 2008.) This acclaimed 1918 autobiography, written in the third person, describes Adams's difficulty coming to terms with the social, scientific, and technological changes of the dawning 20th century and criticizes his formal education grounded mostly in the humanities. This introspective volume reflects on not only Adams's personal history but also the history of 19th-century America. The book is a treasure trove of insights, such as "The chief wonder of education is that it does not ruin everybody concerned in it, teachers and taught"; "Politics, as a practice, whatever its professions, has always been the systematic organization of hatreds"; and "Nature, to be commanded, must be obeyed." Henry Adams was the grandson of President John Quincy Adams and the great-grandson of President John Adams.

51. *Iron Curtain: The Crushing of Eastern Europe, 1945–1956.* Written by Anne Applebaum. (Doubleday, 2012.) Drawing on newly available East European archival information and interviews, Anne Applebaum vividly describes the dark decades when millions of people were caught in the Soviet occupation of Poland, Hungary, and East Germany following World War II. She chronicles the systematic destruction of civil societies—the arts, education, media, judiciary, small business, church, and the entertainment industries—all in the service of communist totalitarianism. In the face of fear, intimidation, and mass propaganda, people coped through passive compliance, active collaboration, or heroic dissent. There is no better account of the destructiveness and brutality of Soviet rule of Eastern Europe. *Iron Curtain* is a follow-up to Applebaum's Pulitzer Prize–winning *Gulag* (2003), a history of the Soviet concentration camps.

52. *The Electric Kool-Aid Acid Test.* Written by Tom Wolfe. (Picador, 2008.) Wolfe's book is considered a canonical text of the hippie movement and the Beat Generation. *The Electric Kool-Aid Acid Test* is the story of Ken Kesey, known as the pioneer of the techniques of New Journalism, and his group of Merry Pranksters, who traveled around the country taking psychedelic drugs with the goal of achieving spiritual release. Kesey, who wrote the counterculture classic *One Flew over the Cuckoo's Nest* (1962), is depicted as a charismatic figure. Wolfe's book is often said to have defined the 1960s generation, just as the image of the carefree Pranksters aboard their colorfully decorated school bus became a symbol of the generation's overindulgence and liberation. *The Electric Kool-Aid Acid Test* was first published in 1968.

53. *The First Tycoon: The Epic Life of Cornelius Vanderbilt.* Written by T. J. Stiles. (Knopf, 2009.) Stiles provides a comprehensive and authoritative portrait of the robber baron who amassed one of the largest fortunes in the world, launched a transportation revolution, and was instrumental in creating the model of corporate capitalism we know today. Stiles describes Cornelius Vanderbilt's rise from the job of lowly boatman to becoming a corporate titan capable of building the country's largest fleet of steamships, creating a railroad empire, and advising President Lincoln on Civil War strategy. Vanderbilt is shown practicing a take-no-prisoners brand of capitalism,

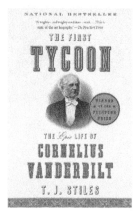

where he would first destroy all competition and then raise his prices. The gruff-and-unschooled individualist provided transportation for the California gold rush and built New York's original Grand Central Station, yet struggled to gain the respect of the city's social and cultural elite.

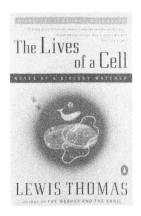

54. *The Lives of a Cell: Notes of a Biology Watcher.* Written by Lewis Thomas. (Penguin Books, 1978.) This scientific classic is a collection of 29 elegant essays originally published in the *New England Journal of Medicine* between 1971 and 1973 that examine the interdependence of living things. Lewis Thomas, an impressively credentialed physician and etymologist, extends his reach beyond biology, touching upon topics as wide-ranging as language, music, technology, and social behavior. In his first essay, Thomas regards the planet as a giant cellular system with humans as just one part. In his concluding essay, "The World's Biggest Membrane," he praises the atmosphere as "a miraculous achievement" and "the grandest product of collaboration in all of nature."

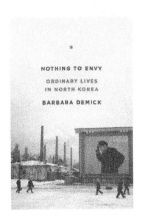

55. *Nothing to Envy: Ordinary Lives in North Korea.* Written by Barbara Demick. (Spiegel & Grau, 2008.) "If you look at satellite photographs of the far east by night, you'll see a large splotch curiously lacking in light. This area of darkness is the Democratic People's Republic of Korea. Next to this mysterious black hole, South Korea, Japan, and now China fairly gleam with prosperity." So begins *Los Angeles Times* reporter Barbara Demick's gripping and apt description of life in the planet's most repressive totalitarian regime. Her account traces the lives of six North Korean defectors over a span of 15 years who finally risk everything to leave this hellishly cruel, impoverished, and isolated country. This is a great book of literary nonfiction and a rare personalized glimpse of a long-suffering people.

56. *Fast Food Nation: The Dark Side of the All-American Meal.* Written by Eric Schlosser. (Houghton Mifflin Company, 2001.) We all know that fast food is an unhealthy choice and a main cause of the American obesity epidemic, but investigative journalist Eric Schlosser's book digs deeper to describe other ways that this industry has degraded our society and the world. His historical account and exposé highlights unsanitary and discriminatory practices, and links the business model to ugly urban sprawl, child-targeted marketing, an underpaid workforce, and the standardization of American society. Part 1 traces the development of fast food from its origins in post–World War II Southern California. Part 2 includes a revealing discussion of the virtually unregulated meatpacking industry that has invited comparisons to Upton Sinclair's *The Jungle* (1906).

57. *Outliers: The Story of Success.* Written by Malcolm Gladwell. (Little, Brown, 2008.) Malcolm Gladwell has again probed the idea of elusive patterns residing behind everyday appearances. In *The Tipping Point* (2000) and *Blink* (2005), he revealed the subtle ways we understand our external and internal worlds, and in *Outliers*, he discloses the unseen factors that determine success. Gladwell asserts that high achievers are almost always "the beneficiaries of hidden advantages and extraordinary opportunities and cultural legacies that allow them to learn and work hard and make sense of the world in ways others cannot." Having innate ability is simply not enough. Attacking the myth of the self-made man, Gladwell promotes the idea that unlocking human potential is deeply dependent on factors such as culture, timing, history, community, and circumstance.

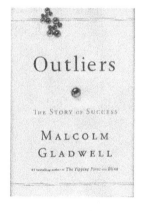

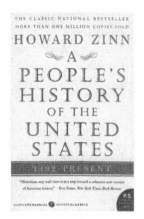

58. *A People's History of the United States: 1492 to Present.* Written by Howard Zinn. (Harper Perennial Modern Classics, 2005.) This provocative history tells America's story from the perspective of common people rather than that of rich and powerful elites. First published in 1980, Zinn's classic is most noteworthy for giving voice to groups that have often been overlooked: women, factory workers, labor organizers, pacifists, socialists, African Americans, Native Americans, working poor, and immigrants. His heroes are not robber barons or war makers, but men and women who have been kept socially and economically powerless. "The history of any country," writes Zinn, "conceals the fierce conflicts of interest (sometimes exploding, often repressed) between conquerors and conquered, masters and slaves, capitalists and workers, dominators and dominated in race and sex. And in such a world of conflict, a world of victims and executioners, it is the job of thinking people, as Albert Camus suggested, not to be on the side of the executioners."

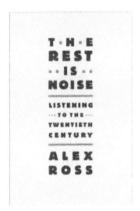

59. *The Rest Is Noise: Listening to the Twentieth Century.* Written by Alex Ross. (Farrar, Straus & Giroux, 2007.) The *New Yorker*'s music critic Alex Ross used music as the organizing principle for writing a history of the 20th century. *The Rest Is Noise* exudes scholarship and erudition in weaving together major historical events, accomplishments of prominent composers, and cultural developments from 1900 through 2000. One of the book's subjects is the increasing gap between classical and contemporary popular music, the latter judged to fall short of other artistic enterprises. Readers will be amazed by the connections Ross makes among different composers, musical styles, and the culture at large. His book will also influence how they listen to classical music and make them reconsider which recordings are most worth their attention.

60. *The Year of Magical Thinking.* Written by Joan Didion. (Knopf, 2005.) Joan Didion's masterpiece recounts her grief and mourning for her husband, novelist and literary critic John Gregory Dunne. In this memoir of the year following his death, Didion also describes her daughter Quintana's dire illness. This intense portrait of a wife and mother struggling to cope with death and illness is interlaced with recollections of her husband's final days, thoughts on the care of her daughter, and research on medical and psychological aspects of bereavement. "Grief turns out to be a place none of us know until we reach it," writes the acclaimed novelist and literary journalist. "We might expect that we will be prostrate, inconsolable, crazy with loss. We do not expect to be literally crazy, cool customers who believe their husband is about to return and need his shoes."

JOAN DIDION
THE YEAR OF MAGICAL THINKING

61. *Steve Jobs.* Written by Walter Isaacson. (Simon & Schuster, 2011.) *Steve Jobs* is the authorized but unvarnished portrait of the entrepreneurial giant who used Apple to transform how we use personal computers, phones, and tablets in the realms of music, digital publishing, music, and animated movies. Known for his creativity and intensity, Jobs comes across as a visionary leader who was tough and sometimes even mean. One reviewer called the book an "encyclopedic survey of all that Mr. Jobs accomplished," while another commentator described the book as "a textbook study of the rise and fall and rise of Apple." Walter Isaacson, who previously wrote best-selling biographies of Benjamin Franklin and Albert Einstein, conducted scores of exclusive interviews with Jobs and his closest associates. *Steve Jobs* is likely to remain the authoritative work on this American icon.

Steve Jobs by Walter Isaacson

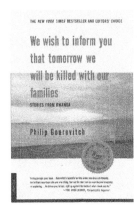

62. *We Wish to Inform You That Tomorrow We Will Be Killed with Our Families: Stories from Rwanda.* Written by Philip Gourevitch. (Picador, 1999.) In 1994, over 800,000 people were killed over the course of 100 days in Rwanda mostly, and almost unimaginably, at the hands of human beings wielding machetes. While the world stood by and watched what was unfolding in this East African country, the majority Hutu tribe engaged in a genocidal mass slaughter of the minority Tutsi population. Gourevitch spent several years interviewing survivors and assembling a history that absolutely must be read. In a world filled with ethnic hatreds, readers and policy makers need to learn from this horrible tragedy and do whatever is humanly possible to make sure that other cases of bitter conflict do not devolve into violence.

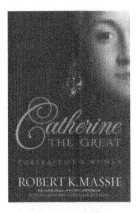

63. *Catherine the Great: Portrait of a Woman.* Written by Robert K. Massie. (Random House, 2011.) Born into minor German nobility, Catherine rose to become the empress of Russia, ruling for 34 years over the world's largest empire. Massie's description of Catherine's multifaceted life includes many love affairs and correspondence with the great Enlightenment philosophers Voltaire, Diderot, and Montesquieu, as well as Marie Antoinette and other 18th-century leaders. Massie chiefly recognizes the ruler for modernizing Russia and importing European culture, while casting her on a personal level as cultured, passionate, and voraciously curious. Massie is no stranger to quality writing or Russian royalty, having written *Nicholas and Alexandra: An Intimate Account of the Last of the Romanovs and the Fall of Imperial Russia* (1967) and *Peter the Great: His Life and World* (1980) for which he won the Pulitzer Prize.

64. *Desert Solitaire: A Season in the Wilderness.* Written by Edward Abbey. (McGraw-Hill, 1968.) Written while he was a park ranger in Utah, Abbey's acclaimed environmental and autobiographical classic is a tribute to the beauty of the American Southwest, a rejection of the values of the mainstream techno-industrialized American culture, and a polemic against ceaseless encroachments on the wilderness contained in our national parks. "No more cars in national parks. Let the people walk. Or ride horses, bicycles, mules, wild pigs—anything—but keep the automobiles and the motorcycles and all their motorized relatives out," writes Abbey. "We have agreed not to drive our automobiles into cathedrals, concert halls, art museums, legislative assemblies, private bedrooms and the other sanctums of our culture; we should treat our national parks with the same deference, for they, too, are holy places."

65. *The Gnostic Gospels.* Written by Elaine Pagels. (Vintage, 1989.) Elaine Pagels's *The Gnostic Gospels* is a provocative, scholarly, and highly readable account of the roots of Christianity with profound implications. Her study shows that early Christians were much more diverse than was previously believed and the religion would have been different if the Gnostic Gospels had not been excluded from the standard biblical canon. By analyzing the gospels, 52 early Christian manuscripts unearthed in Egypt, Pagels shows that God was portrayed by the Gnostics in both masculine and feminine terms, and, not unlike Buddhists and Hindus, they believed that the Christian path to God could be achieved through self-knowledge. The Gnostic Gospels were excluded from Christianity, Pagels argues, because church leaders wanted to consolidate political power. *The Gnostic Gospels* was first published in 1979.

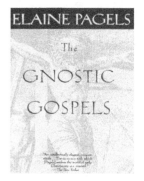

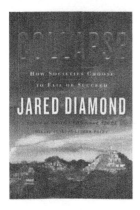

66. *Collapse: How Societies Choose to Fail or Succeed.* Written by Jared Diamond. (Viking, 2004.) "This book employs the comparative method to understand societal collapses to which environmental problems contribute," writes Jared Diamond in his prologue, taking on the opposite problem of societal buildup and success that he pursued in his award-winning *Guns, Germs, and Steel: The Fates of Human Societies.* Some of the past victims of environmental damage he examines are the Greenland Norse, the Polynesians of Pitcairn Island, the Anasazi of southwestern North America, and the Maya of Central America. The leading problems that have led to the collapses of past societies include deforestation and habitat destruction; soil erosion, salinization, and fertility losses; water management issues; overpopulation; overhunting; and overfishing. Diamond has few equals in his ability to look at vast swaths of historical, cultural, and scientific information to draw large-scale conclusions.

67. *Gulag: A History of the Soviet Camps.* Written by Anne Applebaum. (Doubleday, 2003.) Anne Applebaum wrote the first fully documented history of the Soviet Union's concentration camp system from its inception during the Russian Revolution in 1918 to its dissolution in the 1980s during the glasnost era. She highlights Stalin's role in expanding this massive network of punishment, repression, and forced labor to promote industrialization that reached its apex in the 1950s. For over a half century, millions of people were sent to the gulags, but only a small portion returned. This landmark history vividly details the arrest and interrogations of alleged dissidents and describes their daily conditions of extreme hardship, disease, starvation, and death. Applebaum wonders why this monstrous system, in place for so long, never got the attention from the former Soviet Union and Western societies that it deserved.

68. *Destiny of the Republic: A Tale of Madness, Medicine and the Murder of a President.* Written by Candice Millard. (Anchor, 2012.) A neglected chapter of history is brought to life in Candice Millard's dramatic telling of the story of President James A. Garfield and his assassin Charles Guiteau, who shot the 20th president, barely four months into his term, in the back in 1881. By Millard's account, Garfield was a gifted man and a capable leader. His rags-to-riches career included scholarship and Civil War heroism, but he was an unlikely selection as the Republican candidate for president. Guiteau is portrayed as a delusional figure who killed the president because he could not get a job in his administration. After 10 excruciating weeks of suffering, Garfield died because of an infection brought on by incompetent medical care.

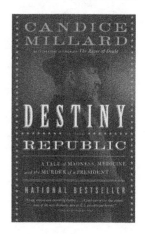

69. *Freakonomics: A Rogue Economist Explores the Hidden Side of Everything.* Written by Steven D. Levitt and Stephen J. Dubner. (William Morrow, 2009.) Journalist Stephen J. Dubner and award-winning economist Steven D. Levitt team up to prove that economics is not dismal science but an absolutely fascinating intellectual exercise in drawing connections among freakishly unrelated behaviors. Here is a sample of their unlikely pairings: guns and swimming pools, schoolteachers and sumo wrestlers, the Ku Klux Klan and real estate agents, and legalized abortion and crime. When abortion became legal, for example, the number of unwanted births declined, and so did the crime rate 16 years later, when this delinquency-inclined cohort would have started breaking laws. The book's underlying premise—that economics is, at bottom, really the study of incentives—provides some unity to the book's wild assortment of topics.

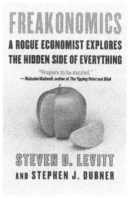

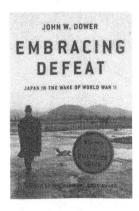

70. *Embracing Defeat: Japan in the Wake of World War II.* Written by John W. Dower. (W. W. Norton, 1999.) Supported by many excellent documentary photographs, MIT historian John W. Dower describes in detail how American forces imposed a social and political transformation over six years of their occupation of Japan, converting the imperial country into a democracy. The story of the change is nothing less than revolutionary, considering how rapidly the country moved from being distinctly militaristic to constitutionally enthroning peace by prohibiting its military from being deployed abroad. Dower's history is not just a chronicle of American ideas and intentions but also an account that focuses on the relationship between the victor and the vanquished, and the personal stories of citizens of this shattered nation. *Embracing Defeat* is a splendid piece of scholarship and the most authoritative account of postwar Japan.

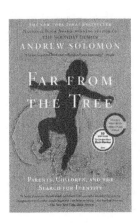

71. *Far from the Tree: Parents, Children, and the Search for Identity.* Written by Andrew Solomon. (Scribner, 2012.) Books about topics such as the nature of diversity, disability, and familiar love can often be described as handy, helpful, or insightful, but rarely can they be considered profound. Andrew Solomon's book deserves this description for its thoughtful exploration of the many ways that children can be fundamentally different from their parents and how everyone copes with the experience. He begins with his own life as a gay person born to heterosexual parents and expands to an extraordinary range of possibilities: deafness, dwarfism, prodigies, transgenders, Down's syndrome, autism, schizophrenia, criminality, physical deformity, and children who are the product of rape. Soloman's compassionate and informative book probes the primal question that every parent must confront about the extent to which they will love and accept their children for who they really are. *Far from the Tree* includes cases of failure, but by and large, it is a compendium of the triumph of understanding over prejudice.

72. *The Hemingses of Monticello: An American Family.* Written by Annette Gordon-Reed. (W. W. Norton, 2008.) In this sequel to Gordon-Reed's highly regarded *Thomas Jefferson and Sally Hemings: An American Controversy* (1997), the professor of law and history comprehensively traces the Hemingses from their origins as an enslaved family in Virginia to their dispersal after Thomas Jefferson's death. Gordon-Reed skillfully shows how the members of the family navigated within the repressive paradigm of institutionalized slavery to achieve a modicum of success. True to his word, Jefferson kept his promise to Sally Hemings to free their children, but Jefferson's other slaves were sold to pay his debts. Through shrewd detective work and careful deduction from scant documentary evidence, the author has assembled a compelling and complex portrait of a now-famous American family spanning three generations.

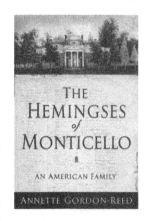

73. *The General Theory of Employment, Interest, and Money.* Written by John Maynard Keynes. (Harcourt, Brace & World, 1965.) "The outstanding faults of the economic society in which we live are its failure to provide for full employment and its arbitrary and inequitable distribution of wealth and incomes," wrote the prescient economist John Maynard Keynes in words that are as true today as they were in 1936. Keynes's magnum opus, one of the most influential books of the 20th century, emphasizes the role of government in stimulating and regulating a nation's economy. With this book, the English economist provided the cornerstone of what is now called "Keynesian thought" and is largely credited with creating the field of macroeconomics. Keynes's book fundamentally changed how the world views economic problems and the workings of capitalism.

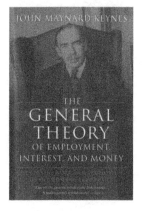

74. *Quiet: The Power of Introverts in a World That Can't Stop Talking.* Written by Susan Cain. (Crown, 2012.) *Quiet* is an introvert's manifesto that provides startling new insights into how people think, work, and interact. In a world seemingly overrun by the loud and gregarious, Cain's psychological classic presents impressive research that portrays quiet, reflective solitude seekers not as maladjusted, but as indispensible contributors to society. Among this diverse band of contributors are Gandhi, Joe DiMaggio, Mother Teresa, and Bill Gates. By profiling a number of introverts, Cain shows that the bias against them is misguided and the cause of an enormous waste of talent. Cain convincingly establishes that many of mankind's most capable people have not conformed to the extrovert ideal. She offers advice on how people with different temperaments can better accept and support each other.

75. *Hiroshima.* Written by John Hersey. (Knopf, 1946.) War correspondent John Hersey was one of the first Western journalists allowed to view Hiroshima after the atomic bomb was dropped on August 6, 1945. His story of six survivors was published a year later in the *New Yorker* and then two months later in book form. It covers one year prior and one year after the nuclear holocaust that killed an estimated 135,000 people. Before Hersey's book, reports of the bombing had not fully considered the human consequences of the event, so the magazine coverage and book were a national sensation. In 1985, Hersey added a final chapter to update the lives of the six survivors. Still relevant to the lingering moral debate over whether dropping the atomic bomb was the right thing to do, *Hiroshima* is considered one of the most important books of the nuclear age.

76. *Legacy of Ashes: The History of the CIA.* Written by Tim Weiner. (Doubleday, 2007.) Pulitzer Prize–winning journalist Weiner's definitive history of the CIA is such a catalog of failure and ineptitude that one wonders how the agency was able to stay intact from administration to administration. This exhaustively researched book, which includes analysis of mountains of CIA archival documents and interviews of 10 former CIA directors, is unrelenting in its criticism. Despite having enormous manpower and resources, the agency is shown repeatedly failing in its core mission to foresee world events, and instead focused on assassinating foreign leaders, overthrowing governments, and violating human rights. From the botched Bay of Pigs invasion, to the unpredicted collapse of the Soviet Union, to the massive intelligence failures in Iraq, the CIA is portrayed going from bad to worse, ultimately doing more to jeopardize than to protect national security. Readers looking for real-life stories to match the CIA's formidable media hype will not find it here.

77. *The Souls of Black Folks.* Written by W. E. B. Du Bois. (Simon & Schuster, 2005.) "The problem of the twentieth century is the problem of the color line," declares W. E. B. Du Bois in his classic work of American literature and sociology. Originally published in 1903, it argues for equality and justice for African Americans as reflected in the right to vote and the right to receive a good education. Du Bois argues against Booker T. Washington's focus on vocational education for black men, preferring a classical education to develop leadership and the full realization of human potential. A graduate from Harvard and the first African American to earn a doctorate, Du Bois went on to help found the National Association for the Advancement of Colored People.

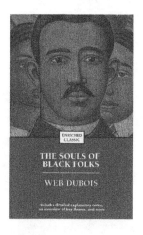

78. *Lit: A Memoir.* Written by Mary Karr. (Harper, 2009.) With honesty and edgy humor, poet and essayist Mary Karr tells the story of the adult chapter of her life in *Lit*, picking up where she left off in her two prior memoirs, *The Lion's Club* (1995), on her difficult childhood, and *Cherry* (2000), on her adolescent sexual coming of age. In this latest installment, Karr describes the dissolution of her marriage, her life as a mother, her descent into alcoholism, and her salvation through conversion to Catholicism. Karr's

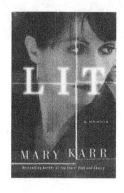

current confessional covers the years from age 17 to 50. Her fans will no doubt be expecting at least one more turbulent ride from this frequent memoirist.

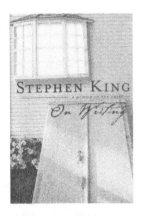

79. *On Writing: A Memoir of the Craft.* Written by Stephen King. (Scribner, 1999.) This massively productive and popular horror and science fiction novelist has a few things to say about his life and some practical advice on how to go from being a competent writer to a good one. The beginning and ending of King's uncharacteristically brief book are autobiographical and include an account of being struck by a van and his painful recovery. Sandwiched in between compelling facts about his life are his thoughts on plot, character, grammar, and the need to eliminate unnecessary words. You would think that an author whose books have sold more than 350,000,000 copies would be more confident about his qualifications for dispensing writing tips, but he compares his novels to fast food: "Colonel Sanders sold a hell of a lot of fried chicken, but I'm not sure anyone wants to know how he made it."

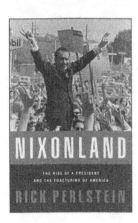

80. *Nixonland: The Rise of a President and the Fracturing of America.* Written by Rick Perlstein. (Scribner, 2008.) Rick Perlstein's book richly describes America's turbulent 1960s and early 1970s, providing vivid accounts of the era's most important events and leaders. Richard Nixon is central to this historical drama in the way that he rallies his "Silent Majority" to win election in 1968 and score a landslide victory in 1972. But in Nixon's manner of winning and governing, Perlstein finds the former president culpable for creating a new dividing line in American politics so potent that it is still with us in today's extreme ideological polarization. Nixon, he argues, was so effective in harvesting resentments and demonizing the liberal counterculture of the 1960s that it left our society enduringly divided. Readers will appreciate Perlstein's account of Nixon's machinations, but they may remain skeptical about adding today's political dysfunction to Richard Nixon's already long list of misdeeds.

81. Mayflower: *A Story of Courage, Community, and War.* Written by Nathaniel Philbrick. (Viking, 2006.) Philbrick's revisionist history of the voyage of the *Mayflower* and the settlement of Plymouth Colony is noteworthy for its success in separating complex facts from cherished myths. The author does recognize the courage of the settlers and praises the cases of Pilgrim-Indian cooperation, but he completes the story with descriptions of their bloody attacks and counterattacks. Instead of a Norman Rockwell painting of settlers and Native Americans sitting around the Thanksgiving dinner table, readers encounter the far more likely scene of the mixed group squatting around an outdoor fire roasting deer and eating from pots of stew. Among the most shocking realities is the fact that some colonists captured Native Americans and sold them into slavery.

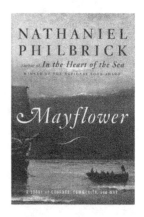

82. *Parting the Waters: America in the King Years, 1954–63.* Written by Taylor Branch. (Simon & Schuster, 1988.) *Parting the Waters*, the first book in a trilogy, describes King's rise to prominence, the Montgomery Bus Boycott, the 1961 Freedom Rides, the 1963 March on Washington for Jobs and Freedom, the lunch-counter sit-ins, the church bombings, and the tragedy of John F. Kennedy's assassination. This Pulitzer Prize–winning account of the early civil rights movement is considered one of the most reliable histories of the key players and events of this period. Taylor Branch's other two King books, *Pillar of Fire* (1998) and *At Canaan's Edge* (2006), cover other pivotal events including King's acceptance of the Nobel Peace Prize and the events leading up to his assassination.

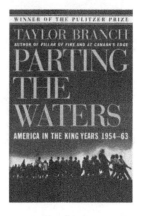

83. *A Short History of Nearly Everything.* Written by Bill Bryson. (Broadway Books, 2003.) Writing a history of almost everything is a tall order, but if anyone could pull it off, Bill Bryson would be up to the challenge. In actuality, Bryson has written a very wide-ranging and accessible science book that explains things through lively stories of people who have made

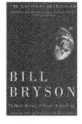

groundbreaking discoveries. Bryson's main interests
are the huge topics such as the primordial Big Bang,
the ascendency of Homo sapiens, the cataclysmic erup-
tion of Krakatoa, and the possibility that earth might
be struck by a civilization-ending meteor. Along the
way, with the extraordinary skill of a true storyteller, he
manages to impart the basic facts of physics, chemistry,
paleontology, astronomy, biology, botany, climatol-
ogy, and more. This entertaining and informative
book will work for both children and adults.

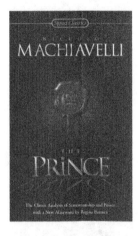

84. *The Prince.* Written by Niccolò Machiavelli.
(Signet Classics, 2008.) First published in 1532, *The
Prince* is a practical guide for rulers on how to acquire
and maintain political power. This classic book is
noteworthy for outlining the principles of a princely
government based not on grand ethical or philosophical ideals but on the practical consequences that flow
from political action. Its 26 chapters discuss different
types of states and armies, and the correct conduct of
a prince, and reflect on Italy's political situation. *The
Prince*, an affirmation of the power of self-determi-
nation and calculated action, over the years has been
negatively and unfairly interpreted as merely ruthless
and manipulative; hence, "Machiavellian."

85. *Slouching towards Bethlehem.* Written by Joan
Didion. (Farrar, Straus & Giroux, 1968.) This book
is Joan Didion's first collection of nonfiction writing
widely hailed for its journalistic excellence. Originally
published in the *Saturday Evening Post* and other
magazines, her essays are an important portrait of
American tumult during the 1960s, especially the
Haight-Ashbury district of San Francisco during its
peak as a countercultural center. The book's title and
opening essay on Haight-Ashbury comes from Yeats's
apocalyptic poem "The Second Coming," reflecting
the somber view that the hippies represented society
falling apart rather than achieving social progress.
Didion is the author of many critically acclaimed
books and screenplays and is regarded as one of
America's most astute culture critics.

86. The Holy Bible. (Zondervan, 2013.) The Bible is a canonical compilation of texts considered scared to Christians and Jews. In the Christian religion, the Bible is composed of the Old and New Testaments. Even among nonbelievers, the book is recognized for its unrivaled influence on culture, law, morality, and literature. The Gutenberg Bible was the world's first mass-printed book and a main driver of literacy in early America. Written by many authors over a period of approximately 1,500 years, it is widely considered the inspired word of God. There are still important differences in opinion about what material should be included in the Bible and what interpretation and emphasis should be ascribed to its passages, giving rise to different religions.

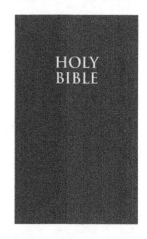

87. *A Supposedly Fun Thing I'll Never Do Again: Essays and Arguments.* Written by David Foster Wallace. (Little, Brown, 1997.) This highly praised collection of entertaining, insightful, and sometimes autobiographical essays gets its title from a piece about Wallace's experience on a Caribbean luxury cruise. Other essays discuss such things as the impact of television on contemporary literature, the nature of professional athletics, the excesses of the Illinois State Fair, the author's involvement in competitive tennis, and his interest in mathematics as a youth. Wallace was an American novelist, short-story writer, essayist, and English professor best known for his 1996 novel *Infinite Jest* (1996). More of Wallace's unique essays can be found in *Everything and More* (2003), and *Consider the Lobster* (2007).

88. *Anti-intellectualism in American Life.* Written by Richard Hofstadter. (Vintage, 1966.) Historian Richard Hofstadter was twice awarded the Pulitzer Prize, for *The Age of Reform* (1956) and for *Anti-intellectualism in American Life* (1963). In Hofstadter's view, intellectuals have throughout American history been marginalized as outsiders, servants, scapegoats, and cartoonish eggheads. The noted scholar believes that suspiciousness toward the life of the mind and a dumbing down of American society are cyclical,

but that they are very much a part of the national character. Hofstadter would be dismayed but hardly surprised by the 2012 Pew Research Center report that nearly a quarter of American adults had not read a single book in the past year and that the number of non–book-readers has nearly tripled since the late 1970s. Readers who have ever felt stigmatized rather than prized for their "elitist" fascination with ideas or books will appreciate this classic cultural history.

89. *The Swerve: How the World Became Modern.* Written by Stephen Greenblatt. (W. W. Norton, 2011.) Part biography and part intellectual history, Stephen Greenblatt's book describes how Poggio Bracciolini discovered by chance a lost ancient manuscript that changed the course of history, planting the seeds of the Renaissance and what we now see as secular modernity. What this alert apostolic secretary found in 1417 in an obscure library was a poem by Roman philosopher Titus Lucretius that suggested, in Greenblatt's words, that "there is no master plan, no divine architect, no intelligent design" and thus no gods necessary to explain the workings of the universe. Among other things, it made more sense, said Lucretius, to think of the world as being made up of small particles moving in constant motion. Bracciolini widely distributed the heretical manuscript, creating a historic swerve toward a new world governed by science and reason.

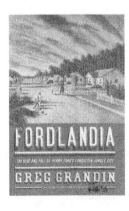

90. *Fordlandia: The Rise and Fall of Henry Ford's Forgotten Jungle City.* Written by Greg Grandin. (Metropolitan Books, 2009.) Greg Grandin, a professor of Latin American history at New York University, provides the first comprehensive account of Henry Ford's failed effort to transform part of the Brazilian rain forest into a Ford company town. This quixotic effort, spanning 1927 to 1945, began as a plan to establish a rubber plantation, but it evolved into a kind of social experiment to re-create small-town America. Leaf blight and the arrival of synthetic rubbers forced

Ford to abandon his colony but not before he threw millions of dollars into an infrastructure to support such amenities as golf courses, square dancing, and ice-cream shops. This is a fascinating story of the folly of applying techniques of mass production to a complex and unyielding jungle ecosystem and of trying to reclaim a quaint, bygone way of life that Ford's own industrial revolution undermined in America.

91. *Thinking, Fast and Slow.* Written by Daniel Kahneman. (Farrar, Straus & Giroux, 2011.) In this landmark book, Nobel Prize winner Daniel Kahneman lays bare the psychological mechanisms that control how and why we make the choices we make. The book summarizes a career's worth of experimental research, often in collaboration with Amos Tversky. Irrationality is the book's central concern, and he explains it as an interplay and dichotomy between two mental systems. The first system is fast, automatic, intuitive, instinctive, and emotional; the second is slower, more deliberative, calculating, logical, and infrequent. "Intelligence is not only the ability to reason; it is also the ability to find relevant material in memory and to deploy attention when needed," advises Kahneman. Readers will be immediately attracted to this book and then, over time, recognize its relevance to both their professional and personal lives.

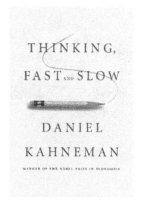

92. *The Origin of Species.* Written by Charles Darwin. (Simon & Schuster, 2008.) First published in 1859, Darwin's *The Origin of Species* is one of the most consequential books in human history. It lays out the theory of evolution by natural selection, with its branching model of common descent, and is the uniting framework of all the life sciences. Darwin powerfully explains the diversity of living organisms and how they adapt to their environment. Although the theory of evolution is accepted as fact by the scientific world, it continues to be contested for religious reasons, mostly in the United States. This groundbreaking book fundamentally redefined our

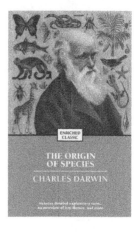

understanding of the nature of humankind and its place in the natural world.

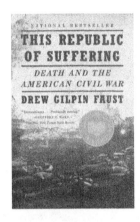

93. *This Republic of Suffering: Death and the American Civil War.* Written by Drew Gilpin Faust. (Knopf, 2008.) "The United States embarked on a new relationship with death, entering into a civil war that proved bloodier than any other conflict in American history," writes Harvard University president Drew Gilpin Faust. "The number of soldiers who died between 1861 and 1865, an estimated 620,000, is approximately equal to the total American fatalities in the Revolution, the War of 1812, the Mexican War, the Spanish-American War, World War I, World War II, and the Korean War combined." Fashioning her cogent story from a copious volume of letters and other Civil War documentation, Faust describes how the bereaved survivors of the war coped with the unprecedented carnage, both in its immediate aftermath and afterward, exploring how the suffering transformed American society, culture, and politics.

94. *The Beauty Myth: How Images of Beauty Are Used against Women.* Written by Naomi Wolf. (Harper Perennial, 2002.) The basic thesis of *The Beauty Myth* is that even as women have gained power and prominence in society, they have been forced to adhere to unattainable standards of physical beauty. "More women have more money and power and scope and legal recognition than we have ever had before," Naomi Wolf writes, "but in terms of how we feel about ourselves physically, we may actually be worse off than our unliberated grandmothers." Fueled by a still patriarchal society and the multibillion-dollar fashion and cosmetic industries, Wolf discusses how the beauty myth impacts the workplace, mass media, religion, sex, violence against women, and eating disorders. *The Beauty Myth* is an important call for women's liberation and the freedom of women to accept their bodies and faces as they are.

95. *The Right Stuff.* Written by Tom Wolfe. (Picador, 2007.) Before the original 1979 publication of *The Right Stuff,* few people really understood the inner drive and courage of the first American astronauts that constituted Project Mercury, NASA's first manned space-flight program. Wolfe's extensively researched book contrasts the Mercury Seven—Scott Carpenter, Gordon Cooper, John Glenn, Gus Grissom, Wally Schirra, Alan Shepard, and Deke Slayton—with legendary military test pilots such as Chuck Yeager and surveys the critical aspects of their training and mission. Against the backdrop of a desperate space race with the Soviet Union, Wolfe profiles this remarkable fraternity of contemporary warriors in what is surely the best book about the early adventures of the American space program.

96. *The Tipping Point: How Little Things Can Make a Big Difference.* Written by Malcolm Gladwell. (Back Bay Books, 2002.) Based on his considerable research into many different fields, Malcolm Gladwell has identified the key factors that determine whether a particular trend will "tip" into exponential popularity. "Ideas and products and messages and behaviors spread like viruses," writes the well-known journalist. The processes and mechanisms by which some trends sped like wildfire are amazingly similar and quite amenable to analysis. Gladwell has three rules: the "Law of the Few," the "Stickiness Factor," and the "Power of Context," and he argues that they can explain everything from the popularity of teenage smoking to the resurgent interest in Hush Puppies shoes. Readers may be left wondering if Gladwell knew that the publication of his very popular book would illustrate the very patterns he described.

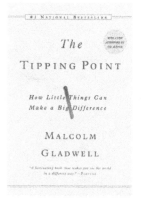

97. *Travels in Siberia*. Written by Ian Frazier. (Farrar, Straus & Giroux, 2010.) Siberia occupies three-quarters of Russian territory but just a sliver of its population. In America's mind, Siberia is a vast, frigid, and hostile wilderness that one is exiled to for punishment. So naturally, *New Yorker* journalist and author Ian Frazier took several road trips there over a 16-year period to probe its bleak history and produce a travelogue. Frazier, a gifted writer and humorist who was once on the staff of the *Harvard Lampoon*, proves he is worthy of the challenge by producing a nonfiction masterpiece. *Travels in Siberia* is both fun and soberly informative, as suggested by nearly 40 pages of endnotes and bibliography. Among Frazier's observations is his discovery that there are no historical markers to acknowledge what happened in the Siberian death camps.

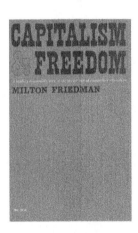

98. *Capitalism and Freedom*. Written by Milton Friedman. (University of Chicago Press, 1968.) Winner of the Nobel Prize, Milton Friedman was the most influential economist of the latter half of the 20th century, and *Capitalism and Freedom* is his magnum opus. This influential book promotes the virtues of the free market and limited government and advocates for the adoption of a flat income tax, free floating exchange rates, the abolishment of medical licenses, a volunteer military, and education vouchers. Friedman's central thesis is that political freedom requires economic freedom and the government should limit itself to protecting property rights and enforcing law and order, ideas which have been widely embraced by conservatives and libertarians.

99. *A Walk in the Woods: Rediscovering America on the Appalachian Trail*. Written by Bill Bryson. (HarperCollins, 1998.) Part adventure, part commentary, and part comedy, this travel-writing classic describes Bill Bryson's attempt, accompanied by his old college roommate, to hike the 2,100-mile Appalachian Trail. Heading north from Georgia, the pair soon realize how tough this trek is gong to be. They shed supplies and equipment to lighten their loads, skip big parts of the trail, and, like most people who attempt the difficult walk from Georgia to Maine, ultimately do not finish. But along the way, Bryson describes lots of interesting characters he meets on the trail, interspersed with discussions of the trail's history and ecology. There is no better comic story of men totally unprepared to engage the American wilderness than *A Walk in the Woods*.

100. *Black Hawk Down: A Story of Modern War.* Written by Mark Bowden. (Signet Books, 1999.) This classic of war reporting provides a dramatic, moment-by-moment account of the Battle of Mogadishu, one of American history's most intense clashes, pitting elite U.S. commandos against an overwhelming number of local militia. When their Blackhawk helicopter was shot down in 1993, 99 soldiers were trapped overnight in the African city, surrounded by thousands of gunmen. Journalist Mark Bowden describes how the U.S. soldiers got into such dire straits and how they heroically fought their way out. He based his book on hundreds of interviews and mountains of official documents, and he succeeds in conveying both the terror and chaos of combat. This military debacle, resulting in the deaths of 18 heroic American soldiers and upward of 500 Somalis, led to the resignation of Les Aspin, President Clinton's secretary of defense, and the withdrawal of troops from Somalia.

CHAPTER 6

Special Interests

At long last, the educational spotlight is shining on nonfiction.

—Kathleen Odean

Adventure

PRESCHOOLERS

Little Dog Lost: The True Story of a Brave Dog Named Baltic. Written and illustrated by Mônica Carnesi.
Redwoods. Written and illustrated by Jason Chin.

EARLY READERS

Astronaut Handbook. Written and illustrated by Meghan McCarthy.
Balto and the Great Race. Written by Elizabeth Cody Kimmel. Illustrated by Nora Koerber.
The Chiru of High Tibet. Written by Jacqueline Briggs Martin. Illustrated by Linda Wingerter.
Coral Reefs. Written and illustrated by Jason Chin.
Moonshot: The Flight of Apollo 11. Written and illustrated by Brian Floca.
One Giant Leap. Written by Robert Burleigh. Illustrated by Mike Wimmer.

MIDDLE READERS

Adventure beneath the Sea: Living in an Underwater Science Station. Written by Kenneth Mallory. Illustrated by Brian Skerry.
Amelia Lost: The Life and Disappearance of Amelia Earhart. Written by Candace Fleming.
Around the World. Written and illustrated by Matt Phelan.
Bomb: The Race to Build—and Steal—the World's Most Dangerous Weapon. Written by Steve Sheinkin.
Far from Shore: Chronicles of an Open Ocean Voyage. Written by Sophie Webb.
Into the Unknown: How Great Explorers Found Their Way by Land, Sea, and Air. Written by Stuart Ross. Illustrated by Stephen Biesty.
The Journey That Saved Curious George: The True Wartime Escape of Margret and H. A. Rey. Written by Louise Borden. Illustrated by Allan Drummond.
My Season with Penguins: An Antarctic Journal. Written and illustrated by Sophie Webb.
Queen of the Falls. Written and illustrated by Chris van Allsburg.
Shipwrecked! The True Adventures of a Japanese Boy. Written by Rhoda Blumberg.

YOUNG ADULTS

The Impossible Rescue: The True Story of an Amazing Arctic Adventure. Written by Martin W. Sandler.

The Mighty Mars Rovers: The Incredible Adventures of Spirit *and* Opportunity. Written by Elizabeth Rusch.

The Notorious Benedict Arnold: A True Story of Adventure, Heroism and Treachery. Written by Steve Sheinkin.

The Quest for the Tree Kangaroo: An Expedition to the Cloud Forest of New Guinea. Written by Sy Montgomery. Illustrated by Nic Bishop.

Shipwreck at the Bottom of the World: The Extraordinary True Story of Shackleton and the Endurance. Written by Jennifer Armstrong.

Sir Walter Raleigh and the Quest for El Dorado. Written by Marc Aronson.

ADULTS

The Lost City of Z: A Tale of Deadly Obsession in the Amazon. Written by David Grann.

The Right Stuff. Written by Tom Wolfe.

African American Experience

PRESCHOOLERS

Dave the Potter: Artist, Poet, Slave. Written by Laban Carrick Hill. Illustrated by Bryan Collier.

Harlem's Little Blackbird. Written by Renée Watson. Illustrated by Christian Robinson.

The Story of Ruby Bridges. Written by Robert Coles. Illustrated by George Ford.

Underground: Finding the Light to Freedom. Written and illustrated by Shane W. Evans.

EARLY READERS

Black Jack: The Ballad of Jack Johnson. Written by Charles R. Smith Jr. Illustrated by Shane W. Evans.

Harriet and the Promised Land. Written and illustrated by Jacob Lawrence.

I Have a Dream. Written by Martin Luther King Jr. Illustrated by Kadir Nelson.

It Jes' Happened: When Bill Traylor Started to Draw. Written by Don Tate. Illustrated by Gregory Christie.

A Nation's Hope: The Story of Boxing Legend Joe Louis. Written by Matt De La Pena. Illustrated by Kadir Nelson.

A Weed Is a Flower: The Life of George Washington Carver. Written and illustrated by Aliki.

When Marian Sang: The True Recital of Marian Anderson. Written by Pam Munoz Ryan. Illustrated by Brian Selznick.

Wilma Unlimited: How Wilma Rudolph Became the World's Fastest Woman. Written by Kathleen Krull. Illustrated by David Diaz.

MIDDLE READERS

Abraham Lincoln and Frederick Douglass: The Story behind an American Friendship. Written by Russell Freedman.

Discovering Black America: From the Age of Exploration to the Twenty-First Century. Written by Linda Tarrant-Reid.

A Dream of Freedom: The Civil Rights Movement from 1954 to 1968. Written by Diane McWhorter.

Freedom Riders: John Lewis and Jim Zwerg on the Front Lines of the Civil Rights Movement. Written by Ann Bausum.

Freedom Walkers: The Story of the Montgomery Bus Boycott. Written by Russell Freedman.

George Washington Carver. Written by Tonya Bolden.

Hand in Hand: Ten Black Men Who Changed America. Written by Andrea Davis Pinkney. Illustrated by Brian Pinkney.

Harriet Tubman: Conductor on the Underground Railroad. Written by Ann Petry.

Heart and Soul: The Story of America and African Americans. Written and illustrated by Kadir Nelson.

Seven Miles to Freedom: The Robert Smalls Story. Written by Janet Halfmann. Illustrated by Duane Smith.

Sit-In: How Four Friends Stood Up by Sitting Down. Written by Andrea Davis Pinkney. Illustrated by Brian Pinkney.

Spirit Seeker: John Coltrane's Musical Journey. Written by Gary Golio. Illustrated by Rudy Gutierrez.

We Are the Ship: The Story of Negro League Baseball. Written and illustrated by Kadir Nelson.

YOUNG ADULTS

The Autobiography of Malcolm X. Written by Malcolm X and Alex Haley.

Bad Boy. Written by Walter Dean Myers.

Birmingham Sunday. Written by Larry Dane Brimner.

Claudette Colvin: Twice toward Justice. Written by Phillip Hoose.

Getting Away with Murder: The True Story of the Emmett Till Case. Written by Chris Crowe.

Harlem Stomp! A Cultural History of the Harlem Renaissance. Written by Laban Carrick Hill.

I Know Why the Caged Bird Sings. Written by Maya Angelou.

Marching for Freedom: Walk Together Children and Don't You Grow Weary. Written by Elizabeth Partridge.

Miles to Go for Freedom: Segregation and Civil Rights in the Jim Crow Years. Written by Linda Barrett Osborne.

Narrative of the Life of Frederick Douglass: An American Slave. Written by Frederick Douglass.

Spies of Mississippi: The True Story of the Spy Network That Tried to Destroy the Civil Rights Movement. Written by Rick Bowers.

Sugar Changed the World: A Story of Magic, Spice, Slavery, Freedom, and Science. Written by Marc Aronson and Marina Budhos.

They Called Themselves the KKK: The Birth of an American Terrorist Group. Written by Susan Campbell Bartoletti.

We've Got a Job: The 1963 Birmingham Children's March. Written by Cynthia Levinson.

ADULTS

The Hemingses of Monticello: An American Family. Written by Annette Gordon-Reed.

Malcolm X: A Life of Reinvention. Written by Manning Marable.

Parting the Waters: America in the King Years, 1954–63. Written by Taylor Branch.

The Souls of Black Folks. Written by W. E. B. Du Bois.

The Warmth of Other Suns: The Epic Story of America's Great Migration. Written by Isabel Wilkerson.

Animal Rescue

PRESCHOOLERS

Leo the Snow Leopard: The True Story of an Amazing Rescue. Written by Craig Hatkoff. Illustrated by Isabella Hatkoff.

Little Dog Lost: The True Story of a Brave Dog Named Baltic. Written and illustrated by Mônica Carnesi.

Pale Male: Citizen Hawk of New York City. Written by Janet Schulman. Illustrated by Meilo So.

Slow Down for Manatees. Written and illustrated by Jim Arnosky.

Two Bobbies: A True Story of Hurricane Katrina, Friendship, and Survival. Written by Kirby Larson and Mary Nethery. Illustrated by Jean Cassels.

Winter's Tail: How One Little Dolphin Learned to Swim Again. Written by Craig Hatkoff, Juliana Hatkoff, and Isabella Hatkoff.

Animals

PRESCHOOLERS

African Animal Alphabet. Written by Beverly Joubert and Dereck Joubert.

Alex the Parrot: No Ordinary Bird. Written by Stephanie Spinner. Illustrated by Meilo So.

Animal Dads. Written by Sneed B. Collard III. Illustrated by Steve Jenkins.

Biggest, Strongest, Fastest. Written and illustrated by Steve Jenkins.

Elephants Can Paint, Too! Written and illustrated by Katya Arnold.

Hachiko. Written by Pamela S. Turner. Illustrated by Yan Nascimbene.

How Many Baby Pandas? Written and illustrated by Sandra Markle.

In the Wild. Written by David Elliott. Illustrated by Holly Meade.

Just One Bite. Written by Lola Schaefer. Illustrated by Geoff Waring.

Koko's Kitten. Written by Francine Patterson. Illustrated by Ronald H. Cohn.

Life-Size Zoo: From Tiny Rodents to Gigantic Elephants, An Actual Size Animal Encyclopedia. Written by Teruyuki Komiya. Illustrated by Toyofumi Fukuda.

May I Pet Your Dog? The How-to Guide for Kids Meeting Dogs (and Dogs Meeting Kids). Written by Stephanie Calmenson. Illustrated by Jan Ormerod.

Meet the Dogs of Bedlam Farm. Written and illustrated by Jon Katz.

Meet the Howlers! Written by April Pulley Sayre. Illustrated by Woody Miller.

My First Day. Written by Steve Jenkins and Robin Page. Illustrated by Steve Jenkins.

My Visit to the Zoo. Written and illustrated by Aliki.

Never Smile at a Monkey: And 17 Other Important Things to Remember. Written and illustrated by Steve Jenkins.

On the Farm. Written by David Elliott. Illustrated by Holly Meade.

Out of Sight. Written by Francesco Pittau and Bernadette Gervais.

Over and Under the Snow. Written by Kate Messner.

Rosie, a Visiting Dog's Story. Written by Stephanie Calmenson. Illustrated by Justin Sutcliffe.

What Do You Do with a Tail like This? Written by Steve Jenkins and Robin Page.

Where in the Wild? Camouflaged Creatures Concealed . . . and Revealed. Written by David M. Schwartz and Yael Schy. Illustrated by Dwight Kuhn.

Zoo Borns! Zoo Babies from around the World. Written by Andrew Bleiman and Chris Eastland.

EARLY READERS

Actual Size. Written and illustrated by Steve Jenkins.

Animal Talk: How Animals Communicate through Sight, Sound and Smell. Written by Etta Kaner. Illustrated by Greg Douglas.

Around One Cactus: Owls, Bats and Leaping Rats. Written by Anthony D. Fredericks. Illustrated by Jennifer DiRubbio.

Can We Save the Tiger? Written by Martin Jenkins. Illustrated by Vicky White.

The Chiru of High Tibet. Written by Jacqueline Briggs Martin. Illustrated by Linda Wingerter.

Dogs and Cats. Written and illustrated by Steve Jenkins.

Dolphin Baby! Written by Nicola Davies. Illustrated by Brita Granström.

An Egg Is Quiet. Written by Dianna Hutts Aston. Illustrated by Sylvia Long.

Exploding Ants: Amazing Facts about How Animals Adapt. Written by Joanne Settel.

Face to Face with Lions. Written by Beverly and Dereck Joubert.

Guess What Is Growing inside This Egg. Written and illustrated by Mia Posada.

How to Clean a Hippopotamus: A Look at Unusual Animal Partnerships. Written by Steve Jenkins and Robin Page. Illustrated by Steve Jenkins.

One Tiny Turtle. Written by Nicola Davies. Illustrated by Jane Chapman.

Owen and Mzee: The True Story of a Remarkable Friendship. Written by Isabella Hatkoff, Craig Hatkoff, and Paula Kahumbu. Illustrated by Peter Greste.

Polar Bears. Written and illustrated by Mark Newman.

MIDDLE READERS

Animals Up Close. Written and illustrated by Igor Siwanowicz.

Dogs on Duty: Soldiers' Best Friends on the Battlefield and Beyond. Written by Dorothy Hinshaw Patent.

The Elephant Scientist. Written by Caitlin O'Connell and Donna M. Jackson. Illustrated by Timothy Rodwell.

Extreme Animals: The Toughest Creatures on Earth. Written by Nicola Davies.

The Horse and the Plains Indians: A Powerful Partnership. Written by Dorothy Hinshaw Patent. Illustrated by William Muñoz.

Ubiquitous: Celebrating Nature's Survivors. Written by Joyce Sidman. Illustrated by Beckie Prange.

YOUNG ADULTS

The Bat Scientists. Written by Mary Kay Carson. Illustrated by Tom Uhlman.
A Life in the Wild: George Schaller's Struggle to Save the Last Great Beasts. Written by Pamela S. Turner.
The Manatee Scientists: Saving Vulnerable Species. Written by Peter Lourie.
The Quest for the Tree Kangaroo: An Expedition to the Cloud Forest of New Guinea. Written by Sy Montgomery. Illustrated by Nic Bishop.
Wild Horse Scientists. Written by Kay Frydenborg.

ADULTS

The Origin of Species. Written by Charles Darwin.

Art

PRESCHOOLERS

Dave the Potter: Artist, Poet, Slave. Written by Laban Carrick Hill. Illustrated by Bryan Collier.
Elephants Can Paint, Too! Written and illustrated by Katya Arnold.
My Painted House, My Friendly Chicken and Me. Written by Maya Angelou. Illustrated by Margaret Courtney-Clarke.
Museum ABC. Written by Metropolitan Museum of Art.

EARLY READERS

The Boy on Fairfield Street: How Ted Geisel Grew Up to Become Dr. Seuss. Written by Kathleen Krull. Illustrated by Steve Johnson and Lou Fancher.
The Boy Who Drew Birds: A Story of John James Audubon. Written by Jacqueline Davies. Illustrated by Melissa Sweet.
Dinosaurs of Waterhouse Hawkins: An Illuminating History of Mr. Waterhouse Hawkins, Artist and Lecturer. Written by Barbara Kerley. Illustrated by Brian Selznick.

Dreaming Up: A Celebration of Building. Written and illustrated by Christy Hale.

Frida. Written by Jonah Winter. Illustrated by Ana Juan.

It Jes' Happened: When Bill Traylor Started to Draw. Written by Don Tate. Illustrated by Gregory Christie.

MIDDLE READERS

Action Jackson. Written by Jan Greenberg and Sandra Jordan. Illustrated by Robert Andrew Parker.

Boys of Steel: The Creators of Superman. Written by Marc Tyler Nobleman. Illustrated by Ross Macdonald.

Built to Last: Building America's Amazing Bridges, Dams, Tunnels, and Skyscrapers. Written by George Sullivan.

Cathedral: The Story of Its Construction. Written and illustrated by David Macaulay.

Chuck Close Face Book. Written by Chuck Close.

Drawing from Memory. Written and illustrated by Allen Say.

The Emperor's Silent Army: Terracotta Warriors of Ancient China. Written by Jane O'Connor.

For the Birds: The Life of Roger Tory Peterson. Written by Peggy Thomas. Illustrated by Laura Jacques.

Harlem Stomp! A Cultural History of the Harlem Renaissance. Written by Laban Carrick Hill.

Michelangelo. Written and illustrated by Diane Stanley.

The Wall: Growing Up behind the Iron Curtain. Written by Peter Sis.

YOUNG READERS

Andy Warhol: Prince of Pop. Written by Jan Greenberg and Sandra Jordan.

Terezín: Voices from the Holocaust. Written by Ruth Thomson.

Vincent van Gogh: Portrait of an Artist. Written by Jan Greenberg and Sandra Jordan.

ADULTS

Just Kids. Written by Patti Smith.

Bilingual Books

PRESCHOOLERS

My Shapes/Mis Formas. Written and illustrated by Rebecca Emberley.

EARLY READERS

Pelé, King of Soccer/El rey del fútbol. Written by Monica Brown. Illustrated by Rudy Gutiérrez.

Sonia Sotomayor: A Judge Grows in the Bronx/La juez que creció en el Bronx. Written by Jonah Winter. Illustrated by Edel Rodriguez.

Biography

PRESCHOOLERS

The Boy Who Loved Math: The Improbable Life of Paul Erdös. Written by Deborah Heiligman. Illustrated by LeUyen Pham.

Harlem's Little Blackbird. Written by Renée Watson. Illustrated by Christian Robinson.

Here Come the Girl Scouts! The Amazing All-True Story of Juliette "Daisy" Gordon Low and Her Great Adventure. Written by Shana Corey. Illustrated by Hadley Hooper.

Me . . . Jane. Written and illustrated by Patrick McDonnell.

Pop! The Invention of Bubble Gum. Written and illustrated by Meghan McCarthy.

Strong Man: The Story of Charles Atlas. Written and illustrated by Meghan McCarthy.

EARLY READERS

Black Jack: The Ballad of Jack Johnson. Written by Charles R. Smith Jr. Illustrated by Shane W. Evans.

The Boy on Fairfield Street: How Ted Geisel Grew Up to Become Dr. Seuss. Written by Kathleen Krull. Illustrated by Steve Johnson and Lou Fancher.

The Boy Who Drew Birds: A Story of John James Audubon. Written by Jacqueline Davies. Illustrated by Melissa Sweet.

The Boy Who Invented TV: The Story of Philo Farnsworth. Written by Kathleen Krull. Illustrated by Greg Couch.

Dinosaurs of Waterhouse Hawkins: An Illuminating History of Mr. Waterhouse Hawkins, Artist and Lecturer. Written by Barbara Kerley. Illustrated by Brian Selznick.

Eleanor, Quiet No More. Written by Doreen Rappaport. Illustrated by Gary Kelley.

The Extraordinary Mark Twain (according to Susy). Written by Barbara Kerley. Illustrated by Edwin Fotheringham.

Fifty Cents and a Dream: Young Booker T. Washington. Written by Jabari Asim. Illustrated by Bryan Collier.

Frida. Written by Jonah Winter. Illustrated by Ana Juan.

Harvesting Hope: The Story of Cesar Chavez. Written by Kathleen Krull. Illustrated by Yuyi Morales.

It Jes' Happened: When Bill Traylor Started to Draw. Written by Don Tate. Illustrated by Gregory Christie.

Life in the Ocean: The Story of Oceanographer Sylvia Earle. Written and illustrated by Claire A. Nivola.

Looking at Lincoln. Written and illustrated by Maira Kalman.

Martin's Big Words: The Life of Dr. Martin Luther King, Jr. Written by Doreen Rappaport. Illustrated by Bryan Collier.

Mermaid Queen: The Spectacular True Story of Annette Kellerman, Who Swam Her Way to Fame, Fortune and Swimsuit History. Written by Shana Corey. Illustrated by Edwin Fotheringham.

Monsieur Marceau: Actor without Words. Written by Leda Schubert. Illustrated by Gerard DuBois.

A Nation's Hope: The Story of Boxing Legend Joe Louis. Written by Matt De La Peña. Illustrated by Kadir Nelson.

Noah Webster and His Words. Written by Jeri Chase Ferris. Illustrated by Vincent X. Kirsch.

Pelé, King of Soccer/El rey del fútbol. Written by Monica Brown. Illustrated by Rudy Gutiérrez.

Roberto Clemente: Pride of the Pittsburgh Pirates. Written by Jonah Winter. Illustrated by Raúl Colón.

Snowflake Bentley. Written by Jacqueline Briggs Martin. Illustrated by Mary Azarian.

So You Want to Be President? Written by Judith St. George. Illustrated by David Small.

Soar, Elinor! Written by Tami Lewis Brown. Illustrated by François Roca.

Sonia Sotomayor: A Judge Grows in the Bronx/La juez que creció en el Bronx. Written by Jonah Winter. Illustrated by Edel Rodriguez.

The Story of Ruby Bridges. Written by Robert Coles. Illustrated by George Ford.

There Goes Ted Williams: The Greatest Hitter Who Ever Lived. Written and illustrated by Matt Tavares.

Those Rebels, John and Tom. Written by Barbara Kerley. Illustrated by Edwin Fotheringham.

A Weed Is a Flower: The Life of George Washington Carver. Written and illustrated by Aliki.

What Presidents Are Made Of. Written and illustrated by Hanoch Piven.

What to Do about Alice? How Alice Roosevelt Broke the Rules, Charmed the World, and Drove Her Father Teddy Crazy! Written by Barbara Kerley. Illustrated by Edwin Fotheringham.

When Marian Sang: The True Recital of Marian Anderson. Written by Pam Muñoz Ryan. Illustrated by Brian Selznick.

Wilma Unlimited: How Wilma Rudolph Became the World's Fastest Woman. Written by Kathleen Krull. Illustrated by David Diaz.

You Forgot Your Skirt, Amelia Bloomer! Written by Shana Corey. Illustrated by Chesley Mclaren.

You Never Heard of Sandy Koufax?! Written by Jonah Winter. Illustrated by Andre Carrilho.

MIDDLE READERS

Abraham Lincoln and Frederick Douglass: The Story behind an American Friendship. Written by Russell Freedman.

Action Jackson. Written by Jan Greenberg and Sandra Jordan. Illustrated by Robert Andrew Parker.

Airborne: A Photobiography of Wilbur and Orville Wright. Written by Mary Collins.

Almost Astronauts: 13 Women Who Dared to Dream. Written by Tanya Lee Stone.

Amelia Lost: The Life and Disappearance of Amelia Earhart. Written by Candace Fleming.

And Then What Happened, Paul Revere? Written by Jean Fritz.

Ben Franklin's Almanac: Being a True Account of the Good Gentleman's Life. Written by Candace Fleming.

Black Elk's Vision: A Lakota Story. Written by S. D. Nelson.

Boys of Steel: The Creators of Superman. Written by Marc Tyler Nobleman. Illustrated by Ross MacDonald.

Candy Bomber: The Story of the Berlin Airlift's "Chocolate Pilot." Written by Michael O. Tunnell.

Chuck Close Face Book. Written by Chuck Close.

The Day-Glo Brothers. Written by Chris Barton. Illustrated by Tony Persiani.

Drawing from Memory. Written and illustrated by Allen Say.

Eleanor Roosevelt: A Life of Discovery. Written by Russell Freedman.

Electric Ben: The Amazing Life and Times of Benjamin Franklin. Written and illustrated by Robert Byrd.

The Endless Steppe: Growing Up in Siberia. Written by Esther Hautzig.

Escape! The Story of the Great Houdini. Written by Sid Fleischman.

For the Birds: The Life of Roger Tory Peterson. Written by Peggy Thomas. Illustrated by Laura Jacques.

George vs. George: The American Revolution as Seen from Both Sides. Written and illustrated by Rosalyn Schanzer.

George Washington Carver. Written by Tonya Bolden.

The Great and Only Barnum: The Tremendous, Stupendous Life of Showman P. T. Barnum. Written by Candace Fleming. Illustrated by Ray Fenwick.

Hand in Hand: Ten Black Men Who Changed America. Written by Andrea Davis Pinkney. Illustrated by Brian Pinkney.

Harriet Tubman: Conductor on the Underground Railroad. Written by Ann Petry.

How Angel Peterson Got His Name. Written by Gary Paulsen.

Jimi: Sounds Like a Rainbow: A Story of the Young Jimi Hendrix. Written by Gary Golio. Illustrated by Javaka Steptoe.

John Muir: America's First Environmentalist. Written by Kathryn Lasky. Illustrated by Stan Fellows.

The Journey That Saved Curious George: The True Wartime Escape of Margret and H. A. Rey. Written by Louise Borden. Illustrated by Allan Drummond.

Knucklehead: Tall Tales and Mostly True Stories about Growing Up Scieszka. Written and illustrated by Jon Scieszka.

Kubla Khan: The Emperor of Everything. Written by Kathleen Krull. Illustrated by Robert Byrd.

Lincoln: A Photobiography. Written by Russell Freedman.

Michelangelo. Written and illustrated by Diane Stanley.

Nurse, Soldier, Spy: The Story of Sarah Edmonds, a Civil War Hero. Written by Marissa Moss.

Phineas Gage: A Gruesome but True Story about Brain Science. Written by John Fleischman.

Queen of the Falls. Written and illustrated by Chris van Allsburg.

Sadako and the Thousand Paper Cranes. Written by Eleanor Coerr. Illustrated by Ronald Himler.

Seven Miles to Freedom: The Robert Smalls Story. Written by Janet Halfmann. Illustrated by Duane Smith.

Shipwrecked! The True Adventures of a Japanese Boy. Written by Rhoda Blumberg.

Spirit Seeker: John Coltrane's Musical Journey. Written by Gary Golio. Illustrated by Rudy Gutierrez.

Temple Grandin: How the Girl Who Loved Cows Embraced Autism and Changed the World. Written by Sy Montgomery and Temple Grandin.

The Wall: Growing Up behind the Iron Curtain. Written by Peter Sis.

William Shakespeare and the Globe. Written and illustrated by Aliki.

YOUNG ADULTS

21: The Story of Roberto Clemente. Written and illustrated by Wilfred Santiago.

The Amazing Harry Kellar: Great American Magician. Written by Gail Jarrow.

Andy Warhol: Prince of Pop. Written by Jan Greenberg and Sandra Jordan.

The Autobiography of Benjamin Franklin. Written by Benjamin Franklin.

The Autobiography of Malcolm X. Written by Malcolm X and Alex Haley.

Bad Boy. Written by Walter Dean Myers.

Charles and Emma: The Darwins' Leap of Faith. Written by Deborah Heiligman.

Charles Dickens and the Street Children of London. Written by Andrea Warren.

Claudette Colvin: Twice toward Justice. Written by Phillip Hoose.

The Diary of a Young Girl. Written by Anne Frank.

Escape from Saigon: How a Vietnam War Orphan Became an American Boy. Written by Andrea Warren.

Feynman. Written by Jim Ottaviani. Illustrated by Leland Myrick.

Freedom Riders: John Lewis and Jim Zwerg on the Front Lines of the Civil Rights Movement. Written by Ann Bausum.

George Washington and the Founding of a Nation. Written by Albert Marrin.

Good Brother, Bad Brother: The Story of Edwin Booth and John Wilkes Booth. Written by James Cross Giblin.

Hole in My Life. Written by Jack Gantos.

I Am Scout: The Biography of Harper Lee. Written by Charles J. Shields.

I Know Why the Caged Bird Sings. Written by Maya Angelou.

Janis Joplin: Rise Up Singing. Written by Ann Angel.

John Lennon: All I Want Is the Truth. Written by Elizabeth Partridge.

King of the Mild Frontier: An Ill-Advised Autobiography. Written by Chris Crutcher.

Lafayette and the American Revolution. Written by Russell Freedman.

The Life and Death of Adolf Hitler. Written by James Cross Giblin.

A Life in the Wild: George Schaller's Struggle to Save the Last Great Beasts. Written by Pamela S. Turner.

The Lincolns: A Scrapbook Look at Abraham and Mary. Written by Candace Fleming.

A Long Way Gone: Memoirs of a Boy Soldier. Written by Ishmael Beah.

The Longitude Prize. Written by Joan Dash. Illustrated by Dusan Petricic.

Lost Boy, Lost Girl: Escaping Civil War in Sudan. Written by John Bul Dau.

Narrative of the Life of Frederick Douglass: An American Slave. Written by Frederick Douglass.

Night. Written by Elie Wiesel.

The Notorious Benedict Arnold: A True Story of Adventure, Heroism, and Treachery. Written by Steve Sheinkin.

The Poet Slave of Cuba: A Biography of Juan Francisco Manzano. Written by Margarita Engle. Illustrated by Sean Qualls.

Profiles in Courage. Written by John F. Kennedy.

Sir Charlie Chaplin: The Funniest Man in the World. Written by Sid Fleischman.

Sir Walter Raleigh and the Quest for El Dorado. Written by Marc Aronson.

Something out of Nothing: Marie Curie and Radium. Written by Carla Killough McClafferty.

Soul Surfer: A True Story of Faith, Family, and Fighting to Get Back on the Board. Written by Bethany Hamilton, Sheryl Berk, and Rick Bundschuh.

Tasting the Sky: A Palestinian Childhood. Written by Ibtisam Barakat.

This Land Was Made for You and Me: The Life and Songs of Woody Guthrie. Written by Elizabeth Partridge.

To Dance: A Ballerina's Graphic Novel. Written by Siena Cherson Siegel. Illustrated by Mark Siegel.

Vincent van Gogh: Portrait of an Artist. Written by Jan Greenberg and Sandra Jordan.

The Wright Brothers: How They Invented the Airplane. Written by Russell Freedman.

ADULTS

The Age of Wonder: How the Romantic Generation Discovered the Beauty and Terror of Science. Written by Richard Holmes.

Angela's Ashes: A Memoir. Written by Frank McCourt.

Catherine the Great: Portrait of a Woman. Written by Robert K. Massie.

Cheever: A Life. Written by Blake Bailey.

Cleopatra: A Life. Written by Stacy Schiff.

Desert Solitaire: A Season in the Wilderness. Written by Edward Abbey.

Destiny of the Republic: A Tale of Madness, Medicine and the Murder of a President. Written by Candice Millard.

The Education of Henry Adams. Written by Henry Adams.
The First Tycoon: The Epic Life of Cornelius Vanderbilt. Written by T. J. Stiles.
A Heartbreaking Work of Staggering Genius. Written by Dave Eggers.
John Adams. Written by David McCullough.
Just Kids. Written by Patti Smith.
Lit: A Memoir. Written by Mary Karr.
Malcolm X: A Life of Reinvention. Written by Manning Marable.
Nixonland: The Rise of a President and the Fracturing of America. Written by Rick Perlstein.
On Writing: A Memoir of the Craft. Written by Stephen King.
The Passage of Power: The Years of Lyndon Johnson. Written by Robert Caro.
The Silent Woman: Sylvia Plath and Ted Hughes. Written by Janet Malcolm.
Speak, Memory: An Autobiography Revisited. Written by Vladimir Nabokov.
Steve Jobs. Written by Walter Isaacson.
A Supposedly Fun Thing I'll Never Do Again: Essays and Arguments. Written by David Foster Wallace.
The Swerve: How the World Became Modern. Written by Stephen Greenblatt.
Unbroken: A World War II Story of Survival, Resilience, and Redemption. Written by Laura Hillenbrand.

Birds

PRESCHOOLERS

About Hummingbirds: A Guide for Children. Written by Cathryn Sill. Illustrated by John Sill.
Bring On the Birds. Written and illustrated by Susan Stockdale.
The Emperor's Egg. Written by Martin Jenkins. Illustrated by Jane Chapman.
What Bluebirds Do. Written and illustrated by Pamela F. Kirby.

EARLY READERS

The Boy Who Drew Birds: A Story of John James Audubon. Written by Jacqueline Davies. Illustrated by Melissa Sweet.
Just Ducks! Written by Nicola Davies. Illustrated by Salvatore Rubbino.
Thunder Birds: Nature's Flying Predators. Written and illustrated by Jim Arnosky.
Vulture View. Written by April Pulley Sayre. Illustrated by Steve Jenkins.

MIDDLE READERS

For the Birds: The Life of Roger Tory Peterson. Written by Peggy Thomas. Illustrated by Laura Jacques.

Kakapo Rescue: Saving the World's Strangest Parrot. Written by Sy Montgomery. Illustrated by Nic Bishop.

Moonbird: A Year on the Wind with the Great Survivor B95. Written by Phillip Hoose.

My Season with Penguins: An Antarctic Journal. Written and illustrated by Sophie Webb.

YOUNG ADULTS

The Race to Save the Lord God Bird. Written by Phillip Hoose.

Business and Economics

PRESCHOOLERS

How Did That Get in My Lunchbox? The Story of Food. Written by Chris Butterworth. Illustrated by Lucia Gaggiotti.

Market! Written and illustrated by Ted Lewin.

An Orange in January. Written by Dianna Hutts Aston. Illustrated by Julie Maren.

Pop! The Invention of Bubble Gum. Written and illustrated by Meghan McCarthy.

EARLY READERS

All the Way to America: The Story of a Big Italian Family and a Little Shovel. Written and illustrated by Dan Yaccarino.

The Boy Who Invented TV: The Story of Philo Farnsworth. Written by Kathleen Krull. Illustrated by Greg Couch.

Harvesting Hope: The Story of Cesar Chavez. Written by Kathleen Krull. Illustrated by Yuyi Morales.

MIDDLE READERS

The Great and Only Barnum: The Tremendous, Stupendous Life of Showman P. T. Barnum. Written by Candace Fleming. Illustrated by Ray Fenwick.

YOUNG ADULTS

Flesh and Blood So Cheap: The Triangle Fire and Its Legacy. Written by Albert Marrin.
Sugar Changed the World: A Story of Magic, Spice, Slavery, Freedom, and Science. Written by Marc Aronson and Marina Budhos.

ADULTS

The Big Short: Inside the Doomsday Machine. Written by Michael Lewis.
Capitalism and Freedom. Written by Milton Friedman.
Fast Food Nation: The Dark Side of the All-American Meal. Written by Eric Schlosser.
The First Tycoon: The Epic Life of Cornelius Vanderbilt. Written by T. J. Stiles.
Fordlandia: The Rise and Fall of Henry Ford's Forgotten Jungle City. Written by Greg Grandin.
Freakonomics: A Rogue Economist Explores the Hidden Side of Everything. Written by Steven D. Levitt and Stephen J. Dubner.
The General Theory of Employment, Interest, and Money. Written by John Maynard Keynes.
Nickel and Dimed: On (Not) Getting By in America. Written by Barbara Ehrenreich.
Outliers: The Story of Success. Written by Malcolm Gladwell.
Silent Spring. Written by Rachel Carson.
Steve Jobs. Written by Walter Isaacson.
The Tipping Point: How Little Things Can Make a Big Difference. Written by Malcolm Gladwell.

Classics

YOUNG ADULTS

The Autobiography of Benjamin Franklin. Written by Benjamin Franklin.
The Autobiography of Malcolm X. Written by Malcolm X and Alex Haley.

Bury My Heart at Wounded Knee: An Indian History of the American West. Written by Dee Brown.

Common Sense, Rights of Man, and Other Essential Writings of Thomas Paine. Written by Thomas Paine.

Democracy in America. Written by Alexis de Tocqueville.

The Diary of a Young Girl. Written by Anne Frank.

The Federalist Papers. Written by Alexander Hamilton, James Madison, and John Jay.

I Know Why the Caged Bird Sings. Written by Maya Angelou.

Narrative of the Life of Frederick Douglass: An American Slave. Written by Frederick Douglass.

Night. Written by Elie Wiesel.

Profiles in Courage. Written by John F. Kennedy.

Walden and "Civil Disobedience." Written by Henry David Thoreau.

ADULTS

Anti-intellectualism in American Life. Written by Richard Hofstadter.

Capitalism and Freedom. Written by Milton Friedman.

The Double Helix: A Personal Account of the Discovery of the Structure of DNA. Written by James D. Watson.

The Education of Henry Adams. Written by Henry Adams.

The Electric Kool-Aid Acid Test. Written by Tom Wolfe.

The Elements of Style. Written by William Strunk Jr. and E. B. White.

The Feminine Mystique. Written by Betty Friedan.

The General Theory of Employment, Interest, and Money. Written by John Maynard Keynes.

The Holy Bible.

Homage to Catalonia. Written by George Orwell.

In Cold Blood. Written by Truman Capote.

The Origin of Species. Written by Charles Darwin.

A People's History of the United States: 1492 to Present. Written by Howard Zinn.

The Prince. Written by Niccolò Machiavelli.

A Room of One's Own. Written by Virginia Woolf.

Silent Spring. Written by Rachel Carson.

The Souls of Black Folks. Written by W. E. B. Du Bois.

Speak, Memory: An Autobiography Revisited. Written by Vladimir Nabokov.

The Structure of Scientific Revolutions. Written by Thomas S. Kuhn.

Concept Books

PRESCHOOLERS

African Animal Alphabet. Written by Beverly Joubert and Dereck Joubert.

Alphabeasties and Other Amazing Types. Written by Sharon Werner and Sarah Forss.

Fabulous Fishes. Written and illustrated by Susan Stockdale.

First the Egg. Written and illustrated by Laura Vaccaro Seeger.

The Handiest Things in the World. Written by Andrew Clements. Illustrated by Raquel Jaramillo.

How Many Baby Pandas? Written and illustrated by Sandra Markle.

If Rocks Could Sing: A Discovered Alphabet. Written and illustrated by Leslie McGuirk.

In My Backyard. Written by Valarie Giogas. Illustrated by Katherine Zecca.

Museum ABC. Written by Metropolitan Museum of Art.

My Favorite Word Book: Words and Pictures for the Very Young. Written and illustrated by Selina Young.

My Shapes/Mis Formas. Written and illustrated by Rebecca Emberley.

One Boy. Written and illustrated by Laura Vaccaro Seeger.

One Foot Two Feet: An Exceptional Counting Book. Written by Peter Maloney and Felicia Zekauskas.

Ones and Twos. Written and illustrated by Marthe Jocelyn and Nell Jocelyn.

A Second Is a Hiccup: A Child's Book of Time. Written by Hazel Hutchins. Illustrated by Kady MacDonald Denton.

Sign Language ABC. Written and illustrated by Lora Heller.

What Do Wheels Do All Day? Written by April Jones Prince. Illustrated by Giles Laroche.

The Wing on a Flea: A Book about Shapes. Written and illustrated by Ed Emberley.

EARLY READERS

Actual Size. Written and illustrated by Steve Jenkins.

How Much Is a Million? Written by David M. Schwartz. Illustrated by Steven Kellogg.

Just a Second. Written and illustrated by Steve Jenkins.

Crime

YOUNG ADULTS

Bootleg: Murder, Moonshine, and the Lawless Years of Prohibition. Written by Karen Blumenthal.

Flesh and Blood So Cheap: The Triangle Fire and Its Legacy. Written by Albert Marrin.

Getting Away with Murder: The True Story of the Emmett Till Case. Written by Chris Crowe.

Hole in My Life. Written by Jack Gantos.

The Notorious Benedict Arnold: A True Story of Adventure, Heroism, and Treachery. Written by Steve Sheinkin.

Written in Bone: Buried Lives of Jamestown and Colonial Maryland. Written by Sally M. Walker.

ADULTS

Columbine. Written by Dave Cullen.

The Devil in the White City: Murder, Magic, and Madness at the Fair That Changed America. Written by Erik Larson.

In Cold Blood. Written by Truman Capote.

Zeitoun. Written by Dave Eggers.

Disasters

PRESCHOOLERS

Two Bobbies: A True Story of Hurricane Katrina, Friendship, and Survival. Written by Kirby Larson and Mary Nethery. Illustrated by Jean Cassels.

MIDDLE READERS

America Is under Attack: September 11, 2001: The Day the Towers Fell. Written and illustrated by Don Brown.

An American Plague: The True and Terrifying Story of the Yellow Fever Epidemic of 1793. Written by Jim Murphy.

Blizzard of Glass: The Halifax Explosion of 1917. Written by Sally M. Walker.

Bodies from the Ash: Life and Death in Ancient Pompeii. Written by James M. Deem.

The Great Fire. Written by Jim Murphy.

YOUNG ADULTS

Flesh and Blood So Cheap: The Triangle Fire and Its Legacy. Written by Albert Marrin.

Titanic: *Voices from the Disaster.* Written by Deborah Hopkinson.

Witches! The Absolutely True Tale of Disaster in Salem. Written and illustrated by Rosalyn Schanzer.

ADULTS

Into Thin Air: A Personal Account of the Mt. Everest Disaster. Written by Jon Krakauer.

Zeitoun. Written by Dave Eggers.

Diversity

PRESCHOOLERS

The Boy Who Loved Math: The Improbable Life of Paul Erdös. Written by Deborah Heiligman. Illustrated by LeUyen Pham.

Frida. Written by Jonah Winter. Illustrated by Ana Juan.

Hachiko. Written by Pamela S. Turner. Illustrated by Yan Nascimbene.

Market! Written and illustrated by Ted Lewin.

My Shapes/Mis Formas. Written and illustrated by Rebecca Emberley.

Sign Language ABC. Written and illustrated by Lora Heller.

Ten Little Fingers and Ten Little Toes. Written by Mem Fox. Illustrated by Helen Oxenbury.

EARLY READERS

Harvesting Hope: The Story of Cesar Chavez. Written by Kathleen Krull. Illustrated by Yuyi Morales.

If You Lived Here: Houses of the World. Written and illustrated by Giles Laroche.

Orani: My Father's Village. Written and illustrated by Claire A. Nivola.

Sixteen Years in Sixteen Seconds: The Sammy Lee Story. Written by Paula Yoo. Illustrated by Dom Lee.

The Story of Ruby Bridges. Written by Robert Coles. Illustrated by George Ford.

MIDDLE READERS

The Horse and the Plains Indians: A Powerful Partnership. Written by Dorothy Hinshaw Patent. Illustrated by William Muñoz.

How to Talk to an Autistic Kid. Written by Daniel Stefanski.

My Librarian Is a Camel: How Books Are Brought to Children around the World. Written by Margriet Ruurs.

Temple Grandin: How the Girl Who Loved Cows Embraced Autism and Changed the World. Written by Sy Montgomery and Temple Grandin.

What the World Eats. Written by Faith D'Aluisio. Illustrated by Peter Menzel.

YOUNG ADULTS

21: The Story of Roberto Clemente. Written and illustrated by Wilfred Santiago.

Navajo Code Talkers. Written by Nathan Aaseng.

The Poet Slave of Cuba: A Biography of Juan Francisco Manzano. Written by Margarita Engle. Illustrated by Sean Qualls.

Pyongyang: A Journey in North Korea. Written by Guy Delisle.

ADULTS

Behind the Beautiful Forevers: Life, Death, and Hope in a Mumbai Undercity. Written by Katherine Boo.

Embracing Defeat: Japan in the Wake of World War II. Written by John W. Dower.

Far from the Tree: Parents, Children, and the Search for Identity. Written by Andrew Solomon.

Nothing to Envy: Ordinary Lives in North Korea. Written by Barbara Demick.

Quiet: The Power of Introverts in a World That Can't Stop Talking. Written by Susan Cain.

Families and Relationships

PRESCHOOLERS

Animal Dads. Written by Sneed B. Collard III. Illustrated by Steve Jenkins.

The Boy Who Loved Math: The Improbable Life of Paul Erdös. Written by Deborah Heiligman. Illustrated by LeUyen Pham.

How to Be a Baby . . . By Me, the Big Sister. Written by Sally Lloyd-Jones. Illustrated by Sue Heap.

Meet the Dogs of Bedlam Farm. Written and illustrated by Jon Katz.

Tarra and Bella: The Elephant and Dog Who Became Best Friends. Written and illustrated by Carol Buckley.

EARLY READERS

All the Way to America: The Story of a Big Italian Family and a Little Shovel. Written and illustrated by Dan Yaccarino.

Brothers at Bat: The True Story of an Amazing All-Brother Baseball Team. Written by Audrey Vernick. Illustrated by Steven Salerno.

Caterpillar, Caterpillar. Written by Vivian French. Illustrated by Charlotte Voake.

Orani: My Father's Village. Written and illustrated by Claire A. Nivola.

Owen and Mzee: The True Story of a Remarkable Friendship. Written by Isabella Hatkoff, Craig Hatkoff, and Paula Kahumbu. Illustrated by Peter Greste.

MIDDLE READERS

The Day-Glo Brothers. Written by Chris Barton. Illustrated by Tony Persiani.

Dogs on Duty: Soldiers' Best Friends on the Battlefield and Beyond. Written by Dorothy Hinshaw Patent.

Drawing from Memory. Written and illustrated by Allen Say.

How It Feels When Parents Divorce. Written by Jill Krementz.

Sit-In: How Four Friends Stood Up by Sitting Down. Written by Andrea Davis Pinkney. Illustrated by Brian Pinkney.

YOUNG ADULTS

Bad Boy. Written by Walter Dean Myers.

Charles and Emma: The Darwins' Leap of Faith. Written by Deborah Heiligman.

The Diary of a Young Girl. Written by Anne Frank.

Good Brother, Bad Brother: The Story of Edwin Booth and John Wilkes Booth. Written by James Cross Giblin.

King of the Mild Frontier: An Ill-Advised Autobiography. Written by Chris Crutcher.

The Letter Q: Queer Writers' Notes to Their Younger Selves. Written by Sarah Moon and James Lecesne.

The Lincolns: A Scrapbook Look at Abraham and Mary. Written by Candace Fleming.

Soul Surfer: A True Story of Faith, Family, and Fighting to Get Back on the Board. Written by Bethany Hamilton, Sheryl Berk, and Rick Bundschuh.

The Year of Goodbyes: A True Story of Friendship, Family and Farewells. Written by Debbie Levy.

ADULTS

Cheever: A Life. Written by Blake Bailey.

Far from the Tree: Parents, Children, and the Search for Identity. Written by Andrew Solomon.

Hemingses of Monticello: An American Family. Written by Annette Gordon-Reed.

Quiet: The Power of Introverts in a World That Can't Stop Talking. Written by Susan Cain.

The Silent Woman: Sylvia Plath and Ted Hughes. Written by Janet Malcolm.

Food

PRESCHOOLERS

How Did That Get in My Lunchbox? The Story of Food. Written by Chris Butterworth. Illustrated by Lucia Gaggiotti.

On the Farm. Written by David Elliott. Illustrated by Holly Meade.

An Orange in January. Written by Dianna Hutts Aston. Illustrated by Julie Maren.

Rah, Rah, Radishes! A Vegetable Chant. Written and illustrated by April Pulley Sayre.

EARLY READERS

Country Road ABC: An Illustrated Journey through America's Farmland. Written and illustrated by Arthur Geisert.

A Weed Is a Flower: The Life of George Washington Carver. Written and illustrated by Aliki.

MIDDLE READERS

George Washington Carver. Written by Tonya Bolden.
What the World Eats. Written by Faith D'Aluisio. Illustrated by Peter Menzel.

ADULTS

Fast Food Nation: The Dark Side of the All-American Meal. Written by Eric Schlosser.
Guns, Germs, and Steel: The Fates of Human Societies. Written by Jared Diamond.
The Omnivore's Dilemma: A Natural History of Four Meals. Written by Michael Pollan.

Graphic Novel

MIDDLE READERS

Around the World. Written and illustrated by Matt Phelan.

YOUNG ADULTS

21: The Story of Roberto Clemente. Written and illustrated by Wilfred Santiago.
The Complete Maus: A Survivor's Tale. Written by Art Spiegelman.
Feynman. Written by Jim Ottaviani. Illustrated by Leland Myrick.
Pyongyang: A Journey in North Korea. Written by Guy Delisle.
To Dance: A Ballerina's Graphic Novel. Written by Siena Cherson Siegel. Illustrated by Mark Siegel.

Health and Disease

PRESCHOOLERS

The Busy Body Book: A Kid's Guide to Fitness. Written and illustrated by Lizzy Rockwell.

Rah, Rah, Radishes! A Vegetable Chant. Written and illustrated by April Pulley Sayre.

EARLY READERS

Balto and the Great Race. Written by Elizabeth Cody Kimmel. Illustrated by Nora Koerber.

I Feel Better with a Frog in My Throat: History's Strangest Cures. Written and illustrated by Carlyn Beccia.

MIDDLE READERS

An American Plague: The True and Terrifying Story of the Yellow Fever Epidemic of 1793. Written by Jim Murphy.

Bones: Skeletons and How They Work. Written and illustrated by Steve Jenkins.

Guinea Pig Scientists: Bold Self-Experimenters in Science and Medicine. Written by Leslie Dendy and Mel Boring. Illustrated by C. B. Mordan.

How They Croaked: The Awful Ends of the Awfully Famous. Written by Georgia Bragg. Illustrated by Kevin O'Malley.

Invincible Microbe: Tuberculosis and the Never-Ending Search for a Cure. Written by Jim Murphy and Alison Blank.

Phineas Gage: A Gruesome but True Story about Brain Science. Written by John Fleischman.

Poop Happened! A History of the World from the Bottom Up. Written by Sarah Albee. Illustrated by Robert Leighton.

Sadako and the Thousand Paper Cranes. Written by Eleanor Coerr. Illustrated by Ronald Himler.

What the World Eats. Written by Faith D'Aluisio. Illustrated by Peter Menzel.

Zombie Makers: True Stories of Nature's Undead. Written by Rebecca L. Johnson.

YOUNG ADULTS

The Secret of the Yellow Death: A True Story of Medical Sleuthing. Written by Suzanne Jurmain.

ADULTS

Destiny of the Republic: A Tale of Madness, Medicine and the Murder of a President. Written by Candice Millard.

The Emperor of All Maladies: A Biography of Cancer. Written by Siddhartha Mukherjee.

Fast Food Nation: The Dark Side of the All-American Meal. Written by Eric Schlosser.

Guns, Germs, and Steel: The Fates of Human Societies. Written by Jared Diamond.

The Immortal Life of Henrietta Lacks. Written by Rebecca Skloot.

The Year of Magical Thinking. Written by Joan Didion.

History

PRESCHOOLERS

Dave the Potter: Artist, Poet, Slave. Written by Laban Carrick Hill. Illustrated by Bryan Collier.

Harlem's Little Blackbird. Written by Renée Watson. Illustrated by Christian Robinson.

Lightship. Written and illustrated by Brian Floca.

Looking at Lincoln. Written and illustrated by Maira Kalman.

Pop! The Invention of Bubble Gum. Written and illustrated by Meghan McCarthy.

Underground: Finding the Light to Freedom. Written and illustrated by Shane W. Evans.

EARLY READERS

14 Cows for America. Written by Carmen Agra Deedy. Illustrated by Thomas Gonzalez.

Ballet for Martha: Making Appalachian Spring. Written by Jan Greenberg and Sandra Jordan. Illustrated by Brian Floca.

Black Jack: The Ballad of Jack Johnson. Written by Charles R. Smith Jr. Illustrated by Shane W. Evans.

The Camping Trip That Changed America. Written by Barb Rosenstock. Illustrated by Mordicai Gerstein.

Eleanor, Quiet No More. Written by Doreen Rappaport. Illustrated by Gary Kelley.

Fireboat: The Heroic Adventures of the John J. Harvey. Written and illustrated by Maira Kalman.

Harriet and the Promised Land. Written and illustrated by Jacob Lawrence.

I Have a Dream. Written by Martin Luther King Jr. Illustrated by Kadir Nelson.

It Jes' Happened: When Bill Traylor Started to Draw. Written by Don Tate. Illustrated by Gregory Christie.

Martin's Big Words: The Life of Dr. Martin Luther King, Jr. Written by Doreen Rappaport. Illustrated by Bryan Collier.

Meadowlands: A Wetland Survival Story. Written and illustrated by Thomas F. Yezerski.

Monsieur Marceau: Actor without Words. Written by Leda Schubert. Illustrated by Gerard DuBois.

Moonshot: The Flight of Apollo 11. Written and illustrated by Brian Floca.

My Senator and Me: A Dog's-Eye View of Washington, D.C. Written by Edward M. Kennedy. Illustrated by David Small.

A Nation's Hope: The Story of Boxing Legend Joe Louis. Written by Matt De La Peña. Illustrated by Kadir Nelson.

Noah Webster and His Words. Written by Jeri Chase Ferris. Illustrated by Vincent X. Kirsch.

One Giant Leap. Written by Robert Burleigh. Illustrated by Mike Wimmer.

So You Want to Be President? Written by Judith St. George. Illustrated by David Small.

Those Rebels, John and Tom. Written by Barbara Kerley. Illustrated by Edwin Fotheringham.

A Weed Is a Flower: The Life of George Washington Carver. Written and illustrated by Aliki.

What Presidents Are Made Of. Written and illustrated by Hanoch Piven.

MIDDLE READERS

10,000 Days of Thunder: A History of the Vietnam War. Written by Philip Caputo.

Abraham Lincoln and Frederick Douglass: The Story behind an American Friendship. Written by Russell Freedman.

Almost Astronauts: 13 Women Who Dared to Dream. Written by Tanya Lee Stone.

Amelia Lost: The Life and Disappearance of Amelia Earhart. Written by Candace Fleming.

America Is under Attack: September 11, 2001: The Day the Towers Fell. Written and illustrated by Don Brown.

An American Plague: The True and Terrifying Story of the Yellow Fever Epidemic of 1793. Written by Jim Murphy.

And Then What Happened, Paul Revere? Written by Jean Fritz.

Ben Franklin's Almanac: Being a True Account of the Good Gentleman's Life. Written by Candace Fleming.

Beyond Courage: The Untold Story of Jewish Resistance during the Holocaust. Written by Doreen Rappaport.

Big Wig: A Little History of Hair. Written by Kathleen Krull. Illustrated by Peter Malone.

Black Elk's Vision: A Lakota Story. Written by S. D. Nelson.

Blizzard of Glass: The Halifax Explosion of 1917. Written by Sally M. Walker.

Bodies from the Ash: Life and Death in Ancient Pompeii. Written by James M. Deem.

Bodies from the Ice: Melting Glaciers and the Recovery of the Past. Written by James M. Deem.

The Boston Tea Party. Written by Russell Freedman. Illustrated by Peter Malone.

Candy Bomber: The Story of the Berlin Airlift's "Chocolate Pilot." Written by Michael O. Tunnell.

Case Closed? Nine Mysteries Unlocked by Modern Science. Written by Susan Hughes. Illustrated by Michael Wandelmaier.

Cathedral: The Story of Its Construction. Written and illustrated by David Macaulay.

Discovering Black America: From the Age of Exploration to the Twenty-First Century. Written by Linda Tarrant-Reid.

A Dream of Freedom: The Civil Rights Movement from 1954 to 1968. Written by Diane McWhorter.

Eleanor Roosevelt: A Life of Discovery. Written by Russell Freedman.

Electric Ben: The Amazing Life and Times of Benjamin Franklin. Written and illustrated by Robert Byrd.

The Emperor's Silent Army: Terracotta Warriors of Ancient China. Written by Jane O'Connor.

The Endless Steppe: Growing Up in Siberia. Written by Esther Hautzig.

The Fairy Ring, or, Elsie and Frances Fool the World. Written by Mary Losure.

Freedom Walkers: The Story of the Montgomery Bus Boycott. Written by Russell Freedman.

George vs. George: The American Revolution as Seen from Both Sides. Written and illustrated by Rosalyn Schanzer.

Girls Think of Everything: Stories of Ingenious Inventions by Women. Written by Catherine Thimmesh. Illustrated by Melissa Sweet.

The Great Fire. Written by Jim Murphy.

Harriet Tubman: Conductor on the Underground Railroad. Written by Ann Petry.

Heart and Soul: The Story of America and African Americans. Written and illustrated by Kadir Nelson.

The Horse and the Plains Indians: A Powerful Partnership. Written by Dorothy Hinshaw Patent. Illustrated by William Muñoz.

How They Croaked: The Awful Ends of the Awfully Famous. Written by Georgia Bragg. Illustrated by Kevin O'Malley.

Into the Unknown: How Great Explorers Found Their Way by Land, Sea, and Air. Written by Stuart Ross. Illustrated by Stephen Biesty.

Invincible Microbe: Tuberculosis and the Never-Ending Search for a Cure. Written by Jim Murphy and Alison Blank.

Kubla Khan: The Emperor of Everything. Written by Kathleen Krull. Illustrated by Robert Byrd.

Lincoln: A Photobiography. Written by Russell Freedman.

Mission Control, This Is Apollo: The Story of the First Voyages to the Moon. Written by Andrew Chaikin and Victoria Kohl. Illustrated by Alan Bean.

Nurse, Soldier, Spy: The Story of Sarah Edmonds, a Civil War Hero. Written by Marissa Moss.

One Times Square: A Century of Change at the Crossroads of the World. Written and illustrated by Joe McKendry.

Poop Happened! A History of the World from the Bottom Up. Written by Sarah Albee. Illustrated by Robert Leighton.

Seven Miles to Freedom: The Robert Smalls Story. Written by Janet Halfmann. Illustrated by Duane Smith.

Shipwrecked! The True Adventures of a Japanese Boy. Written by Rhoda Blumberg.

Sit-In: How Four Friends Stood Up by Sitting Down. Written by Andrea Davis
   Pinkney. Illustrated by Brian Pinkney.
Team Moon: How 400,000 People Landed Apollo 11 on the Moon. Written by
   Catherine Thimmesh.
Truce: The Day the Soldiers Stopped Fighting. Written by Jim Murphy.
The Wall: Growing Up behind the Iron Curtain. Written by Peter Sis.
We Are the Ship: The Story of Negro League Baseball. Written and illustrated by
   Kadir Nelson.
Who Was First? Discovering the Americas. Written by Russell Freedman.
William Shakespeare and the Globe. Written and illustrated by Aliki.

YOUNG ADULTS

1776. Written by David McCullough.
The Autobiography of Benjamin Franklin. Written by Benjamin Franklin.
The Autobiography of Malcolm X. Written by Malcolm X and Alex Haley.
Birmingham Sunday. Written by Larry Dane Brimner.
Bootleg: Murder, Moonshine, and the Lawless Years of Prohibition. Written by
   Karen Blumenthal.
Bury My Heart at Wounded Knee: An Indian History of the American West. Written by Dee Brown.
Charles Dickens and the Street Children of London. Written by Andrea Warren.
Children of the Great Depression. Written by Russell Freedman.
Claudette Colvin: Twice toward Justice. Written by Phillip Hoose.
The Complete Maus: A Survivor's Tale. Written by Art Spiegelman.
The Dark Game: True Spy Stories from Invisible Ink to CIA Moles. Written by
   Paul Janeczko.
*Dear Miss Breed: True Stories of the Japanese American Incarceration during World
   War II and a Librarian Who Made a Difference.* Written by Joanne Oppenheim.
The Diary of a Young Girl. Written by Anne Frank.
Escape from Saigon: How a Vietnam War Orphan Became an American Boy. Written by Andrea Warren.
Flesh and Blood So Cheap: The Triangle Fire and Its Legacy. Written by Albert
   Marrin.
*Freedom Riders: John Lewis and Jim Zwerg on the Front Lines of the Civil Rights
   Movement.* Written by Ann Bausum.
George Washington and the Founding of a Nation. Written by Albert Marrin.
Getting Away with Murder: The True Story of the Emmett Till Case. Written by
   Chris Crowe.

Ghosts in the Fog: The Untold Story of Alaska's WWII Invasion. Written by Samantha Seiple.

Good Brother, Bad Brother: The Story of Edwin Booth and John Wilkes Booth. Written by James Cross Giblin.

The Good Fight: How World War II Was Won. Written by Stephen E. Ambrose.

Harlem Stomp! A Cultural History of the Harlem Renaissance. Written by Laban Carrick Hill.

The Impossible Rescue: The True Story of An Amazing Arctic Adventure. Written by Martin W. Sandler.

In Defiance of Hitler: The Secret Mission of Varian Fry. Written by Carla Killough McClafferty.

Lafayette and the American Revolution. Written by Russell Freedman.

The Life and Death of Adolf Hitler. Written by James Cross Giblin.

The Lincolns: A Scrapbook Look at Abraham and Mary. Written by Candace Fleming.

The Longitude Prize. Written by Joan Dash. Illustrated by Dusan Petricic.

Marching for Freedom: Walk Together Children and Don't You Grow Weary. Written by Elizabeth Partridge.

The Mighty Mars Rovers: The Incredible Adventures of Spirit *and* Opportunity. Written by Elizabeth Rusch.

Miles to Go for Freedom: Segregation and Civil Rights in the Jim Crow Years. Written by Linda Barrett Osborne.

Mysterious Messages: A History of Codes and Ciphers. Written by Gary Blackwood.

Navajo Code Talkers. Written by Nathan Aaseng.

Night. Written by Elie Wiesel.

The Notorious Benedict Arnold: A True Story of Adventure, Heroism, and Treachery. Written by Steve Sheinkin.

Parting the Waters: America in the King Years, 1954–63. Written by Taylor Branch.

Profiles in Courage. Written by John F. Kennedy.

Shipwreck at the Bottom of the World: The Extraordinary True Story of Shackleton and the Endurance. Written by Jennifer Armstrong.

Sir Walter Raleigh and the Quest for El Dorado. Written by Marc Aronson.

Spies of Mississippi: The True Story of the Spy Network That Tried to Destroy the Civil Rights Movement. Written by Rick Bowers.

Sugar Changed the World: A Story of Magic, Spice, Slavery, Freedom, and Science. Written by Marc Aronson and Marina Budhos.

Tasting the Sky: A Palestinian Childhood. Written by Ibtisam Barakat.

They Called Themselves the KKK: The Birth of an American Terrorist Group. Written by Susan Campbell Bartoletti.

This Land Was Made for You and Me: The Life and Songs of Woody Guthrie. Written by Elizabeth Partridge.

Titanic: *Voices from the Disaster.* Written by Deborah Hopkinson.

Unraveling Freedom: The Battle for Democracy on the Home Front during World War I. Written by Ann Bausum.

The War to End All Wars: World War I. Written by Russell Freedman.

We've Got a Job: The 1963 Birmingham Children's March. Written by Cynthia Levinson.

Wheels of Change: How Women Rode the Bicycle to Freedom (with a Few Flat Tires along the Way). Written by Sue Macy.

Witches! The Absolutely True Tale of Disaster in Salem. Written and illustrated by Rosalyn Schanzer.

The Year of Goodbyes: A True Story of Friendship, Family and Farewells. Written by Debbie Levy.

ADULTS

The Age of Wonder: How the Romantic Generation Discovered the Beauty and Terror of Science. Written by Richard Holmes.

Anti-intellectualism in American Life. Written by Richard Hofstadter.

Catherine the Great: Portrait of a Woman. Written by Robert K. Massie.

The Civil War: A Narrative (3 vols.). Written by Shelby Foote.

Cleopatra: A Life. Written by Stacy Schiff.

Collapse: How Societies Choose to Fail or Succeed. Written by Jared Diamond.

Destiny of the Republic: A Tale of Madness, Medicine and the Murder of a President. Written by Candice Millard.

The Devil in the White City: Murder, Magic, and Madness at the Fair That Changed America. Written by Erik Larson.

The Education of Henry Adams. Written by Henry Adams.

Electric Universe: How Electricity Switched on the Modern World. Written by David Bodanis.

Embracing Defeat: Japan in the Wake of World War II. Written by John W. Dower.

The Emperor of All Maladies: A Biography of Cancer. Written by Siddhartha Mukherjee.

Fast Food Nation: The Dark Side of the All-American Meal. Written by Eric Schlosser.

Fordlandia: The Rise and Fall of Henry Ford's Forgotten Jungle City. Written by Greg Grandin.

The Gnostic Gospels. Written by Elaine Pagels.

Gulag: A History of the Soviet Camps. Written by Anne Applebaum.

Guns, Germs, and Steel: The Fates of Human Societies. Written by Jared Diamond.

Hemingses of Monticello: An American Family. Written by Annette Gordon-Reed.

Hiroshima. Written by John Hersey.

Homage to Catalonia. Written by George Orwell.

The Immortal Life of Henrietta Lacks. Written by Rebecca Skloot.

In the Garden of Beasts: Love, Terror, and an American Family in Hitler's Berlin. Written by Erik Larson.

The Information: A History, a Theory, a Flood. Written by James Gleick.

Iron Curtain: The Crushing of Eastern Europe, 1945–1956. Written by Anne Applebaum.

John Adams. Written by David McCullough.

Legacy of Ashes: The History of the CIA. Written by Tim Weiner.

The Looming Tower: Al-Qaeda and the Road to 9/11. Written by Lawrence Wright.

The Lost City of Z: A Tale of Deadly Obsession in the Amazon. Written by David Grann.

The Making of the Atomic Bomb. Written by Richard Rhodes.

Mayflower: *A Story of Courage, Community, and War.* Written by Nathaniel Philbrick.

Nixonland: The Rise of a President and the Fracturing of America. Written by Rick Perlstein.

The Passage of Power: The Years of Lyndon Johnson. Written by Robert Caro.

A People's History of the United States: 1492 to Present. Written by Howard Zinn.

Postwar: A History of Europe since 1945. Written by Tony Judt.

The Rest Is Noise: Listening to the Twentieth Century. Written by Alex Ross.

The Right Stuff. Written by Tom Wolfe.

A Short History of Nearly Everything. Written by Bill Bryson.

Slouching towards Bethlehem. Written by Joan Didion.

The Structure of Scientific Revolutions. Written by Thomas S. Kuhn.

The Swerve: How the World Became Modern. Written by Stephen Greenblatt.

This Republic of Suffering: Death and the American Civil War. Written by Drew Gilpin Faust.

Travels in Siberia. Written by Ian Frazier.

Unbroken: A World War II Story of Survival, Resilience, and Redemption. Written by Laura Hillenbrand.

The Warmth of Other Suns: The Epic Story of America's Great Migration. Written by Isabel Wilkerson.

We Wish to Inform You That Tomorrow We Will Be Killed with Our Families: Stories from Rwanda. Written by Philip Gourevitch.

Insects and Spiders

PRESCHOOLERS

Are You a Snail? Written by Judy Allen. Illustrated by Tudor Humphries.
Bugs! Bugs! Bugs! Written and illustrated by Bob Barner.
The Bumblebee Queen. Written by April Pulley Sayre. Illustrated by Patricia J. Wynne.
In the Trees, Honey Bees. Written by Lori Mortensen. Illustrated by Cris Arbo.
It's a Butterfly's Life. Written and illustrated by Irene Kelly.
Ladybugs: Red, Fiery, and Bright. Written and illustrated by Mia Posada.
Monarch and Milkweed. Written by Helen Frost. Illustrated by Leonid Gore.
Step Gently Out. Written by Helen Frost. Illustrated by Rick Lieder.

EARLY READERS

The Beetle Book. Written and illustrated by Steve Jenkins.
Bug Zoo. Written by Nick Baker.
Bugs Are Insects. Written by Anne Rockwell. Illustrated by Steve Jenkins.
A Butterfly Is Patient. Written by Dianna Hutts Aston. Illustrated by Sylvia Long.
Caterpillar, Caterpillar. Written by Vivian French. Illustrated by Charlotte Voake.
Creep and Flutter: The Secret World of Insects and Spiders. Written and illustrated by Jim Arnosky.
Exploding Ants: Amazing Facts about How Animals Adapt. Written by Joanne Settel.
Insect Detective. Written by Steve Voake. Illustrated by Charlotte Voake.
Ladybugs. Written by Gail Gibbons.
Nic Bishop Spiders. Written and illustrated by Nic Bishop.
UnBEElievables: Honeybee Poems and Paintings. Written and illustrated by Douglas Florian.

MIDDLE READERS

An Extraordinary Life: The Story of a Monarch Butterfly. Written by Laurence Pringle. Illustrated by Bob Marstall.

YOUNG ADULTS

The Hive Detectives: Chronicle of a Honey Bee Catastrophe. Written by Loree Griffin Burns. Illustrated by Ellen Harasimowicz.
The Tarantula Scientist. Written by Sy Montgomery. Illustrated by Nic Bishop.

Inspiration

PRESCHOOLERS

Hachiko. Written by Pamela S. Turner. Illustrated by Yan Nascimbene.
Koko's Kitten. Written by Francine Patterson. Illustrated by Ronald H. Cohn.
Leo the Snow Leopard: The True Story of an Amazing Rescue. Written by Craig Hatkoff. Illustrated by Isabella Hatkoff.
Little Dog Lost: The True Story of a Brave Dog Named Baltic. Written and illustrated by Mônica Carnesi.
Rosie, a Visiting Dog's Story. Written by Stephanie Calmenson. Illustrated by Justin Sutcliffe.
Snowflakes Fall. Written by Patricia MacLachlan. Illustrated by Steven Kellogg.
Tarra and Bella: The Elephant and Dog Who Became Best Friends. Written and illustrated by Carol Buckley.
Two Bobbies: A True Story of Hurricane Katrina, Friendship, and Survival. Written by Kirby Larson and Mary Nethery. Illustrated by Jean Cassels.
Winter's Tail: How One Little Dolphin Learned to Swim Again. Written by Craig Hatkoff, Juliana Hatkoff, and Isabella Hatkoff.

EARLY READERS

14 Cows for America. Written by Carmen Agra Deedy. Illustrated by Thomas Gonzalez.
Fifty Cents and a Dream: Young Booker T. Washington. Written by Jabari Asim. Illustrated by Bryan Collier.
Harriet and the Promised Land. Written and illustrated by Jacob Lawrence.
I Have a Dream. Written by Martin Luther King Jr. Illustrated by Kadir Nelson.
Martin's Big Words: The Life of Dr. Martin Luther King, Jr. Written by Doreen Rappaport. Illustrated by Bryan Collier.
Roberto Clemente: Pride of the Pittsburgh Pirates. Written by Jonah Winter. Illustrated by Raúl Colón.

Sixteen Years in Sixteen Seconds: The Sammy Lee Story. Written by Paula Yoo. Illustrated by Dom Lee.

The Story of Ruby Bridges. Written by Robert Coles. Illustrated by George Ford.

There Goes Ted Williams: The Greatest Hitter Who Ever Lived. Written and illustrated by Matt Tavares.

A Weed Is a Flower: The Life of George Washington Carver. Written and illustrated by Aliki.

Wilma Unlimited: How Wilma Rudolph Became the World's Fastest Woman. Written by Kathleen Krull. Illustrated by David Diaz.

MIDDLE READERS

Beyond Courage: The Untold Story of Jewish Resistance during the Holocaust. Written by Doreen Rappaport.

Candy Bomber: The Story of the Berlin Airlift's "Chocolate Pilot." Written by Michael O. Tunnell.

Chuck Close Face Book. Written by Chuck Close.

Temple Grandin: How the Girl Who Loved Cows Embraced Autism and Changed the World. Written by Sy Montgomery and Temple Grandin.

YOUNG ADULTS

21: The Story of Roberto Clemente. Written and illustrated by Wilfred Santiago.

The Boy Who Harnessed the Wind. Written by William Kamkwamba and Bryan Mealer.

The Diary of a Young Girl. Written by Anne Frank.

The Letter Q: Queer Writers' Notes to Their Younger Selves. Written by Sarah Moon and James Lecesne.

Soul Surfer: A True Story of Faith, Family, and Fighting to Get Back on the Board. Written by Bethany Hamilton, Sheryl Berk, and Rick Bundschuh.

Life Cycles

PRESCHOOLERS

Are You a Snail? Written by Judy Allen. Illustrated by Tudor Humphries.

How Many Baby Pandas? Written and illustrated by Sandra Markle.

It's a Butterfly's Life. Written and illustrated by Irene Kelly.

Ladybugs: Red, Fiery, and Bright. Written and illustrated by Mia Posada.
Monarch and Milkweed. Written by Helen Frost. Illustrated by Leonid Gore.
One Small Place in a Tree. Written by Barbara Brenner. Illustrated by Tom Leonard.
Seahorses. Written by Jennifer Keats Curtis. Illustrated by Chad Wallace.
The Tiny Seed. Written and illustrated by Eric Carle.
What Bluebirds Do. Written and illustrated by Pamela F. Kirby.

EARLY READERS

A Butterfly Is Patient. Written by Dianna Hutts Aston. Illustrated by Sylvia Long.
Caterpillar, Caterpillar. Written by Vivian French. Illustrated by Charlotte Voake.
From Seed to Plant. Written and illustrated by Gail Gibbons.
Growing Frogs. Written by Vivian French. Illustrated by Alison Bartlett.

MIDDLE READERS

Come Back, Salmon: How a Group of Dedicated Kids Adopted Pigeon Creek and Brought It Back to Life. Written by Molly Cone. Illustrated by Sidnee Wheelwright.
An Extraordinary Life: The Story of a Monarch Butterfly. Written by Laurence Pringle. Illustrated by Bob Marstall.
Zombie Makers: True Stories of Nature's Undead. Written by Rebecca L. Johnson.

Nature

PRESCHOOLERS

All the Water in the World. Written by George Ella Lyon.
The Bumblebee Queen. Written by April Pulley Sayre. Illustrated by Patricia J. Wynne.
Creep and Flutter: The Secret World of Insects and Spiders. Written and illustrated by Jim Arnosky.
Hottest, Coldest, Highest, Deepest. Written and illustrated by Steve Jenkins.
It's a Butterfly's Life. Written and illustrated by Irene Kelly.
Monarch and Milkweed. Written by Helen Frost. Illustrated by Leonid Gore.

My Light. Written and illustrated by Molly Bang.

One Small Place in a Tree. Written by Barbara Brenner. Illustrated by Tom Leonard.

Over and Under the Snow. Written by Kate Messner.

Redwoods. Written and illustrated by Jason Chin.

Stars beneath Your Bed: The Surprising Story of Dust. Written by April Pulley Sayre. Illustrated by Ann Jonas.

Swirl by Swirl: Spirals in Nature. Written by Joyce Sidman. Illustrated by Beth Krommes.

The Tiny Seed. Written and illustrated by Eric Carle.

Where in the Wild? Camouflaged Creatures Concealed . . . and Revealed. Written by David M. Schwartz and Yael Schy. Illustrated by Dwight Kuhn.

Why? The Best Ever Question and Answer Book about Nature, Science and the World around You. Written by Catherine Ripley. Illustrated by Scot Ritchie.

You Are Stardust. Written by Elin Kelsey. Illustrated by Soyeon Kim.

EARLY READERS

Around One Cactus: Owls, Bats and Leaping Rats. Written by Anthony D. Fredericks. Illustrated by Jennifer DiRubbio.

Living Sunlight: How Plants Bring the Earth to Life. Written by Molly Bang and Penny Chisholm.

Vulture View. Written by April Pulley Sayre. Illustrated by Steve Jenkins.

MIDDLE READERS

Ubiquitous: Celebrating Nature's Survivors. Written by Joyce Sidman. Illustrated by Beckie Prange.

YOUNG ADULTS

Hidden Worlds: Looking through a Scientist's Microscope. Written by Stephen P. Kramer. Illustrated by Dennis Kunkel.

Walden and "Civil Disobedience." Written by Henry David Thoreau.

ADULTS

The Lives of a Cell: Notes of a Biology Watcher. Written by Lewis Thomas.

Pilgrim at Tinker Creek. Written by Annie Dillard.

A Walk in the Woods: Rediscovering America on the Appalachian Trail. Written by Bill Bryson.

Ocean Life

PRESCHOOLERS

Big Blue Whale. Written by Nicola Davies. Illustrated by Nick Maland.
Fabulous Fishes. Written and illustrated by Susan Stockdale.
Gentle Giant Octopus. Written by Karen Wallace. Illustrated by Mike Bostock.
An Island Grows. Written by Lola M. Schaefer. Illustrated by Cathie Felstead.
Seahorses. Written by Jennifer Keats Curtis. Illustrated by Chad Wallace.
Slow Down for Manatees. Written and illustrated by Jim Arnosky.
Starfish. Written by Edith Thacher Hurd.

EARLY READERS

Amazing Sharks! Written by Sarah L. Thomson.
Coral Reefs. Written and illustrated by Jason Chin.
Down, Down, Down: A Journey to the Bottom of the Sea. Written and illustrated by Steve Jenkins.
Life in the Ocean: The Story of Oceanographer Sylvia Earle. Written and illustrated by Claire A. Nivola.
Ocean Sunlight: How Tiny Plants Feed the Seas. Written by Molly Bang and Penny Chisholm.
One Tiny Turtle. Written by Nicola Davies. Illustrated by Jane Chapman.
Sea Horse: The Shyest Fish in the Sea. Written by Chris Butterworth. Illustrated by John Lawrence.

MIDDLE READERS

Adventure beneath the Sea: Living in an Underwater Science Station. Written by Kenneth Mallory. Illustrated by Brian Skerry.
Far from Shore: Chronicles of an Open Ocean Voyage. Written by Sophie Webb.

YOUNG ADULTS

Tracking Trash: Flotsam, Jetsam, and the Science of Ocean Motion. Written by Loree Griffin Burns.

Performing Arts

PRESCHOOLERS

Stay: The True Story of Ten Dogs. Written by Michaela Muntean. Illustrated by K. C. Bailey and Stephen Kazmierski.

EARLY READERS

Ballet for Martha: Making Appalachian Spring. Written by Jan Greenberg and Sandra Jordan. Illustrated by Brian Floca.
Monsieur Marceau: Actor without Words. Written by Leda Schubert. Illustrated by Gerard DuBois.

MIDDLE READERS

Escape! The Story of the Great Houdini. Written by Sid Fleischman.
The Great and Only Barnum: The Tremendous, Stupendous Life of Showman P. T. Barnum. Written by Candace Fleming. Illustrated by Ray Fenwick.
Jimi: Sounds Like a Rainbow: A Story of the Young Jimi Hendrix. Written by Gary Golio. Illustrated by Javaka Steptoe.
Spirit Seeker: John Coltrane's Musical Journey. Written by Gary Golio. Illustrated by Rudy Gutierrez.

YOUNG ADULTS

The Amazing Harry Kellar: Great American Magician. Written by Gail Jarrow.
Harlem Stomp! A Cultural History of the Harlem Renaissance. Written by Laban Carrick Hill.
Janis Joplin: Rise Up Singing. Written by Ann Angel.
John Lennon: All I Want Is the Truth. Written by Elizabeth Partridge.
Sir Charlie Chaplin: The Funniest Man in the World. Written by Sid Fleischman.
This Land Was Made for You and Me: The Life and Songs of Woody Guthrie. Written by Elizabeth Partridge.
To Dance: A Ballerina's Graphic Novel. Written by Siena Cherson Siegel. Illustrated by Mark Siegel.

ADULTS

Just Kids. Written by Patti Smith.
The Rest Is Noise: Listening to the Twentieth Century. Written by Alex Ross.

Religion

EARLY READERS

Martin's Big Words: The Life of Dr. Martin Luther King, Jr. Written by Doreen
    Rappaport. Illustrated by Bryan Collier.
The Story of Ruby Bridges. Written by Robert Coles. Illustrated by George Ford.

MIDDLE READERS

Spirit Seeker: John Coltrane's Musical Journey. Written by Gary Golio. Illustrated
    by Rudy Gutierrez.
Truce: The Day the Soldiers Stopped Fighting. Written by Jim Murphy.

YOUNG ADULTS

Charles and Emma: The Darwins' Leap of Faith. Written by Deborah Heiligman.
Night. Written by Elie Wiesel.
Soul Surfer: A True Story of Faith, Family, and Fighting to Get Back on the Board.
    Written by Bethany Hamilton, Sheryl Berk, and Rick Bundschuh.

ADULTS

The Gnostic Gospels. Written by Elaine Pagels.
The Holy Bible.
Lit: A Memoir. Written by Mary Karr.
Unbroken: A World War II Story of Survival, Resilience, and Redemption. Written
    by Laura Hillenbrand.

Reptiles

PRESCHOOLERS

Chameleon, Chameleon. Written by Joy Cowley. Illustrated by Nic Bishop.
Chameleons Are Cool. Written by Martin Jenkins. Illustrated by Sue Shields.
Dinosaurs, Dinosaurs. Written and illustrated by Byron Barton.
Red-Eyed Tree Frog. Written by Joy Cowley. Illustrated by Nic Bishop.

EARLY READERS

Growing Frogs. Written by Vivian French. Illustrated by Alison Bartlett.
Nic Bishop Snakes. Written and illustrated by Nic Bishop.

MIDDLE READERS

The Case of the Vanishing Golden Frogs: A Scientific Mystery. Written by Sandra Markle.

Science

PRESCHOOLERS

Biggest, Strongest, Fastest. Written and illustrated by Steve Jenkins.
Hottest, Coldest, Highest, Deepest. Written and illustrated by Steve Jenkins.
I Face the Wind. Written by Vicki Cobb. Illustrated by Julia Gorton.
I Fall Down. Written by Vicki Cobb. Illustrated by Julia Gorton.
An Island Grows. Written by Lola M. Schaefer. Illustrated by Cathie Felstead.
Me . . . Jane. Written and illustrated by Patrick McDonnell.
My Light. Written and illustrated by Molly Bang.
Oscar and the Bird: A Book about Electricity. Written and illustrated by Geoff Waring.
Stars beneath Your Bed: The Surprising Story of Dust. Written by April Pulley Sayre. Illustrated by Ann Jonas.
Why? The Best Ever Question and Answer Book about Nature, Science and the World around You. Written by Catherine Ripley. Illustrated by Scot Ritchie.

EARLY READERS

Amazing Sharks! Written by Sarah L. Thomson.

The Beetle Book. Written and illustrated by Steve Jenkins.

Dinosaurs of Waterhouse Hawkins: An Illuminating History of Mr. Waterhouse Hawkins, Artist and Lecturer. Written by Barbara Kerley. Illustrated by Brian Selznick.

Dogs and Cats. Written and illustrated by Steve Jenkins.

Down, Down, Down: A Journey to the Bottom of the Sea. Written and illustrated by Steve Jenkins.

A Drop of Water: A Book of Science and Wonder. Written and illustrated by Walter Wick.

Exploding Ants: Amazing Facts about How Animals Adapt. Written by Joanne Settel.

From Seed to Plant. Written and illustrated by Gail Gibbons.

Growing Frogs. Written by Vivian French. Illustrated by Alison Bartlett.

Guess What Is Growing inside This Egg. Written and illustrated by Mia Posada.

How to Clean a Hippopotamus: A Look at Unusual Animal Partnerships. Written by Steve Jenkins and Robin Page. Illustrated by Steve Jenkins.

I Feel Better with a Frog in My Throat: History's Strangest Cures. Written and illustrated by Carlyn Beccia.

Insect Detective. Written by Steve Voake. Illustrated by Charlotte Voake.

Just a Second. Written and illustrated by Steve Jenkins.

Living Sunlight: How Plants Bring the Earth to Life. Written by Molly Bang. Illustrated by Penny Chisholm.

Nic Bishop Snakes. Written and illustrated by Nic Bishop.

Nic Bishop Spiders. Written and illustrated by Nic Bishop.

Ocean Sunlight: How Tiny Plants Feed the Seas. Written by Molly Bang and Penny Chisholm.

On Earth. Written and illustrated by G. Brian Karas.

Snowflake Bentley. Written by Jacqueline Briggs Martin. Illustrated by Mary Azarian.

Thunder Birds: Nature's Flying Predators. Written and illustrated by Jim Arnosky.

What Do You Do with a Tail like This? Written by Steve Jenkins and Robin Page.

What Is the World Made Of? All about Solids, Liquids, and Gases. Written by Kathleen Weidner Zoehfeld.

MIDDLE READERS

Adventure beneath the Sea: Living in an Underwater Science Station. Written by Kenneth Mallory. Illustrated by Brian Skerry.

Alex the Parrot: No Ordinary Bird. Written by Stephanie Spinner. Illustrated by Meilo So.

Animals Up Close. Written by Igor Siwanowicz.

A Black Hole Is NOT a Hole. Written by Carolyn Cinami DeCristofano. Illustrated by Michael Carroll.

Bodies from the Ash: Life and Death in Ancient Pompeii. Written by James M. Deem.

Bodies from the Ice: Melting Glaciers and the Recovery of the Past. Written by James M. Deem.

Bomb: The Race to Build—and Steal—The World's Most Dangerous Weapon. Written by Steve Sheinkin.

Bones: Skeletons and How They Work. Written and illustrated by Steve Jenkins.

Case Closed? Nine Mysteries Unlocked by Modern Science. Written by Susan Hughes. Illustrated by Michael Wandelmaier.

The Case of the Vanishing Golden Frogs: A Scientific Mystery. Written by Sandra Markle.

Citizen Scientists: Be a Part of Scientific Discovery from Your Own Backyard. Written by Loree Griffin Burns. Illustrated by Ellen Harasimowicz.

The Elephant Scientist. Written by Caitlin O'Connell and Donna M. Jackson. Illustrated by Timothy Rodwell.

Far from Shore: Chronicles of an Open Ocean Voyage. Written by Sophie Webb.

Guinea Pig Scientists: Bold Self-Experimenters in Science and Medicine. Written by Leslie Dendy and Mel Boring. Illustrated by C. B. Mordan.

If Stones Could Speak: Unlocking the Secrets of Stonehenge. Written by Mark Aronson.

Little People and a Lost World: An Anthropological Mystery. Written by Linda Goldenberg.

Mission Control, This Is Apollo: The Story of the First Voyages to the Moon. Written by Andrew Chaikin and Victoria Kohl. Illustrated by Alan Bean.

Moonbird: A Year on the Wind with the Great Survivor B95. Written by Phillip Hoose.

My Season with Penguins: An Antarctic Journal. Written and illustrated by Sophie Webb.

Phineas Gage: A Gruesome but True Story about Brain Science. Written by John Fleischman.

Ubiquitous: Celebrating Nature's Survivors. Written by Joyce Sidman. Illustrated by Beckie Prange.

Zombie Makers: True Stories of Nature's Undead. Written by Rebecca L. Johnson.

YOUNG ADULTS

The Bat Scientists. Written by Mary Kay Carson. Illustrated by Tom Uhlman.

Charles and Emma: The Darwins' Leap of Faith. Written by Deborah Heiligman.

Every Bone Tells a Story: Hominin Discoveries, Deductions, and Debates. Written by Jill Rubalcaba and Peter Robertshaw.

Faces from the Past: Forgotten People of North America. Written by James M. Deem.

Feynman. Written by Jim Ottaviani. Illustrated by Leland Myrick.

The Hive Detectives: Chronicle of a Honey Bee Catastrophe. Written by Loree Griffin Burns. Illustrated by Ellen Harasimowicz.

The Manatee Scientists: Saving Vulnerable Species. Written by Peter Lourie.

The Mighty Mars Rovers: The Incredible Adventures of Spirit and Opportunity. Written by Elizabeth Rusch.

The Mysteries of Beethoven's Hair. Written by Russell Martin and Lydia Nibley.

The Quest for the Tree Kangaroo: An Expedition to the Cloud Forest of New Guinea. Written by Sy Montgomery. Illustrated by Nic Bishop.

The Radioactive Boy Scout: The True Story of a Boy and His Backyard Nuclear Reactor. Written by Ken Silverstein.

Secrets of a Civil War Submarine: Solving the Mysteries of the H. L. Hunley. Written by Sally M. Walker.

Something out of Nothing: Marie Curie and Radium. Written by Carla Killough McClafferty.

The Tarantula Scientist. Written by Sy Montgomery. Illustrated by Nic Bishop.

Tracking Trash: Flotsam, Jetsam, and the Science of Ocean Motion. Written by Loree Griffin Burns.

Wild Horse Scientists. Written by Kay Frydenborg.

Written in Bone: Buried Lives of Jamestown and Colonial Maryland. Written by Sally M. Walker.

ADULTS

A Brief History of Time: From the Big Bang to Black Holes. Written by Stephen Hawking.

Chaos: Making a New Science. Written by James Gleick.

The Double Helix: A Personal Account of the Discovery of the Structure of DNA. Written by James D. Watson.

Electric Universe: How Electricity Switched on the Modern World. Written by David Bodanis.

The Emperor of All Maladies: A Biography of Cancer. Written by Siddhartha Mukherjee.

Gödel, Escher, Bach: An Eternal Golden Braid. Written by Douglas R. Hofstadter.

The Immortal Life of Henrietta Lacks. Written by Rebecca Skloot.

The Information: A History, a Theory, a Flood. Written by James Gleick.

The Lives of a Cell: Notes of a Biology Watcher. Written by Lewis Thomas.

The Making of the Atomic Bomb. Written by Richard Rhodes.

The Origin of Species. Written by Charles Darwin.

Outliers: The Story of Success. Written by Malcolm Gladwell.

The Selfish Gene. Written by Richard Dawkins.

A Short History of Nearly Everything. Written by Bill Bryson.

Silent Spring. Written by Rachel Carson.

The Structure of Scientific Revolutions. Written by Thomas S. Kuhn.

Thinking, Fast and Slow. Written by Daniel Kahneman.

The Tipping Point: How Little Things Can Make a Big Difference. Written by Malcolm Gladwell.

Sports

EARLY READERS

Black Jack: The Ballad of Jack Johnson. Written by Charles R. Smith Jr. Illustrated by Shane W. Evans.

Brothers at Bat: The True Story of an Amazing All-Brother Baseball Team. Written by Audrey Vernick. Illustrated by Steven Salerno.

Mermaid Queen: The Spectacular True Story of Annette Kellerman, Who Swam Her Way to Fame, Fortune and Swimsuit History. Written by Shana Corey. Illustrated by Edwin Fotheringham.

A Nation's Hope: The Story of Boxing Legend Joe Louis. Written by Matt De La Peña. Illustrated by Kadir Nelson.

Pelé, King of Soccer/El rey del fútbol. Written by Monica Brown. Illustrated by Rudy Gutiérrez.

Roberto Clemente: Pride of the Pittsburgh Pirates. Written by Jonah Winter. Illustrated by Raúl Colón.

Sixteen Years in Sixteen Seconds: The Sammy Lee Story. Written by Paula Yoo. Illustrated by Dom Lee.

There Goes Ted Williams: The Greatest Hitter Who Ever Lived. Written and illustrated by Matt Tavares.

Wilma Unlimited: How Wilma Rudolph Became the World's Fastest Woman. Written by Kathleen Krull. Illustrated by David Diaz.

You Never Heard of Sandy Koufax?! Written by Jonah Winter. Illustrated by André Carrilho.

MIDDLE READERS

We Are the Ship: The Story of Negro League Baseball. Written and illustrated by Kadir Nelson.

YOUNG ADULTS

21: The Story of Roberto Clemente. Written and illustrated by Wilfred Santiago.
Friday Night Lights: A Town, a Team, and a Dream. Written by H. G. Bissinger.

Technology

PRESCHOOLERS

Dig Dig Digging. Written by Margaret Mayo. Illustrated by Alex Ayliffe.
Goodnight, Goodnight Construction Site. Written by Sherri Duskey Rinker. Illustrated by Tom Lichtenheld.
Machines Go to Work in the City. Written and illustrated by William Low.
My Light. Written and illustrated by Molly Bang.
Oscar and the Bird: A Book about Electricity. Written and illustrated by Geoff Waring.
What Do Wheels Do All Day? Written by April Jones Prince. Illustrated by Giles Laroche.

EARLY READERS

Astronaut Handbook. Written and illustrated by Meghan McCarthy.
The Boy Who Invented TV: The Story of Philo Farnsworth. Written by Kathleen Krull. Illustrated by Greg Couch.
Energy Island: How One Community Harnessed the Wind and Changed Their World. Written and illustrated by Allan Drummond.
Moonshot: The Flight of Apollo 11. Written and illustrated by Brian Floca.

MIDDLE READERS

Airborne: A Photobiography of Wilbur and Orville Wright. Written by Mary Collins.

Built to Last: Building America's Amazing Bridges, Dams, Tunnels, and Skyscrapers. Written by George Sullivan.

Cathedral: The Story of Its Construction. Written and illustrated by David Macaulay.

Team Moon: How 400,000 People Landed Apollo 11 on the Moon. Written by Catherine Thimmesh.

YOUNG ADULTS

The Boy Who Harnessed the Wind. Written by William Kamkwamba and Bryan Mealer.

Hidden Worlds: Looking through a Scientist's Microscope. Written by Stephen P. Kramer. Illustrated by Dennis Kunkel.

The Longitude Prize. Written by Joan Dash. Illustrated by Dusan Petricic.

The Mighty Mars Rovers: The Incredible Adventures of Spirit *and* Opportunity. Written by Elizabeth Rusch.

The Way Things Work. Written by David Macaulay and Neil Ardley.

Wheels of Change: How Women Rode the Bicycle to Freedom (with a Few Flat Tires along the Way). Written by Sue Macy.

The Wright Brothers: How They Invented the Airplane. Written by Russell Freedman.

ADULTS

Electric Universe: How Electricity Switched on the Modern World. Written by David Bodanis.

Guns, Germs, and Steel: The Fates of Human Societies. Written by Jared Diamond.

The Information: A History, a Theory, a Flood. Written by James Gleick.

War

MIDDLE READERS

10,000 Days of Thunder: A History of the Vietnam War. Written by Philip Caputo.

America Is under Attack: September 11, 2001: The Day the Towers Fell. Written and illustrated by Don Brown.

Beyond Courage: The Untold Story of Jewish Resistance during the Holocaust. Written by Doreen Rappaport.

Blizzard of Glass: The Halifax Explosion of 1917. Written by Sally M. Walker.

Bomb: The Race to Build—and Steal—the World's Most Dangerous Weapon. Written by Steve Sheinkin.

Dogs on Duty: Soldiers' Best Friends on the Battlefield and Beyond. Written by Dorothy Hinshaw Patent.

Nurse, Soldier, Spy: The Story of Sarah Edmonds, a Civil War Hero. Written by Marissa Moss.

Sadako and the Thousand Paper Cranes. Written by Eleanor Coerr. Illustrated by Ronald Himler.

Truce: The Day the Soldiers Stopped Fighting. Written by Jim Murphy.

The Wall: Growing Up behind the Iron Curtain. Written by Peter Sis.

YOUNG ADULTS

1776. Written by David McCullough.

The Complete Maus: A Survivor's Tale. Written by Art Spiegelman.

Dear Miss Breed: True Stories of the Japanese American Incarceration during World War II and a Librarian Who Made a Difference. Written by Joanne Oppenheim.

The Diary of a Young Girl. Written by Anne Frank.

Escape from Saigon: How a Vietnam War Orphan Became an American Boy. Written by Andrea Warren.

Ghosts in the Fog: The Untold Story of Alaska's WWII Invasion. Written by Samantha Seiple.

The Good Fight: How World War II Was Won. Written by Stephen E. Ambrose.

Hitler Youth: Growing Up in Hitler's Shadow. Written by Susan Campbell Bartoletti.

In Defiance of Hitler: The Secret Mission of Varian Fry. Written by Carla Killough McClafferty.

Lafayette and the American Revolution. Written by Russell Freedman.

The Life and Death of Adolf Hitler. Written by James Cross Giblin.

A Long Way Gone: Memoirs of a Boy Soldier. Written by Ishmael Beah.

Lost Boy, Lost Girl: Escaping Civil War in Sudan. Written by John Bul Dau.

Navajo Code Talkers. Written by Nathan Aaseng.

Night. Written by Elie Wiesel.

Secrets of a Civil War Submarine: Solving the Mysteries of the H. L. Hunley. Written by Sally M. Walker.

Tasting the Sky: A Palestinian Childhood. Written by Ibtisam Barakat.
Terezín: Voices from the Holocaust. Written by Ruth Thomson.
Unraveling Freedom: The Battle for Democracy on the Home Front during World War I. Written by Ann Bausum.
The War to End All Wars: World War I. Written by Russell Freedman.

ADULTS

The Assassins' Gate: America in Iraq. Written by George Packer.
Black Hawk Down: A Story of Modern War. Written by Mark Bowden.
The Civil War: A Narrative (3 vols.). Written by Shelby Foote.
The Dark Side: The Inside Story of How the War on Terror Turned into a War on American Ideals. Written by Jane Mayer.
The Forever War. Written by Dexter Filkins.
The Great War and Modern Memory. Written by Paul Fussell.
Hiroshima. Written by John Hersey.
Homage to Catalonia. Written by George Orwell.
In the Garden of Beasts: Love, Terror, and an American Family in Hitler's Berlin. Written by Erik Larson.
The Looming Tower: Al-Qaeda and the Road to 9/11. Written by Lawrence Wright.
This Republic of Suffering: Death and the American Civil War. Written by Drew Gilpin Faust.
We Wish to Inform You That Tomorrow We Will Be Killed with Our Families: Stories from Rwanda. Written by Philip Gourevitch.

Wildlife and Environmental Conservation

PRESCHOOLERS

Elephants Can Paint, Too! Written and illustrated by Katya Arnold.
Leo the Snow Leopard: The True Story of an Amazing Rescue. Written by Craig Hatkoff. Illustrated by Isabella Hatkoff.
Pale Male: Citizen Hawk of New York City. Written by Janet Schulman. Illustrated by Meilo So.
What Bluebirds Do. Written and illustrated by Pamela F. Kirby.

EARLY READERS

The Camping Trip That Changed America. Written by Barb Rosenstock. Illustrated by Mordicai Gerstein.

Can We Save the Tiger? Written by Martin Jenkins. Illustrated by Vicky White.

The Chiru of High Tibet. Written by Jacqueline Briggs Martin. Illustrated by Linda Wingerter.

Energy Island: How One Community Harnessed the Wind and Changed Their World. Written and illustrated by Allan Drummond.

Face to Face with Lions. Written by Beverly and Dereck Joubert.

Life in the Ocean: The Story of Oceanographer Sylvia Earle. Written and illustrated by Claire A. Nivola.

Meadowlands: A Wetland Survival Story. Written and illustrated by Thomas F. Yezerski.

Planting the Trees of Kenya: The Story of Wangari Maathai. Written and illustrated by Claire A. Nivola.

Sea Horse: The Shyest Fish in the Sea. Written by Chris Butterworth. Illustrated by John Lawrence.

MIDDLE READERS

Come Back, Salmon: How a Group of Dedicated Kids Adopted Pigeon Creek and Brought It Back to Life. Written by Molly Cone. Illustrated by Sidnee Wheelwright.

For the Birds: The Life of Roger Tory Peterson. Written by Peggy Thomas. Illustrated by Laura Jacques.

George Washington Carver. Written by Tonya Bolden.

John Muir: America's First Environmentalist. Written by Kathryn Lasky. Illustrated by Stan Fellows.

Kakapo Rescue: Saving the World's Strangest Parrot. Written by Sy Montgomery. Illustrated by Nic Bishop.

Moonbird: A Year on the Wind with the Great Survivor B95. Written by Phillip Hoose.

YOUNG ADULTS

The Bat Scientists. Written by Mary Kay Carson. Illustrated by Tom Uhlman.

A Life in the Wild: George Schaller's Struggle to Save the Last Great Beasts. Written by Pamela S. Turner.

The Manatee Scientists: Saving Vulnerable Species. Written by Peter Lourie.
The Race to Save the Lord God Bird. Written by Phillip Hoose.
Tracking Trash: Flotsam, Jetsam, and the Science of Ocean Motion. Written by
   Loree Griffin Burns.

ADULTS

Collapse: How Societies Choose to Fail or Succeed. Written by Jared Diamond.
Desert Solitaire: A Season in the Wilderness. Written by Edward Abbey.
The Omnivore's Dilemma: A Natural History of Four Meals. Written by Michael
   Pollan.
Silent Spring. Written by Rachel Carson.

Women's Accomplishments and Struggles

EARLY READERS

Eleanor, Quiet No More. Written by Doreen Rappaport. Illustrated by Gary
   Kelley.
*Mermaid Queen: The Spectacular True Story of Annette Kellerman, Who Swam
   Her Way to Fame, Fortune and Swimsuit History.* Written by Shana Corey.
   Illustrated by Edwin Fotheringham.
Planting the Trees of Kenya: The Story of Wangari Maathai. Written and illus-
   trated by Claire A. Nivola.
Soar, Elinor! Written by Tami Lewis Brown. Illustrated by François Roca.
Sonia Sotomayor: A Judge Grows in the Bronx/La juez que creció en el Bronx. Writ-
   ten by Jonah Winter. Illustrated by Edel Rodriguez.
*What to Do about Alice? How Alice Roosevelt Broke the Rules, Charmed the World,
   and Drove Her Father Teddy Crazy!* Written by Barbara Kerley. Illustrated
   by Edwin Fotheringham.
You Forgot Your Skirt, Amelia Bloomer! Written by Shana Corey. Illustrated by
   Chesley McLaren.

MIDDLE READERS

Almost Astronauts: 13 Women Who Dared to Dream. Written by Tanya Lee
   Stone.
Eleanor Roosevelt: A Life of Discovery. Written by Russell Freedman.

Girls Think of Everything: Stories of Ingenious Inventions by Women. Written by Catherine Thimmesh. Illustrated by Melissa Sweet.

Harriet Tubman: Conductor on the Underground Railroad. Written by Ann Petry.

Nurse, Soldier, Spy: The Story of Sarah Edmonds, a Civil War Hero. Written by Marissa Moss.

Queen of the Falls. Written and illustrated by Chris van Allsburg.

YOUNG ADULTS

Claudette Colvin: Twice toward Justice. Written by Phillip Hoose.

I Know Why the Caged Bird Sings. Written by Maya Angelou.

Something out of Nothing: Marie Curie and Radium. Written by Carla Killough McClafferty.

Wheels of Change: How Women Rode the Bicycle to Freedom (with a Few Flat Tires along the Way). Written by Sue Macy.

Witches! The Absolutely True Tale of Disaster in Salem. Written and illustrated by Rosalyn Schanzer.

ADULTS

The Beauty Myth: How Images of Beauty Are Used against Women. Written by Naomi Wolf.

Catherine the Great: Portrait of a Woman. Written by Robert K. Massie.

Cleopatra: A Life. Written by Stacy Schiff.

The Feminine Mystique. Written by Betty Friedan.

The Gnostic Gospels. Written by Elaine Pagels.

A Room of One's Own. Written by Virginia Woolf.

CHAPTER 7

25 Contemporary Writers You Should Know

The writer is an explorer. Every step is an advance into a new land.

—Ralph Waldo Emerson

The Mother of All Booklists is a very selective guide. To have one book chosen for inclusion by such a distinguished cross section of experts is impressive; to have several titles chosen is amazing. Representing a broad range of backgrounds, interests, and age-group specializations, the following group of modern researchers, illustrators, and storytellers has each made multiple contributions to this volume. Listed alphabetically, each sketch begins with the works cited in *The Mother of All Booklists*.

Anne Applebaum, courtesy of Anne Applebaum.

ANNE APPLEBAUM (B. 1964)

Gulag: A History of the Soviet Camps (2003)
Iron Curtain: The Crushing of Eastern Europe, 1945–1956 (2012)

Anne Applebaum is a leading journalist and Pulitzer Prize–winning author best known for her foreign policy writing and her books about the former Soviet Union and its satellite countries. She has written for countless international publications and once served on the editorial board of the *Washington Post*. Applebaum is a product of the most selective education, having graduated from the Sidwell Friends School, Yale University, and the London School of Economics. She speaks French, Polish, and Russian and is married to Polish foreign minister Radoslaw Sikorski. "To me, the point of writing history is to transmit the sense of a particular time and place—to explain why people in a particular era thought, spoke, acted, and felt as they did—and not just to say what happened. To do so, one of course needs to do more than just find the bare facts. One has to speak with people who lived at the time if at all possible, to read their memoirs, [and] to read archives," Applebuam told an interviewer when she was a finalist for the 2012 National Book Award.[1] She is the editor of *Gulag Voices: An Anthology* (2011) and cowrote *From a Polish Country House Kitchen: 90 Recipes for the Ultimate Comfort Food* (2012).

Susan Campbell Bartoletti, photo by Kim Winey Photography.

SUSAN CAMPBELL BARTOLETTI (B. 1958)

Hitler Youth: Growing Up in Hitler's Shadow (2005)
They Called Themselves the KKK: The Birth of an American Terrorist Group (2010)

Susan Campbell Bartoletti grew up in rural Moscow, Pennsylvania, attended college at nearby Marywood University and the University of Scranton, and worked locally for many years as an English teacher at North Pocono Middle School. Flourishing as a writer in this rustic setting, Bartoletti has produced poetry, short stories, picture books, novels, and especially nonfiction for young readers, for which she is most recognized. Her many awards include the Newbery Honor, Robert F. Sibert Award for Nonfiction, Orbis Pictus Award for Nonfiction, Golden Kite Award for Nonfiction, Jane Addams Children's Book Award, and the Washington Post's Children's Book Guild Award for her body of nonfiction work. Bartoletti has a Ph.D. in English from Binghamton University and is a member of the Pennsylvania State University's World Campus faculty for children's literature. "I often tell aspiring writers to write about what you like, to write about what you know, to write about what you'd like to know, and to write about what you don't like and don't understand," says the author who has delved into difficult topics such as child labor, the Third Reich, and the Ku Klux Klan. "In my work, I explore the lives of those who were victimized, exploited, disenfranchised, and silenced."[2] She recently published *Down the Rabbit Hole: The Diary of Pringle Rose* (2013), a novel for middle and young-adult readers featuring a boy with Down's syndrome.

Nic Bishop, photo by Nic Bishop.

NIC BISHOP (B. 1955)

Red-Eyed Tree Frog (1999)
Chameleon, Chameleon (2005)
The Quest for the Tree Kangaroo: An Expedition to the Cloud Forest of New Guinea (2006)
The Tarantula Scientist (2007)
Nic Bishop Spiders (2007)
Kakapo Rescue: Saving the World's Strangest Parrot (2010)
Nic Bishop Snakes (2012)

Acclaimed photographer Nic Bishop, known for his stunning images of bugs, frogs, and reptiles, is the author and illustrator of more than 60 children's and young-adult books. Born in England, the son of biologists, Bishop was raised in Bangladesh, Sudan, and Papua New Guinea, and his work has kept him traveling around the world. In New Zealand, he earned a Ph.D. in plant physiology at Canterbury University. He started taking photographs at age 9 while in Africa and had many other opportunities to take pictures in a childhood and adolescence full of travel and adventure. After publishing several photo books about New Zealand's natural history, he was persuaded to try his hand at children's nonfiction books, which he says are actually more fun to create. Bishop employs two distinct photographic styles, controlled studio shots for extreme close-ups of small animals, and opportunistic shots that are taken on expedition to some of the most remote regions on earth. Bishop has received several book awards in New Zealand, and in the United States, he has been recognized with the Robert F. Sibert Informational Honor, the International Reading Association Children's Book Award, and the Boston Globe–Horn Book Award. Unlike many nonfiction writers, Bishop relies mostly on firsthand observation rather than from content from other books. His children's titles often do not have bibliographies.[3]

Bill Bryson, courtesy of Durham University.

BILL BRYSON (B. 1951)

A Walk in the Woods: Rediscovering America on the Appalachian Trail (1998)
A Short History of Nearly Everything (2003)

Known for his books observing life in North America, Britain, Europe, and Australia, Bryson was born and raised in Des Moines, Iowa. On a visit to England, Bryson got a temporary job at a psychiatric hospital, where he met and married a nurse. The couple lived in England from 1977 to 1995, where he worked as a journalist and editor for the *Times* and the *Independent*. He spent several years back in America before returning to England where he was awarded an honorary Order of the British Empire and served as the chancellor of Durham University. Bryson has said that the best job in the world is to be a travel writer. "I think the main thing is to just write," the jovial scribe recommends to aspiring authors. "There are an awful lot of people that just talk about a book they are going to write, but they never get round to writing it. I think that unless you just get on with the writing, there's no way to tell whether you're a good writer or not."[4] Two of Bryson's recent acclaimed titles are *At Home: A Short History of Private Life* (2010), a history of domesticity, and *One Summer: America, 1927* (2013), a look at epochal events and personalities of this forgotten year. He has written a humorous memoir, *The Life and Times of the Thunderbolt Kid* (2006), about his Iowa childhood.

Nicola Davies, courtesy of Nicola Davies.

NICOLA DAVIES (B. 1958)

Big Blue Whale (2001)
One Tiny Turtle (2005)
Extreme Animals: The Toughest Creatures on Earth (2009)
Dolphin Baby! (2012)
Just Ducks! (2012)

With a degree in zoology and experience as a television host for a BBC wildlife program, Nicola Davies is best recognized in America for her animal books for children. Davies has always been intrigued by animals and has traveled all over the world to study them. Her subjects of study include Madagascan chameleons, Arctic walruses, Kenyan foxes, Australian crocodiles, and Welsh birds near her home. As a teenager, she had the opportunity to study dolphins in Newfoundland and the Indian Ocean, leading her to study zoology at Kings College in Cambridge. "I am interested in communication," says Davies, "communication about zoology, about science and about how we as humans experience and interpret our existence. I'm convinced that art and science are all part of the same picture and can contribute enormously to each other. It's the crossovers and combinations of fields of interest that motivate me in life and work."[5] Davies began writing in her 30s, first on scripts for children's television and then articles, books, and novels. The author is also known for her humorous and well-regarded *Poop: A Natural History of the Unmentionable* (2004) and *Gaia Warriors* (2011), a book about global warming that she coauthored with James Lovelock. Under the pseudonym Stevie Morgan, Davies has also written several novels for adults.

JARED DIAMOND (B. 1937)

Collapse: How Societies Choose to Fail or Succeed (2004)
Guns, Germs, and Steel: The Fates of Human Societies (2005)

Polymath Jared Diamond is a scientist who has distinguished himself by writing popular-science books that synthesize information from a diverse array of fields. He is an accomplished pianist who began playing at age 6; he attended the Roxbury Latin School, Harvard College, and Trinity College at the University of Cambridge. Diamond has expertise in physiology, biophysics, ornithology, environmental science, history, geography, evolutionary biology, and anthropology; he also speaks 12 languages.

Jared Diamond, courtesy of Geography Department, UCLA.

Currently a professor of geography at the University of California, Los Angeles, Diamond has been elected to the National Academy of Sciences, the American Academy of Arts and Sciences, and the American Philosophical Society. Among his many awards are the National Medal of Science and the Pulitzer Prize for *Guns, Germs, and Steel*. He divides his time between teaching, doing field research in the South Pacific, writing books for a broad readership, and helping to direct international environmental organizations. "Working in academia, and writing about geography and environmental history, are things that I love. It's not work: it's fun. I happen to get paid for that fun, but if someone tomorrow gave me ten million dollars, I would continue my job as professor of geography at UCLA, because it's what I most enjoy." Two of Diamond's other noteworthy books are *The Third Chimpanzee: The Evolution and Future of the Human Animal* (1992) and *The World until Yesterday: What Can We Learn from Traditional Societies?* (2012).[6]

Joan Didion, courtesy of Tulane University.

JOAN DIDION (B. 1934)

Slouching towards Bethlehem (1968)
A Year of Magical Thinking (2005)

This author of many works of fiction, nonfiction, and screenplays had a roving childhood that left her anxious and detached, qualities that are recognizable in some of her books. Her father's job as a military finance officer required the family to relocate often, which she says left her feeling that she never got properly socialized,[7] yet she became one of the most distinguished writers of the 20th century. Didion majored in English at the University of California, Berkeley, and, after winning a writing contest sponsored by *Vogue* (the same essay prize won a few years earlier by Jacqueline Bouvier), she was offered a job at the magazine's New York headquarters. Didion's first novel, *Run River* (1963), was published to generally tepid reviews, while her collection of nonfiction essays, *Slouching towards Bethlehem* (1968), received such critical acclaim that it got her nominated by the *Los Angeles Times* for Woman of the Year.[8] Didion is not politically predictable—over the course of her career, she has gone from being moderately conservative to liberal. "I came out of what was called the silent generation—and the whole bottom line was that we didn't really think there were any social answers to the problems of humanity," she once told a newspaper interviewer. In an article she wrote for the *New York Times Book Review*, Didion promoted the unorthodox view that writing was an act of aggression. "There's no getting around the fact that setting words on paper is the tactic of a secret bully, an invasion, an imposition of the writer's sensibility on the reader's most private space."[9] In *Slouching towards Bethlehem* the iconoclastic author famously observed, "Writers are always selling somebody out."

Dave Eggers, photo by Duke Photography.

DAVE EGGERS (B. 1970)

A Heartbreaking Work of Staggering Genius (2001)
Zeitoun (2009)

Dave Eggers is a critically acclaimed author, editor, publisher, and philanthropist who burst upon the literary scene with his memoir, *A Heartbreaking Work of Staggering Genius*, that recounts how, at age 21, he raised his 8-year-old brother after the death of both parents. Eggers is the founder and editor of McSweeney's—named in memory of his mother—an independent publishing house in San Francisco. He is one of the founders of 826 Valencia, a nonprofit tutoring center in San Francisco that now has chapters in several cities. He is also the founder of ScholarMatch, a program that helps needy students raise money to attend college. Eggers's *What Is the What* (2006), a finalist for the National Book Critics Circle Award, is about a survivor of the civil war in Sudan; it has spawned a foundation that operates a secondary school in the war-torn African country. In 2009, Eggers was given the "Courage in Media" Award by the Council on American-Islamic Relations for *Zeitoun*, the story of a Syrian immigrant who was unjustly imprisoned while helping neighbors after Hurricane Katrina. Humanitarian Eggers does his writing in long stretches in a modest backyard shed, punctuating his time by teaching kids to write once a week at 826 Valencia. "When you spend eight hours in a shed to get a few hundred words down, you need every bit of inspiration you can get. And the best place to find inspiration, for me at least, is to see the effect of great writing on the young. Their reactions can be hard to predict, and they're always brutally honest, but when they love something, their enthusiasm is completely without guile, utterly without cynicism."[10]

Candace Fleming, courtesy of Michael Lionstar.

CANDACE FLEMING (B. 1962)

Ben Franklin's Almanac: Being a True Account of the Good Gentleman's Life (2003)
The Lincolns: A Scrapbook Look at Abraham and Mary (2008)
The Great and Only Barnum: The Tremendous, Stupendous Life of Showman P. T. Barnum (2009)
Amelia Lost: The Life and Disappearance of Amelia Earhart (2011)

Candace Fleming is the productive and award-winning author of more than 20 books for children who at an early age started telling creative stories about her family. Encouraged by her parents, by the second grade she began recording her thoughts on paper, an activity that grew through her teenage years. In college she joined her love of language with the love of history. Fleming's experience of reading to her own children is what motivated her to begin creating entertaining picture books for younger readers and creative and original biographies of historical figures for middle readers. In 2014, the Children's Book Guild presented its annual Nonfiction Award to Fleming for her body of excellent nonfiction books for children of various ages. She has received the Golden Kite Award for Nonfiction, the Boston Globe–Horn Book award for Nonfiction, and has been recognized by the ALA, *Publishers Weekly*, and the *New York Times* for her exemplary writing. "I'm one of those writers who tend to get lost in their research. In fact, I want to get lost in the research. It's the only way to uncover those overlooked tidbits of truth," Fleming says. To write *Amelia Lost*, Fleming spent weeks sifting through documents at the Purdue University Library; visited historical societies in Kansas, New Mexico, California; took a flight along Amelia's route over Southeast Asia; and even considered taking flying lessons.[11]

Russell Freedman, courtesy of Houghton Mifflin Harcourt.

RUSSELL FREEDMAN (B. 1929)

Lincoln: A Photobiography (1987)
The Wright Brothers: How They Invented the Airplane (1994)
Eleanor Roosevelt: A Life of Discovery (1997)
Children of the Great Depression (2005)
Freedom Walkers: The Story of the Montgomery Bus Boycott (2006)
Who Was First? Discovering the Americas (2007)
Lafayette and the American Revolution (2010)
Abraham Lincoln and Frederick Douglass: The Story behind an American Friendship (2012)
The Boston Tea Party (2012)
The War to End All Wars: World War I (2013)

Of the many books that have won the prestigious Newbery Medal since the inception of the award in 1922, only a handful have been recognized for nonfiction. Russell Freedman's *Lincoln: A Photobiography* is one of those few winners. The author of over 50 books for young people, Freedman is a favorite among teachers and librarians because of his reputation for consistently producing high quality books. His rich and varied life includes attending college at the University of California, working as a reporter and editor for the Associated Press, fighting in the Korean War, working for an ad agency and writing publicity copy for the television shows *Father Knows Best* and *The Real McCoys*, and living in Greenwich Village during the 1960s. To get inspiration for his books, Freedman has traveled all over the world; for example, he wrote *Confucius: The Golden Rule* (2002) after touring mainland China. To write Lincoln's biography, Freedman visited the Kentucky log cabin of the president's birth; the Indiana home of his childhood; Ford's Theater, where he was assassinated; and many other historical sites. "There is something magical about laying your eyes on the real thing—something you can't get from your reading alone," the author advises.[12] Besides his Newbery Medal and honors, Freedman has received the Laura Ingalls Wilder Medal, Sibert Medal, Regina Medal, Anne V. Zarrow Award for Young Readers' Literature, Jane Addams Children's Book Award, Orbis Pictus Award, and the National Humanities Medal. A recent noteworthy title is *Angel Island: Gateway to Gold Mountain* (2013).

Malcolm Gladwell, courtesy of Nick Gangemi, the Miami Hurricane.

MALCOLM GLADWELL (B. 1963)

The Tipping Point: How Little Things Can Make a Big Difference (2000)
Outliers: The Story of Success (2008)

Born in England, journalist Malcolm Gladwell grew up in Canada and has written five *New York Times* best sellers that mine social science research, identifying unforeseen implications. His books are encouraging and optimistic and have found a wide audience among businesspeople and others looking to comprehend and profit from the complexities of modern society. While in high school, he was a championship middle-distance runner, and he graduated from the University of Toronto. Reflecting on his method for writing books and articles, Gladwell said, "I have two parallel things I'm interested in. One is, I'm interested in collecting interesting stories, and the other is I'm interested in collecting interesting research. What I'm looking for is cases where they overlap."[13] In his *What the Dog Saw and Other Adventures* (2009), he explained, "Good writing does not succeed or fail on the strength of its ability to persuade. It succeeds or fails on the strength of its ability to engage you, to make you think, to give you a glimpse into someone else's head." Gladwell has been appointed to the Order of Canada, was named by *Time* one of its 100 most influential people, selected as one of *Foreign Policy*'s top global thinkers, and received the American Sociological Association's first Award for Excellence in the Reporting of Social Issues. Gladwell has a trademark crop of curly hair and is known as a gifted speaker, sometimes commanding fees of $40,000 per lecture. Gladwell's other books are *Blink: The Power of Thinking without Thinking* (2005) and *David and Goliath: Underdogs, Misfits, and the Art of Battling Giants* (2013).

JAMES GLEICK (B. 1954)

Chaos: Making a New Science (2008)
The Information: A History, a Theory, a Flood (2011)

Ten years a reporter and editor for the *New York Times*, acclaimed science writer James Gleick's gift is making complex and arcane topics intelligible to the average reader. He attended Riverdale Country School, where JFK once studied, and excelled in mathematics and science. Gleick attended Harvard University, wrote for the *Harvard Crimson*, and graduated with degrees in English and linguistics. His first book, *Chaos*, originally published in 1987, was a National Book Award and Pulitzer Prize finalist. It was followed by several other books, including the biographies *Genius: The Life and Science of Richard Feynman* (1992) and *Isaac Newton* (2003); both titles also made the short list for the Pulitzer Prize. He has lectured at Princeton University, cofounded a pioneering Internet service company in New York City, and edited *The Best American Science Writing* (2000), the first of the series. Gleick faced personal tragedy in 1997 when he crashed an experimental plane he was piloting, killing his 8-year-old son, losing his leg, and requiring five months of hospitalization.[14] During his rehabilitation, he began writing *Faster: Our Race against Time* (1999), based on his Fast Forward newspaper columns in the *New York Times*. As a writer, Gleick admits, "I'm often at the very edge of what I'm able to understand myself. I'm writing books about things that I care about, telling the stories that I think matter to our culture and our culture is more and more about scientific things." He acknowledges that science writing is often a humbling experience because "it often requires asking smart people a lot of dumb questions."[15]

Jan Greenberg, courtesy of Jan Greenberg.

JAN GREENBERG (B. 1942) AND SANDRA JORDAN (B. 1947)

Vincent van Gogh: Portrait of an Artist (2001)
Action Jackson (2007)
Andy Warhol: Prince of Pop (2007)
Ballet for Martha: Making Appalachian Spring (2010)

Jan Greenberg is a writer, teacher, and art educator who lives in St. Louis, and Sandra Jordan is a writer, editor, and photographer based in New York City. Working together since 1989,

Sandra Jordan, courtesy of Sandra Jordan.

this writing team has left its mark by producing outstanding books about art. They met in 1978 when Greenberg submitted a manuscript to Farrar, Straus & Giroux, where Sandra was then editor in chief of Children's Books. After 10 years of friendship, they decided to work together to write *The Painter's Eye: Learning to Look at Contemporary American Art* (1991), which describes the basic elements of artistic composition. Greenberg was on the staff at Webster University and working toward a doctorate degree at Washington University but decided to pursue a writing career when she published her first novel, *A Season In-Between* (1979). Jordan decided in high school that she wanted to be an editor and, after graduating from Simmons College, found a job with a publisher. In addition to Farrar, Straus & Giroux, she has been an editor at New American Library, and she is one of the founders of the U.S. branch of Orchard Books. The writing team has earned numerous book awards from the most esteemed organizations. While they live in different parts of the country, Greenberg says that she and Jordan have a close partnership. "We do work well together, and we rewrite each other's sentences. We revise endlessly." Jordan says that writing involves self-discovery, explaining that "I often find that I don't know what I think until I write it."[16] Some of Greenberg and Jordan's noteworthy books are *Runaway Girl: The Artist Louise Bourgeois* (2003), *Christo and Jeanne-Claude: Through the Gates and Beyond* (2008), and *The Mad Potter: George E. Ohr, Eccentric Genius* (2013).

Steve Jenkins, photo by Jamie Jenkins.

STEVE JENKINS (B. 1952)

Biggest, Strongest, Fastest (1995)
Hottest, Coldest, Highest, Deepest (1998)
Animal Dads (2000)
Bugs Are Insects (2001)
What Do You Do with a Tail like This? (2003)
Vulture View (2007)
Never Smile at a Monkey: And 17 Other Important Things to Remember (2009)
Down, Down, Down: A Journey to the Bottom of the Sea (2009)

How to Clean a Hippopotamus: A Look at Unusual Animal Partnerships (2010)
Bones: Skeletons and How They Work (2010)
Just a Second (2011)
Actual Size (2011)
The Beetle Book (2012)
Dogs and Cats (2012)
My First Day (2013)

Prolific writer and illustrator Steve Jenkins is known for his distinctive cut-and-torn collages that make his books so attractive and identifiable to young readers. Jenkins has written and illustrated dozens of books, many in collaboration with his wife, Robin Page, making him one of the biggest names in children's nonfiction. He has teamed up with an impressive array of children's authors and written and illustrated many books that are a mainstay of school libraries across the United States. As a youngster, Jenkins's family moved often and the constant thread was his interest in art and the natural world, passions encouraged by his physicist father. In his childhood travels, Jenkins collected lizards, mice, insects, rocks, and fossils—the types of things that he would later feature in his books. He attended the School of Design at North Carolina State University, where he met his wife. They moved to New York City and did commercial graphic design work for several years before segueing into children's book publishing. Jenkins has accumulated many honors and awards including the Caldecott Honor and the Boston Globe–Horn Book Award, and he has been recognized by organizations such as *Scientific American, Booklist, School Library Journal,* the Bank Street College of Education, the New York Public Library, the National Science Teachers Association, and the National Council of Teachers of English. In his work, Jenkins dismisses the cultural misconception that exaggerates the gulf between art and science. "I believe that understanding how things work, what they're called, and what they do increases our sense of awe and reverence. I believe we should teach science as a process, [and] tool, not just a collection of facts."[17]

Barbara Kerley, courtesy of
Barbara Kerley.

BARBARA KERLEY (B. 1960)

Dinosaurs of Waterhouse Hawkins: An Illuminating History of Mr. Waterhouse Hawkins, Artist and Lecturer (2001)
What to Do about Alice? How Alice Roosevelt Broke the Rules, Charmed the World, and Drove Her Father Teddy Crazy! (2008)
The Extraordinary Mark Twain (according to Susy) (2010)
Those Rebels, John and Tom (2012)

One of the foremost writers of historical biographies for children, Barbara Kerley, the youngest of three children, grew up in the suburbs of Washington, D.C., and was active in sports and theater groups. After majoring in English at the University of Chicago, Kerley joined the Peace Corps and taught math, science, and English in Nepal. While in Nepal, she hiked the approach to Mount Everest up to 14,000 feet. When she returned to the United States, she worked as a bartender and later as a baker while going to graduate school at the University of Washington, where she received a masters degree in "English as a Second Language." She then taught English in Guam and used her experiences abroad as inspiration to write *Songs from Papa's Island* (1995) and *A Cool Drink of Water* (2002). She has also written *Walt Whitman: Words for America* (2004), *A Home for Mr. Emerson* (2014), and other award-winning titles. Kerley advises aspiring writers to start with a biography of a family member the way Susy Clemens did as described in Kerley's book *The Extraordinary Mark Twain (according to Susy)*. She suggests paying attention to personal habits, observing likes and dislikes, and taking copious notes. Wherever possible, Kerley says, writers should strive to show rather than tell. "To make your biography lively, instead of just telling your readers that your subject is funny, give them an example of one of your subject's jokes."[18] She now lives in Portland, Oregon, and her hobbies include reading, hiking, cooking, canoeing, movie watching, and banjo playing.

Kathleen Krull, photo by Lili Gonzalez.

KATHLEEN KRULL (B. 1952)

Wilma Unlimited: How Wilma Rudolph Became the World's Fastest Woman (2000)
Harvesting Hope: The Story of Cesar Chavez (2003)
The Boy Who Invented TV: The Story of Philo Farnsworth (2009)
Kubla Khan: The Emperor of Everything (2010)
The Boy on Fairfield Street: How Ted Geisel Grew Up to Become Dr. Seuss (2010)
Big Wig: A Little History of Hair (2011)

Kathleen Krull's more than 60 books have earned her dozens of awards and accolades, including the Children's Book Guild Award for her total body of quality nonfiction for children. When she was a teenager, Krull played the organ at church, served doughnuts at a bakery, gave piano lessons, and worked at the library, where she was fired for reading on the job. She is a graduate of Lawrence University in Appleton, Wisconsin, and now lives in San Diego with her husband, a book illustrator and occasional publishing partner. Before she became a full-time writer, Krull worked for 11 years as a children's book editor. Krull has written many biographies of prominent people, including Charles Darwin, Marie Curie, Sigmund Freud, Albert Einstein, Leonardo da Vinci, Isaac Newton, Hillary Rodham Clinton, Franklin Delano Roosevelt, Jim Henson, Houdini, and the Beatles. She has written several books that pull together the lives of accomplished people by occupation, supplying fascinating mini-biographies of writers, scientists, athletes, musicians, presidents, and others. "I see my role as taking the valuable work of scholars and distilling it into a form that I hope will make children love, or at least like, history. I take a mountain of notes on what is most interesting, and then revise, tinker, revise, edit, whittle, and then revise some more. If there is a key to what I do, it's that I don't use most of my information. As Voltaire said, 'The best way to be boring is to leave nothing out.'"[19]

ERIK LARSON (B. 1954)

The Devil in the White City: Murder, Magic, and Madness at the Fair That Changed America (2003)
In the Garden of Beasts: Love, Terror, and an American Family in Hitler's Berlin (2011)

Erik Larson, courtesy of Erik Larson, photo by Benjamin Benschneider.

Larson grew up on Long Island and made his first attempts at publication by submitting cartoons to the *New Yorker*, which the magazine declined to publish. Next he wrote a novel. "It was 75 pages long and had a sex scene, even though I had no idea what sex was." Larson studied Russian history, language, and culture as an undergraduate at the University of Pennsylvania and received a master's degree in journalism from Columbia University. His first job as a reporter was with a newspaper in the Philadelphia suburbs followed by a job with the *Wall Street Journal*. Larson has written stories for *Time*, the *New Yorker*, the *Atlantic Monthly*, and *Harper's* and has taught nonfiction writing at San Francisco State University and Johns Hopkins University. *The Devil in the White City* was a finalist for the National Book Award and a *San Francisco Chronicle* Best Book of the Year. *In the Garden of Beasts* was short listed for a Chautauqua Prize and selected by *Christian Science Monitor* as a best nonfiction book. "I always advise writers to work in manageable, relatively short periods, and always to stop at a point where they know they can pick up the next day. I'd also quote my favorite maxim: if you don't ask, the answer is always no. If you don't send that short story to the *New Yorker*, one thing is certain, it will never be published in the *New Yorker*."[20] Two of Larson's other notable titles are *Isaac's Storm: A Man, a Time, and the Deadliest Hurricane in History* (1999) and *Thunderstruck* (2006).

DAVID MCCULLOUGH (B. 1933)

David McCullough, courtesy of Scranton Public Library.

John Adams (2001)
1776 (2005)

It would be hard to find an American author with a more distinguished record than David McCullough. He is a two-time winner of both the Pulitzer Prize and the National Book Award, and he has been recognized by the National Book Foundation for a lifetime of achievement. He has been given over 50 honorary degrees, is the recipient of the Presidential Medal of Freedom, has spoken before a joint session of Congress, and been asked to lecture at some of America's most prestigious institutions. He hosted PBS's *American Experience* for 12 years and has narrated many documentaries. He graduated from Yale University in 1955 with the intention of becoming a novelist. McCullough was born and raised in Pittsburgh, Pennsylvania, and while working as an editor at *American Heritage*, he wrote his first book, *The Johnstown Flood* (1968). McCullough writes for the general reader rather than for fellow historians, and his general rule of thumb is to write the book that he would like to read. He became a historian by accident when he saw pictures of the devastation at Johnstown, a city not far from Pittsburgh. He read some books on the topic and found them wanting, so he decided to write one himself. "I was about 29 at the time. I'd never done historical research. So I had a lot to learn, but I had found what I wanted to do with my life."[21] McCullough has also written *The Great Bridge* (1972), *The Path between the Seas* (1977), *Mornings on Horseback* (1981), *Brave Companions* (1992), *Truman* (1992), and *The Greater Journey* (2011).

SY MONTGOMERY (B. 1958)

The Quest for the Tree Kangaroo: An Expedition to the Cloud Forest of New Guinea (2006)
The Tarantula Scientist (2007)
Kakapo Rescue: Saving the World's Strangest Parrot (2010)
Temple Grandin: How the Girl Who Loved Cows Embraced Autism and Changed the World (2012)

Sy Montgomery, photo by Nic Bishop.

Sy Montgomery is an author, conservationist, and scriptwriter who, in the course of doing her research for her many projects, has been bitten by vampire bats, chased by irate silverback gorillas, worked with crawling snakes, swum with piranhas, handled tarantulas, and been hunted by tigers. She has written 15 books and received many honors and awards. Born in Frankfurt, Germany, she graduated from Syracuse University, majoring in journalism, French language and literature, and psychology. After college, she worked as a reporter but was eager to move on to books. Her first book was *Walking with the Great Apes: Jane Goodall, Dian Fossey, Birute Galdikas* (1991). Montgomery has narrated and scripted a National Geographic documentary based on her book *Spell of the Tiger: The Man-Eaters of Sundarbans* (1995). She has also written *The Good Good Pig: The Extraordinary Life of Christopher Hogwood* (2006), a popular book about her adoption of a sickly runt from a litter of pigs who grew into a 750-pound barnyard pet and a celebrity in her New Hampshire hometown. "I loved writing for newspapers, but the thing is, when you write for a newspaper, your story is on the bottom of someone's birdcage within 24 hours. It's nice to write a book that's going to last forever." Montgomery's animal books, she says, follow a basic pattern: "Look at this fantastic creature. Look at the abilities this creature has. Don't you love it? . . . Don't you want to join in the effort to protect and preserve this animal?"[22]

JIM MURPHY (B. 1947)

An American Plague: The True and Terrifying Story of the Yellow Fever Epidemic of 1793 (2003)
Truce: The Day the Soldiers Stopped Fighting (2009)
The Great Fire (2010)
Invincible Microbe: Tuberculosis and the Never-Ending Search for a Cure (2012)

Jim Murphy, photo by Arthur Cohen.

Award-winning author Jim Murphy is the author of more than 30 books about American history. He grew up in a New Jersey industrial town near New York City and attended Rutgers University and Radcliffe College. Murphy says he had no interest in reading until a teacher mentioned a book that students were absolutely forbidden to read: naturally, he searched out the book and soon got hooked on the printed word. Murphy landed a job in publishing as an editorial secretary and worked his way up to managing editor, finally leaving to work on his own books.[23] His first title was *Weird and Wacky Inventions* (1978), and it dealt with strange creations such as a suitcase that transforms into a bathtub and a hair-cutting machine. Murphy's subsequent books followed a more serious vein and led to his receipt of the ALA's Margaret A. Edwards Award for lifetime achievement in young-adult literature. The 2010 award referenced five of his most noteworthy books: *The Long Road to Gettysburg* (1992), *A Young Patriot: The American Revolution as Experienced by One Boy* (1996), *Blizzard! The Storm That Changed America* (2000), *The Great Fire* (2010), and *An American Plague: The True and Terrifying Story of the Yellow Fever Epidemic of 1793* (2003). In his several books about war for a young audience, Murphy has endeavored to write truthfully and frankly, largely focusing on the perspectives and emotions of those who were actually in combat situations. He wants to avoid the history he was exposed to as a child that "talked almost solely about important individuals making important decisions [and] discussed battles as if they were well-mannered chess matches."[24]

KADIR NELSON (B. 1974)

Kadir Nelson, photo by David Harrison.

We Are the Ship: The Story of Negro League Baseball (2008)
Heart and Soul: The Story of America and African Americans (2011)
A Nation's Hope: The Story of Boxing Legend Joe Louis (2011)
I Have a Dream (2012)

Kadir Nelson is a critically acclaimed artist, illustrator, and author whose works have been exhibited in national and international publications, institutions, art galleries, and museums, and he is recognized for his work on African American culture and history. He grew up in San Diego, started drawing at age 3, and was apprenticed to his artist uncle. After entering paintings in art contests, he was awarded a scholarship to attend the Pratt Institute in New York City, where he graduated with honors. He has illustrated over two dozen books and is a two-time winner of the Caldecott Honor Award and a Coretta Scott King Award winner. In 2010, the gifted artist created a pair of U.S. postage stamps in honor of Negro League Baseball, and he designed the cover art for Michael Jackson's posthumous album *Michael*. Many of Nelson's paintings can be found in institutional collections such as the U.S. House of Representatives, U.S. Postal Service, U.S. Sports Academy, and International Olympic Committee, and in private collections, such as Denzel Washington, Will Smith, Spike Lee, Venus Williams, Sharon Stone, and Shaquille O'Neal. He has also done paintings for *Sports Illustrated*, the Coca-Cola Company, and Major League Baseball. Nelson recently wrote and illustrated *Nelson Mandela* (2013) and *Baby Bear* (2014). "I find that when you're doing an illustration, it's always for someone else, when you're doing a piece of fine art it's usually for yourself, or it should be." He finds that doing art for his own purposes energizes him and better develops his ability.[25]

April Pulley Sayre, photo by Jeff Sayre.

APRIL PULLEY SAYRE (B. 1966)

Stars beneath Your Bed: The Surprising Story of Dust (2005)
The Bumblebee Queen (2006)
Vulture View (2007)
Meet the Howlers! (2010)
Rah, Rah, Radishes! A Vegetable Chant (2011)

April Pulley Sayre has written over 55 natural-history books for children and adults. Born and raised in Greenville, South Carolina, she credits her mother for introducing her to the wonders of birds, plants, and wildflowers. Sayre has a bachelor's degree in biology from Duke University and a master's degree in creative writing from Vermont College. An accomplished speaker on science and writing, she often speaks to over 15,000 students a year. She has worked at the National Wildlife Federation and the National Geographic Society. Sayre has traveled to 27 countries and frequently visits Panama, a setting that is significant in several of her books, including *Army Ant Parade* (2002), *Secrets of Sound: Studying the Calls and Songs of Whales, Elephants, and Birds* (2002), and *Meet the Howlers!* (2010). In partnership with her husband, Sayre has engaged in wildlife gardening for 20 years and published an introduction to the topic, *Touch a Butterfly: Wildlife Gardening with Kids* (2013). To prepare for all of her books, she follows many avenues of research. "I read adult science books. I read scientific papers. I do a lot of interviews with scientists. But a lot of the nature books just flow naturally from our goofy, exploratory daily lives. So I spend time studying squirrels or investigating bees. Then, it becomes a picture book." With the publication of *Rah, Rah Radishes!* (2011) and *Go, Go, Grapes!* (2012), Sayre began using her own photographs, adding a new dimension to her work.[26]

JONAH WINTER (B. 1962)

Frida (2002)
Roberto Clemente: Pride of the Pittsburgh Pirates (2008)
You Never Heard of Sandy Koufax?! (2009)
Sonia Sotomayor: A Judge Grows in the Bronx/La juez que creció en el Bronx (2009)

This recognized master of picture-book biographies spent most of his childhood painting pictures, playing musical instruments, composing poems, and collecting baseball cards in Fort Worth, Texas, passions that have continued into his adulthood. Jonah Winter, the son of noted author and illustrator Jeannette Winter, entered the family business when his mother asked him to write the text for *Diego* (1991), the story of Diego Rivera, Mexico's greatest muralist. Winter has a B.A. from George Mason University and an M.F.A. from the University of Virginia and has worked as a llama rancher, a flower deliverer, a member of a rock band, and a children's-book editor. His favorite subjects are individuals who struggled against discrimination and convention. His biographies include Pablo Picasso, Hildegard von Bingen, Willie Mays, Pablo Picasso, Gertrude Stein, Beethoven, Muhammad Ali, Dizzy Gillespie, and Barack Obama (before he was elected president). Winter's *Peaceful Heroes* (2009) is a collection of profiles of individuals who have acted heroically without using violence. He has also written *Fair Ball! 14 Great Stars from Baseball's Negro Leagues* (1999) and *Born and Bred in the Great Depression* (2011), about his father growing up in East Texas during the 1930s. "Where I grew up in Texas, my classmates used racial epithets on a regular basis. In my neighborhood, people would not sell their houses to African Americans," Winter says. "As a nonfiction children's book writer . . . if I can make a difference in raising the tolerance and knowledge levels of today's children, then I feel as if I'm doing my job."[27]

TOM WOLFE (B. 1931)

The Electric Kool-Aid Acid Test (1968)
The Right Stuff (1979)

Tom Wolfe is known for his trademark white suits and is acclaimed for the quality and influence of his writing, introducing such phrases as "the right stuff," "radical chic," "the Me Generation," and "good ol' boy" into the popular vernacular. Born and raised in Richmond, Virginia, even as a child he assumed he would be a writer, modeling himself after his father who was the editor of an agriculture magazine. Wolfe received his undergraduate degree from Washington and Lee University and his Ph.D. in American Studies from Yale University and is the recipient of many literary awards, including the National Book Award, the Columbia Journalism Award, and National Book Critics Circle Finalist honor, all for *The Right Stuff*. *The Electric Kool-Aid Acid Test* is recognized for helping to usher in the literary style known as the "New Journalism" and for being the defining book of 1960s countercultural era. Wolfe is also recognized for writing *The Kandy-Kolored Tangerine-Flake Streamline Baby* (1965) and *Radical Chic and Mau-Mauing the Flak Catchers* (1970) and for his novels *The Bonfire of the Vanities* (1987) and *A Man in Full* (1998). The iconic writer is a great believer in outlines, both for his fiction and nonfiction, and he always works with a clock in sight. In an interview with George Plimpton in the *Paris Review*, Wolfe said this about his work routine: "I set myself a quota—ten pages a day, triple-spaced, which means about eighteen hundred words. If I can finish that in three hours, then I'm through for the day. I just close up the lunch box and go home—that's the way I think of it anyway. If it takes me twelve hours, that's too bad, I've got to do it."[28]

Notes

1. Mira Ptacin, interview of Anne Applebaum regarding Applebaum's book *Iron Curtain: The Crushing of Eastern Europe, 1945–1956*, National Book Foundation (website), accessed February 1, 2014, http://www.nationalbook.org/nba2012_nf_applebaum_interv.html#.Uu1uv_1teu6.

2. "Susan Campbell Bartoletti, a Writer, a Teacher, a Work-in-Progress," accessed February 2, 2014, http://www.scbartoletti.com/?page_id=2.

3. "Nick Bishop, How I Research My Books," accessed February 2, 2014, http://www.nicbishop.com/nic_bishop_029.htm.

4. Rob Savage, "Rob Savage Meets Travel Writer Extraordinaire—Bill Bryson," St. Christopher's Inns (website), accessed February 3, 2014, http://www.st-christophers.co.uk/travel-tips/blogs/interviews/bill-bryson-interview.

5. "Nicola Davies," Encyclopedia.com, accessed February 3, 2014, http://www.encyclopedia.com/topic/Nicola_Davies.aspx.

6. Jared Diamond (personal website), accessed February 3, 2014, http://www.jared diamond.org/Jared_Diamond/Welcome.html.

7. Susanna Rustin, "Legends of the Fall," *Guardian*, May 20, 2005, http://www.theguardian.com/books/2005/may/21/usnationalbookawards.society.

8. Michelle Dean, "Becoming Joan Didion," The Awl (website), May 23, 2012, http://www.theawl.com/2012/05/becoming-joan-didion.

9. "Joan Didion, Excerpts from 'Why I Write,'" *New York Times*, December 5, 1976, http://www.idiom.com/~rick/html/why_i_write.htm.

10. Dave Eggers, "Dave Eggers's Writing Life," *Washington Post*, December 10, 2010, http://www.washingtonpost.com/wp-dyn/content/article/2010/12/10/AR2010121003215.html.

11. "Meet the Biographer: Candace Fleming," *Kidsbiographer's Blog*, August 6, 2012, http://kidsbiographer.com/2012/08/06/452/.

12. *The Newbery and Caldecott Medal Books, 1986–2000: A Comprehensive Guide to the Winners* (Boston: The Horn Book and Association for Library Service to Children, 2001), 71–84.

13. "Malcolm Gladwell," Dallas Museum of Art (website), accessed February 4, 2014, http://www.dallasmuseumofart.org/programs/event/malcolm-gladwell.

14. David Diamond, "James Gleick's Survival Lessons," *Wired*, accessed February 6, 2014, http://www.wired.com/wired/archive/7.08/gleick.html.

15. "Science Writing: How Do You Make Complex Issues Accessible and Readable?," *Guardian*, December 1, 2012, http://www.theguardian.com/books/2012/dec/02/science-writing-debate-pinker-gleick-greene-frank-foer.

16. "Transcript from an Interview with Jan Greenberg and Sandra Jordan," Reading Rockets (website), accessed February 7, 2014, http://www.readingrockets.org/books/interviews/greenbergjordan/transcript.

17. "Meet Authors and Illustrators: Steve Jenkins," Children's Literature (website), accessed February 7, 2014, http://www.childrenslit.com/childrenslit/mai_jenkins_steve.html.

18. Barbara Kerley, Children's Book Author (personal website), accessed February 7, 2014, http://www.barbarakerley.com/Site/Welcome.html.

19. "Illuminating a Life through Research: Author Interview with Kathleen Krull," TheWriteChris—On Writing (website), accessed February 7, 2014, http://thewritechris.blogspot.com/2013_07_01_archive.html.

20. Erik Larson, "How I Write," *Daily Beast*, October 31, 2012, http://www.thedailybeast.com/articles/2012/10/31/how-i-write-erik-larson-revisits-isaac-s-storm.html.

21. David McCullough, "On History and Writing," *Brigham Young University Magazine*, accessed February 7, 2014, http://magazine.byu.edu/?act=view&a=1752.

22. "Sy Montgomery: In-depth Written Interview," TeachingBooks.net, February 27, 2012, http://www.teachingbooks.net/interview.cgi?id=100&a=1.

23. Jim Murphy: Making History Come Alive (website), accessed February 9, 2014, http://www.jimmurphybooks.com/about.htm.

24. Jim Murphy, "Writing about War and Peace," *The Nonfiction Life*, a blog by Jim Murphy, June 15, 2010, http://www.jimmurphybooks.com/blog/.

25. Karen Rostadha, "San Diego Artist Wins National Award," KPBS (National Public Radio), accessed February 9, 2014, https://www.kadirnelson.com/press/KPBS.htm.

26. *Michelle Cusolito, Polliwog on Safari* (blog), "Author Interview: April Pulley Sayre," April 23, 2013, http://michellecusolito.blogspot.com/2013/04/author-interview-april-pulley-sayre.html.

27. Monessa Tinsley, "Jonah Winter's Work Focuses on Famous People of Color," *Pittsburgh Post-Gazette*, February 5, 2008, http://www.post-gazette.com/ae/2008/02/05/Jonah-Winter-s-work-focuses-on-famous-people-of-color/stories/200802050209.

28. George Plimpton, "Tom Wolfe, the Art of Fiction No. 123," interview of Tom Wolfe, *Paris Review*, accessed February 11, 2014, http://www.theparisreview.org/interviews/2226/the-art-of-fiction-no-123-tom-wolfe.

APPENDIX 1

Preschool Booklist

1. *Me . . . Jane*. Written and illustrated by Patrick McDonnell. (Little, Brown Books for Young Readers, 2011.)
2. *Dave the Potter: Artist, Poet, Slave*. Written by Laban Carrick Hill. Illustrated by Bryan Collier. (Little, Brown Books for Young Readers, 2010.)
3. *Stay: The True Story of Ten Dogs*. Written by Michaela Muntean. Illustrated by K. C. Bailey and Stephen Kazmierski. (Scholastic Press, 2012.)
4. *In My Backyard*. Written by Valarie Giogas. Illustrated by Katherine Zecca. (Sylvan Dell Publishing, 2007.)
5. *Lightship*. Written and illustrated by Brian Floca. (Atheneum/Richard Jackson Books, 2007.)
6. *It's a Butterfly's Life*. Written and illustrated by Irene Kelly. (Holiday House, 2007.)
7. *Where in the Wild? Camouflaged Creatures Concealed . . . and Revealed*. Written by David M. Schwartz and Yael Schy. Illustrated by Dwight Kuhn. (Tricycle Press, 2007.)
8. *Fabulous Fishes*. Written and illustrated by Susan Stockdale. (Peachtree Publishers, 2008.)
9. *Big Blue Whale*. Written by Nicola Davies. Illustrated by Nick Maland. (Candlewick, 2001.)
10. *All the Water in the World*. Written by George Ella Lyon. Illustrated by Katherine Tillotson. (Atheneum/Richard Jackson Books, 2011.)
11. *Over and Under the Snow*. Written by Kate Messner. Illustrated by Christopher Silas Neal. (Chronicle Books, 2011.)
12. *Red-Eyed Tree Frog*. Written by Joy Cowley. Illustrated by Nic Bishop. (Scholastic Paperbacks, 1999.)
13. *Leo the Snow Leopard: The True Story of an Amazing Rescue*. Written by Craig Hatkoff. Illustrated by Isabella Hatkoff. (Scholastic Press, 2010.)

14. *Underground: Finding the Light to Freedom.* Written and illustrated by Shane W. Evans. (Roaring Brook Press, 2011.)

15. *Never Smile at a Monkey: And 17 Other Important Things to Remember.* Written and illustrated by Steve Jenkins. (HMH Books for Young Readers, 2009.)

16. *Chameleon!* Written by Joy Cowley. Illustrated by Nic Bishop. (Scholastic, 2005.)

17. *Starfish.* Written by Edith Thacher Hurd. Illustrated by Robin Brickman. (HarperCollins, 2000.)

18. *Winter's Tail: How One Little Dolphin Learned to Swim Again.* Written by Craig Hatkoff, Juliana Hatkoff, and Isabella Hatkoff. (Scholastic, 2009.)

19. *About Hummingbirds: A Guide for Children.* Written by Cathryn Sill. Illustrated by John Sill. (Peachtree Publishers, 2011.)

20. *Machines Go to Work in the City.* Written and illustrated by William Low. (Henry Holt, 2012.)

21. *Little Dog Lost: The True Story of a Brave Dog Named Baltic.* Written and illustrated by Mônica Carnesi. (Nancy Paulsen Books, 2012.)

22. *Koko's Kitten.* Written by Francine Patterson. Illustrated by Ronald H. Cohn. (Scholastic, 1985.)

23. *Just One Bite.* Written by Lola Schaefer. Illustrated by Geoff Waring. (Chronicle Books, 2010.)

24. *Elephants Can Paint, Too!* Written and illustrated by Katya Arnold. (Atheneum Books for Young Readers, 2005.)

25. *Bring On the Birds.* Written and illustrated by Susan Stockdale. (Peachtree Publishers, 2011.)

26. *My Shapes/Mis Formas.* Written and illustrated by Rebecca Emberley. (Little, Brown, 2000.)

27. *May I Pet Your Dog? The How-To Guide for Kids Meeting Dogs (and Dogs Meeting Kids).* Written by Stephanie Calmenson. Illustrated by Jan Ormerod. (Clarion Books, 2007.)

28. *A Second Is a Hiccup: A Child's Book of Time.* Written by Hazel Hutchins. Illustrated by Kady MacDonald Denton. (Arthur A. Levine Books, 2007.)

29. *The Tiny Seed.* Written and illustrated by Eric Carle. (Crowell, 1970.)

30. *What Do Wheels Do All Day?* Written by April Jones Prince. Illustrated by Giles Laroche. (HMH Books for Young Readers, 2006.)

31. *Animal Dads.* Written by Sneed B. Collard III. Illustrated by Steve Jenkins. (HMH Books for Young Readers, 2000.)

32. *Zoo Borns! Zoo Babies from around the World.* Written by Andrew Bleiman and Chris Eastland. (Simon & Schuster, 2010.)

33. *Ten Little Fingers and Ten Little Toes.* Written by Mem Fox. Illustrated by Helen Oxenbury. (HMH Books for Young Readers, 2010.)

34. *Biggest, Strongest, Fastest.* Written and illustrated by Steve Jenkins. (HMH Books for Young Readers, 1995.)
35. *The Bumblebee Queen.* Written by April Pulley Sayre. Illustrated by Patricia J. Wynne. (Charlesbridge Publishing, 2006.)
36. *My Favorite Word Book: Words and Pictures for the Very Young.* Written and illustrated by Selina Young.
37. *Here Come the Girl Scouts! The Amazing All-True Story of Juliette "Daisy" Gordon Low and Her Great Adventure.* Written by Shana Corey. Illustrated by Hadley Hooper. (Scholastic Press, 2012.)
38. *The Emperor's Egg.* Written by Martin Jenkins. Illustrated by Jane Chapman. (Candlewick, 2002.)
39. *Hottest, Coldest, Highest, Deepest.* Written and illustrated by Steve Jenkins. (Houghton Mifflin, 1998.)
40. *How to Be a Baby . . . by Me, the Big Sister.* Written by Sally Lloyd-Jones. Illustrated by Sue Heap. (Schwartz & Wade, 2007.)
41. *Tarra & Bella: The Elephant and Dog Who Became Best Friends.* Written and illustrated by Carol Buckley. (Putnam Juvenile, 2009.)
42. *If Rocks Could Sing: A Discovered Alphabet.* Written and illustrated by Leslie McGuirk. (Tricycle Press, 2011.)
43. *One Small Place in a Tree.* Written by Barbara Brenner. Illustrated by Tom Leonard. (HarperCollins, 2004.)
44. *Meet the Dogs of Bedlam Farm.* Written and illustrated by Jon Katz. (Henry Holt, 2011.)
45. *Pale Male: Citizen Hawk of New York City.* Written by Janet Schulman. Illustrated by Meilo So. (Knopf Books for Young Readers, 2008.)
46. *Rosie, a Visiting Dog's Story.* Written by Stephanie Calmenson. Illustrated by Justin Sutcliffe. (HMH Books for Young Readers, 1998.)
47. *Strong Man: The Story of Charles Atlas.* Written and illustrated by Meghan McCarthy. (Knopf Books for Young Readers, 2007.)
48. *My Visit to the Zoo.* Written and illustrated by Aliki. (HarperCollins, 1999.)
49. *Step Gently Out.* Written by Helen Frost. Illustrated by Rick Lieder. (Candlewick, 2012.)
50. *What Bluebirds Do.* Written and illustrated by Pamela F. Kirby. (Boyds Mills Press, 2013.)
51. *Stars beneath Your Bed: The Surprising Story of Dust.* Written by April Pulley Sayre. Illustrated by Ann Jonas. (Greenwillow Books, 2005.)
52. *Two Bobbies: A True Story of Hurricane Katrina, Friendship, and Survival.* Written by Kirby Larson and Mary Nethery. Illustrated by Jean Cassels. (Walker Childrens, 2008.)
53. *African Animal Alphabet.* Written by Beverly Joubert and Dereck Joubert. (National Geographic Children's Books, 2011.)

54. *Dinosaurs, Dinosaurs.* Written and illustrated by Byron Barton. (HarperCollins, 1989.)
55. *Alphabeasties and Other Amazing Types.* Written by Sharon Werner and Sarah Forss. (Blue Apple Books, 2009.)
56. *The Wing on a Flea: A Book about Shapes.* Written and illustrated by Ed Emberley. (Little, Brown, 1961.)
57. *Bugs! Bugs! Bugs!* Written and illustrated by Bob Barner. (Chronicle Books, 1999.)
58. *The Handiest Things in the World.* Written by Andrew Clements. Illustrated by Raquel Jaramillo. (Atheneum Books for Young Readers, 2010.)
59. *I Face the Wind.* Written by Vicki Cobb. Illustrated by Julia Gorton. (HarperCollins, 2003.)
60. *How Many Baby Pandas?* Written and illustrated by Sandra Markle. (Walker Childrens 2011.)
61. *Chameleons Are Cool.* Written by Martin Jenkins. Illustrated by Sue Shields. (Candlewick, 1998.)
62. *Harlem's Little Blackbird.* Written by Renée Watson. Illustrated by Christian Robinson. (Random House Books for Young Readers, 2012.)
63. *Gentle Giant Octopus.* Written by Karen Wallace. Illustrated by Mike Bostock. (Candlewick, 2002.)
64. *Dig Dig Digging.* Written by Margaret Mayo. Illustrated by Alex Ayliffe. (Henry Holt, 2002.)
65. *Seahorses.* Written by Jennifer Keats Curtis. Illustrated by Chad Wallace. (Henry Holt, 2012.)
66. *Out of Sight.* Written by Francesco Pittau and Bernadette Gervais. (Chronicle Books, 2010.)
67. *Ladybugs: Red, Fiery, and Bright.* Written and illustrated by Mia Posada. (Carolrhoda Books, 2002.)
68. *Oscar and the Bird: A Book about Electricity.* Written and illustrated by Geoff Waring. (Candlewick, 2011.)
69. *I Fall Down.* Written by Vicki Cobb. Illustrated by Julia Gorton. (HarperCollins, 2004.)
70. *Ones and Twos.* Written and illustrated by Marthe Jocelyn and Nell Jocelyn. (Tundra Books, 2011.)
71. *How Did That Get in My Lunchbox? The Story of Food.* Written by Chris Butterworth. Illustrated by Lucia Gaggiotti. (Candlewick, 2011.)
72. *One Foot Two Feet: An Exceptional Counting Book.* Written by Peter Maloney and Felicia Zekauskas. (Putnam Juvenile, 2011.)
73. *The Busy Body Book: A Kid's Guide to Fitness.* Written and illustrated by Lizzy Rockwell. (Dragonfly Books, 2008.)

74. *One Boy*. Written and illustrated by Laura Vaccaro Seeger. (Roaring Brook Press, 2008.)
75. *My Painted House, My Friendly Chicken and Me*. Written by Maya Angelou. Illustrated by Margaret Courtney-Clarke. (Crown Books for Young Readers, 2003.)
76. *Rah, Rah, Radishes! A Vegetable Chant*. Written and illustrated by April Pulley Sayre. (Beach Lane Books, 2011.)
77. *Museum ABC*. Written by Metropolitan Museum of Art. (Little, Brown Books for Young Readers, 2002.)
78. *In the Trees, Honey Bees*. Written by Lori Mortensen. Illustrated by Cris Arbo. (Dawn Publications, 2009.)
79. *Monarch and Milkweed*. Written by Helen Frost. Illustrated by Leonid Gore. (Atheneum Books for Young Readers, 2008.)
80. *Slow Down for Manatees*. Written and illustrated by Jim Arnosky. (Putnam Juvenile, 2010.)
81. *Meet the Howlers!* Written by April Pulley Sayre. Illustrated by Woody Miller. (Charlesbridge Publishing, 2010.)
82. *Life-Size Zoo: From Tiny Rodents to Gigantic Elephants, An Actual Size Animal Encyclopedia*. Written by Teruyuki Komiya. Illustrated by Toyofumi Fukuda. (Seven Footer Press, 2009.)
83. *An Island Grows*. Written by Lola M. Schaefer. Illustrated by Cathie Felstead. (Greenwillow Books, 2006.)
84. *An Orange in January*. Written by Dianna Hutts Aston. Illustrated by Julie Maren. (Dial, 2007.)
85. *In the Wild*. Written by David Elliott. Illustrated by Holly Meade. (Candlewick, 2013.)
86. *Sign Language ABC*. Written and illustrated by Lora Heller. (Sterling Children's Books, 2012.)
87. *First the Egg*. Written and illustrated by Laura Vaccaro Seeger. (Roaring Brook Press, 2007.)
88. *On the Farm*. Written by David Elliott. Illustrated by Holly Meade. (Candlewick, 2008.)
89. *The Boy Who Loved Math: The Improbable Life of Paul Erdös*. Written by Deborah Heiligman. Illustrated by LeUyen Pham. (Roaring Brook Press, 2013.)
90. *Why? The Best Ever Question and Answer Book about Nature, Science and the World around You*. Written by Catherine Ripley. Illustrated by Scot Ritchie. (Owlkids Books, 2010.)
91. *My Light*. Written and illustrated by Molly Bang. (Scholastic, 2004.)
92. *Pop! The Invention of Bubble Gum*. Written and illustrated by Meghan McCarthy. (Simon & Schuster/Paula Wiseman Books, 2010.)

93. *Are You a Snail?* Written by Judy Allen. Illustrated by Tudor Humphries. (Kingfisher, 2000.)
94. *Snowflakes Fall.* Written by Patricia MacLachlan. Illustrated by Steven Kellogg. (Random House Books for Young Readers, 2013.)
95. *Hachiko.* Written by Pamela S. Turner. Illustrated by Yan Nascimbene. (HMH Books for Young Readers, 2004.)
96. *Market!* Written and illustrated by Ted Lewin. (HarperCollins, 1996.)
97. *Redwoods.* Written and illustrated by Jason Chin. (Flash Point, 2009.)
98. *My First Day.* Written by Steve Jenkins and Robin Page. Illustrated by Steve Jenkins. (HMH Books for Young Readers, 2013.)
99. *Swirl by Swirl: Spirals in Nature.* Written by Joyce Sidman. Illustrated by Beth Krommes. (HMH Books for Young Readers, 2011.)
100. *Goodnight, Goodnight Construction Site.* Written by Sherri Duskey Rinker. Illustrated by Tom Lichtenheld. (Chronicle Books, 2011.)

Early-Reader Booklist

1. *Actual Size*. Written and illustrated by Steve Jenkins. (HMH Books for Young Readers, 2011.)
2. *The Beetle Book*. Written and illustrated by Steve Jenkins. (HMH Books for Young Readers, 2012.)
3. *Black Jack: The Ballad of Jack Johnson*. Written by Charles R. Smith Jr. Illustrated by Shane W. Evans. (Roaring Brook Press, 2010.)
4. *Monsieur Marceau: Actor without Words*. Written by Leda Schubert. Illustrated by Gerard DuBois. (Flash Point, 2012.)
5. *When Marian Sang: The True Recital of Marian Anderson*. Written by Pam Muñoz Ryan. Illustrated by Brian Selznick. (Scholastic Press, 2002.)
6. *Astronaut Handbook*. Written and illustrated by Meghan McCarthy. (Knopf Books for Young Readers, 2008.)
7. *On Earth*. Written and illustrated by G. Brian Karas. (Perfection Learning, 2008.)
8. *Country Road ABC: An Illustrated Journey through America's Farmland*. Written and illustrated by Arthur Geisert. (HMH Books for Young Readers, 2010.)
9. *Soar, Elinor!* Written by Tami Lewis Brown. Illustrated by François Roca. (Farrar, Straus & Giroux, 2010.)
10. *Just a Second*. Written and illustrated by Steve Jenkins. (HMH Books for Young Readers, 2011.)
11. *A Weed Is a Flower: The Life of George Washington Carver*. Written and illustrated by Aliki. (Prentice Hall, 1965.)
12. *Around One Cactus: Owls, Bats and Leaping Rats*. Written by Anthony D. Fredericks. Illustrated by Jennifer DiRubbio. (Dawn Publications, 2003.)
13. *Ballet for Martha: Making Appalachian Spring*. Written by Jan Greenberg and Sandra Jordan. Illustrated by Brian Floca. (Flash Point, 2010.)

14. *Life in the Ocean: The Story of Oceanographer Sylvia Earle.* Written and illustrated by Claire A. Nivola. (Farrar, Straus & Giroux, 2012.)

15. *Living Sunlight: How Plants Bring the Earth to Life.* Written by Molly Bang and Penny Chisholm. (Blue Sky Press, 2009.)

16. *An Egg Is Quiet.* Written by Dianna Hutts Aston. Illustrated by Sylvia Long. (Chronicle Books, 2006.)

17. *The Extraordinary Mark Twain (according to Susy).* Written by Barbara Kerley. Illustrated by Edwin Fotheringham. (Scholastic Press, 2010.)

18. *Can We Save the Tiger?* Written by Martin Jenkins. Illustrated by Vicky White. (Candlewick, 2011.)

19. *How to Clean a Hippopotamus: A Look at Unusual Animal Partnerships.* Written by Robin Page and Steve Jenkins. Illustrated by Steve Jenkins. (HMH Books for Young Readers, 2010.)

20. *Insect Detective.* Written by Steve Voake. Illustrated by Charlotte Voake. (Candlewick, 2012.)

21. *Pelé, King of Soccer/El rey del fútbol.* Written by Monica Brown. Illustrated by Rudy Gutiérrez. (Rayo, 2008.)

22. *Sea Horse: The Shyest Fish in the Sea.* Written by Chris Butterworth. Illustrated by John Lawrence. (Candlewick, 2006.)

23. *Coral Reefs.* Written and illustrated by Jason Chin. (Flash Point, 2011.)

24. *Energy Island: How One Community Harnessed the Wind and Changed Their World.* Written and illustrated by Allan Drummond. (Farrar, Straus & Giroux, 2011.)

25. *Looking at Lincoln.* Written and illustrated by Maira Kalman. (Nancy Paulsen Books, 2012.)

26. *One Tiny Turtle.* Written by Nicola Davies. Illustrated by Jane Chapman. (Candlewick, 2005.)

27. *So You Want to Be President?* Written by Judith St. George. Illustrated by David Small. (Philomel, 2004.)

28. *Brothers at Bat: The True Story of an Amazing All-Brother Baseball Team.* Written by Audrey Vernick. Illustrated by Steven Salerno. (Clarion Books, 2012.)

29. *Fifty Cents and a Dream: Young Booker T. Washington.* Written by Jabari Asim. Illustrated by Bryan Collier. (Little, Brown Books for Young Readers, 2012.)

30. *How Much Is a Million?* Written by David M. Schwartz. Illustrated by Steven Kellogg. (HarperCollins, 1985.)

31. *Martin's Big Words: The Life of Dr. Martin Luther King, Jr.* Written by Doreen Rappaport. Illustrated by Bryan Collier. (Hyperion, 2007.)

32. *Nic Bishop Spiders.* Written and illustrated by Nic Bishop. (Scholastic, 2012.)

33. *Owen & Mzee: The True Story of a Remarkable Friendship.* Written by Isabella Hatkoff, Craig Hatkoff, and Paula Kahumbu. Illustrated by Peter Greste. (Scholastic Press, 2006.)

34. *You Never Heard of Sandy Koufax?!* Written by Jonah Winter. Illustrated by André Carrilho. (Schwartz & Wade, 2009.)

35. *Snowflake Bentley.* Written by Jacqueline Briggs Martin. Illustrated by Mary Azarian. (HMH Books for Young Readers, 1998.)

36. *The Boy Who Invented TV: The Story of Philo Farnsworth.* Written by Kathleen Krull. Illustrated by Greg Couch. (Knopf Books for Young Readers, 2009.)

37. *Down, Down, Down: A Journey to the Bottom of the Sea.* Written and illustrated by Steve Jenkins. (HMH Books for Young Readers, 2009.)

38. *Moonshot: The Flight of Apollo 11.* Written and illustrated by Brian Floca. (Atheneum/Richard Jackson Books, 2009.)

39. *A Drop of Water: A Book of Science and Wonder.* Written and illustrated by Walter Wick. (Scholastic Press, 1997.)

40. *It Jes' Happened: When Bill Traylor Started to Draw.* Written by Don Tate. Illustrated by Gregory Christie. (Lee & Low Books, 2012.)

41. *Sonia Sotomayor: A Judge Grows in the Bronx/La juez que creció en el Bronx.* Written by Jonah Winter. Illustrated by Edel Rodriguez. (Atheneum Books for Young Readers, 2009.)

42. *Nic Bishop Snakes.* Written and illustrated by Nic Bishop. (Scholastic, 2012.)

43. *Planting the Trees of Kenya: The Story of Wangari Maathai.* Written and illustrated by Claire A. Nivola. (Farrar, Straus & Giroux, 2008.)

44. *The Camping Trip That Changed America.* Written by Barb Rosenstock. Illustrated by Mordicai Gerstein. (Dial, 2012.)

45. *Eleanor, Quiet No More.* Written by Doreen Rappaport. Illustrated by Gary Kelley. (Disney-Hyperion, 2009.)

46. *The Dinosaurs of Waterhouse Hawkins: An Illuminating History of Mr. Waterhouse Hawkins, Artist and Lecturer.* Written by Barbara Kerley. Illustrated by Brian Selznick. (Scholastic Press, 2001.)

47. *Meadowlands: A Wetland Survival Story.* Written and illustrated by Thomas F. Yezerski. (Farrar, Straus & Giroux, 2011.)

48. *Thunder Birds: Nature's Flying Predators.* Written and illustrated by Jim Arnosky. (Sterling, 2011.)

49. *Ocean Sunlight: How Tiny Plants Feed the Seas.* Written by Molly Bang and Penny Chisholm. (The Blue Sky Press, 2012.)

50. *Roberto Clemente: Pride of the Pittsburgh Pirates.* Written by Jonah Winter. Illustrated by Raúl Colón. (Perfection Learning, 2008.)

51. *UnBEElievables: Honeybee Poems and Paintings.* Written and illustrated by Douglas Florian. (Beach Lane Books, 2012.)

52. *What Do You Do with a Tail like This?* Written by Steve Jenkins and Robin Page. (HMH Books for Young Readers, 2003.)
53. *I Have a Dream.* Written by Martin Luther King Jr. Illustrated by Kadir Nelson. (Schwartz & Wade, 2012.)
54. *What Presidents Are Made Of.* Written and illustrated by Hanoch Piven. (Atheneum Books for Young Readers, 2012.)
55. *Harvesting Hope: The Story of Cesar Chavez.* Written by Kathleen Krull. Illustrated by Yuyi Morales. (HMH Books for Young Readers, 2003.)
56. *Wilma Unlimited: How Wilma Rudolph Became the World's Fastest Woman.* Written by Kathleen Krull. Illustrated by David Diaz. (HMH Books for Young Readers, 2000.)
57. *14 Cows for America.* Written by Carmen Agra Deedy and Wilson Kimeli Naiyomah. Illustrated by Thomas Gonzalez. (Peachtree Publishers, 2009.)
58. *All the Way to America: The Story of a Big Italian Family and a Little Shovel.* Written and illustrated by Dan Yaccarino. (Knopf Books for Young Readers, 2011.)
59. *The Boy Who Drew Birds: A Story of John James Audubon.* Written by Jacqueline Davies. Illustrated by Melissa Sweet. (HMH Books for Young Readers, 2004.)
60. *Growing Frogs.* Written by Vivian French. Illustrated by Alison Bartlett. (Candlewick, 2003.)
61. *Harriet and the Promised Land.* Written and illustrated by Jacob Lawrence. (Aladdin, 1997.)
62. *Mermaid Queen: The Spectacular True Story of Annette Kellerman, Who Swam Her Way to Fame, Fortune and Swimsuit History.* Written by Shana Corey. Illustrated by Edwin Fotheringham. (Scholastic Press, 2009.)
63. *Bug Zoo.* Written by Nick Baker. (DK Publishing, 2010.)
64. *Dogs and Cats.* Written and illustrated by Steve Jenkins. (HMH Books for Young Readers, 2012.)
65. *The Chiru of High Tibet.* Written by Jacqueline Briggs Martin. Illustrated by Linda Wingerter. (Houghton Mifflin Books for Children, 2010.)
66. *My Senator and Me: A Dog's Eye-View of Washington, D.C.* Written by Edward M. Kennedy. Illustrated by David Small. (Scholastic, 2006.)
67. *Ladybugs.* Written by Gail Gibbons. (Holiday House, 2012.)
68. *Vulture View.* Written by April Pulley Sayre. Illustrated by Steve Jenkins. (Henry Holt, 2007.)
69. *A Butterfly Is Patient.* Written by Dianna Hutts Aston. Illustrated by Sylvia Long. (Chronicle Books, 2011.)
70. *Noah Webster and His Words.* Written by Jeri Chase Ferris. Illustrated by Vincent X. Kirsch. (HMH Books for Young Readers, 2012.)

71. *What to Do about Alice? How Alice Roosevelt Broke the Rules, Charmed the World, and Drove Her Father Teddy Crazy!* Written by Barbara Kerley. Illustrated by Edwin Fotheringham. (Scholastic Press, 2008.)

72. *A Nation's Hope: The Story of Boxing Legend Joe Louis.* Written by Matt De La Peña. Illustrated by Kadir Nelson. (Dial, 2011.)

73. *Polar Bears.* Written and illustrated by Mark Newman. (Henry Holt, 2010.)

74. *The Story of Ruby Bridges.* Written by Robert Coles. Illustrated by George Ford. (Scholastic, 2010.)

75. *Orani: My Father's Village.* Written and illustrated by Claire A. Nivola. (Farrar, Straus & Giroux, 2011.)

76. *Sixteen Years in Sixteen Seconds: The Sammy Lee Story.* Written by Paula Yoo. Illustrated by Dom Lee. (Lee & Low Books, 2010.)

77. *Those Rebels, John and Tom.* Written by Barbara Kerley. Illustrated by Edwin Fotheringham. (Scholastic Press, 2012.)

78. *One Giant Leap.* Written by Robert Burleigh. Illustrated by Mike Wimmer. (Philomel, 2009.)

79. *You Are Stardust.* Written by Elin Kelsey. Illustrated by Soyeon Kim. (Owlkids Books, 2012.)

80. *Amazing Sharks!* Written by Sarah L. Thomson. (HarperCollins, 2006.)

81. *You Forgot Your Skirt, Amelia Bloomer!* Written by Shana Corey. Illustrated by Chesley McLaren. (Scholastic Press, 2000.)

82. *The Boy on Fairfield Street: How Ted Geisel Grew Up to Become Dr. Seuss.* Written by Kathleen Krull. Illustrated by Steve Johnson and Lou Fancher. (Dragonfly Books, 2010.)

83. *Frida.* Written by Jonah Winter. Illustrated by Ana Juan. (Arthur A. Levine Books, 2002.)

84. *Bugs Are Insects.* Written by Anne Rockwell. Illustrated by Steve Jenkins. (HarperCollins, 2001.)

85. *Dolphin Baby!* Written by Nicola Davies. Illustrated by Brita Granström. (Candlewick, 2012.)

86. *Caterpillar, Caterpillar.* Written by Vivian French. Illustrated by Charlotte Voake. (Candlewick, 2009.)

87. *Fireboat: The Heroic Adventures of the* John J. Harvey. Written and illustrated by Maira Kalman. (Putnam Juvenile, 2002.)

88. *Creep and Flutter: The Secret World of Insects and Spiders.* Written and illustrated by Jim Arnosky. (Sterling Children's Books, 2012.)

89. *Dreaming Up: A Celebration of Building.* Written and illustrated by Christy Hale. (Lee & Low Books, 2012.)

90. *Animal Talk: How Animals Communicate through Sight, Sound and Smell.* Written by Etta Kaner. Illustrated by Greg Douglas. (Kids Can Press, 2002.)

91. *Exploding Ants: Amazing Facts about How Animals Adapt.* Written by Joanne Settel. (Atheneum Books for Young Readers, 1999.)

92. *Just Ducks!* Written by Nicola Davies. Illustrated by Salvatore Rubbino. (Candlewick, 2012.)

93. *Face to Face with Lions.* Written by Beverly and Dereck Joubert. (National Geographic Children's Books, 2008.)

94. *From Seed to Plant.* Written and illustrated by Gail Gibbons. (Holiday House, 1993.)

95. *Guess What Is Growing inside This Egg.* Written and illustrated by Mia Posada. (Millbrook Press, 2006.)

96. *I Feel Better with a Frog in My Throat: History's Strangest Cures.* Written and illustrated by Carlyn Beccia. (Houghton Mifflin Books for Children, 2010.)

97. *Balto and the Great Race.* Written by Elizabeth Cody Kimmel. Illustrated by Nora Koerber. (Paw Prints, 2008.)

98. *If You Lived Here: Houses of the World.* Written and illustrated by Giles Laroche. (HMH Books for Young Readers, 2011.)

99. *There Goes Ted Williams: The Greatest Hitter Who Ever Lived.* Written and illustrated by Matt Tavares. (Candlewick, 2012.)

100. *What Is the World Made Of? All about Solids, Liquids, and Gases.* Written by Kathleen Weidner Zoehfeld. Illustrated by Paul Meisel. (HarperCollins, 1998.)

Middle-Reader Booklist

1. *Amelia Lost: The Life and Disappearance of Amelia Earhart.* Written by Candace Fleming. (Schwartz & Wade, 2011.)
2. *Temple Grandin: How the Girl Who Loved Cows Embraced Autism and Changed the World.* Written by Sy Montgomery and Temple Grandin. (HMH Books for Young Readers, 2012.)
3. *Chuck Close Face Book.* Written by Chuck Close. (Abrams Books for Young Readers, 2012.)
4. *Moonbird: A Year on the Wind with the Great Survivor B95.* Written by Phillip Hoose. (Farrar, Straus & Giroux, 2012.)
5. *Almost Astronauts: 13 Women Who Dared to Dream.* Written by Tanya Lee Stone. (Candlewick, 2009.)
6. *Heart and Soul: The Story of America and African Americans.* Written and illustrated by Kadir Nelson. (Balzer & Bray, 2011.)
7. *Michelangelo.* Written and illustrated by Diane Stanley. (HarperCollins, 2003.)
8. *Beyond Courage: The Untold Story of Jewish Resistance during the Holocaust.* Written by Doreen Rappaport. (Candlewick, 2012.)
9. *Drawing from Memory.* Written and illustrated by Allen Say. (Scholastic Press, 2011.)
10. *Bomb: The Race to Build—and Steal—the World's Most Dangerous Weapon.* Written by Steve Sheinkin. (Flash Point, 2012.)
11. *We Are the Ship: The Story of Negro League Baseball.* Written and illustrated by Kadir Nelson. (Hyperion Books for Children, 2008.)
12. *A Black Hole Is NOT a Hole.* Written by Carolyn Cinami DeCristofano. Illustrated by Michael Carroll. (Charlesbridge Publishing, 2012.)
13. *Abraham Lincoln and Frederick Douglass: The Story behind an American Friendship.* Written by Russell Freedman. (Clarion Books, 2012.)

14. *An American Plague: The True and Terrifying Story of the Yellow Fever Epidemic of 1793.* Written by Jim Murphy. (Clarion Books, 2003.)
15. *Invincible Microbe: Tuberculosis and the Never-Ending Search for a Cure.* Written by Jim Murphy and Alison Blank. (Clarion Books, 2012.)
16. *The Day-Glo Brothers.* Written by Chris Barton. Illustrated by Tony Persiani. (Charlesbridge Publishing, 2009.)
17. *Hand in Hand: Ten Black Men Who Changed America.* Written by Andrea Davis Pinkney. Illustrated by Brian Pinkney. (Hyperion, 2012.)
18. *The Great and Only Barnum: The Tremendous, Stupendous Life of Showman P. T. Barnum.* Written by Candace Fleming. Illustrated by Ray Fenwick. (Schwartz & Wade, 2009.)
19. *Kakapo Rescue: Saving the World's Strangest Parrot.* Written by Sy Montgomery. Illustrated by Nic Bishop. (HMH Books for Young Readers, 2010.)
20. *Bones: Skeletons and How They Work.* Written and illustrated by Steve Jenkins. (Scholastic, 2010.)
21. *Extreme Animals: The Toughest Creatures on Earth.* Written by Nicola Davies. Illustrated by Neal Layton. (Candlewick, 2009.)
22. *The Wall: Growing Up behind the Iron Curtain.* Written by Peter Sis. (Farrar, Straus & Giroux, 2007.)
23. *The Great Fire.* Written by Jim Murphy. (Scholastic, 2010.)
24. *Into the Unknown: How Great Explorers Found Their Way by Land, Sea, and Air.* Written by Stuart Ross. Illustrated by Stephen Biesty. (Candlewick, 2011.)
25. *Team Moon: How 400,000 People Landed Apollo 11 on the Moon.* Written by Catherine Thimmesh. (Houghton Mifflin Company, 2006.)
26. *Knucklehead: Tall Tales and Mostly True Stories about Growing Up Scieszka.* Written and illustrated by Jon Scieszka. (Viking Juvenile, 2008.)
27. *Electric Ben: The Amazing Life and Times of Benjamin Franklin.* Written and illustrated by Robert Byrd. (Dial, 2012.)
28. *America Is under Attack: September 11, 2001: The Day the Towers Fell.* Written and illustrated by Don Brown. (Flash Point, 2011.)
29. *Boys of Steel: The Creators of Superman.* Written by Marc Tyler Nobleman. Illustrated by Ross MacDonald. (Knopf Books for Young Readers, 2008.)
30. *Cathedral: The Story of Its Construction.* Written and illustrated by David Macaulay. (HMH Books for Young Readers, 1973.)
31. *Phineas Gage: A Gruesome but True Story about Brain Science.* Written by John Fleischman. (HMH Books for Young Readers, 2002.)
32. *Candy Bomber: The Story of the Berlin Airlift's "Chocolate Pilot."* Written by Michael O. Tunnell. (Charlesbridge Publishing, 2010.)
33. *Zombie Makers: True Stories of Nature's Undead.* Written by Rebecca L. Johnson. (21st Century, 2012.)

34. *Citizen Scientists: Be a Part of Scientific Discovery from Your Own Backyard.* Written by Loree Griffin Burns. Illustrated by Ellen Harasimowicz. (Henry Holt, 2012.)
35. *The Elephant Scientist.* Written by Caitlin O'Connell and Donna M. Jackson. Illustrated by Timothy Rodwell. (HMH Books for Young Readers, 2011.)
36. *My Season with Penguins: An Antarctic Journal.* Written and illustrated by Sophie Webb. (HMH Books for Young Readers, 2000.)
37. *Freedom Walkers: The Story of the Montgomery Bus Boycott.* Written by Russell Freedman. (Holiday House, 2006.)
38. *Blizzard of Glass: The Halifax Explosion of 1917.* Written by Sally M. Walker. (Henry Holt, 2011.)
39. *The Case of the Vanishing Golden Frogs: A Scientific Mystery.* Written by Sandra Markle. (Millbrook Press, 2011.)
40. *A Dream of Freedom: The Civil Rights Movement from 1954 to 1968.* Written by Diane McWhorter. (Scholastic, 2004.)
41. *For the Birds: The Life of Roger Tory Peterson.* Written by Peggy Thomas. Illustrated by Laura Jacques. (Boyds Mills Press, 2011.)
42. *Lincoln: A Photobiography.* Written by Russell Freedman. (Clarion Books, 1987.)
43. *George Washington Carver.* Written by Tonya Bolden. (Scholastic, 2009.)
44. *How They Croaked: The Awful Ends of the Awfully Famous.* Written by Georgia Bragg. Illustrated by Kevin O'Malley. (Walker Childrens, 2012.)
45. *Seven Miles to Freedom: The Robert Smalls Story.* Written by Janet Halfmann. Illustrated by Duane Smith. (Lee & Low Books, 2012.)
46. *Nurse, Soldier, Spy: The Story of Sarah Edmonds, a Civil War Hero.* Written by Marissa Moss. Illustrated by John Hendrix. (Harry N. Abrams, 2011.)
47. *Poop Happened! A History of the World from the Bottom Up.* Written by Sarah Albee. Illustrated by Robert Leighton. (Walker Childrens, 2010.)
48. *Shipwrecked! The True Adventures of a Japanese Boy.* Written by Rhoda Blumberg. (HarperCollins, 2003.)
49. *Bodies from the Ash: Life and Death in Ancient Pompeii.* Written by James M. Deem. (HMH Books for Young Readers, 2005.)
50. *Queen of the Falls.* Written and illustrated by Chris van Allsburg. (HMH Books for Young Readers, 2011.)
51. *And Then What Happened, Paul Revere?* Written by Jean Fritz. Illustrated by Margot Tomes. (Puffin, 1996.)
52. *Ubiquitous: Celebrating Nature's Survivors.* Written by Joyce Sidman. Illustrated by Beckie Prange. (HMH Books for Young Readers, 2010.)
53. *Sadako and the Thousand Paper Cranes.* Written by Eleanor Coerr. Illustrated by Ronald Himler. (Penguin Group, 2009.)

54. *Spirit Seeker: John Coltrane's Musical Journey.* Written by Gary Golio. Illustrated by Rudy Gutierrez. (Clarion Books, 2012.)

55. *Bodies from the Ice: Melting Glaciers and the Recovery of the Past.* Written by James M. Deem. (HMH Books for Young Readers, 2008.)

56. *Come Back, Salmon: How a Group of Dedicated Kids Adopted Pigeon Creek and Brought It Back to Life.* Written by Molly Cone. Illustrated by Sidnee Wheelwright. (Sierra Club Books for Children, 2001.)

57. *Escape! The Story of the Great Houdini.* Written by Sid Fleischman. (Greenwillow Books, 2006.)

58. *The Endless Steppe.* Written by Esther Hautzig. (Penguin, 1971.)

59. *The Fairy Ring, or, Elsie and Frances Fool the World.* Written by Mary Losure. (Candlewick, 2012.)

60. *George vs. George: The American Revolution as Seen from Both Sides.* Written and illustrated by Rosalyn Schanzer. (National Geographic Children's Books, 2007.)

61. *The Horse and the Plains Indians: A Powerful Partnership.* Written by Dorothy Hinshaw Patent. Illustrated by William Muñoz. (Clarion Books, 2012.)

62. *Black Elk's Vision: A Lakota Story.* Written by S. D. Nelson. (Harry N. Abrams, 2010.)

63. *Kubla Khan: The Emperor of Everything.* Written by Kathleen Krull. Illustrated by Robert Byrd. (Viking Juvenile, 2010.)

64. *How Angel Peterson Got His Name.* Written by Gary Paulsen. (Perfection Learning, 2004.)

65. *Jimi: Sounds Like a Rainbow: A Story of the Young Jimi Hendrix.* Written by Gary Golio. Illustrated by Javaka Steptoe. (Clarion Books, 2010.)

66. *My Librarian Is a Camel: How Books Are Brought to Children around the World.* Written by Margriet Ruurs. (Boyds Mills Press, 2005.)

67. *Sit-In: How Four Friends Stood Up by Sitting Down.* Written by Andrea Davis Pinkney. Illustrated by Brian Pinkney. (Little, Brown Books for Young Readers, 2010.)

68. *Truce: The Day the Soldiers Stopped Fighting.* Written by Jim Murphy. (Scholastic, 2009.)

69. *Action Jackson.* Written by Jan Greenberg and Sandra Jordan. Illustrated by Robert Andrew Parker. (Square Fish, 2007.)

70. *William Shakespeare and the Globe.* Written and illustrated by Aliki. (HarperCollins, 2000.)

71. *Adventure beneath the Sea: Living in an Underwater Science Station.* Written by Kenneth Mallory. Illustrated by Brian Skerry. (Boyds Mills Press, 2010.)

72. *Airborne: A Photobiography of Wilbur and Orville Wright.* Written by Mary Collins. (National Geographic Children's Books, 2003.)

73. *Mission Control, This Is Apollo: The Story of the First Voyages to the Moon.* Written by Andrew Chaikin and Victoria Kohl. Illustrated by Alan Bean. (Viking Juvenile, 2009.)

74. *Alex the Parrot: No Ordinary Bird.* Written by Stephanie Spinner. Illustrated by Meilo So. (Knopf Books for Young Readers, 2012.)

75. *If Stones Could Speak: Unlocking the Secrets of Stonehenge.* Written by Mark Aronson. (National Geographic Children's Books, 2010.)

76. *Animals Up Close.* Written and illustrated by Igor Siwanowicz. (DK Publishing, 2009.)

77. *How to Talk to an Autistic Kid.* Written by Daniel Stefanski. (Free Spirit Publishing, 2011.)

78. *Ben Franklin's Almanac: Being a True Account of the Good Gentleman's Life.* Written by Candace Fleming. (Atheneum Books for Young Readers, 2003.)

79. *Little People and a Lost World: An Anthropological Mystery.* Written by Linda Goldenberg. (Twenty-First Century Books, 2006.)

80. *Big Wig: A Little History of Hair.* Written by Kathleen Krull. Illustrated by Peter Malone. (Arthur A. Levine Books, 2011.)

81. *Around the World.* Written and illustrated by Matt Phelan. (Candlewick, 2011.)

82. *The Boston Tea Party.* Written by Russell Freedman. Illustrated by Peter Malone. (Holiday House, 2012.)

83. *One Times Square: A Century of Change at the Crossroads of the World.* Written and illustrated by Joe McKendry. (David R. Godine, 2012.)

84. *The Emperor's Silent Army: Terracotta Warriors of Ancient China.* Written by Jane O'Connor. (Viking Juvenile, 2002.)

85. *Built to Last: Building America's Amazing Bridges, Dams, Tunnels, and Skyscrapers.* Written by George Sullivan. (Scholastic, 2005.)

86. *10,000 Days of Thunder: A History of the Vietnam War.* Written by Philip Caputo. (Atheneum Books for Young Readers, 2005.)

87. *The Journey That Saved Curious George: The True Wartime Escape of Margret and H. A. Rey.* Written by Louise Borden. Illustrated by Allan Drummond. (HMH Books, 2005.)

88. *Discovering Black America: From the Age of Exploration to the Twenty-First Century.* Written by Linda Tarrant-Reid. (Harry N. Abrams, 2012.)

89. *What the World Eats.* Written by Faith D'Aluisio. Illustrated by Peter Menzel. (Tricycle Press, 2008.)

90. *Eleanor Roosevelt: A Life of Discovery.* Written by Russell Freedman. (HMH Books for Young Readers, 1997.)

91. *Who Was First? Discovering the Americas.* Written by Russell Freedman. (Clarion Books, 2007.)

92. *Far from Shore: Chronicles of an Open Ocean Voyage.* Written by Sophie Webb. (HMH Books for Young Readers, 2011.)

93. *Girls Think of Everything: Stories of Ingenious Inventions by Women.* Written by Catherine Thimmesh. Illustrated by Melissa Sweet. (HMH Books for Young Readers, 2002.)

94. *An Extraordinary Life: The Story of a Monarch Butterfly.* Written by Laurence Pringle. Illustrated by Bob Marstall. (Scholastic, 1996.)

95. *Harriet Tubman: Conductor on the Underground Railroad.* Written by Ann Petry. (Amistad, 2007.)

96. *Dogs on Duty: Soldiers' Best Friends on the Battlefield and Beyond.* Written by Dorothy Hinshaw Patent. (Walker Childrens, 2012.)

97. *How It Feels When Parents Divorce.* Written by Jill Krementz. (Knopf, 1984.)

98. *Case Closed? Nine Mysteries Unlocked by Modern Science.* Written by Susan Hughes. Illustrated by Michael Wandelmaier. (Kids Can Press, 2010.)

99. *Guinea Pig Scientists: Bold Self-Experimenters in Science and Medicine.* Written by Leslie Dendy and Mel Boring. Illustrated by C. B. Mordan. (Henry Holt, 2005.)

100. *John Muir: America's First Environmentalist.* Written by Kathryn Lasky. Illustrated by Stan Fellows. (Candlewick, 2006.)

APPENDIX 4

Young-Adult Booklist

1. *The Diary of a Young Girl.* Written by Anne Frank. (Bantam, 1993.)
2. *The Mighty Mars Rovers: The Incredible Adventures of Spirit and Opportunity.* Written by Elizabeth Rusch. (HMH Books for Young Readers, 2012.)
3. *The Quest for the Tree Kangaroo: An Expedition to the Cloud Forest of New Guinea.* Written by Sy Montgomery. Illustrated by Nic Bishop. (HMH Books for Young Readers, 2006.)
4. *We've Got a Job: The 1963 Birmingham Children's March.* Written by Cynthia Levinson. (Peachtree Publishers, 2012.)
5. *The Notorious Benedict Arnold: A True Story of Adventure, Heroism, and Treachery.* Written by Steve Sheinkin. (Flash Point, 2010.)
6. *Charles and Emma: The Darwins' Leap of Faith.* Written by Deborah Heiligman. (Square Fish, 2011.)
7. *Walden and Civil "Disobedience."* Written by Henry David Thoreau. (Signet Classics, 2012.)
8. *Claudette Colvin: Twice toward Justice.* Written by Phillip Hoose. (Farrar, Straus & Giroux, 2009.)
9. *The Tarantula Scientist.* Written by Sy Montgomery. Illustrated by Nic Bishop. (HMH Books for Young Readers, 2007.)
10. *Written in Bone: Buried Lives of Jamestown and Colonial Maryland.* Written by Sally M. Walker. (Carolrhoda Books, 2009.)
11. *The Autobiography of Malcolm X.* Written by Malcolm X and Alex Haley. (Ballantine Books, 1992.)
12. *Flesh and Blood So Cheap: The Triangle Fire and Its Legacy.* Written by Albert Marrin. (Knopf Books for Young Readers, 2011.)
13. *Hitler Youth: Growing Up in Hitler's Shadow.* Written by Susan Campbell Bartoletti. (Scholastic, 2005.)

14. *Janis Joplin: Rise Up Singing.* Written by Ann Angel. (Harry N. Abrams, 2010.)
15. *Lafayette and the American Revolution.* Written by Russell Freedman. (Holiday House, 2010.)
16. *Something out of Nothing: Marie Curie and Radium.* Written by Carla Killough McClafferty. (Farrar, Straus & Giroux, 2006.)
17. *The Way Things Work.* Written by David Macaulay and Neil Ardley. Illustrated by David Macaulay. (DK Publishing, 2004.)
18. *Tracking Trash: Flotsam, Jetsam, and the Science of Ocean Motion.* Written by Loree Griffin Burns. (HMH Books for Young Readers, 2007.)
19. *I Know Why the Caged Bird Sings.* Written by Maya Angelou. (Ballantine Books, 2009.)
20. *Hole in My Life.* Written by Jack Gantos. (Farrar, Straus & Giroux, 2002.)
21. *The Impossible Rescue: The True Story of an Amazing Arctic Adventure.* Written by Martin W. Sandler. (Candlewick, 2012.)
22. *The Race to Save the Lord God Bird.* Written by Phillip Hoose. (Farrar, Straus & Giroux, 2010.)
23. *Secrets of a Civil War Submarine: Solving the Mysteries of the* H. L. Hunley. Written by Sally M. Walker. (Carolrhoda Books, 2005.)
24. *Tasting the Sky: A Palestinian Childhood.* Written by Ibtisam Barakat. (Farrar, Straus & Giroux, 2007.)
25. *The Federalist Papers.* Written by Alexander Hamilton, James Madison, and John Jay. (Simon & Schuster, 2004.)
26. Titanic: *Voices from the Disaster.* Written by Deborah Hopkinson. (Scholastic, 2012.)
27. *Bury My Heart at Wounded Knee: An Indian History of the American West.* Written by Dee Brown. (Holt, Rinehart & Winston, 1970.)
28. *Dear Miss Breed: True Stories of the Japanese American Incarceration during World War II and a Librarian Who Made a Difference.* Written by Joanne Oppenheim. (Scholastic, 2006.)
29. *Marching for Freedom: Walk Together Children and Don't You Grow Weary.* Written by Elizabeth Partridge. (Viking Juvenile, 2009.)
30. *A Life in the Wild: George Schaller's Struggle to Save the Last Great Beasts.* Written by Pamela S. Turner. (Farrar, Straus & Giroux, 2008.)
31. *Narrative of the Life of Frederick Douglass: An American Slave.* Written by Frederick Douglass. (Simon & Schuster, 2004.)
32. *Shipwreck at the Bottom of the World: The Extraordinary True Story of Shackleton and the* Endurance. Written by Jennifer Armstrong. (Paw Prints, 2008.)
33. *The War to End All Wars: World War I.* Written by Russell Freedman. (HMH Books for Young Readers, 2013.)

34. *Sir Walter Raleigh and the Quest for El Dorado.* Written by Marc Aronson. (Clarion Books, 2000.)
35. *Spies of Mississippi: The True Story of the Spy Network That Tried to Destroy the Civil Rights Movement.* Written by Rick Bowers. (National Geographic Children's Books, 2010.)
36. *Terezín: Voices from the Holocaust.* Written by Ruth Thomson. (Candlewick Press, 2011.)
37. *1776.* Written by David McCullough. (Simon & Schuster, 2005.)
38. *They Called Themselves the KKK: The Birth of an American Terrorist Group.* Written by Susan Campbell Bartoletti. (HMH Books for Young Readers, 2010.)
39. *Unraveling Freedom: The Battle for Democracy on the Home Front during World War I.* Written by Ann Bausum. (National Geographic Children's Books, 2010.)
40. *Birmingham Sunday.* Written by Larry Dane Brimner. (Calkins Creek, 2010.)
41. *Vincent van Gogh: Portrait of an Artist.* Written by Jan Greenberg and Sandra Jordan. (Delacorte Books for Young Readers, 2001.)
42. *Wild Horse Scientists.* Written by Kay Frydenborg. (HMH Books for Young Readers, 2012.)
43. *Common Sense, Rights of Man, and Other Essential Writings of Thomas Paine.* Written by Thomas Paine. (Penguin Group, 2003.)
44. *The Wright Brothers: How They Invented the Airplane.* Written by Russell Freedman. (Holiday House, 1994.)
45. *21: The Story of Roberto Clemente.* Written and illustrated by Wilfred Santiago. (Fantagraphics, 2011.)
46. *Bad Boy.* Written by Walter Dean Myers. (Amistad, 2002.)
47. *Night.* Written by Elie Wiesel. (Hill & Wang, 2006.)
48. *Bootleg: Murder, Moonshine, and the Lawless Years of Prohibition.* Written by Karen Blumenthal. (Flash Point, 2011.)
49. *Every Bone Tells a Story: Hominin Discoveries, Deductions, and Debates.* Written by Jill Rubalcaba and Peter Robertshaw. (Charlesbridge Publishing, 2010.)
50. *Children of the Great Depression.* Written by Russell Freedman. (Clarion Books, 2005.)
51. *Feynman.* Written by Jim Ottaviani. Illustrated by Leland Myrick. (First Second, 2011.)
52. *Witches! The Absolutely True Tale of Disaster in Salem.* Written and illustrated by Rosalyn Schanzer. (National Geographic Children's Books, 2011.)
53. *Freedom Riders: John Lewis and Jim Zwerg on the Front Lines of the Civil Rights Movement.* Written by Ann Bausum. (National Geographic Children's Books, 2005.)

54. *Harlem Stomp! A Cultural History of the Harlem Renaissance.* Written by Laban Carrick Hill. (Little, Brown Books for Young Readers, 2009.)

55. *Democracy in America.* Written by Alexis de Tocqueville. (Library of America, 2004.)

56. *The Hive Detectives: Chronicle of a Honey Bee Catastrophe.* Written by Loree Griffin Burns. Illustrated by Ellen Harasimowicz. (HMH Books for Young Readers, 2013.)

57. *Lost Boy, Lost Girl: Escaping Civil War in Sudan.* Written by John Bul Dau, Martha Arual Akech, Michael S. Sweeney, and K. M. Kostyal. (National Geographic Children's Books, 2010.)

58. *I Am Scout: The Biography of Harper Lee.* Written by Charles J. Shields. (Henry Holt, 2008.)

59. *John Lennon: All I Want Is the Truth.* Written by Elizabeth Partridge. (Viking Juvenile, 2005.)

60. *The Bat Scientists.* Written by Mary Kay Carson. Illustrated by Tom Uhlman. (HMH Books for Young Readers, 2010.)

61. *The Life and Death of Adolf Hitler.* Written by James Cross Giblin. (Clarion Books, 2002.)

62. *The Manatee Scientists: Saving Vulnerable Species.* Written by Peter Lourie. (HMH Books for Young Readers, 2011.)

63. *Soul Surfer: A True Story of Faith, Family, and Fighting to Get Back on the Board.* Written by Bethany Hamilton, Sheryl Berk, and Rick Bundschuh. (MTV Books, 2006.)

64. *This Land Was Made for You and Me: The Life and Songs of Woody Guthrie.* Written by Elizabeth Partridge. (Viking Juvenile, 2002.)

65. *Wheels of Change: How Women Rode the Bicycle to Freedom (with a Few Flat Tires along the Way).* Written by Sue Macy. (National Geographic Children's Books, 2011.)

66. *The Year of Goodbyes: A True Story of Friendship, Family and Farewells.* Written by Debbie Levy. (Disney-Hyperion, 2010.)

67. *The Amazing Harry Kellar: Great American Magician.* Written by Gail Jarrow. (Calkins Creek, 2012.)

68. *Charles Dickens and the Street Children of London.* Written by Andrea Warren. (HMH Books for Young Readers, 2011.)

69. *The Autobiography of Benjamin Franklin.* Written by Benjamin Franklin. (Dover Publications, 1995.)

70. *The Dark Game: True Spy Stories from Invisible Ink to CIA Moles.* Written by Paul Janeczko. (Candlewick, 2010.)

71. *Escape from Saigon: How a Vietnam War Orphan Became an American Boy.* Written by Andrea Warren. (Square Fish, 2008.)

72. *Friday Night Lights: A Town, a Team, and a Dream.* Written by H. G. Bissinger. (Da Capo Press, 1990.)

73. *Faces from the Past: Forgotten People of North America.* Written by James M. Deem. (HMH Books for Young Readers, 2012.)

74. *George Washington and the Founding of a Nation.* Written by Albert Marrin. (Dutton Juvenile, 2001.)

75. *The Letter Q: Queer Writers' Notes to Their Younger Selves.* Written by Sarah Moon and James Lecesne. (Arthur A. Levine Books, 2012.)

76. *Getting Away with Murder: The True Story of the Emmett Till Case.* Written by Chris Crowe. (Dial, 2003.)

77. *The Lincolns: A Scrapbook Look at Abraham and Mary.* Written by Candace Fleming. (Schwartz & Wade, 2008.)

78. *Ghosts in the Fog: The Untold Story of Alaska's WWII Invasion.* Written by Samantha Seiple. (Scholastic, 2011.)

79. *Hidden Worlds: Looking through a Scientist's Microscope.* Written by Stephen P. Kramer. Illustrated by Dennis Kunkel. (HMH Books for Young Readers, 2003.)

80. *Good Brother, Bad Brother: The Story of Edwin Booth and John Wilkes Booth.* Written by James Cross Giblin. (Clarion Books, 2005.)

81. *The Longitude Prize.* Written by Joan Dash. Illustrated by Dusan Petricic. (Farrar, Straus & Giroux, 2000.)

82. *The Good Fight: How World War II Was Won.* Written by Stephen E. Ambrose. (Atheneum Books for Young Readers, 2001.)

83. *A Long Way Gone: Memoirs of a Boy Soldier.* Written by Ishmael Beah. (Sarah Crichton Books, 2008.)

84. *In Defiance of Hitler: The Secret Mission of Varian Fry.* Written by Carla Killough McClafferty. (Farrar, Straus & Giroux, 2008.)

85. *King of the Mild Frontier: An Ill-Advised Autobiography.* Written by Chris Crutcher. (Greenwillow Books, 2003.)

86. *Navajo Code Talkers.* Written by Nathan Aaseng. (Walker Childrens, 1994.)

87. *Miles to Go for Freedom: Segregation and Civil Rights in the Jim Crow Years.* Written by Linda Barrett Osborne. (Harry N. Abrams, 2012.)

88. *The Mysteries of Beethoven's Hair.* Written by Russell Martin and Lydia Nibley. (Charlesbridge Publishing, 2009.)

89. *The Secret of the Yellow Death: A True Story of Medical Sleuthing.* Written by Suzanne Jurmain. (HMH Books for Young Readers, 2009.)

90. *The Poet Slave of Cuba: A Biography of Juan Francisco Manzano.* Written by Margarita Engle. Illustrated by Sean Qualls. (Square Fish, 2011.)

91. *Pyongyang: A Journey in North Korea.* Written by Guy Delisle. (Drawn and Quarterly, 2007.)

92. *Mysterious Messages: A History of Codes and Ciphers.* Written by Gary Blackwood. (Dutton Juvenile, 2009.)

93. *The Radioactive Boy Scout: The True Story of a Boy and His Backyard Nuclear Reactor.* Written by Ken Silverstein. (Random House, 2004.)

94. *The Complete Maus: A Survivor's Tale.* Written by Art Spiegelman. (Pantheon, 1996.)

95. *Sir Charlie Chaplin: The Funniest Man in the World.* Written by Sid Fleischman. (Greenwillow Books, 2010.)

96. *Profiles in Courage.* Written by John F. Kennedy. (Harper, 1964.)

97. *Sugar Changed the World: A Story of Magic, Spice, Slavery, Freedom, and Science.* Written by Marc Aronson and Marina Budhos. (Clarion Books, 2010.)

98. *To Dance: A Ballerina's Graphic Novel.* Written by Siena Cherson Siegel. Illustrated by Mark Siegel. (Atheneum/Richard Jackson Books, 2006.)

99. *The Boy Who Harnessed the Wind.* Written by William Kamkwamba and Bryan Mealer. (Harper Luxe, 2009.)

100. *Andy Warhol: Prince of Pop.* Written by Jan Greenberg and Sandra Jordan. (Random House, 2004.)

APPENDIX 5

Adult Booklist

1. *Silent Spring*. Written by Rachel Carson. (Houghton Mifflin, 1962.)
2. *Behind the Beautiful Forevers: Life, Death, and Hope in a Mumbai Undercity*. Written by Katherine Boo. (Random House, 2012.)
3. *The Emperor of All Maladies: A Biography of Cancer*. Written by Siddhartha Mukherjee. (Scribner, 2010.)
4. *The Warmth of Other Suns: The Epic Story of America's Great Migration*. Written by Isabel Wilkerson. (Random House, 2010.)
5. *The Double Helix: A Personal Account of the Discovery of the Structure of DNA*. Written by James D. Watson. (Atheneum, 1968.)
6. *In Cold Blood*. Written by Truman Capote. (Signet, 1965.)
7. *Malcolm X: A Life of Reinvention*. Written by Manning Marable. (Viking, 2011.)
8. *The Immortal Life of Henrietta Lacks*. Written by Rebecca Skloot. (Crown, 2010.)
9. *A Heartbreaking Work of Staggering Genius*. Written by Dave Eggers. (Vintage, 2001.)
10. *The Passage of Power: The Years of Lyndon Johnson*. Written by Robert Caro. (Knopf, 2012.)
11. *Homage to Catalonia*. Written by George Orwell. (Penguin Books, 1978.)
12. *The Looming Tower: Al-Qaeda and the Road to 9/11*. Written by Lawrence Wright. (Knopf, 2006.)
13. *Cleopatra: A Life*. Written by Stacy Schiff. (Little, Brown and Company, 2010.)
14. *The Information: A History, a Theory, a Flood*. Written by James Gleick. (Pantheon, 2011.)
15. *Nickel and Dimed: On (Not) Getting By in America*. Written by Barbara Ehrenreich. (Picador, 2011.)

16. *Just Kids*. Written by Patti Smith. (Ecco, 2010.)
17. *The Lost City of Z: A Tale of Deadly Obsession in the Amazon*. Written by David Grann. (Vintage, 2010.)
18. *The Elements of Style*. Written by William Strunk Jr. and E. B. White. (Macmillan, 1959.)
19. *The Age of Wonder: How the Romantic Generation Discovered the Beauty and Terror of Science*. Written by Richard Holmes. (Pantheon, 2009.)
20. *Guns, Germs, and Steel: The Fates of Human Societies*. Written by Jared Diamond. (W. W. Norton, 2005.)
21. *The Civil War: A Narrative* (3 vols.). Written by Shelby Foote. (Random House, 1958–1974.)
22. *Gödel, Escher, Bach: An Eternal Golden Braid*. Written by Douglas R. Hofstadter. (Basic Books, 1979.)
23. *A Brief History of Time: From the Big Bang to Black Holes*. Written by Stephen Hawking. (Bantam Books, 1995.)
24. *In the Garden of Beasts: Love, Terror, and an American Family in Hitler's Berlin*. Written by Erik Larson. (Crown, 2011.)
25. *The Making of the Atomic Bomb*. Written by Richard Rhodes. (Simon & Schuster, 2012.)
26. *A Room of One's Own*. Written by Virginia Woolf. (Penguin Books, 2002.)
27. *Columbine*. Written by Dave Cullen. (Twelve Books, 2009.)
28. *Speak, Memory: An Autobiography Revisited*. Written by Vladimir Nabokov. (Penguin Classics, 2000.)
29. *Electric Universe: How Electricity Switched on the Modern World*. Written by David Bodanis. (Broadway Books, 2006.)
30. *The Structure of Scientific Revolutions*. Written by Thomas S. Kuhn. (University of Chicago Press, 1971.)
31. *Into Thin Air: A Personal Account of the Mt. Everest Disaster*. Written by Jon Krakauer. (Pan Books, 2011.)
32. *The Forever War*. Written by Dexter Filkins. (Knopf, 2008.)
33. *John Adams*. Written by David McCullough. (Simon & Schuster, 2001.)
34. *Pilgrim at Tinker Creek*. Written by Annie Dillard. (HarperCollins, 2007.)
35. *The Silent Woman: Sylvia Plath and Ted Hughes*. Written by Janet Malcolm. (Vintage, 1995.)
36. *Postwar: A History of Europe since 1945*. Written by Tony Judt. (Penguin Press, 2005.)
37. *Angela's Ashes: A Memoir*. Written by Frank McCourt. (Scribner, 1996.)
38. *The Selfish Gene*. Written by Richard Dawkins. (Oxford University Press, 2006.)
39. *Chaos: Making a New Science*. Written by James Gleick. (Penguin Books, 2008.)

40. *Unbroken: A World War II Story of Survival, Resilience, and Redemption.* Written by Laura Hillenbrand. (Random House, 2010.)
41. *Cheever: A Life.* Written by Blake Bailey. (Knopf, 2009.)
42. *The Feminine Mystique.* Written by Betty Friedan. (Dell/Laurel, 1984.)
43. *The Omnivore's Dilemma: A Natural History of Four Meals.* Written by Michael Pollan. (Penguin Press, 2007.)
44. *The Big Short: Inside the Doomsday Machine.* Written by Michael Lewis. (W. W. Norton, 2010.)
45. *The Assassins' Gate: America in Iraq.* Written by George Packer. (Farrar, Straus & Giroux, 2005.)
46. *The Dark Side: The Inside Story of How the War on Terror Turned into a War on American Ideals.* Written by Jane Mayer. (Doubleday, 2008.)
47. *Zeitoun.* Written by Dave Eggers. (McSweeney's, 2009.)
48. *The Great War and Modern Memory.* Written by Paul Fussell. (Sterling, 2012.)
49. *The Devil in the White City: Murder, Magic, and Madness at the Fair That Changed America.* Written by Erik Larson. (Crown, 2003.)
50. *The Education of Henry Adams.* Written by Henry Adams. (University of Virginia Press, 2008.)
51. *Iron Curtain: The Crushing of Eastern Europe, 1945–1956.* Written by Anne Applebaum. (Doubleday, 2012.)
52. *The Electric Kool-Aid Acid Test.* Written by Tom Wolfe. (Picador, 2008.)
53. *The First Tycoon: The Epic Life of Cornelius Vanderbilt.* Written by T. J. Stiles. (Knopf, 2009.)
54. *The Lives of a Cell: Notes of a Biology Watcher.* Written by Lewis Thomas. (Penguin Books, 1978.)
55. *Nothing to Envy: Ordinary Lives in North Korea.* Written by Barbara Demick. (Spiegel & Grau, 2008.)
56. *Fast Food Nation: The Dark Side of the All-American Meal.* Written by Eric Schlosser. (Houghton Mifflin Company, 2001.)
57. *Outliers: The Story of Success.* Written by Malcolm Gladwell. (Little, Brown, 2008.)
58. *A People's History of the United States: 1492 to Present.* Written by Howard Zinn. (Harper Perennial Modern Classics, 2005.)
59. *The Rest Is Noise: Listening to the Twentieth Century.* Written by Alex Ross. (Farrar, Straus & Giroux, 2007.)
60. *The Year of Magical Thinking.* Written by Joan Didion. (Knopf, 2005.)
61. *Steve Jobs.* Written by Walter Isaacson. (Simon & Schuster, 2011.)
62. *We Wish to Inform You That Tomorrow We Will Be Killed with Our Families: Stories from Rwanda.* Written by Philip Gourevitch. (Picador, 1999.)

63. *Catherine the Great: Portrait of a Woman.* Written by Robert K. Massie. (Random House, 2011.)
64. *Desert Solitaire: A Season in the Wilderness.* Written by Edward Abbey. (McGraw-Hill, 1968.)
65. *The Gnostic Gospels.* Written by Elaine Pagels. (Vintage, 1989.)
66. *Collapse: How Societies Choose to Fail or Succeed.* Written by Jared Diamond. (Viking, 2004.)
67. *Gulag: A History of the Soviet Camps.* Written by Anne Applebaum. (Doubleday, 2003.)
68. *Destiny of the Republic: A Tale of Madness, Medicine and the Murder of a President.* Written by Candice Millard. (Anchor, 2012.)
69. *Freakonomics: A Rogue Economist Explores the Hidden Side of Everything.* Written by Steven D. Levitt and Stephen J. Dubner. (William Morrow, 2009.)
70. *Embracing Defeat: Japan in the Wake of World War II.* Written by John W. Dower. (W. W. Norton, 1999.)
71. *Far from the Tree: Parents, Children, and the Search for Identity.* Written by Andrew Solomon. (Scribner, 2012.)
72. *The Hemingses of Monticello: An American Family.* Written by Annette Gordon-Reed. (W. W. Norton, 2008.)
73. *The General Theory of Employment, Interest, and Money.* Written by John Maynard Keynes. (Harcourt, Brace & World, 1965.)
74. *Quiet: The Power of Introverts in a World That Can't Stop Talking.* Written by Susan Cain. (Crown, 2012.)
75. *Hiroshima.* Written by John Hersey. (Knopf, 1946.)
76. *Legacy of Ashes: The History of the CIA.* Written by Tim Weiner. (Doubleday, 2007.)
77. *The Souls of Black Folks.* Written by W. E. B. Du Bois. (Simon & Schuster, 2005.)
78. *Lit: A Memoir.* Written by Mary Karr. (Harper, 2009.)
79. *On Writing: A Memoir of the Craft.* Written by Stephen King. (Scribner, 1999.)
80. *Nixonland: The Rise of a President and the Fracturing of America.* Written by Rick Perlstein. (Scribner, 2008.)
81. *Mayflower: A Story of Courage, Community, and War.* Written by Nathaniel Philbrick. (Viking, 2006.)
82. *Parting the Waters: America in the King Years, 1954–63.* Written by Taylor Branch. (Simon and Schuster, 1988.)
83. *A Short History of Nearly Everything.* Written by Bill Bryson. (Broadway Books, 2003.)
84. *The Prince.* Written by Niccolò Machiavelli. (Signet Classics, 2008.)

85. *Slouching towards Bethlehem*. Written by Joan Didion. (Farrar, Straus & Giroux, 1968.)

86. The Holy Bible. (Zondervan, 2013.)

87. *A Supposedly Fun Thing I'll Never Do Again: Essays and Arguments*. Written by David Foster Wallace. (Little, Brown, 1997.)

88. *Anti-intellectualism in American Life*. Written by Richard Hofstadter. (Vintage, 1966.)

89. *The Swerve: How the World Became Modern*. Written by Stephen Greenblatt. (W. W. Norton, 2011.)

90. *Fordlandia: The Rise and Fall of Henry Ford's Forgotten Jungle City*. Written by Greg Grandin. (Metropolitan Books, 2009.)

91. *Thinking, Fast and Slow*. Written by Daniel Kahneman. (Farrar, Straus & Giroux, 2011.)

92. *The Origin of Species*. Written by Charles Darwin. (Simon & Schuster, 2008.)

93. *This Republic of Suffering: Death and the American Civil War*. Written by Drew Gilpin Faust. (Knopf, 2008.)

94. *The Beauty Myth: How Images of Beauty Are Used against Women*. Written by Naomi Wolf. (Harper Perennial, 2002.)

95. *The Right Stuff*. Written by Tom Wolfe. (Picador, 2007.)

96. *The Tipping Point: How Little Things Can Make a Big Difference*. Written by Malcolm Gladwell. (Back Bay Books, 2002.)

97. *Travels in Siberia*. Written by Ian Frazier. (Farrar, Straus & Giroux, 2010.)

98. *Capitalism and Freedom*. Written by Milton Friedman. (University of Chicago Press, 1968.)

99. *A Walk in the Woods: Rediscovering America on the Appalachian Trail*. Written by Bill Bryson. (HarperCollins, 1998.)

100. *Black Hawk Down: A Story of Modern War*. Written by Mark Bowden. (Signet Books, 1999.)

Bibliography

The Mother of All Booklists: The 500 Most Recommended Nonfiction Reads for Ages 3 to 103 integrates 155 English-language book awards, references, web guides, and reading lists from leading magazines, newspapers, consumer and parenting organizations, schools, and libraries. In most cases, award-winner and finalist information was gathered from the date of inception of the award to the most recent material available. Where best-book lists encompassed multiple years, the web address of the most recent year is cited.

The bibliography is organized into three parts. The first two sections, "Child and Young-Adult References" and "Adult References" annotate the sources of the lists that were used to generate The Mother of All Booklists. The third section, "Additional Readings," cites other works mentioned in the book.

Child and Young-Adult References

"100 Best Children's Books of All Time." Parenthood.com. Accessed October 17, 2013. http://www.parenthood.com/article-topics/the_100_best_childrens_books.html/full -view.

> Parents, readers, and children's literature experts present a list of books expected to stand the test of time.

"100 Nonfiction Titles for Young Children." Idaho Commission for Libraries. Accessed October 12, 2013. http://libraries.idaho.gov/files/100-nonfiction-titles.pdf.

> The commission assists libraries to build the capacity to better serve their clientele.

"All Nonfiction Booklists." Carnegie Library of Pittsburgh. Accessed October 15, 2013. http://www.carnegielibrary.org/teens/books/allnonfiction.cfm.

> From baseball to biographies, hip-hop to health, and crafts to community service, the library has many offbeat, quality booklists for teenagers.

"The All-Time Best Books for Preschoolers." Parents.com. Accessed October 17, 2013. http://www.parents.com/fun/entertainment/books/the-all-time-best-books-for-preschoolers/#page=1.
  Parents.com is the online home of *Parents, American Baby,* and *Family Circle* magazines.

"Alphabet Soup: Nonfiction A–Z." Plymouth District Library. Accessed October 6, 2013. http://plymouthlibrary.org/index.php/youth/youth-booklists/638-preschool-alphabet-nonfiction-books.
  The library serves residents in suburban Detroit, Michigan.

"AP Language Non-fiction Outside Reading List." North Yarmouth Academy. Accessed October 21, 2013. http://www2.nya.org/files/2010/06/ap11nonfiction1.pdf.
  This private college-preparatory school is located in Maine.

"Award-Winning Nonfiction Books for Toddlers and Preschoolers." Booknixie. Accessed October 30, 2013. http://www.booknixie.com/books/preschool/nonfiction/all-cultures/all-time.
  This website lists quality books for children and young adults.

Ballweg, Judy. "Picture Books That Nurture Mathematical Thinking." Madison Metropolitan School District. Accessed October 30, 2013. http://oldweb.madison.k12.wi.us/tnl/lilm/docs/judys_picture_book_list_0-3.pdf.
  Ballweg's list of recommended titles gives preference to the interests of toddlers and preschoolers.

Barr, Catherine. *Best Books for Children: Preschool through Grade 6: Supplement to the 9th Edition.* Santa Barbara, CA: Libraries Unlimited, 2013.
  Barr's supplement helps public librarians keep up with thousands of recently published children's books.

"Beehive Book Awards." Children's Literature Association of Utah. Accessed October 20, 2013. http://www.clau.org/brochures-bookmarks--lists.html.
  The association exists to share ideas and to encourage the reading, study, and writing of children's literature. Award information was gathered for the years 1986 through 2013.

"Best Children's Books: Nonfiction." Kirkus Reviews. Accessed October 18, 2013. https://www.kirkusreviews.com/lists/best-childrens-books-2012-nonfiction/.
  The editors pick books for all age groups that will inspire and inform. Booklist information was gathered for the years 2010 through 2012.

"The Best Children's Books.org." Accessed October 15, 2013. http://www.the-best-childrens-books.org/.
  This is a resource for teachers, parents, and homeschoolers with booklists on language arts, history, math, science, and other topics.

"Best Children's Nonfiction." Goodreads. Last modified February 23, 2009. http://www.goodreads.com/list/show/1557.Best_Children_s_Nonfiction.
  The list has books for elementary and high-school-aged students.

"Best Children's Nonfiction." Granite School District. Accessed October 20, 2013. http://www.granitemedia.org/category/best-new-books/best-nonfiction/.

Out of all the books reviewed in this Utah school district, these titles received the highest ratings. Booklist information was gathered for the years 2012 and 2013.

"Best Kids Books." *Washington Post.* Last modified November 13, 2012. http://articles .washingtonpost.com/2012-11-13/lifestyle/35506066_1_kids-books-steve-sheinkin -lois-lowry.

The *Washington Post Book World* reviewers select the best children's books of the year. Booklist information was gathered for the years 2008 through 2012.

"Best of the Best 2013." Chicago Public Library. Accessed October 12, 2013. http:// www.chipublib.org/forkids/kidsbooklists/bestofbest_list.php.

The library recommends 100 great and award-winning books published for kids in 2012.

Blasingame, James. *Books That Don't Bore 'Em: Young Adult Books That Speak to This Generation.* New York: Scholastic Teaching Resources, 2007.

Professor Blasingame presents many annotated best-book lists organized by theme, topic, genre, and reading level.

"The BookHive: Your Guide to Children's Literature." Charlotte Mecklenburg Library. Accessed October 5, 2013. http://www.cmlibrary.org/Bookhive/.

The library has reading lists for different age groups and a searchable database.

"Booklist Editors' Choice: Books for Youth." Booklist Online. Last modified January 1, 2013. http://www.booklistonline.com/Booklist-Editors-Choice-Books-for-Youth -2012-Gillian-Engberg/pid=5893027.

The editors make best-of-the-year selections that mix popular appeal with literary excellence. Booklist information was gathered for the years 1994 through 2012.

"Boston Globe–Horn Book Awards." Accessed October 5, 2013. http://www.hbook .com/2013/05/news/boston-globe-horn-book-awards/2013-boston-globe-horn-book -awards-for-excellence-in-childrens-literature-2/.

These annual awards recognize and reward excellence in literature for children and young adults. Award information was collected for the years 1967 through 2013.

Bradbury, Judy. *The Read-Aloud Scaffold: Best Books to Enhance Content Area Curriculum, Grades Pre-K–3.* Santa Barbara, CA: Libraries Unlimited, 2011.

Bradbury has a wide range of recent noteworthy titles.

Burns, Mary M. "Children's Classics: A Booklist for Parents." *The Horn Book Magazine.* Accessed October 21, 2013. http://archive.hbook.com/pdf/childrensclassics.pdf.

This is a list of outstanding titles from a magazine with a reputation for recommending quality children's literature.

Capizzo, Louise, and Cathy Potter. "Top Ten Science and Math Books of 2012." The Nonfiction Detectives. Last modified December 24, 2012. http://www.nonfictionde tectives.com/2012/12/top-ten-science-and-math-books-of-2012.html.

Two librarians recommend the best nonfiction books for children.

"Carter G. Woodson Book Awards." National Council for the Social Studies. Accessed October 17, 2013.

The annual awards are given for the most distinguished books for young readers that depict ethnicity in the United States. Award information was gathered for the years 1974 through 2012.

"Children's and Young Adult Bloggers' Literary Awards." Accessed September 25, 2013. http://www.cybils.com/2013/02/the-2012-cybils-awards.html#more.

CYBILS awards are given annually, and nominations are open to the public. Award information was gathered for the years 2006 through 2012.

"Children's Books 2012: 100 Titles for Reading and Sharing." New York Public Library. http://www.nypl.org/collections/nypl-recommendations/lists/childrens2012.

Accessed September 25, 2013. The librarians' annual list recommends titles full of imagination and information.

"Common Core State Standards for English Language Arts & Literacy in History/Social Studies, Science, and Technical Subjects." Council of Chief State School Officers and the National Governors Association. Last modified June 2, 2010. http://www.cores tandards.org/assets/Appendix_B.pdf.

Appendix B provides nonfiction text exemplars for the school curriculum.

"Common Sense for the Core: Nonfiction Lists." Scholastic Incorporated. Accessed September 24, 2013. http://www.scholastic.com/commoncore/common-core-book -list-nonfiction.htm.

The publisher lists noteworthy examples of informational texts by grade level.

Corneal, Devon. "Mesmerizing Non-fiction Children's Books." *Huffington Post.* Last modified November 5, 2012. http://www.huffingtonpost.com/devon-corneal/novem ber-books_b_2066539.html.

Devon highlights great biographies and histories.

"CurriConnects Lists." TeachersFirst. Accessed October 10, 2013. http://www.teachers first.com/content/booklist-series.cfm.

This teacher resource has an impressive collection of age-group booklists.

"EDSITEment's Recommended Reading List for College-Bound Students." National Endowment for the Humanities. Accessed October 21, 2013. http://edsitement.neh.gov/ feature/edsitements-recommended-reading-list-college-bound-students#nonfiction.

The NEH recommends the best traditional humanities reads.

"The Essential Guide to Preschool Science." Education.com. Last modified June 30, 2009. http://www.education.com/magazine/article/preschool-science-nature/.

Experts selected the books that are most informative and do the most to make science fun.

"Favorite Books." GreatSchools. Accessed October 12, 2013. http://www.greatschools .org/cgi-bin/showarticle/3607/.

Panels of children's-book experts recommend great books for preschool through fifth grade.

Flowers, Tiffany A., and Lamont A. Flowers. "Nonfiction in the Early Grades: Making Reading and Writing Relevant for All Students." *Journal for the Liberal Arts and Sciences* (Spring 2009). Accessed October 30, 2013. http://www.clemson.edu/centers -institutes/houston/documents/nonfiction.pdf.

> The bibliography includes recommended nonfiction and informational children's texts by subject.

Fraser, Elizabeth. *Reality Rules: A Guide to Teen Nonfiction.* Santa Barbara, CA: Libraries Unlimited, 2008.

> This readers' advisory reference arranges books by genre and school age.

Freeman, Judy. "Nonfiction: 71 Top Books of the Century." Booktalk. Accessed September 24, 2013. http://teacher.scholastic.com/reading/bestpractices/nonfiction/ topBooksCentury.pdf.

> A children's-book author and consultant selected unforgettable titles from a variety of publishers.

"The Golden Kite Awards." Society of Children's Book Writers and Illustrators. Accessed November 1, 2013. http://www.scbwi.org/awards/golden-kite-award/.

> The medallion awards are given annually by a jury of peers to recognize excellence in children's literature. Award information was gathered for the years 1978 through 2013.

"Great Books." Benicia Public Library. Last modified March 19, 2012. http://www .benicialibrary.org/kids/booklists/grade/kindergarten#nonfiction.

> The library has booklists for kindergarten through eighth grade.

"Great Math Books: Preschoolers (3–5 Years Old)." Mother Goose Programs, Vermont Center for the Book. Accessed October 7, 2013. http://www.mothergooseprograms .org/math_books_preschoolers.php.

> The center disseminates information to libraries, schools, and other organizations.

"Great Science Books for Preschoolers." Amazon. Accessed October 10, 2013. http:// www.amazon.com/Great-science-books-for-preschoolers/lm/R3SWAP0TB1WIHP.

> This is a collection of nicely illustrated picture books about science.

"Great Science Books for the Little Ones." Smithsonian.com. Last modified December 13, 2010. http://blogs.smithsonianmag.com/science/2010/12/great-science-books -for-the-little-ones/.

> The article lists the most notable children's science books from 2010.

"Great Science Books: Preschoolers (3–5 Years Old)." Mother Goose Programs, Vermont Center for the Book. Accessed October 7, 2013. http://www.mothergoosepro grams.org/science_books_age_3_5.php.

> The center disseminates information to libraries, schools, and other organizations.

"Informational Picture Books." Office of Commonwealth Libraries, Pennsylvania Department of Education. Accessed October 21, 2013. http://www.portal.state.pa.us/ portal/server.pt/community/library_resources/8722/resources_for_pennsylvania_li- braries/524616.

The state Department of Education advises parents to look for these books at local libraries.

"IRA Children's and Young Adults Book Awards." International Reading Association. Accessed September 25, 2013. http://www.reading.org/resources/AwardsandGrants/ childrens_ira.aspx.
Awards are given to newly published authors who show unusual promise in children's and young-adult books. Award information was gathered for the years 1995 through 2013.

Isaacs, Kathleen T. *Picturing the World: Informational Picture Books for Children.* Chicago: American Library Association, 2013.
This library resource surveys the best nonfiction/informational titles for ages 3 through 10.

Jones, Trevelyn, et al. "Best Books." *School Library Journal.* Last modified November 29, 2012. http://www.slj.com/2012/11/featured/best-books-2012/.
The influential monthly magazine issues an annual best-books list. Booklist information was gathered for the years 2010 through 2012.

"Just the Facts, Ma'am: Non-fiction Books." Middletown Township Public Library. Accessed October 14, 2013. http://mtpl.org/?q=node/91.
This New Jersey library has nonfiction recommendations for first through sixth graders.

Linder, Rozlyn. *The Common Core Guidebook, Grades 6–8: Informational Text Lessons, Guided Practice, Suggested Book Lists, and Reproducible Organizers.* New York: The Literacy Initiative, 2013.
This guide is an essential resource for anyone teaching middle-grade students to navigate informational texts.

Lipson, Eden Ross. *The* New York Times *Parent's Guide to the Best Books for Children.* New York: Three Rivers Press, 2000.
This is an annotated compendium of the best 1001 books for kids.

Lorenzi, Natalie. "Best Nonfiction Kids Books." Scholastic. Accessed October 21, 2013. http://www.scholastic.com/teachers/article/best-nonfiction-kids-books.
Lorenzi recommends noteworthy titles for middle readers.

MacMillan, Meredith. "Books for Young Children about Nature." National Association for the Education of Young Children. Last updated January 2008. http://www.naeyc .org/files/yc/file/200801/BTJRecommendedNatureBooks.pdf.
MacMillan suggests the best informational books in a variety of categories including the alphabet, animals, insects, and plants.

"NCTE Orbis Pictus Awards for Outstanding Nonfiction for Children." National Council of Teachers of English. Accessed September 25, 2013. http://www.ncte.org/ awards/orbispictus.
Award information was gathered for the years 1990 through 2013.

"Newbery Awards." Association for Library Service to Children, American Library Association. Accessed September 24, 2013. http://www.ala.org/alsc/awardsgrants/book media/newberymedal/newberymedal.

The annual Newbery Medal is America's most distinguished and widely recognized award for excellence in children's literature. Award information was collected for the years 1922 through 2013.

Nichols, Mark, ed. *Book Sense Best Children's Books: 240 Favorites for All Ages Recommended by Independent Booksellers.* New York: Newmarket Press, 2005.

Recommendations are offered for different age groups.

"Non-fiction, High School Booklist." ATN Reading Lists. Accessed October 13, 2013. http://atn-reading-lists.wikispaces.com/Non-fiction%2C+High+School.

The All Together Now project is a collaborative website created by librarians.

"Norma Fleck Award for Canadian Children's Non-fiction." Canadian Children's Book Centre. Accessed September 25, 2013. http://www.bookcentre.ca/awards/norma_fleck_award_canadian_childrens_nonfiction.

The awards recognize exceptional books by Canadian authors. Award information was gathered for the years 1999 through 2012.

"Notable Children's Books." *New York Times.* Last modified November 28, 2012. http://www.nytimes.com/2012/12/02/books/review/notable-childrens-books-of-2012.html?ref=review.

The year's best books are selected by the children's-book editor of the *New York Times Book Review.* Booklist information was gathered for the years 2004 through 2012.

"Notable Children's Lists." Association for Library Service to Children, American Library Association. Accessed October 15, 2013. http://www.ala.org/alsc/awardsgrants/notalists.

Each year the ALSC complies best-of-the-best lists of children's books. Booklists were collected for the years 1995 through 2013.

"Notable Social Studies Trade Books for Young People." National Council for the Social Studies. http://www.socialstudies.org/notable. Accessed September 25, 2013.

Each year, the NCSS in cooperation with the Children's Book Council (CBC) publishes a bibliography of noteworthy books. Booklist information was gathered for the years 2000 through 2013.

NoveList Plus. EBSCO Information Services. Accessed October 15, 2013. http://web.ebscohost.com/novp/search?sid=72810cfb-c453-44e4-bfb0-bdda7a5194f0%40sessionmgr111&vid=2&hid=127.

This is a popular online library database with titles and booklists recommended to support the school curriculum.

Odean, Kathleen. "20 Outstanding Nonfiction Books | Core Essentials." *School Library Journal.* Last modified May 7, 2013. http://www.slj.com/2013/05/standards/common-core/20-outstanding-nonfiction-books-core-essentials/#_.

Odean describes outstanding informational titles, suggesting that college preparation requires the reading of full-length books rather than just excerpts.

"Outstanding Books for the College Bound." Young Adult Library Services Association, American Library Association. Accessed October 22, 2013. http://www.ala.org/yalsa/outstanding-books-college-bound.
Every few years the ALA recommends books to introduce a variety of academic subjects to lifetime learners and the college bound. Booklist information was gathered for 1999, 2004, and 2009.

"Outstanding Science Trade Books for Students K–12." National Science Teachers Association. Accessed October 6, 2013. http://www.nsta.org/publications/ostb/.
The recommended books embody a broad and exciting vision of science. Booklist information was gathered for the years 1996 through 2013.

"PW Best Books." *Publisher's Weekly*. Accessed October 6, 2013. http://www.publisher sweekly.com/pw/best-books/2012/childrens-nonfiction#list.
The trade news and book review magazine makes annual recommendations. Booklist information was gathered for the years 2008 through 2012.

"Read-Aloud Favorites." TextProject. Accessed October 22, 2013. http://textproject.org/teachers/read-aloud-favorites/FavoritesSearchForm.
The searchable database produces lists of great books for beginning and struggling readers.

Reid, Rob. "Reid-Aloud Alert: Biographies as Read-Alouds." Booklist. Last modified September 2012. http://www.booklistonline.com/Reid-Aloud-Alert-Biographies-as-Read-Alouds-Rob-Reid/pid=5569027.
Reid recommends biographies that are as compelling as the best fiction.

"The Riverby Award List of Nature Books for Young Readers." John Burroughs Association. Accessed October 22, 2013. http://research.amnh.org/burroughs/young_read ers_list.html.
The annual award is given for outstanding natural-history books for children that contain perceptive and artistic accounts of direct experiences in the world of nature.

"Robert F. Sibert Informational Book Medal." Association for Library Service to Children, American Library Association. Accessed September 25, 2013. http://www.ala .org/alsc/awardsgrants/bookmedia/sibertmedal.
The ALSC gives annual awards to recognize factual books for children. Award information was gathered for the years 2001 through 2013.

Salley, Coleen C., and Terrence E. Young. "Outstanding Science Read-Alouds." *Book Links*, November 2004, 36–40. Accessed October 22, 2013. http://www.coleensalley .com/other_files/Read-Alouds_nov04.pdf.
The books were recommended for school-library media centers.

Silvey, Anita. *100 Best Books for Children: A Parent's Guide to Making the Right Choices for Your Young Reader, Toddler to Preteen*. Boston: Mariner Books, 2004.

This is an annotated list of classic children's books published between 1902 and 2002.

Silvey, Anita. *Children's Book-a-Day Almanac*. New York: Roaring Brook Press, 2012.
The former editor of *Hornbook Magazine* recommends classic books for children of all ages.

Silvey, Anita. *The Essential Guide to Children's Books and Their Creators*. New York: Houghton Mifflin, 2002.
The guide lists important children's books and has a wealth of information on writers and illustrators.

"Suggested Reading for PreK–K." Bethlehem Public Library. Accessed October 30, 2013. http://www.bethlehempubliclibrary.org/pdfs/booklist_preK-K.pdf.
This Pennsylvania library has many quality 2012 and 2013 nonfiction recommendations.

"Summer Book Lists." Boston Public Schools. Accessed October 12, 2013. http://www.bostonpublicschools.org/summer.
Quality informational and other books are recommended for kindergarten through 12th grade. Booklist information was gathered for 2012 and 2013.

"Summer Reads for Kids." Morton Grove Public Library. Accessed October 14, 2013. http://www.mgpl.org/kids/summer-reads/.
This Illinois library has recommended-book lists for kindergarten though sixth grade.

Tanen, Sloane. "16 Great Biographies for Kids." Grandparents.com. Accessed October 15, 2013. http://www.grandparents.com/grandkids/toys-books-and-entertainment/best-biographies-for-children.
The book columnist selects titles that make history come alive.

"Teen Link Biographies." Hennepin County Library. Accessed October 15, 2013. http://www.hclib.org/teens/booklistaction.cfm?list_num=585.
This Minnesota library identifies the best recent reads for young adults.

"Teen Zone Classic Nonfiction." King County Library System. Accessed October 13, 2013. http://www.kcls.org/teens/booklist.cfm?booklistid=15.
This Washington-state library system has an impressive list of titles.

Temple, Emily. "An Essential Nonfiction Reading List for High School and Beyond." Flavorwire. Last modified November 29, 2012. http://flavorwire.com/351082/an-essential-nonfiction-reading-list-for-high-school-and-beyond/view-all/.
Flavorwire reports on cultural events, art, books, music, and pop culture.

"Ten Great Science Books for Kids." Smithsonian.com. Last modified November 22, 2011. http://blogs.smithsonianmag.com/science/2011/11/ten-great-science-books-for-kids/.
The article lists the most notable children's science books from 2011.

Trelease, Jim. *The Read-Aloud Handbook.* New York: Viking Penguin, 2013.
This updated edition offers many excellent read-aloud titles.

Ward, Barbara A., and Terrell A. Young. "Biography for Children Has Never Been Better." *Reading Horizons* 48, no. 4 (2008). Accessed October 15, 2013. http://scholar
works.wmich.edu/cgi/viewcontent.cgi?article=1094&context=reading_horizons.
These Washington State University scholars select the most notable life stories.

"What Kids Are Reading: The Book-Reading Habits of Students in American Schools, 2013." Renaissance Learning. Accessed October 6, 2013. http://doc.renlearn.com/
KMNet/R0055233EDFB0A65.pdf.
Noteworthy nonfiction books are rated by interest level and text complexity.

Wray, Denise. "Non-Fiction 'Must Read' Author List Preschool." First Years. Last modified September 2012. http://firstyears.org/c5/must-reads-non-fiction-Pre.pdf.
Administered by the University of North Carolina at Chapel Hill, the First Years program promotes literacy in the fields of deaf education, speech-language pathology, audiology, and early intervention.

"YALSA Award for Excellence in Nonfiction for Young Adults." Young Adult Library Services Association, American Library Association. Accessed September 25, 2013. http://www.ala.org/yalsa/nonfiction.
The annual award honors the best nonfiction book published for teenagers. Award information was gathered for the years 2010 through 2013.

Young, Terrell A., and Barbara A. Ward. "Classroom Connections: Informational Texts and the Common Core." Booklist Online. Last modified September 2012. http://
booklistonline.com/Classroom-Connections-Informational-Texts-and-the-Common
-Core-Terrell-A-Young/pid=5641482.
The article includes a bibliography emphasizing literary nonfiction and social studies themes.

Young, Terrence E., and Coleen C. Salley. "Outstanding Science Read Alouds 2005–2007." *SB&F*, November/December 2007, 238–46. Accessed October 22, 2013. http://www.coleensalley.com/other_files/Read-Alouds2007.pdf.
The titles were selected to augment classroom instruction.

"Young People's Book Prize." The Royal Society. Accessed September 25, 2013. http://
royalsociety.org/awards/young-people/.
The British book prize celebrates the best books that communicate science to young people. Award information was gathered for the years 1988 through 2012.

Adult References

"The 10 Best Books." *New York Times.* Last modified November 30, 2012. http://www
.nytimes.com/2012/12/09/books/review/10-best-books-of-2012.html.
Booklist information was gathered for the years 1981 through 2012.

"The 25 Best Non-fiction Books Ever: Reader Picks." Open Culture. Last modified June 27, 2011. http://www.openculture.com/2011/06/the_25_best_non-fiction_books_ever_readers_picks.html.
    With a mission of identifying the best media and educational media, Open Culture asked its readers to pick the best nonfiction titles of all time.

"50 Notable Works of Nonfiction." *Washington Post.* Last modified November 16, 2012. http://articles.washingtonpost.com/2012-11-16/entertainment/35506527_1_stephen-r-platt-bedside-book-knopf.
    Booklist information was gathered for the years 2006 through 2012.

"75 Biographies to Read before You Die." Open Education Database. Last modified September 23, 2012. http://oedb.org/ilibrarian/75-biographies-to-read-before-you-die/.
    Open Education Database is a comprehensive collection of online college rankings and free courses.

"100 Best Nonfiction." Modern Library, Random House. Accessed October 3, 2013. http://www.modernlibrary.com/top-100/100-best-nonfiction/.
    The publishing house developed a list of what it considers the world's best books and a parallel reader's list based on public opinion.

"The 100 Best Nonfiction Books of All Time." List Muse. Accessed October 1, 2013. http://www.listmuse.com/best-books-top-100-nonfiction.php.
    The website seeks to provide the best cultural products that are available today.

"The 100 Best Non-fiction Books of the Century." *National Review.* Accessed October 3, 2013. http://old.nationalreview.com/100best/100_books.html.
    Inspired by the Modern Library's 100 recommendations, the *NR* took a stab at creating its own list.

"The 100 Greatest Non-fiction Books." *Guardian.* Last updated June 14, 2011. http://www.theguardian.com/books/2011/jun/14/100-greatest-non-fiction-books.
    The British newspaper recommended what it considers the very best factual writing.

"100 Notable Books." *New York Times.* Last modified November 27, 2012. http://www.nytimes.com/2012/12/02/books/review/100-notable-books-of-2012.html?pagewanted=all.
    This is the newspaper's long list of the year's outstanding books. Booklists were collected for the years 1981 through 2012.

"110 Best Books: The Perfect Library." *Telegraph.* Last modified April 6, 2008. http://www.telegraph.co.uk/culture/books/3672376/110-best-books-The-perfect-library.html.
    The British newspaper recommends a reading list of classics and books that changed the world.

Ackman, Dan. "The 20 Most Influential Business Books." *Forbes.* Last modified September 30, 2002. http://www.forbes.com/2002/09/30/0930booksintro.html.
    A panel of experts selected the 20 most significant business books of the last 20 years.

"All-Time 100 Nonfiction Books." *Time.* Accessed October 5, 2013. http://entertain ment.time.com/2011/08/30/all-time-100-best-nonfiction-books/#ixzz2grMxeRzM. The editors picked best and most influential books written in English since the magazine's 1923 inception.

"Andrew Carnegie Medals for Excellence in Fiction and Nonfiction." Reference and Users Services Association, American Library Association. Accessed September 27, 2013. http://www.ala.org/rusa/awards/carnegie. The annual prizes recognize the best books written for adults that were published in the United States. Award information was gathered for the years 2012 and 2013.

"Arthur Ross Book Award." Council on Foreign Relations. Accessed September 27, 2013. http://www.cfr.org/about/arthur_ross.html. The annual award recognizes books that make an outstanding contribution to the understanding of foreign policy or international relations. Award information was gathered for the years 2002 and 2012.

Bailey, Lauren. "25 Fascinating Biographies Every College Student Should Read." Best Colleges Online. Last modified June 15, 2010. http://www.bestcollegesonline.com/blog/2010/06/15/25-fascinating-biographies-every-college-student-should-read/. Bailey recommends the study of the lives and deeds of famous women and men.

"Bancroft Prize." Columbia University. Accessed September 27, 2013. http://library .columbia.edu/subject-guides/amerihist/bancroft/previous_awards.html. The prize is given out each year by the university trustees for books about diplomacy or American history. Award information was gathered for the years 1948 through 2013.

"Best 100 Non-fiction Books." The Best 100 Lists. Accessed October 10, 2013. http://www.thebest100lists.com/best100nonfictionbooks/index.html. The Best 100 Lists is a website that conducts polls on a variety of cultural topics.

"Best Books of the Year: Nonfiction." Amazon. Accessed October 6, 2013. http://www .amazon.com/b?ie=UTF8&node=5917171011. Booklist information was gathered for the years 2006 through 2012.

"Best Books of the Year: Nonfiction." *Christian Science Monitor.* Accessed September 27, 2013. http://www.csmonitor.com/Books/2012/1203/15-best-books-of-2012-nonfic tion/The-Lady-in-Gold-The-Extraordinary-Tale-of-Gustav-Klimt-s-Masterpiece-Por trait-of-Adele-Bloch-Bauer-by-Anne-Marie-O-Connor. Booklist information was gathered for the years 2003 through 2012.

"The Best Cook Books of All Time." *Village Voice.* Accessed October 5, 2013. http://www.villagevoice.com/slideshow/the-best-cook-books-of-all-time-28718904/. The influential arts and culture weekly overcame its fear of hyperbole to create what it describes as a probably impossible booklist.

"Best Economics Books." Goodreads. Accessed September 30, 2013. http://www .goodreads.com/list/show/7874.Best_Economics_Books. The Goodreads website recommends titles based on user-populated databases.

"Best Non-fiction." Goodreads. Accessed September 30, 2013. http://www.goodreads
.com/list/show/134.Best_Non_Fiction_non_biography_.
The mission of this social cataloging website is to help people find and share information about books.

"Best Nonfiction." Los Angeles Public Library. Last modified April 5, 2013. http://www
.lapl.org/collections-resources/lapl-reads/book-lists/best-2012-non-fiction.
Booklist information was gathered for the years 2011 and 2012.

"The Best Nonfiction." *Wall Street Journal.* Last modified December 14, 2012. http://
online.wsj.com/article/SB10001424127887324481204578179532266739440.html.
The book editors do an annual round up of the best books. Booklist information
was gathered for the years 2008 through 2012.

"Best Nonfiction Books." *Boston Globe.* Last modified December 29, 2012. http://www
.bostonglobe.com/arts/books/2012/12/29/best-nonfiction/vHuDfzPNsWv4c02h
FyCNuM/story.html.
Booklist information was gathered for the years 2005 through 2012.

"Best Nonfiction Books." Inside Higher Ed. Last modified December 20, 2012.
http://www.insidehighered.com/blogs/technology-and-learning/11-best-nonfiction-
books-2012.
The publication recommends the best nonfiction and favors the concise e-book
format. Booklist information was gathered for the years 2011 and 2012.

"Best Nonfiction of the Year." *Entertainment Weekly.* Accessed July 15, 2013. http://
www.ew.com/ew/gallery/0,,20326356_20652530_21246940,00.html#21246940.
Booklist information was gathered for the years 2006 through 2012.

"The Best Southern Nonfiction of All Time." *Oxford American.* Last modified August
31, 2009. http://www.oxfordamerican.org/articles/2009/aug/31/best-southern-non
fiction-all-time/.
The journal compiled a list of celebrated and sometimes underrated masterpieces.

Bowman, Donna, et al. "AV Club Best Books of the 00s." *Onion.* Last modified November 25, 2009. http://www.avclub.com/article/the-best-books-of-the-00s.35774/.
The entertainment newspaper and website came up with its list of best books for
the first decade of the 21st century.

Bratman, Fred, and Scott Lewis. *The Reader's Companion: A Book Lover's Guide to the
Most Important Books in Every Field of Knowledge, as Chosen by the Experts.* New York:
Hyperion, 1994.
Writers, historians, movie stars, and religious and political figures reveal the titles
that have most affected their lives.

"Business Book of the Year Award." Financial Times and Goldman Sachs. Last modified September 19, 2013. http://www.goldmansachs.com/citizenship/business-book
-award/.

The award recognizes the books having the most compelling insight into the modern business world. Award information was gathered for the years 2005 through 2013.

Cords, Sarah Statz. *The Real Story: A Guide to Nonfiction Reading Interests.* Westport, Conn.: Libraries Unlimited, 2006.

Clearly defining various nonfiction genres and subgenres, this is an important addition to the field of readers' advisory services.

Covert, Jack, and Todd Sattersten. *The 100 Best Business Books of All Time: What They Say, Why They Matter, and How They Can Help You.* New York: Portfolio Trade, 2011.

Covert and Sattersten distill the best business titles from the thousands published yearly, selecting those of interest to a wider audience.

"Edgar Award for Best Fact Crime." Mystery Writers of America. Accessed September 30, 2013. http://www.theedgars.com/edgarsDB/.

The Edgar Allan Poe Awards are presented annually for the best works of mystery in a variety of media. Award information was gathered for the years 1948 through 2013.

"The Electric Typewriter 100 Great Nonfiction Books." Accessed September 30, 2013. http://tetw.org/Books.

This website identifies the must-read works of narrative nonfiction, essay collections, and classic journalism.

Ewers, Justin. "Executive Picks." *U.S. News & World Report.* Last modified May 13, 2007. http://www.usnews.com/usnews/biztech/articles/070513/21best.intro.htm.

Culled from a panel of CEOs and experts, the magazine presents a list of best business books of all time.

"Goodreads Choice Awards." Accessed September 30, 2013. http://www.goodreads.com/choiceawards/best-books-2012.

This award is decided by readers who visit the website. Award information was gathered for the years 2009 through 2012.

Kipen, David. "West-Side Stories / Readers Rank the 20th Century's Best Nonfiction This Side of the Rockies." *San Francisco Chronicle.* Last modified May 27, 1999. http://www.sfgate.com/entertainment/article/West-Side-Stories-Readers-rank-the-20th-2928676.php#photo-2254180.

This is the newspaper's list of 100 best nonfiction reads from the American West.

Liebetrau, Eric. "Best Nonfiction of the Year." *Kirkus Reviews.* Accessed October 1, 2013. https://www.kirkusreviews.com/issue/2012-best-of/section/nonfiction/.

A diverse variety of quality titles are represented on this list. Booklist information was gathered for the years 2009 through 2012.

Lindgren, Hugo. "As If You Don't Have Enough to Read." *New York Times Magazine.* Last modified June 17, 2011. http://6thfloor.blogs.nytimes.com/2011/06/17/as-if-you-dont-have-enough-to-read/.

Inspired by the *Guardian*'s list, the magazine staff created its own list of the best nonfiction books of all time.

"LJ's Best Books and Media." *Library Journal.* Last modified December 6, 2012. http://lj.libraryjournal.com/2012/12/publishing/ljs-best-books-and-media-of-2012/.
The recommended lists have a wide range of quality titles. Booklist information was gathered for the years 2011 and 2012.

"Los Angeles Times Book Prize." *Los Angeles Times.* Accessed October 1, 2013. http://events.latimes.com/bookprizes/.
Prizes are presented in several categories including biography, current interest, history, science, and technology. Award information was gathered for the years 1980 through 2012.

McMurtrie, John. "Best Books of the Year." *San Francisco Chronicle.* Last modified February 1, 2013. http://www.sfgate.com/books/article/Best-books-of-2012-100-recommended-books-4139185.php.
Booklist information was gathered for the years 2007 through 2012.

Miller, Laura. "The Best Books of the Decade." *Salon.* Last modified December 9, 2009. http://www.salon.com/2009/12/10/best_books_decade/.
The magazine steered away from trendsetting books in favor of definitive accounts of current events, penetrating histories, and perennial human concerns.

"*Ms.* Readers' 100 Best Non-Fiction Books of All Time." *Ms.* Last modified October 10, 2011. http://msmagazine.com/blog/2011/10/10/ms-readers-100-best-non-fiction-books-of-all-time-the-top-10-and-the-complete-list/.
The list includes the most authoritative feminist titles.

"National Book Award for Nonfiction." National Book Foundation. Accessed October 2, 2013. http://www.nationalbook.org/nba2013.html#.Ukv6jxbvyRs.
The foundation presents annual awards to recognize the best American literature and to enhance the cultural value of good writing. Award information was gathered for the years 1950 through 2013.

"National Book Critics Circle Award." National Book Critics Circle. Accessed April 16, 2013. http://bookcritics.org/awards.
The NBCC is an organization of literary professionals who annually honor the highest quality writing published in English. Award information was collected for the years 1975 through 2012.

"New-York Historical Society American History Book Prize." New-York Historical Society. Accessed October 3, 2013. http://www.nyhistory.org/press/releases/new-york-historical-society-awards-its-annual-american-history-book-prize-robert-caro.
Award information was gathered for the years 2005 through 2013.

Nordquist, Richard. "100 Major Works of Modern Creative Nonfiction." About.com Guide. Accessed September 27, 2013. http://grammar.about.com/od/60essays/a/modnonfiction.htm.
Nordquist's list of major works by British and American writers includes essays, memoirs, autobiographies, biographies, travel writing, history, cultural studies, and nature writing.

"Notable Books Lists." Reference and Users Services Association, American Library Association. Accessed September 27, 2013. http://www.ala.org/rusa/awards/notablebooks.
  The ALA annually lists very good, readable, and important books for the adult reader. Booklist information was gathered for the years 1998 through 2013.

"Page Turners." *Economist.* Accessed July 12, 2013. http://www.economist.com/news/books-and-arts/21567575-best-books-2012-were-about-richard-burton-titian-rin-tin-tin-revolution.
  The weekly international magazine recommends the best reads of the year. Booklist information was gathered for the years 2003 through 2012.

Parini, Jay. *Promised Land: 13 Books That Changed America.* New York: Anchor, 2010.
  Parini discusses the books that most shaped America's perception of itself and the world.

"PEN/E.O. Wilson Literary Science Writing Award." PEN. Accessed October 4, 2013. http://www.pen.org/content/pene-o-wilson-literary-science-writing-award-10000.
  The writer's organization celebrates literary excellence in the physical and biological sciences. Award information was gathered for the years 2011 through 2013.

"PEN/ESPN Award for Literary Sports Writing." PEN. Accessed October 4, 2013. http://www.pen.org/content/penespn-award-literary-sports-writing-5000.
  The award honors an exemplary nonfiction book about sports of a biographical, investigative, historical, or analytical nature. Award information was gathered for the years 2011 through 2013.

"PEN/Jacqueline Bograd Weld Award for Biography." PEN. Accessed October 4, 2013. http://www.pen.org/content/penjacqueline-bograd-weld-award-biography-5000.
  The award is given for a scrupulously researched work of exceptional literary, narrative, and artistic merit. Award information was gathered for the years 2008 through 2013.

"PEN/John Kenneth Galbraith Award for Nonfiction." PEN. Accessed October 4, 2013. http://www.pen.org/content/penjohn-kenneth-galbraith-award-nonfiction-10000.
  This biennial prize goes to the author of a distinguished book of general nonfiction possessing notable literary merit. Award information was gathered for the years 2007 through 2013.

"The Pol Roger Duff Cooper Prize." Duff Cooper Estate. Accessed September 27, 2013. http://www.theduffcooperprize.org.
  This British prize is awarded annually for the best work of history, biography, poetry, or political science published in English. Award information was gathered for the years 1956 through 2012.

"Pulitzer Prize for Biography or Autobiography." Columbia University. Accessed October 5, 2013. http://www.pulitzer.org/bycat/Biography-or-Autobiography.
  The annual award recognizes the most distinguished biography or autobiography by an American writer. Award information was collected for the years 1917 through 2013.

"Pulitzer Prize for General Nonfiction." Columbia University. Accessed October 5, 2013. http://www.pulitzer.org/bycat/General-Nonfiction.
The annual award is presented for a distinguished book of nonfiction by an American author that is not eligible for consideration in another category. Award information was gathered for the years 1962 through 2013.

"Pulitzer Prize for History." Columbia University. Accessed October 5, 2013. http://www.pulitzer.org/bycat/History.
The annual award recognizes the most distinguished work of U.S. history. Award information was collected for the years 1917 through 2013.

"PW Best Books." *Publisher's Weekly.* Accessed October 5, 2013. http://www.publishersweekly.com/pw/best-books/2012/nonfiction#list.
The influential trade news and book review magazine makes annual recommendations. Booklist information was gathered for the years 2008 through 2012.

Randerson, James. "Levi's Memoir Beats Darwin to Win Science Book Title." *Guardian.* Last modified October 20, 2006. http://www.theguardian.com/science/2006/oct/21/uk.books.
The Royal Institution of Great Britain compiled a list of the best science books ever.

"The Reviewer's Ten Most Influential Environmental Books of the 20th Century." The Guide to Outdoor Literature. Accessed October 5, 2013. http://www.ronwatters.com/BkTheRev.htm.
The Internet book-review site invited scholars and readers to nominate the best environmental books.

"Royal Society Winton Prize for Science Books." The Royal Society. Accessed October 5, 2013. http://royalsociety.org/awards/science-books/.
The annual award is given to authors of outstanding science books written for a nonspecialist audience. Award information was gathered for the years 1988 through 2013.

"Samuel Johnson Prize for Non-fiction." British Broadcasting Company. Accessed September 27, 2013. http://www.thesamueljohnsonprize.co.uk/sjnav/books/62.
The Samuel Johnson Prize for Non-fiction is the UK's premier award for nonfiction books. Award information was gathered for the years 1999 through 2013.

"The Top 100 Sports Books of All Time." *Sports Illustrated.* Last modified December 16, 2012. http://sportsillustrated.cnn.com/si_online/features/2002/top_sports_books/1/.
The editors selected books that transcend sports and display the qualities of great literature.

"What Is the Best History Book of 2012?" George Mason University and History News Network. Last modified December 12, 2012. http://hnn.us/article/149717.
Out of 50 books nominated, five were recommended.

Additional Readings

Alvarez, A. *The Savage God.* New York: Random House, 1972.

Applebaum, Anne. *Gulag Voices: An Anthology.* New Haven, Conn.: Yale University Press, 2011.

Applebaum, Anne, and Danielle Crittenden. *From a Polish Country House Kitchen: 90 Recipes for the Ultimate Comfort Food.* San Francisco: Chronicle Books, 2012.

Aston, Dianna Hutts. *A Seed Is Sleepy.* San Francisco: Chronicle Books, 2007.

Bartoletti, Susan Campbell. *Down the Rabbit Hole: The Diary of Pringle Rose.* New York: Scholastic, 2013.

Baum, L. Frank. *The Wonderful Wizard of Oz.* Chicago: George M. Hill Company, 1900.

Branch, Taylor. *At Canaan's Edge.* New York: Simon & Schuster, 2006.

———. *Pillar of Fire.* New York: Simon & Schuster, 1998.

Bryson, Bill. *At Home: A Short History of Private Life.* New York: Doubleday, 2010.

———. *The Life and Times of the Thunderbolt Kid.* New York: Broadway Books, 2006.

———. *One Summer: America, 1927.* New York: Doubleday, 2013.

Caro, Robert. *The Years of Lyndon Johnson.* 4 vols. New York: Knopf, 2013.

Chaikin, Andrew. *A Man on the Moon.* London: Michael Joseph, 2002.

Davies, Nicola, and Neal Layton. *Poop: A Natural History of the Unmentionable.* Somerville, Mass.: Candlewick Press, 2004.

Davies, Nicola, and James Lovelock. *Gaia Warriors.* Somerville, Mass.: Candlewick Press, 2011.

Deem, James M. *Bodies from the Ash.* Boston: Houghton Mifflin, 2005.

———. *Bodies from the Bog.* Boston: Houghton Mifflin, 1998.

Diamond, Jared. *The Third Chimpanzee: The Evolution and Future of the Human Animal.* New York: HarperCollins, 1992.

———. *The World until Yesterday: What Can We Learn from Traditional Societies?* New York: Viking, 2012.

Dickens, Charles. *Oliver Twist.* London: Richard Bentley, 1837–1839.

Didion, Joan. *Run River.* New York: I. Obolensky, 1963.

Eggers, Dave. *What Is the What: The Autobiography of Valentino Achak Deng.* San Francisco: McSweeney's, 2006.

Feynman, Paul, Ralph Leighton, and Edward Hutchings. *"Surely You're Joking, Mr. Feynman!" Adventures of a Curious Character.* W. W. Norton, 1997.

Fleming, Candace. *Our Eleanor: A Scrapbook Look at Eleanor Roosevelt's Remarkable Life.* New York: Atheneum Books for Young Readers, 2005.

Franklin, Benjamin. *Poor Richard's Almanack.* New York: Skyhorse, 2007.

Freedman, Russell. *Angel Island: Gateway to Gold Mountain.* New York: Clarion Books, 2013.

———. *Children of the Wild West.* New York: Houghton Mifflin, 1992.

———. *Confucius: The Golden Rule.* New York: Arthur A. Levine Books, 2002.

Gladwell, Malcolm. *Blink: The Power of Thinking without Thinking.* New York: Little, Brown and Company, 2005.

———. *David and Goliath: Underdogs, Misfits, and the Art of Battling Giants.* New York: Little, Brown and Company, 2013.

———. *What the Dog Saw and Other Adventures.* New York: Little, Brown and Company, 2009.

Gleick, James. *Faster: Our Race against Time.* New York: Little, Brown and Company, 1999.

———. *Genius: The Life and Science of Richard Feynman.* New York: Pantheon Books, 1992.

———. *Isaac Newton.* New York: Pantheon Books, 2003.

Gleick, James, ed. *The Best American Science Writing.* New York, Ecco Press, 2000.

Greenberg, Jan. *A Season In-Between.* New York: Farrar, Straus & Giroux, 1979.

Greenberg, Jan, and Sandra Jordan. *Christo and Jeanne-Claude: Through the Gates and Beyond.* New York: Roaring Brook Press, 2008.

———. *The Mad Potter: George E. Ohr, Eccentric Genius.* New York: Roaring Brook Press, 2013.

———. *The Painter's Eye: Learning to Look at Contemporary American Art.* New York: Delacorte Press, 1991.

———. *Runaway Girl: The Artist Louise Bourgeois.* New York: Harry N. Abrams, 2003.

Karr, Mary. *Cherry.* New York: Viking, 2000.

———. *The Lion's Club.* New York: Penguin Group, 1995.

Kerley, Barbara. *A Cool Drink of Water.* Washington, D.C.: National Geographic Society, 2002.

———. *A Home for Mr. Emerson.* New York: Scholastic Press, 2014.

———. *Songs from Papa's Island.* Boston: Houghton Mifflin, 1995.

———. *Walt Whitman: Words for America.* New York: Scholastic Press, 2004.

Kesey, Ken. *One Flew over the Cuckoo's Nest.* New York: Viking Press, 1962.

Larson, Erik. *Isaac's Storm: A Man, a Time, and the Deadliest Hurricane in History.* New York: Crown Publishers, 1999.

———. *Thunderstruck.* New York: Crown Publishers, 2006.

Lee, Harper. *To Kill a Mockingbird.* Philadelphia: Lippincott, 1960.

Martin, Russell. *Beethoven's Hair.* New York: Broadway Books, 2000.

Massie, Robert K. *Nicholas and Alexandra: An Intimate Account of the Last of the Romanovs and the Fall of Imperial Russia.* New York: Atheneum, 1967.

———. *Peter the Great: His Life and World.* New York: Knopf, 1980.

McCullough, David. *Brave Companions.* New York: Prentice Hall, 1992.

———. *The Great Bridge.* New York: Simon & Schuster, 1972.

———. *The Greater Journey.* New York: Simon & Schuster, 2011.

———. *The Johnstown Flood.* New York: Simon & Schuster, 1968.

———. *Mornings on Horseback.* New York: Simon & Schuster, 1981.

———. *The Path between the Seas.* New York: Simon & Schuster, 1977.

———. *Truman.* New York: Simon & Schuster, 1992.

Montgomery, Sy. *The Good Good Pig: The Extraordinary Life of Christopher Hogwood.* New York: Ballantine Books, 2006.

———. *Spell of the Tiger: The Man-Eaters of Sundarbans.* Boston: Houghton Mifflin, 1995.

———. *Walking with the Great Apes: Jane Goodall, Dian Fossey, Birute Galdikas.* Boston: Houghton Mifflin, 1991.

Murphy, Jim. *Blizzard! The Storm That Changed America.* New York: Scholastic Press, 2000.

———. *The Long Road to Gettysburg.* New York: Clarion Books, 1992.

———. *A Young Patriot: The American Revolution as Experienced by One Boy.* New York: Clarion Books, 1996.

Nabokov, Vladimir. *Lolita.* New York: G. P. Putnam's Sons, 1958.

Nelson, Kadir. *Baby Bear.* New York: Balzer & Bray, 2014.

———. *Nelson Mandela.* New York: Katherine Tegen Books, 2013.

Orwell, George. *Animal Farm.* London: Secker and Warburg, 1945.

———. *Nineteen Eighty-Four.* London: Secker and Warburg, 1949.

Patent, Dorothy Hinshaw. *The Buffalo and the Indians: A Shared Destiny.* New York: Clarion Books, 2006.

Say, Allen. *The Ink-Keeper's Apprentice.* New York: Harper & Row, 1979.

Sayre, April Pulley. *Army Ant Parade.* New York: Henry Holt, 2002.

———. *Go, Go, Grapes!* New York: Beach Lane Books, 2012.

———. *Secrets of Sound: Studying the Calls and Songs of Whales, Elephants, and Birds.* Boston: Houghton Mifflin, 2002.

———. *Touch a Butterfly: Wildlife Gardening with Kids.* Boston: Roost Books, 2013.

Scieszka, Jon. *The Stinky Cheese Man.* New York: Penguin Books, 1992.

———. *The True Story of the 3 Little Pigs!* New York: Puffin Books, 2009.

Shields, Charles A. *Mockingbird: A Portrait of Harper Lee.* New York: Henry Holt, 2006.

Sinclair, Upton. *The Jungle.* New York: Doubleday, Jabber & Company, 1906.

Wallace, David Foster. *Consider the Lobster.* Boston: Little, Brown and Company, 2007.

———. *Everything and More.* New York: Atlas Books, 2003.

———. *Infinite Jest.* Boston: Little, Brown and Company, 1996.

Waring, Geoff. *Oscar and the Bat: A Book about Sound.* Cambridge: Candlewick Press, 2008.

———. *Oscar and the Snail: A Book about Things That We Use.* Cambridge: Candlewick Press, 2009.

Watson, James D. *The Annotated and Illustrated Double Helix.* New York: Simon & Schuster, 2012.

Winter, Jonah. *Born and Bred in the Great Depression.* New York: Schwartz & Wade Books, 2011.

———. *Diego.* New York: Knopf, 1991.

———. *Fair Ball! 14 Great Stars from Baseball's Negro Leagues.* New York: Scholastic Press, 1999.

———. *Peaceful Heroes.* New York: Arthur A. Levine Books, 2009.

Wolfe, Tom. *The Bonfire of the Vanities.* New York: Farrar, Straus & Giroux, 1987.

———. *The Kandy-Kolored Tangerine-Flake Streamline Baby.* New York: Farrar, Straus & Giroux, 1965.

———. *A Man in Full.* New York: Farrar, Straus & Giroux, 1998.

———. *Radical Chic & Mau-Mauing the Flak Catchers.* New York: Farrar, Straus & Giroux, 1970.

Woolf, Virginia. *Mrs Dalloway.* London: Hogarth Press, 1925.

———. *To the Lighthouse.* London: Hogarth Press, 1927.